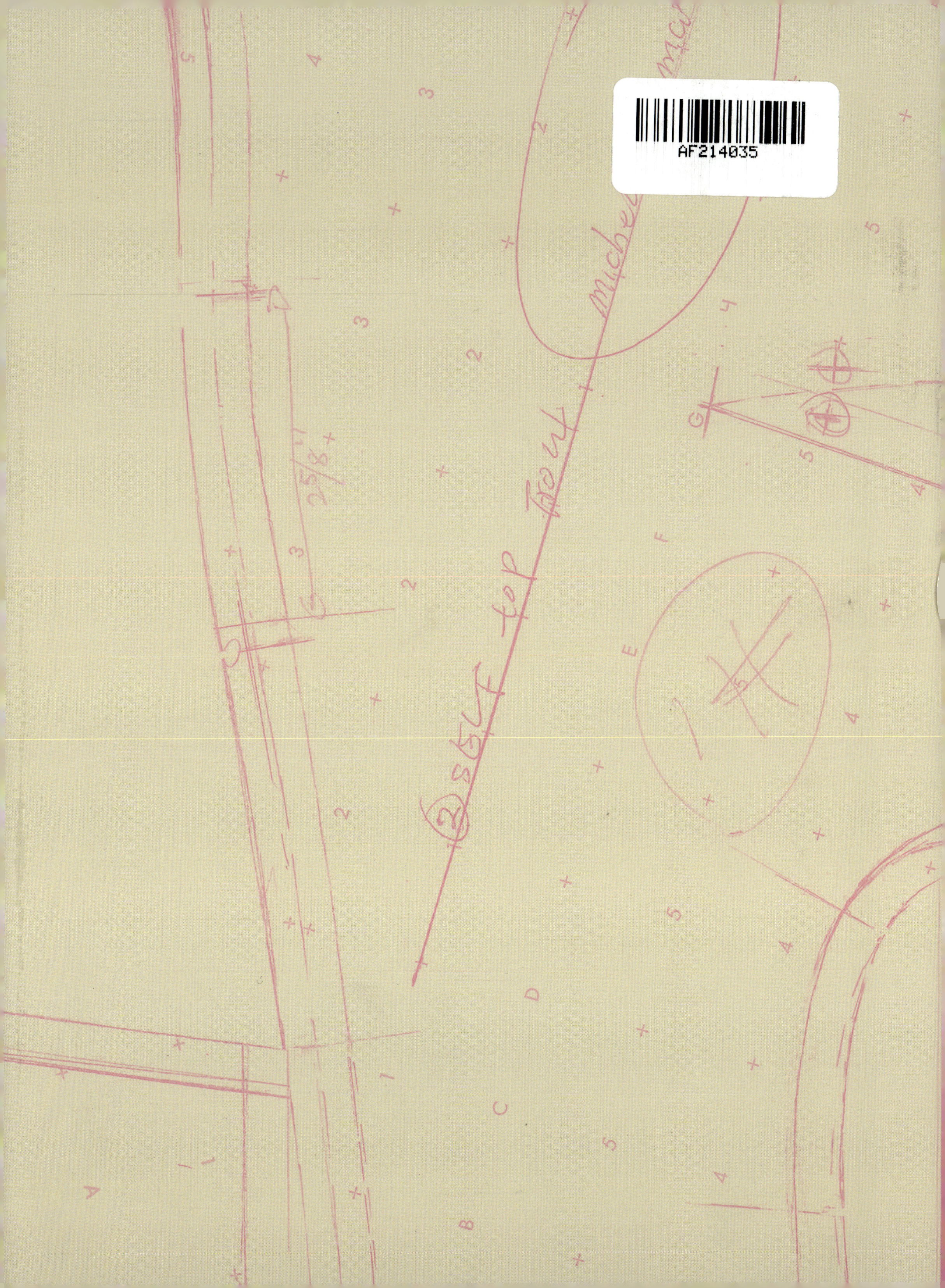
2 self top front
2 5/8"

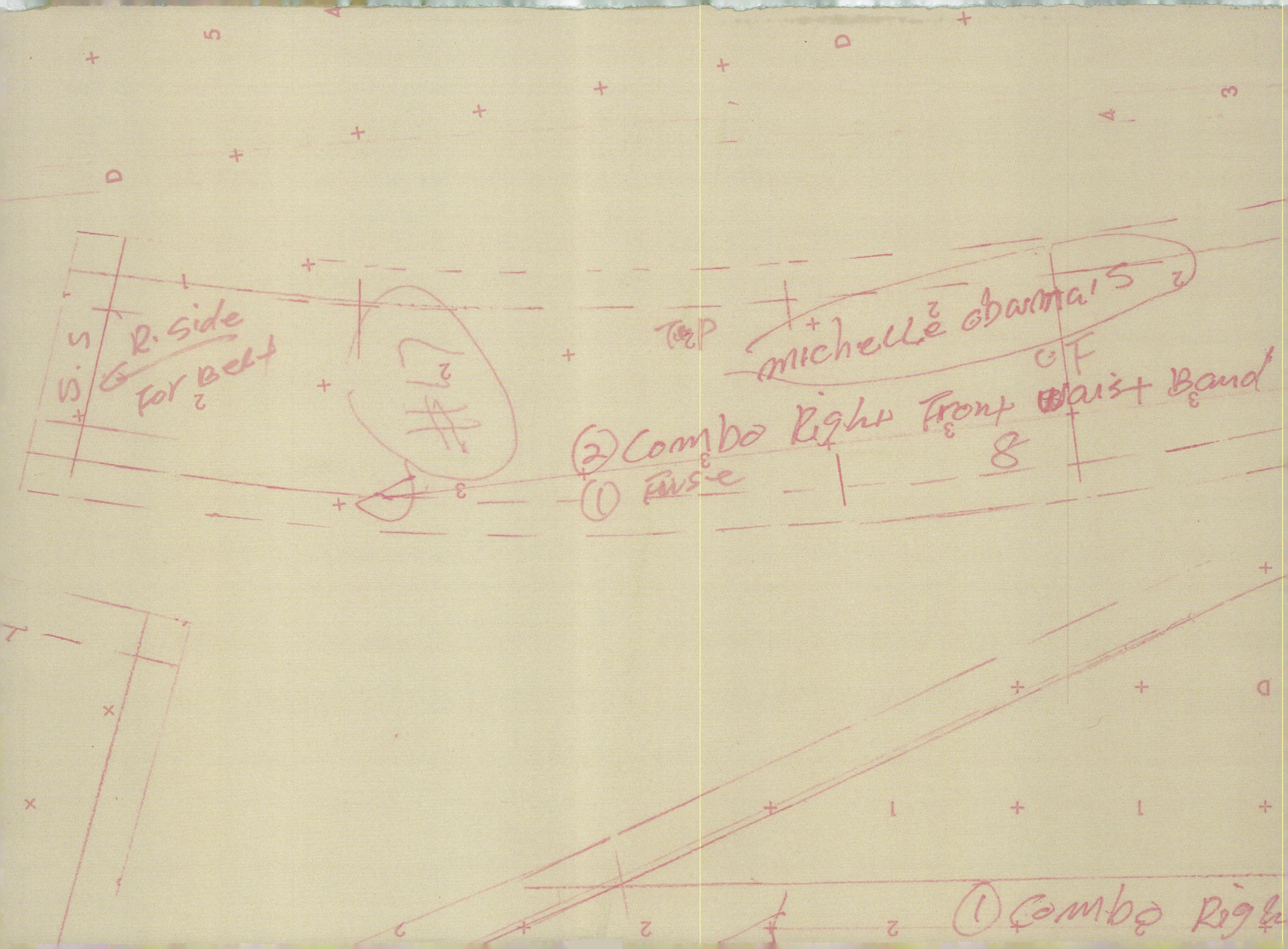
S.S
R. side for Belt
#7
TOP
michelle obama's
CF
(2) Combo Right Front Waist Band
8
(1) Fuse
(1) Combo Righ

DIANE VON FURSTENBERG

WOMAN BEFORE FASHION

EDITED BY
Nicolas Lor

RIZZOLI Electa

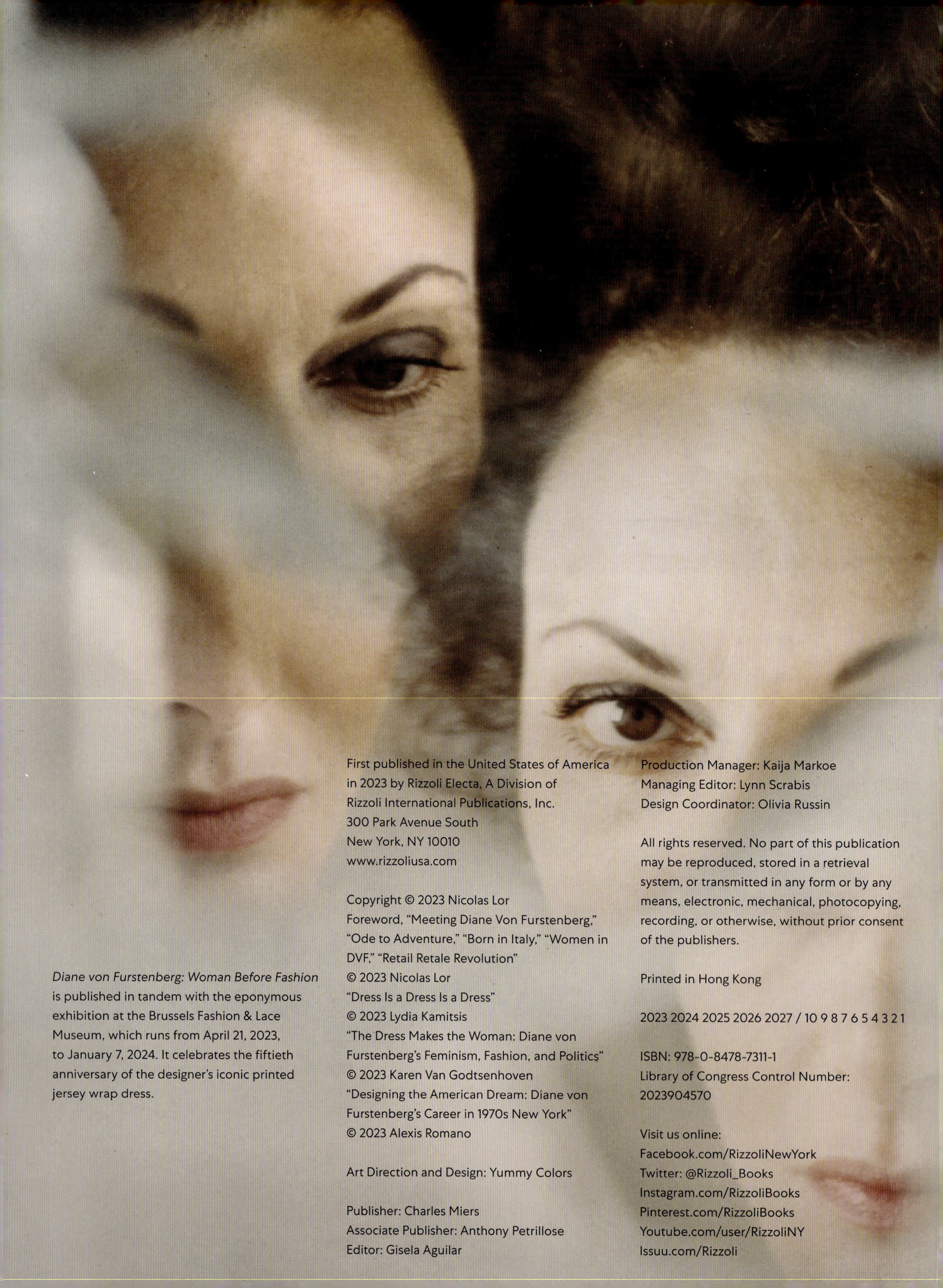

Diane von Furstenberg: Woman Before Fashion is published in tandem with the eponymous exhibition at the Brussels Fashion & Lace Museum, which runs from April 21, 2023, to January 7, 2024. It celebrates the fiftieth anniversary of the designer's iconic printed jersey wrap dress.

First published in the United States of America in 2023 by Rizzoli Electa, A Division of Rizzoli International Publications, Inc.
300 Park Avenue South
New York, NY 10010
www.rizzoliusa.com

Art Direction and Design: Yummy Colors

Publisher: Charles Miers
Associate Publisher: Anthony Petrillose
Editor: Gisela Aguilar
Production Manager: Kaija Markoe
Managing Editor: Lynn Scrabis
Design Coordinator: Olivia Russin

Printed in Hong Kong

2023 2024 2025 2026 2027 / 10 9 8 7 6 5 4 3 2 1

ISBN: 978-0-8478-7311-1
Library of Congress Control Number: 2023904570

Visit us online:
Facebook.com/RizzoliNewYork
Twitter: @Rizzoli_Books
Instagram.com/RizzoliBooks
Pinterest.com/RizzoliBooks
Youtube.com/user/RizzoliNY
Issuu.com/Rizzoli

Contents

4 Foreword

INTRODUCTION 7 Meeting Diane von Furstenberg

9 Ode to Adventure

CHAPTER 01 17 Born in Italy

33 Geometry

49 Dress Is a Dress Is a Dress

CHAPTER 02 81 Women in DVF

97 Nature

113 The Dress Makes the Woman: Diane von Furstenberg's Feminism, Fashion, and Politics

CHAPTER 03 145 Retail Retale Revolution

161 Movement

177 Designing the American Dream: Diane von Furstenberg's Career in 1970s New York

203 Acknowledgments

205 Notes

207 Credits

Woman Before Fashion is doubly a first. It is not only the first exhibition dedicated to Diane von Furstenberg in Europe but also the first exhibition that I am curating for the Fashion & Lace Museum in Brussels.

I could say that it was a natural choice from the outset, but this is not the case. Like my fellow fashion curators and historians, I was well aware of the origins and success of the wrap dress, which often and logically summarizes her person. Yet, as I engaged in preliminary research and after actually meeting Diane, I came to distinguish the myriad facets of her personality and was caught up in the complex and fascinating subject that she embodies. The natural thing to do was then obvious: show the work of this fashion designer, in the true sense of the word, in a new light.

Her achievement lies in how she turns clothing into objects of design that are aesthetic, practical, and replicable. This is what truly makes Diane von Furstenberg a designer in the field of fashion. She is a full personality—more than just a creator of fashion.

In its exhibition form, *Woman Before Fashion* takes as its starting point fashion and closes with the woman, mirroring its title.

The three chapters of this publication are based on the exhibition's texts and delve deeper into its key themes through personal interviews, striking pattern design books, and three previously unpublished scientific articles. These last texts, authored by Lydia Kamitsis, Karen van Godtsenhoven, and Alexis Romano, contextualize Diane von Furstenberg's work within the global history of fashion.

Nicolas Lor

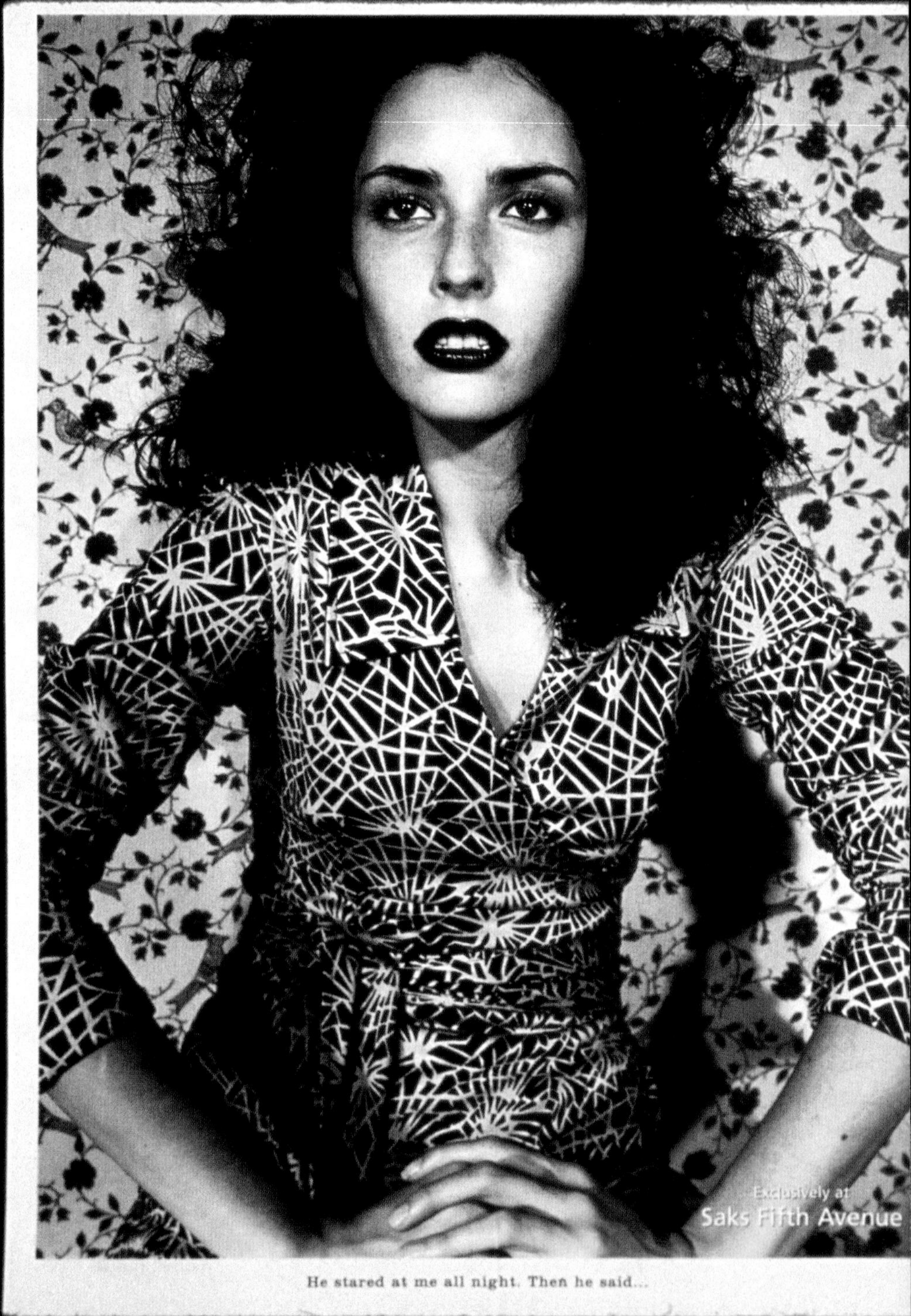

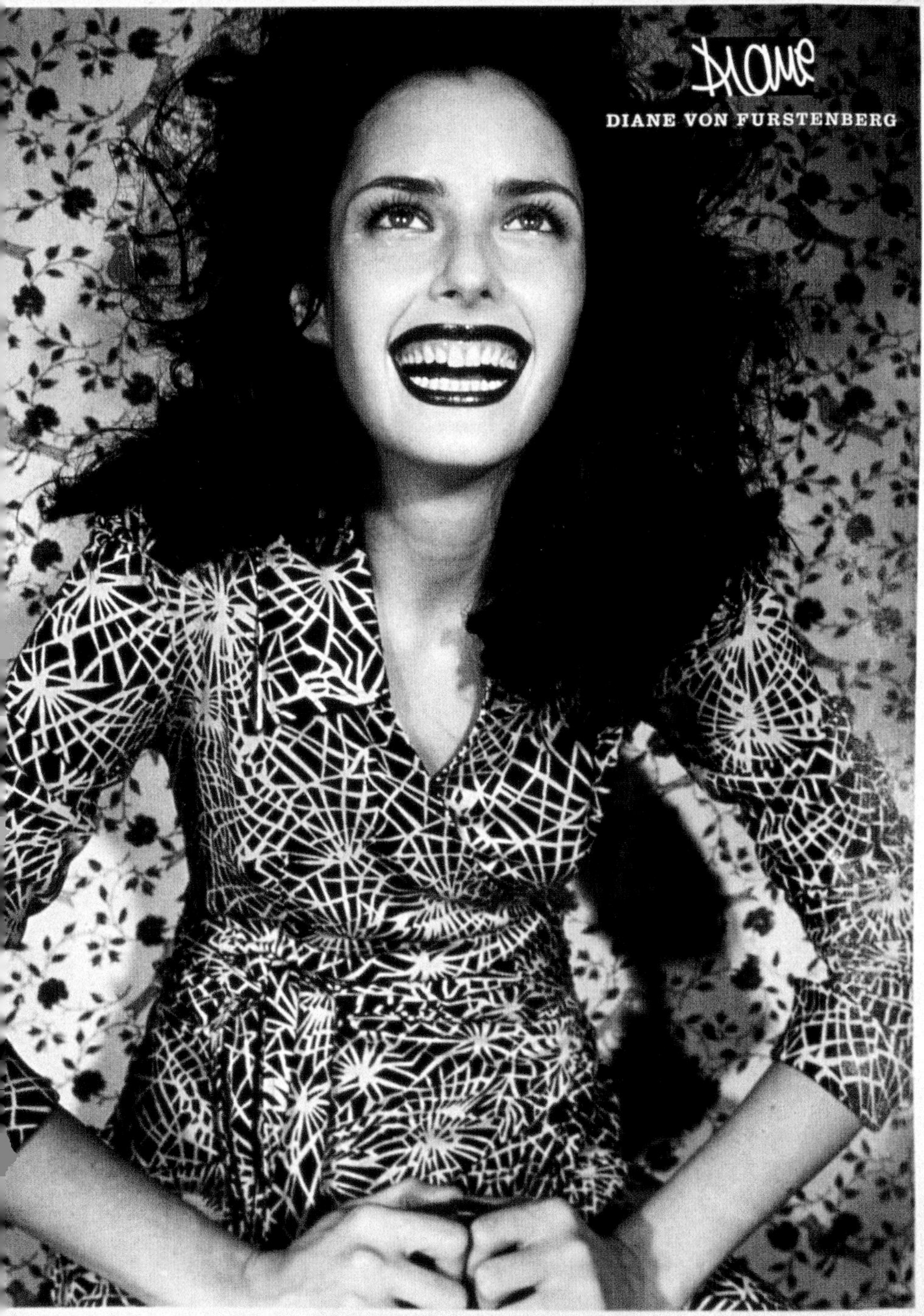

"Something about you reminds me of my mother."

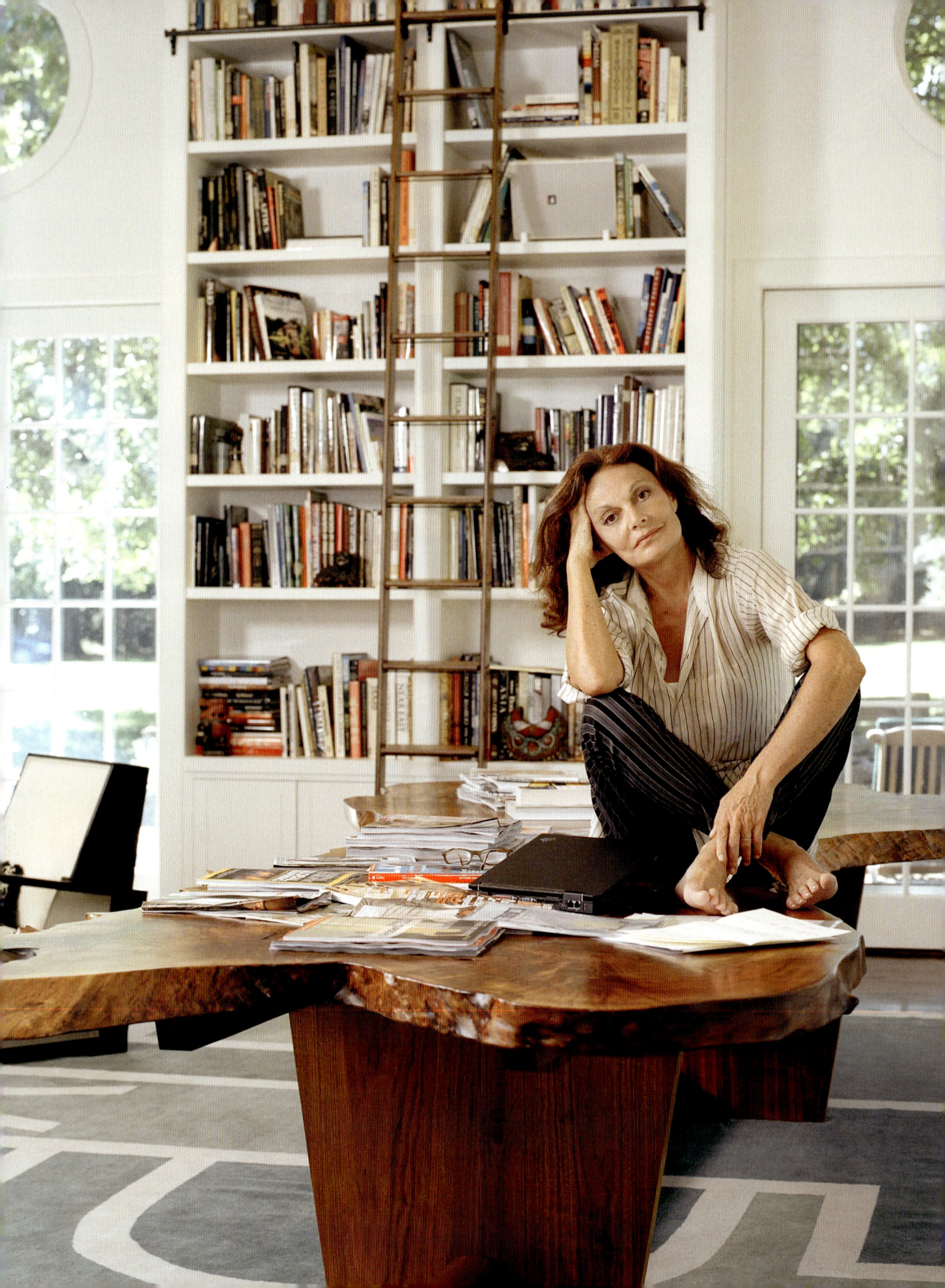

Meeting Diane von Furstenberg

INTRODUCTION

Nicolas Lor

Opposite
Diane von Furstenberg at Cloudwalk, her home in New Milford, Connecticut, ca. 2005.

A truly pertinent approach to putting on an exhibition about Diane von Furstenberg could only be achieved by meeting her in person. Greta Halfin, Diane's sister-in-law and DVF's licensee in Brussels, was kind enough to make the connection. I remember precisely when the name "Diane von Furstenberg" first appeared on my phone at 4:12 P.M. on February 18, 2022. It was with a genuine feeling of awe that I answered the call. After a few minutes of formal introductions, Diane asked me straight up, "What made you decide to choose me for your first show?" I replied, "You were born in Brussels, although you did leave early on. I believe the fiftieth anniversary of the design of your iconic dress is an opportunity to trace it back to its origins. It's not a retrospective, but an original, more modest, and more intimate show—much like the exhibition spaces of the Fashion & Lace Museum."

This first conversation was the starting point for a mutual closeness—a preliminary to the bonds we were to form and to the significant support Diane herself would provide us. Not only did she decide to come and see the museum for herself, she also generously lent many items from her own archives for the exhibition. She eventually offered to work on the present book, and advised and encouraged me at every stage of its writing—at my every interrogation—while allowing me complete freedom.

In July of 2022, I had the chance to set foot in New York City for the first time to meet the house's teams. Visiting the design studio and boutique in the Meatpacking District gave me a better understanding of their aesthetic and working environment. After only two days, DVF's archivist, Costanza Reiser, showed me the brand's rich archives (a large inventory of textiles and documents from 1946 to the present day) that are stored in Cloudwalk, Connecticut. This estate, which the designer bought for her birthday in 1974, has always been a refuge for her. I immediately understood why. Cloudwalk in New Milford is a true haven. It is where Diane spends hours every day working, walking, and meditating.

Each day, I had the opportunity to spend time with Diane in her private family environment and see the way she takes great care to listen attentively to everyone around her. On the last morning, I woke early to head back to the archives. Thinking I would be the only one up at 6.30 A.M., I entered the main building, Diane's home, located above the archives. She called out to me, inviting me to join her for coffee in her room. It was at that very moment that we formed a strong mutual bond. I realized that my presence at Cloudwalk would not only allow me to learn about a great designer but also about the business of fashion. We spent three hours talking and sharing our experiences and views. Since then, Diane and I speak at least once a week. We discuss our projects, talk of her brand, and even broach societal issues. I had hoped to create a unique exhibition but, ultimately, I also met an exceptional soulmate and mentor.

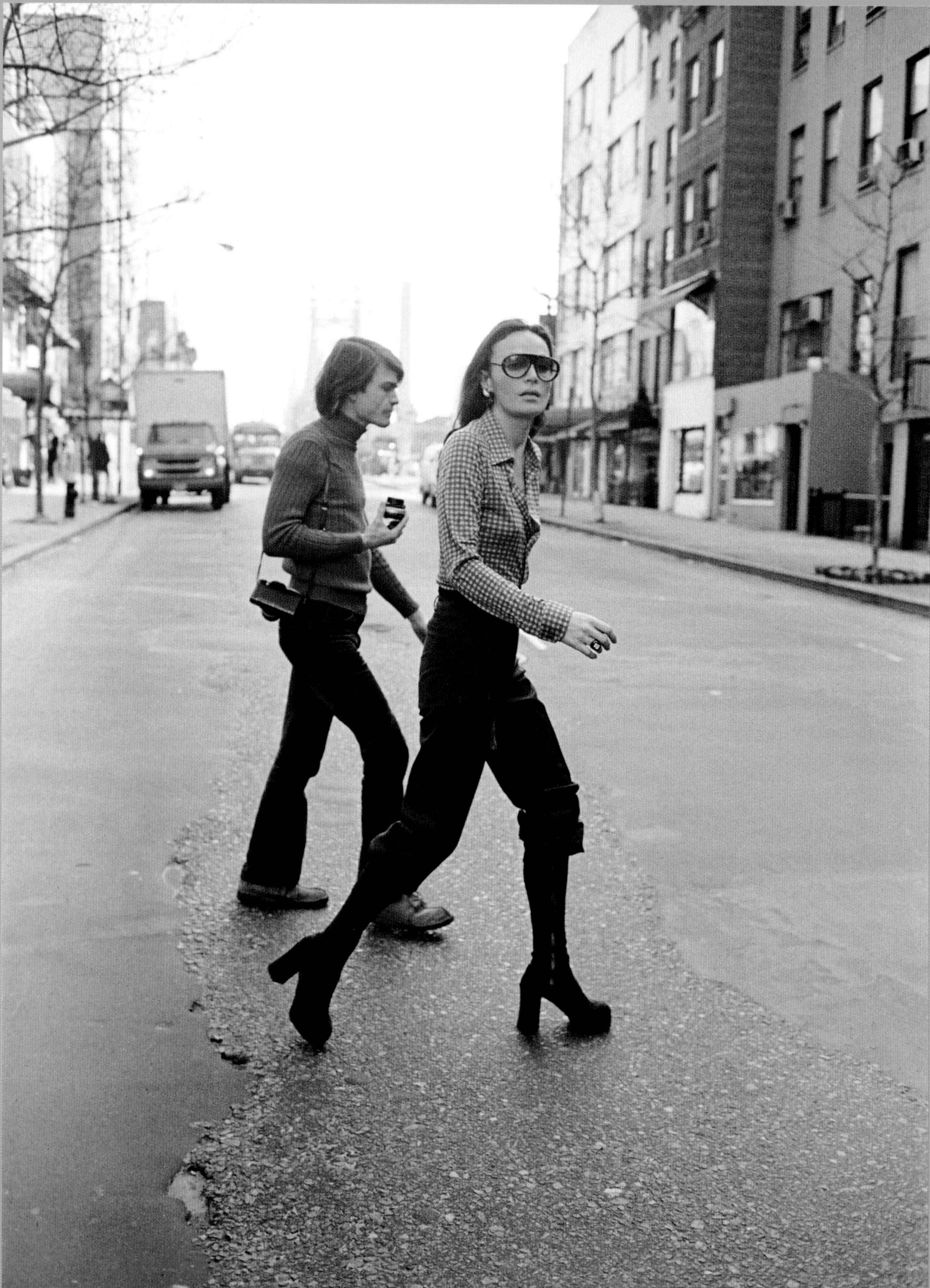

Ode to Adventure

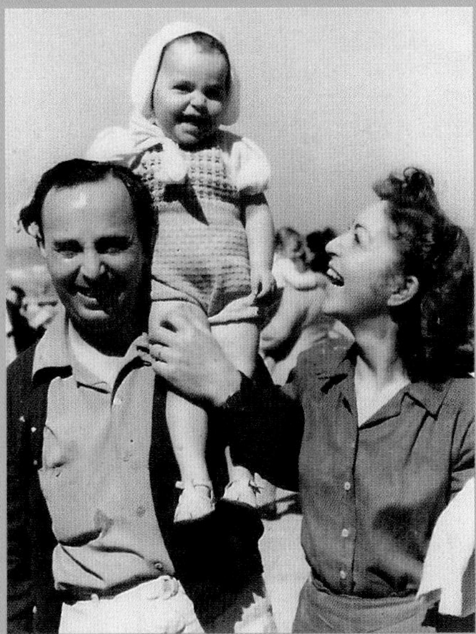

Above
Baby Diane with her parents Lily and Leon, ca. 1947.

Opposite
Diane von Furstenberg crosses a street in New York City, 1970.

Diane Halfin was born in Brussels, Belgium, on December 31, 1946, to Jewish parents—her father of Moldavian origin (born in Kishinev in the former Bessarabia) and her mother Greek (born in Salonika). She embodied her mother's newfound freedom after her detention in the Auschwitz-Birkenau and Ravensbrück camps. The young Diane, an alert child open to the world, attended the Dachsbeck elementary school in Brussels's Sablon district, where she was already dreaming of escape with her friends. In her teens, her fantasies of exploring the world would only grow as she was sent to international schools—first, at the Pensionnat Cuche in Lausanne, Switzerland, between 1959 and 1961, and then at the Stroud Court Boarding School in Eynsham, not far from Oxford, England, from 1962 to 1964. From 1964 to 1965, Diane attended the University of Madrid before transferring to the University of Geneva to study economics from 1965 to 1968.

Despite a family predisposition for fashion (her grandfather worked for the family textile company Maison Dorée in Brussels, and her mother had learned the art of millinery), it was only by chance—or accident—that Diane Halfin came to discover the industry. In the summer of 1968, she began work as an assistant to Albert Koski, a photographers' agent based in Paris. The job provided her with a first behind-the-scenes view of the world of fashion. The makings of press books exposed her to the communication practices between prominent photographers, top models, and leading fashion magazines, and introduced her to the industry's most influential people. Diane did not stay long at the agency, as Angelo Ferretti, a recent acquaintance, invited her to visit his textile manufacturing and printing factory in Italy.

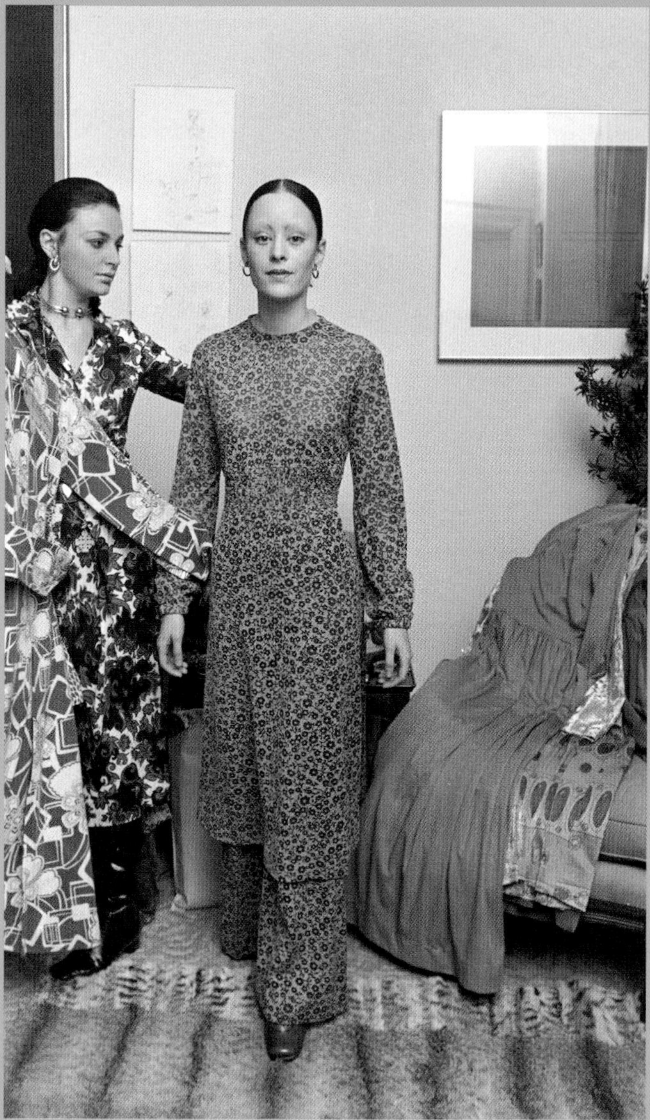

Diane von Furstenberg presents her first collection with model Jane Forth at the Gotham Hotel in New York City, April 1970.

Opposite (above) Diane von Furstenberg and Diana Vreeland at a party, 1973.

Opposite (below) A 1982 advertisement for Diane von Furstenberg's Liquid Assets line.

This factory is where Diane Halfin not only discovered jersey—a fabric she quickly fell in love with—but also the technical side of the trade, cutting methods with Bruna Sequalino, and the world of colors and prints with Mimmo Ferretti.

Her boyfriend at the time was none other than Prince Egon von Furstenberg, one of the most desired and desirable names of the jet set. In January 1969, Diane spent a month with him in New York City. This first trip across the Atlantic was to be a revelation. Egon introduced her to many of his friends, including several designers who were eager to dress Diane. She reveled in the city's energy and, once back in the Ferretti factory, had only one idea in mind: to return to New York. She also began to realize the potential of the factory and its products, and their possible market in the United States. She asked her mentor, Angelo Ferretti, if she could create a few "little dresses" using existing prints, a project that he approved and supported. She chose the simplest and most comfortable styles from Bruna's dress patterns: shirtdresses and tunic-dresses, both long and short.

Married and pregnant with her first child, Princess Diane von Furstenberg left Italy for New York City on September 16, 1969. Her natural dynamism, coupled with Egon's own network, worked wonders. In March 1970, she met Diana Vreeland, US *Vogue's* editor-in-chief. Her Vuitton suitcase packed with printed and plain-colored jersey dresses, she showed them to a delighted Vreeland, who consented to help Diane, advising her to show her collection the following month during New York Fashion Week. In April of that year, Diane set up a showroom in the Gotham Hotel, presenting her first collection of diverse dresses, some of which were very much on trend. Jersey remained central.

The Diane von Furstenberg Limited brand was not launched until April 4, 1972, when she collaborated with Richard Conrad, an experienced salesman based in the city. Together, they opened a showroom on Seventh Avenue and, in barely one year, the company's sales for 1973 reached 1.8 million dollars. With her collaborator Sue Feinberg, an American based in Montevarchi, Italy, she developed new models, leading ultimately to the creation of pattern number T72. The iconic, printed jersey wrap dress was born! Publicized in September 1973, it led to Diane's fast and profitable success, and her apogee between 1974 and 1978, with the famous leopard and snakeskin prints.

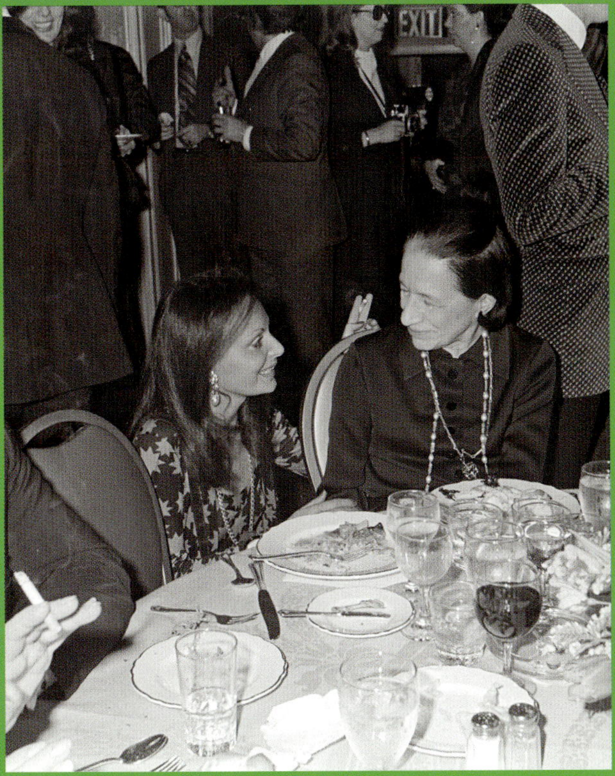

On March 22, 1976, Diane made the cover of *Newsweek* magazine. In the article, journalist Linda Bird Francke described the designer as the "most marketable female in fashion since Coco Chanel." Like Chanel, Diane chose jersey as the starting point for the construction of an item of clothing directly on a woman's body. In a generous and ingenious act of communication, she devised a wardrobe of fashions designed both for herself and for all women rather than seeking to present a "fashionable" collection. Her jersey dresses—especially the wrap dress—were manufactured in industrial quantities. Their comfortable and practical design met the needs of the newly liberated American working woman of the mid-1970s. Diane designed this wardrobe as an alternative to the suit—a basic uniform for work and a signature of independence and liberation, which were the designer's key words. This free and independent state of mind would never leave her; it has continued to inhabit her personality and career to this day.

Diane von Furstenberg's empire was also built on parallel product lines that complemented a woman's kit (cosmetics and perfumes in 1974) and a network of licensing that proved to be extremely profitable throughout the 1970s. Toward the end of the decade, however, the tide turned. The brand's identity was diluted by a plethora of licenses, while Diane continued to create new ranges under her name. In the early 1980s, in collaboration with Stephan Janson, she launched *Liquid Assets*, a fluid, ready-to-wear line featuring only solid colors. With *Diane Fifth Avenue*, she rolled out an unexpected couture collection at the end of 1984.

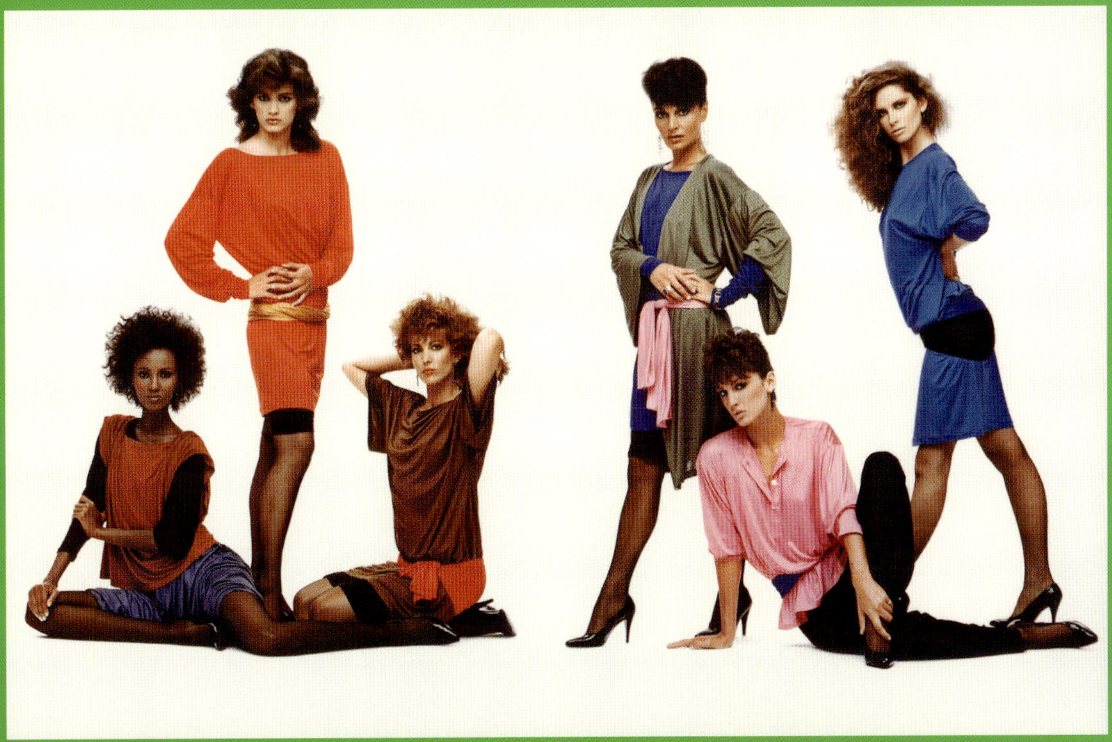

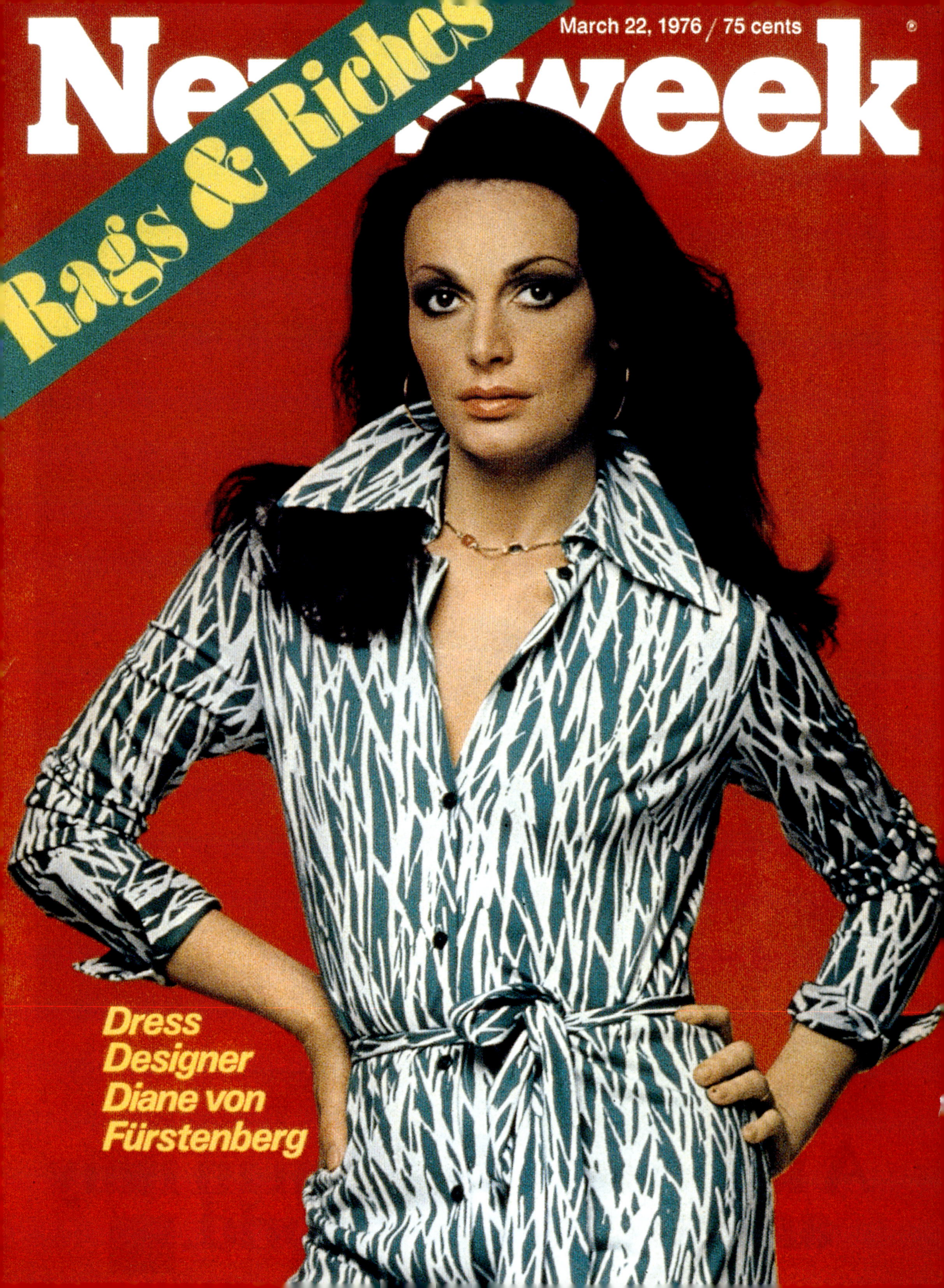
March 22, 1976 / 75 cents
Newsweek
Rags & Riches
Dress
Designer
Diane von
Fürstenberg

Opposite
Diane von Furstenberg wearing one of her dresses on the cover of *Newsweek*, March 22, 1976.

Below
Diane von Furstenberg and Hervé Léger collection presentation in Paris, 1987.

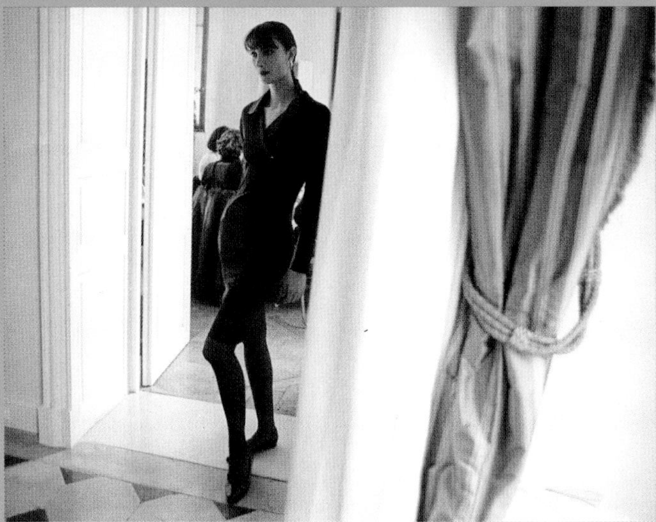

Far different than her initial vision, the boutique carrying the couture line was managed by Diane from Paris, where she resided from 1985 to 1989. The City of Light was a welcome interlude in Diane's fashion career, while her brand remained one of the top ten women-owned businesses in the United States.

In 1987, she teamed up with French designer Hervé Léger to create a new collection. Although extremely wearable and of excellent quality, this collection remains, like her couture boutique, unequal to what made the Diane von Furstenberg signature: printed jersey. The end of the 1980s saw Diane returning to New York to face the chaos of the licenses that she had developed, which were weakening, or worse yet, compromising her name. She took the necessary actions with caution and eventually, in just over five years, completed the process of selecting the best license agreements to protect and ensure the brand's success. During this time, she devised new ways of selling and diversifying her products. This included a new collection of wrap dresses in 1991 and 1992, and the sale of a line that she called *Silk Assets* on American home shopping network QVC. In less than two hours, it generated sales exceeding one million dollars.

The brand made a positive comeback in the second half of the 1990s. Diane moved her offices to the Meatpacking District in New York City and took advantage of the renewed interest in her iconic wrap dress. The resurgence of 1970s nostalgia gave her styles new clout. Women wearing vintage wrap dresses walked the streets again. Designer Todd Oldham named his Spring/Summer 1995 collection *Dotti von Furstenberg* in a tribute to Diane. Her entourage pushed her to relaunch her line. She heeded the call and staged a spectacular comeback on September 9, 1997, in a show on the seventh floor of Saks Fifth Avenue. In 1999, sales of her wrap dresses exceeded 20 million dollars.

Since this reboot, the brand has collaborated with a series of creative directors: Catherine Malandrino from 1998 to 2001, Nathan Jenden from 2001 to 2010 and from 2018 to 2019, Yvan Mispelaere from 2010 to 2012, Michael Herz from 2014 to 2016, and Jonathan Saunders from 2016 to 2018. Working hand in hand with Diane, these designers all contributed in their personal way to the brand's rich image and vocabulary.

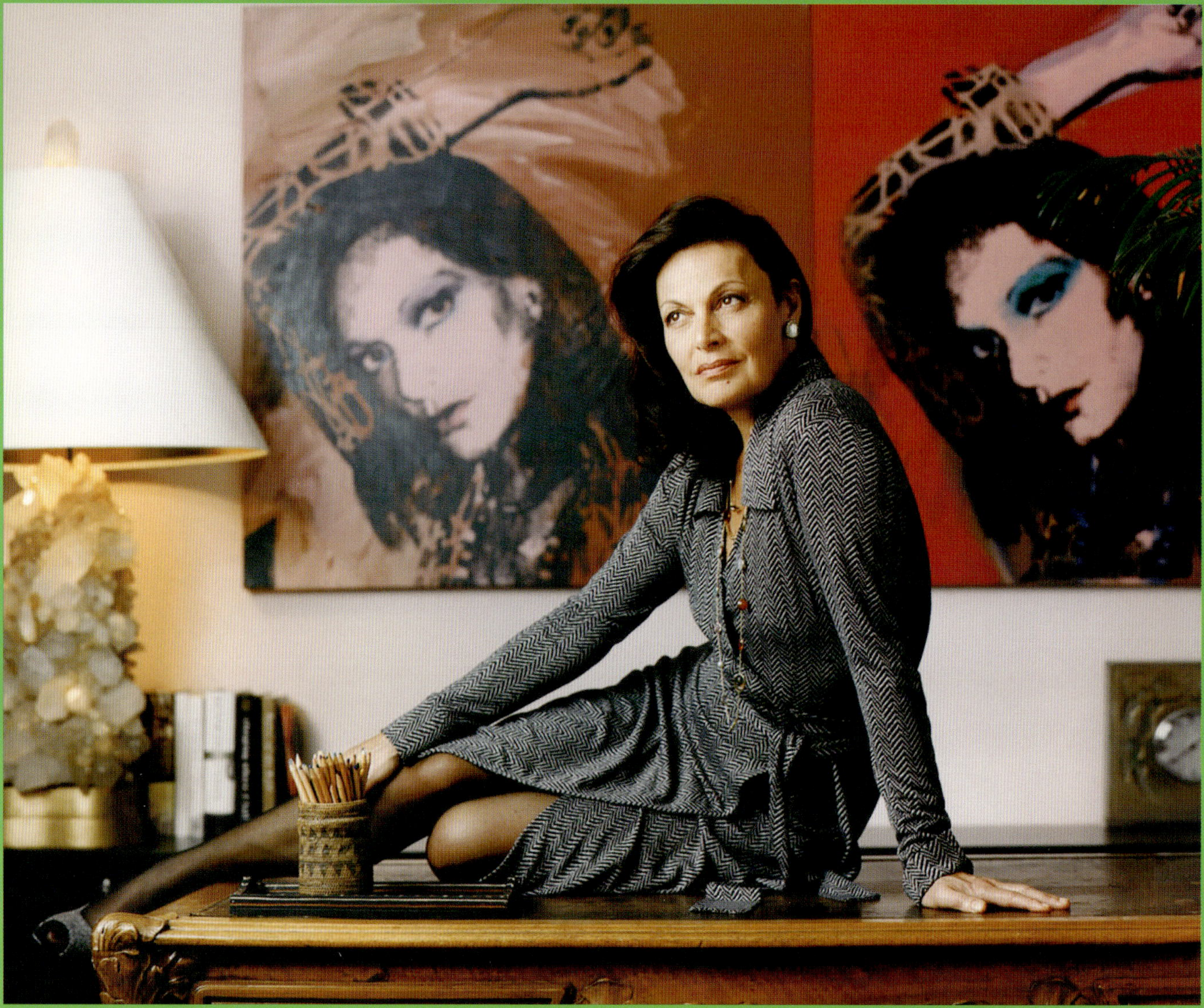

From 2018 onward, the creative studio has been in charge of developing the collections. In 2020, in the aftermath of the Covid-19 pandemic and as the brand approached its fiftieth anniversary, Diane passed the torch on to her granddaughter, Talita von Furstenberg.

Together, they consider the brand's past successes and Diane's commitment to social activism when they envision new designs and products. Although fashion was a vehicle to further the cause of women for the designer, her activism placed women before fashion. In the 1970s, as a self-proclaimed feminist, she became involved in the women's movement—notably, alongside Bella Abzug in 1976, hosting her fundraising dinners. This commitment continues in her name through a number of women's platforms (DVF Awards since 2010, In Charge events since 2019) and many other causes (High Line, Statue of Liberty, and more).

Above
Diane von Furstenberg in her office, 1998.

Opposite
Talita von Furstenberg poses in the iconic chainlink wrap dress, 2016.

Next page
Diane von Furstenberg Winter 2022 collection.

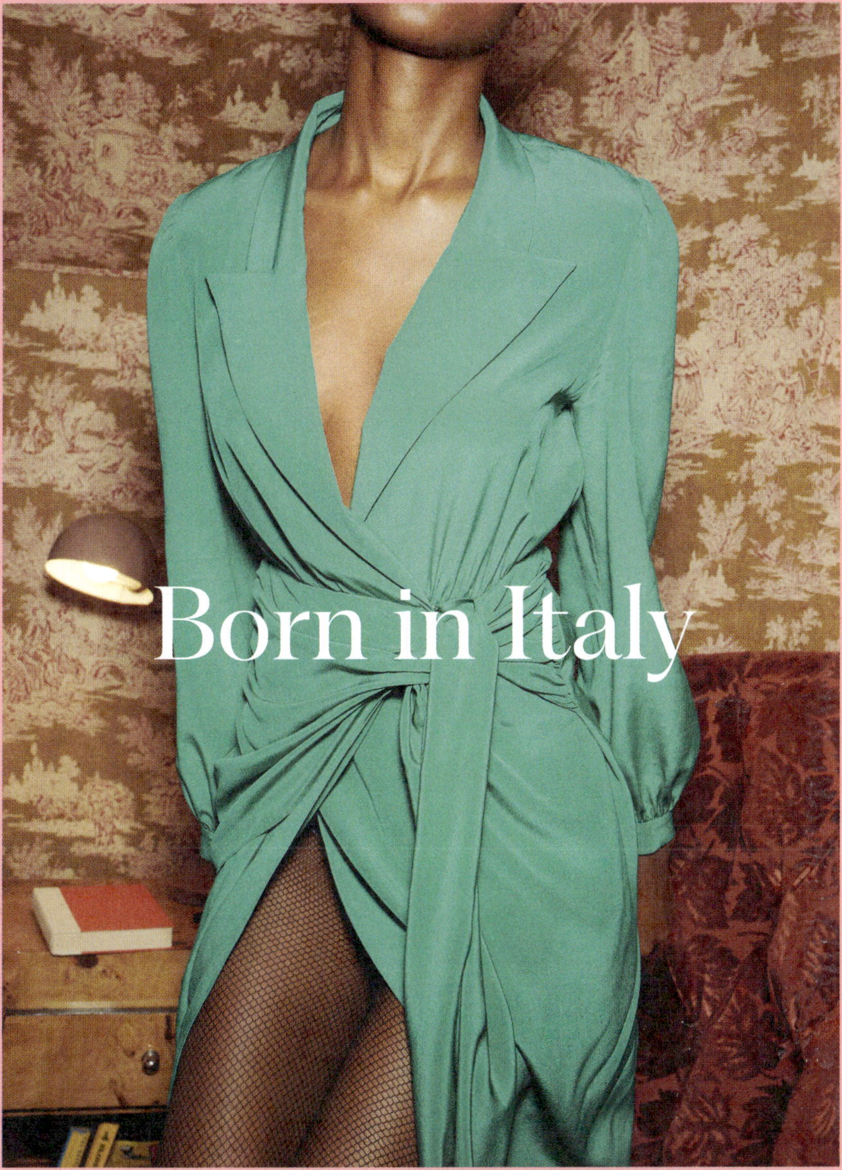

CHAPTER 01

Born in Italy

INTERVIEWS BY

Nicolas Lor

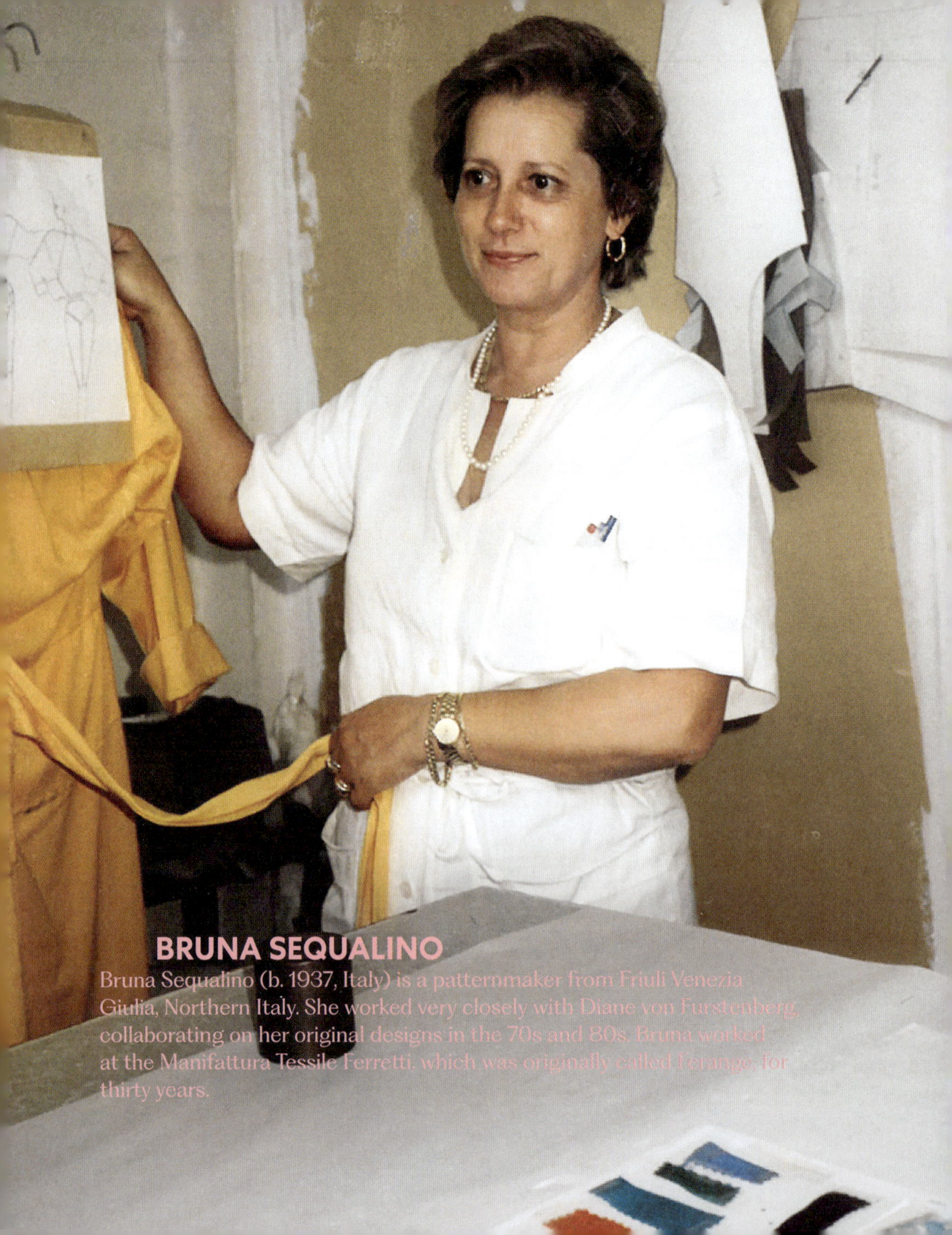

BRUNA SEQUALINO

Bruna Sequalino (b. 1937, Italy) is a patternmaker from Friuli Venezia Giulia, Northern Italy. She worked very closely with Diane von Furstenberg, collaborating on her original designs in the 70s and 80s. Bruna worked at the Manifattura Tessile Ferretti, which was originally called Ferange, for thirty years.

How and when did you begin working with von Furstenberg?

Previous page
Diane von Furstenberg
Winter 2020 collection.

Opposite
Bruna Sequalino works on the development of patterns for Diane von Furstenberg, ca. 1970s.

In 1953, when I was 16 years old, I enrolled in a dressmaking course for two years. After graduating, I worked from home, making clothes for friends and family. Years later, I moved to Montevarchi in Tuscany, where I met my husband. We got engaged and eventually married. From 1960 to 1964, I dedicated myself to my family. In 1964, I returned to work at a lingerie factory called La Toscanina. In December 1969, Angelo Ferretti purchased the factory. Mr. Ferretti was from Milan and had a textile manufacturing plant near Como. He asked me to make women's clothing for his new company called Ferange. After a few days of working at Ferange, I was introduced to a couple, Diane and Egon von Furstenberg. My working relationship with them began when they brought me the sketches of their new ready-to-wear line and asked me to develop the patterns and prototypes.

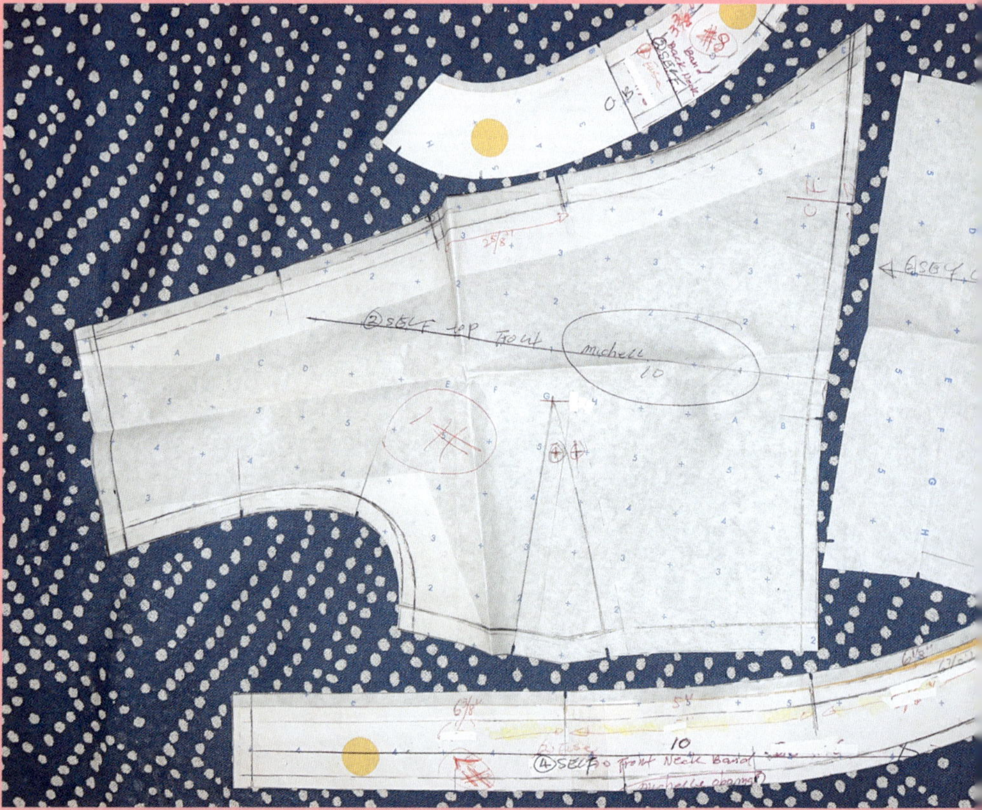

What were your responsibilities as patternmaker for Diane von Furstenberg?

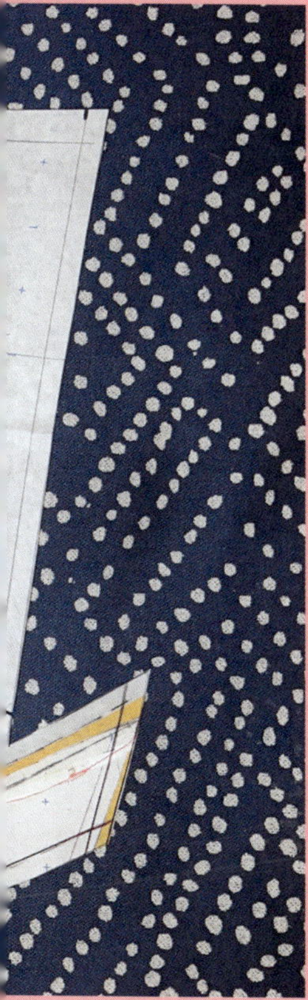

Making a dress consisted of developing the individual pieces necessary to create a garment, such as the front and back, sleeves, collar, and cuffs. Each worker had his or her own task in assembling the pieces to create the final product. From 1972 to 1974, I began to create the first patterns from the designs that Furstenberg's collaborator, Sue Feinberg, provided me. Diane would approve the fit of the first sample. After the first prototype was approved, I would then grade the model into a size range. My collaboration with Furstenberg was my greatest professional achievement. We understood each other perfectly.

A wrap dress pattern.

What patterns did you make for von Furstenberg?

Opposite
T72 dress design.

Diane was Manifattura Tessile Ferretti's main client for many years. The most successful style was the T72. Its pattern was the starting point for the making of Furstenberg's famous wrap dress, which was made with fit-forming printed jersey. This dress was very comfortable but elegant enough for a woman to go from the office directly to an evening cocktail party.

Watching American films today, I still recognize the clothing on which I worked in the 70s, I am very proud of my work. I see the comfortable jersey dresses and the pantsuits for women who travel. They could be packed in a suitcase without wrinkling. In my opinion, these dresses became the epitome of timeless elegance for the American woman.

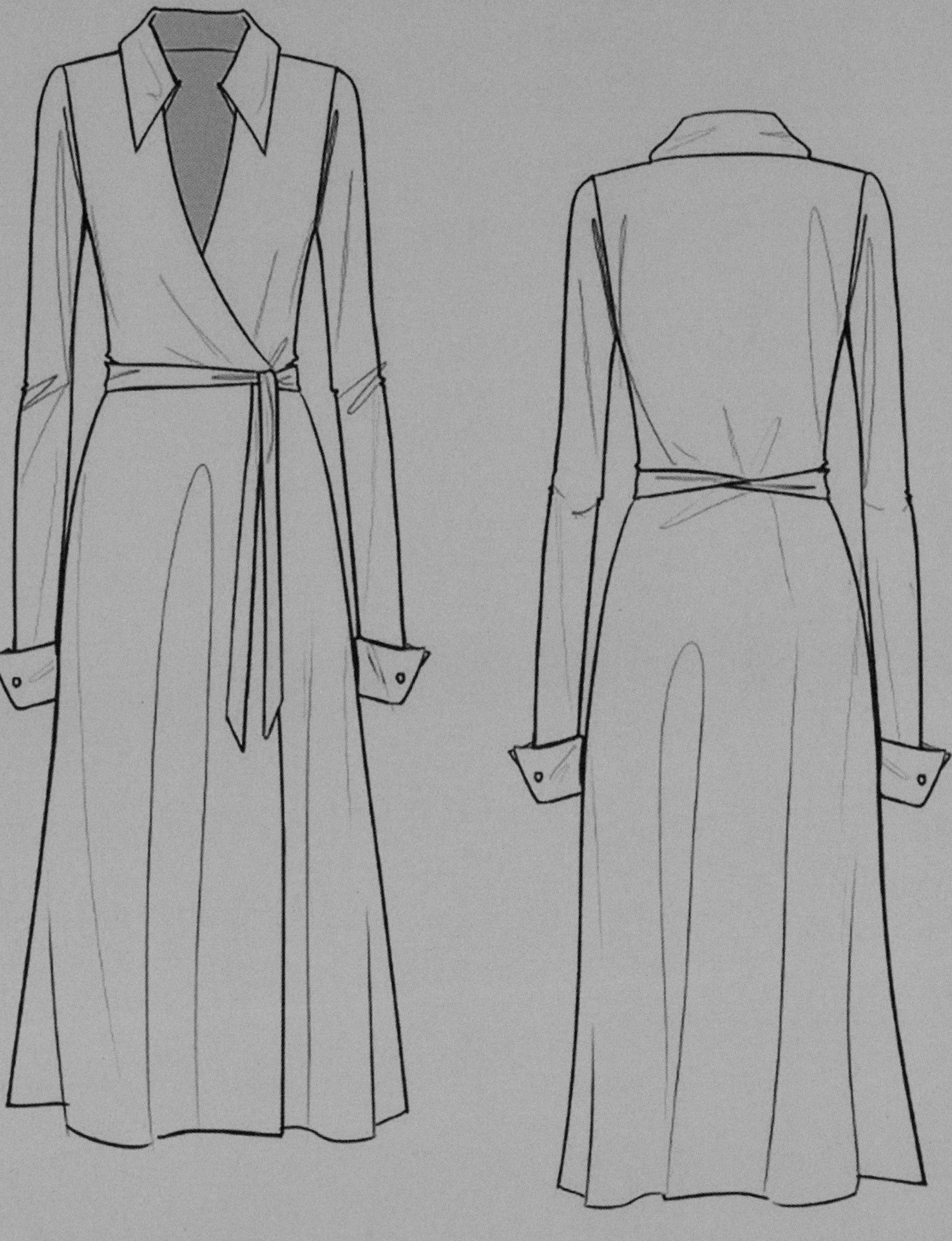

What is your relationship to Diane von Furstenberg?

Opposite
Bruna Sequalino and Diane von Furstenberg in Florence, June 2008.

Diane has always been very nice and affectionate toward me. In June 2008, she invited me to see her 2009 Resort collection in the Torrigiani Gardens in Florence. After so many years, I never imagined that I would meet Diane in Florence in such a beautiful location. That evening, the brand introduced a new collection during Pitti Immagine. On that occasion, I met Mimmo Ferretti, Angelo Ferretti's son; Stephan Janson, one of Diane's stylists with whom I had worked in the past; and Mr. Baldetti. Many years have passed, but I still treasure all the good memories I have working with Diane, and I hope there will be more opportunities to reconnect.

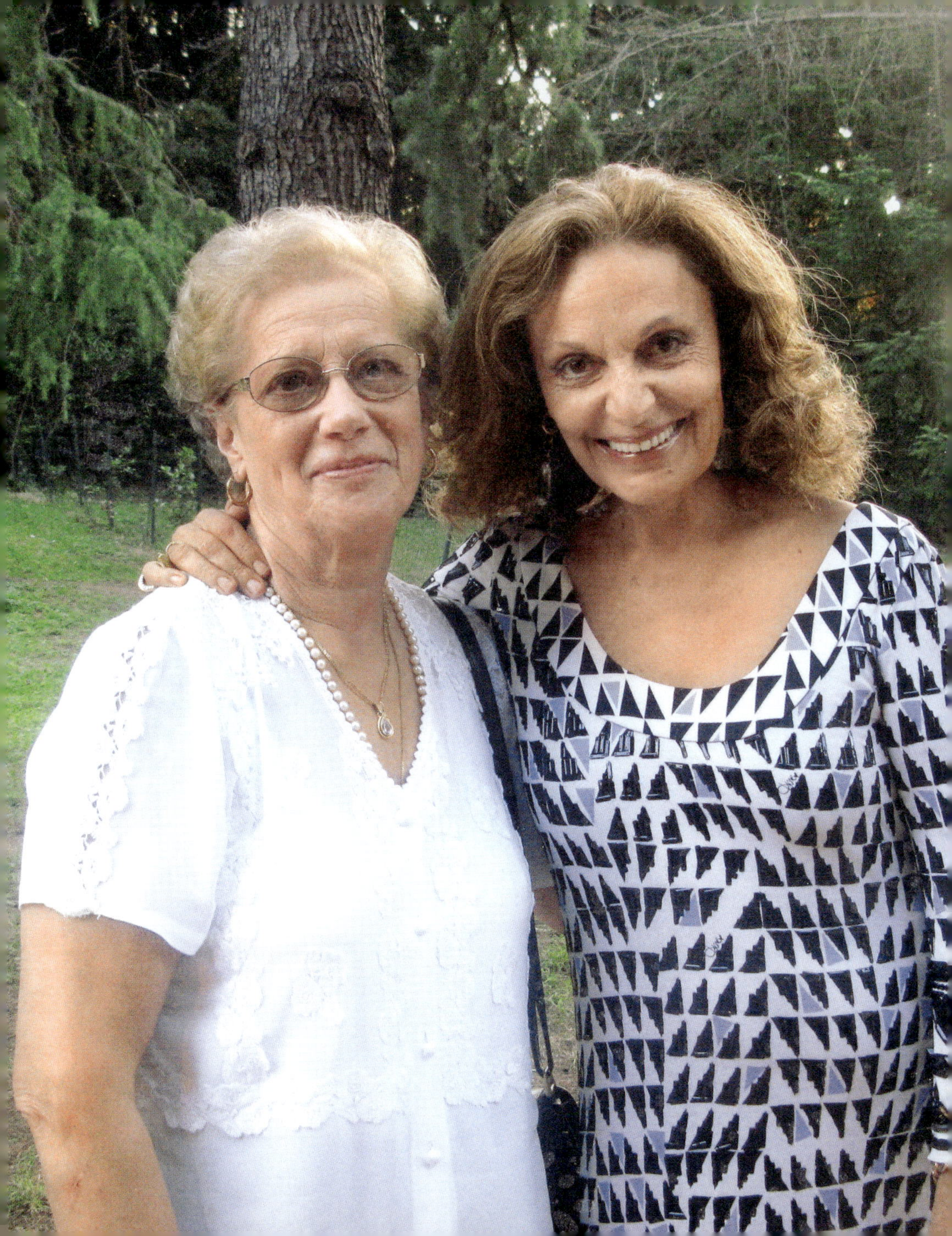

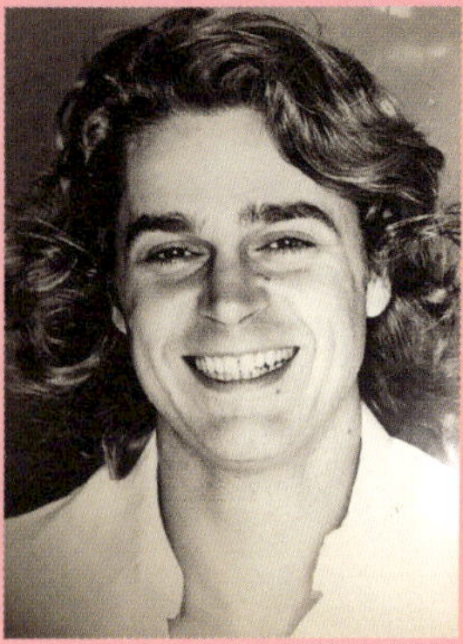

MIMMO FERRETTI

Mimmo Ferretti (b. 1949, Italy) is an entrepreneur; author; and son of Diane von Furstenberg's mentor, Angelo Ferretti, an Italian fashion industrialist who supported von Furstenberg in developing and producing her initial collections. Mimmo Ferretti is a very close friend of von Furstenberg and has worked with her in imagining and fabricating some bold prints at the Como factory.

How and when did you begin working with Diane?

I became Diane's friend around the age of sixteen. She was Egon's new girlfriend. Egon's brother, Sebastiano, was my best friend. We were always very curious about Egon's new girlfriends. Diane was very different from the others. She was very charming and had a distinct and very personal make-up style: white lips and black fingernails—a style ahead of the times. I met her for the first time in Cortina at Egon's mother's home. Later on, in Milan, she became much closer to my family and me.

Diane was very curious about my father's business and started going to his factory in 1969. There, she picked up the first notions about fashion business and learned how textiles are fabricated. When I returned from military duty in 1970, she had already moved to New York City. She had predicted that the Ferretti factories would be sold and she would lose them as resources.

There were two factories: one in Como, where yarn to finished fabric was produced, and one in Levane, near Montevarchi, where the clothing was manufactured. We were sending everything to Levane to be manufactured.

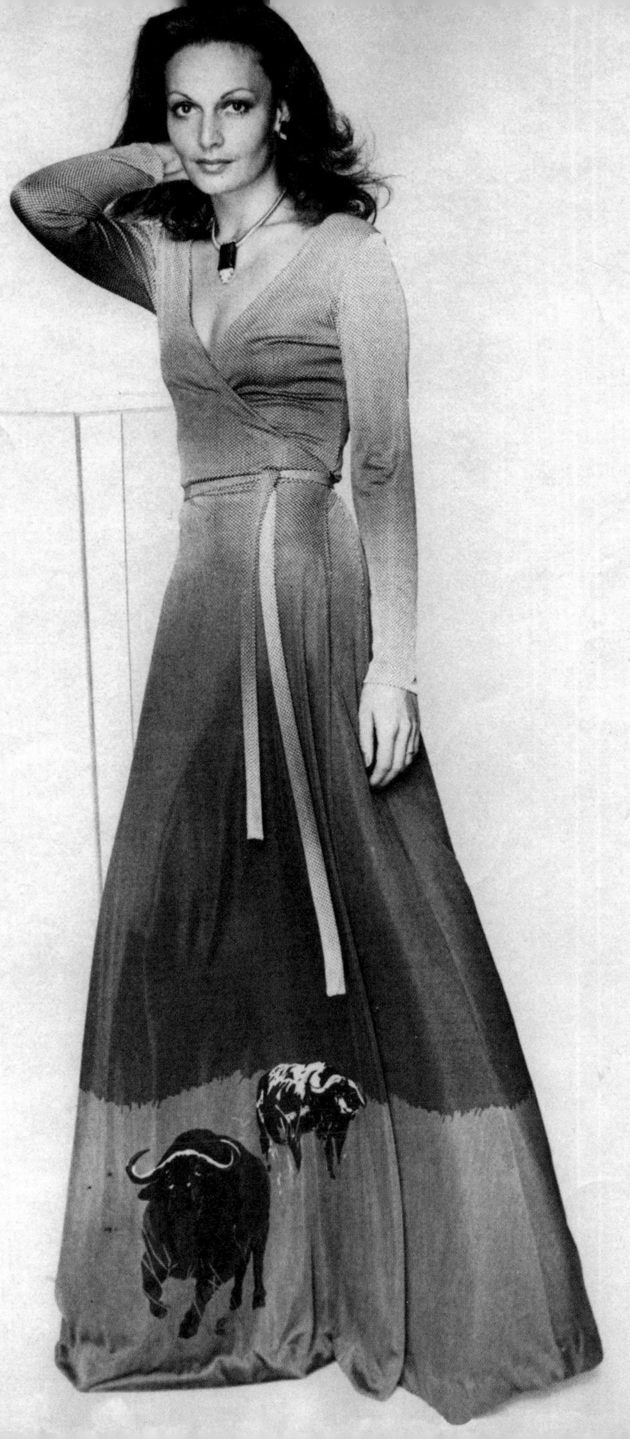

Opposite
Mimmo Ferretti in New York City, ca. 1976.

Right
Diane von Furstenberg wears a long jersey wrap dress printed in one of Mimmo Ferretti's designs, ca. 1974.

What was the specific jersey printing process?

Opposite
A page from a Ferretti sample book with printed jersey, ca. 1974.

I don't quite remember if, at first, we chose the drawings from those in our portfolio, which was already rich with three or four thousand drawings, but almost immediately, we began, together with Diane, to develop designs exclusively for her. I used to make the first choice by viewing the collections on paper of artists who specialized in creating pieces made of jersey. Then, together with Diane, we would choose the definitive ones.

There were no computers in those days, so the development of the variants had to be done by hand. Once we chose the design, we delivered it to the frameworks makers. The framework consists of a light, rigid, and nondeforming frame with metallic edges profiles that kept taut in place the photo-engraved screen printing fabric, called *buratto*. The frame has many tiny holes through which the printing paste passes. Each design element needed a different print frame that added the next color element and so on to get to the final result. We prepared dozen of variations, but only three or four were selected.

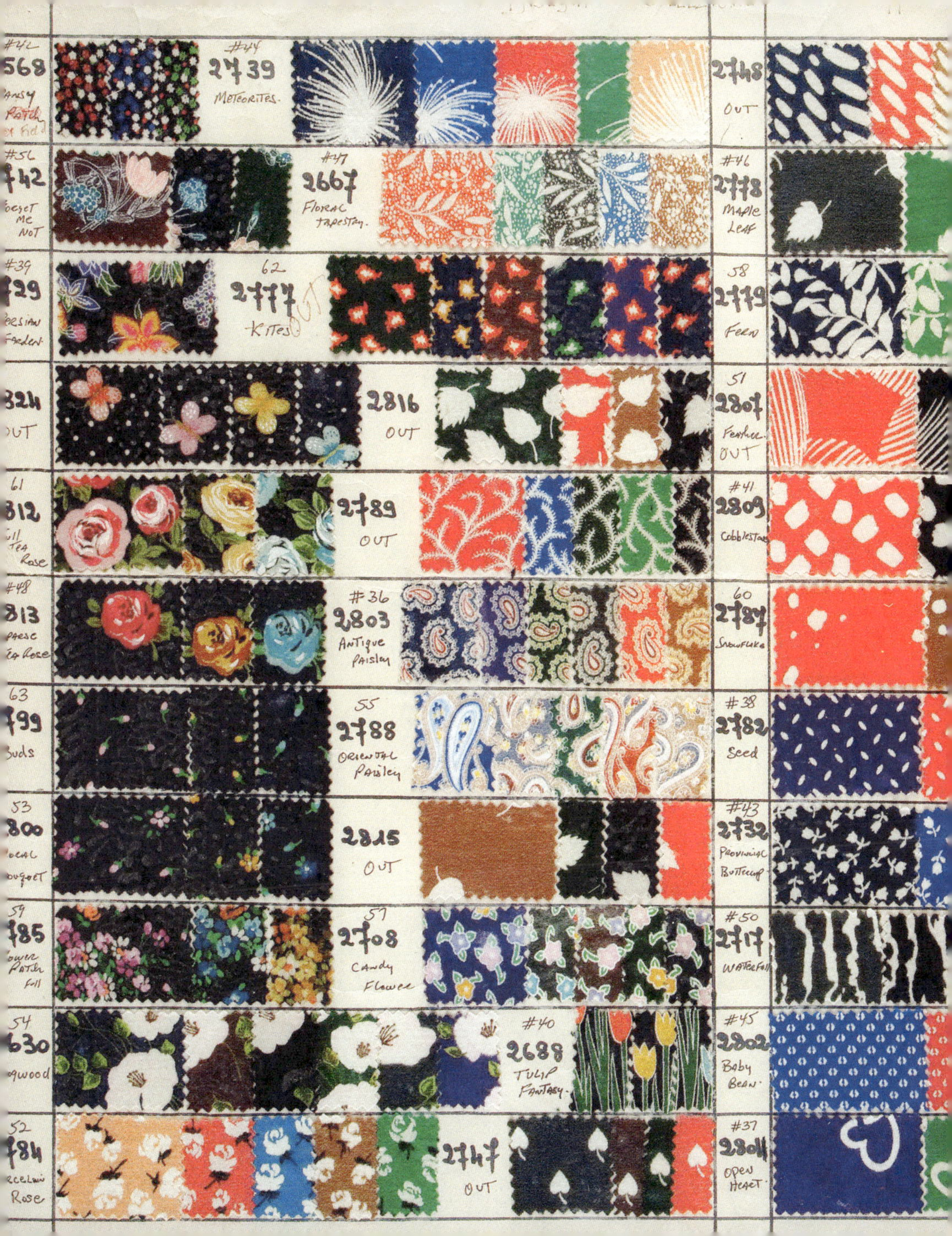

#44
2739
Meteorites
2748
OUT
#47
2667
Floral Tapestry
#46
2778
Maple Leaf
62
2777
Kites
58
2779
Fern
2816
OUT
51
2807
Feather
OUT
2789
OUT
#41
2809
Cobblestone
#36
2803
Antique Paisley
60
2787
Snowflake
55
2788
Oriental Paisley
#38
2782
Seed
2815
OUT
#43
2732
Provincial Buttercup
57
2708
Candy Flower
#50
2717
Waterfall
#40
2688
Tulip Fantasy
#45
2802
Baby Bean
2747
OUT
#37
2804
Open Heart

What did your position as printmaker for Diane von Furstenberg consist of?

After serving military duty, which was mandatory at the time, I returned to my civilian headquarters. As a young apprentice, I found my space in the drawing and color variants department with the assignment of following Diane's collections. Initially, it was a relatively easy task, which went well with my lack of passion for work. As we progressed, the number of drawings multiplied dramatically. Consequently, the number of variants increased exponentially until it took up all of my time.

Most of Diane's prints were one or two colors. The background was often white for the summer collections, which eased the job. On colored backgrounds, even dark ones, we used the corrosion printing technique by applying a corrosive product to erase part of the background color to reserve the space to print on. A corrosive product could alter the softness of the fabric to the touch. But our technicians, who were led by Diego Peverelli, were masters in finishing. In addition to stabilizing the possible shrinkage of cotton blends when washing, they were able to give an extremely pleasant hand to the touch.

When Diane came to Italy to choose the designs to add to the collection, we worked side by side.

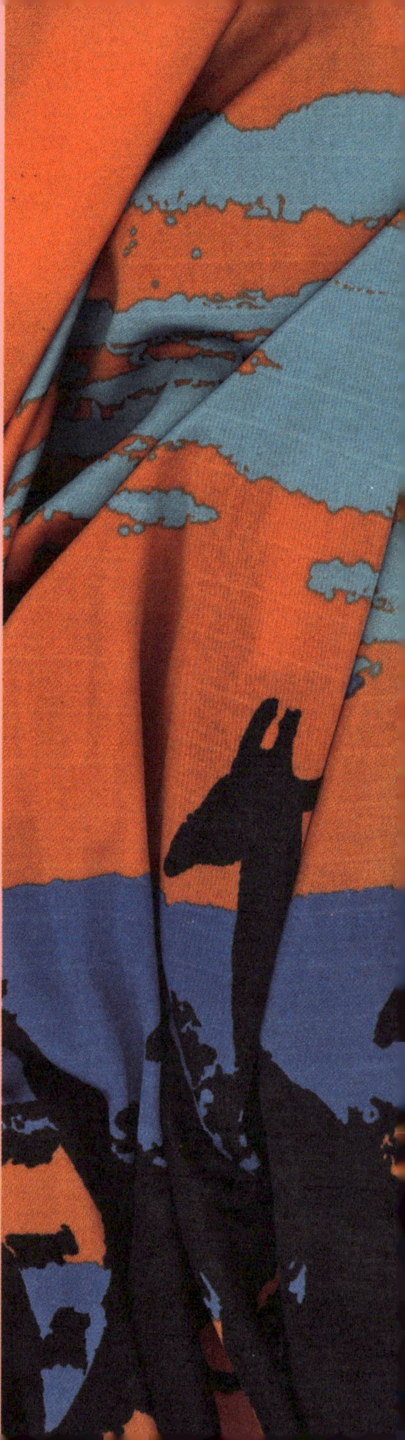

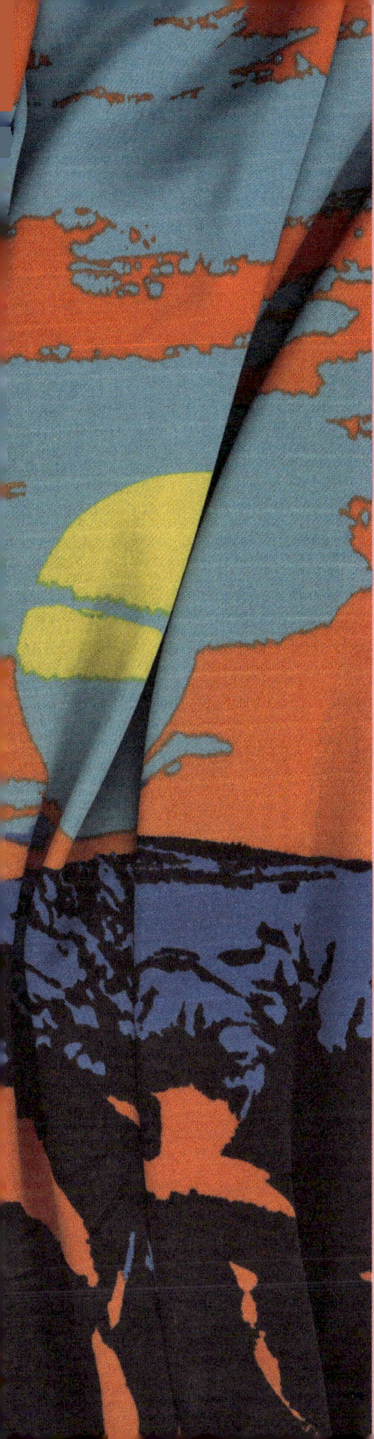

What were your influences in developing the prints?

I was influenced by my travels to Africa. I remember using some of my photos from Africa to make a buffalo and giraffes in a landscape print, as well as a leopard climbing print.

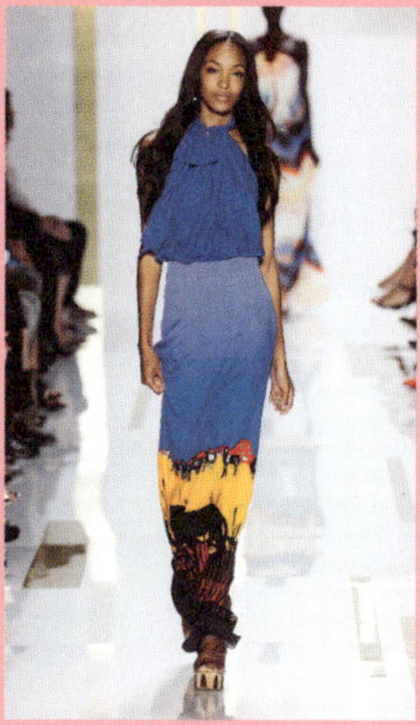

Opposite
Mimmo Ferretti-inspired print detail.

Next page
An article about Diane von Furstenberg and Angelo Ferretti, titled "This Fantastic Woman Has a Fantastic Guy Behind Her," published in the *Burlington County Times*, March 30, 1976.

Above
Model Jourdan Dunn in a Mimmo Ferretti–inspired print skirt at the Diane von Furstenberg Spring 2014 show.

MAR 3 0 1976

BURLINGTON COUNTY TIMES
Willingboro, N.J.
PM-38,716 S-27,389

This fantastic woman has fantastic guy behind her

By LOGAN BENTLEY LESSONA

ROME, ITALY — "Diane von Furstenberg is a fantastic woman," says Angelo Ferretti, a handsome, husky Italian industralist.

"You could compare her to Helena Rubinstein." Fine, but Ferretti, the man behind Diane von Furstenberg and her partner, is a pretty fantastic guy himself.

Typical of the energetic, driving businessmen of Italy's north who contributed to Italy's economic "miracle" after World War II, he has gone from turning out knitted silk jersey on silk stocking machines nobody knew what to do with when women turned to nylon stockings, to running an operation that is shipping to the United States alone some 17,000 dresses a week.

This is remarkable considering that Italy is suffering its worst economic crisis since the end of World War II. The lira is in such bad shape at the moment that the joke making the rounds is that the Olympic skiers used 10,000 lire notes for ski wax so they could go down faster.

Ferretti's is a vertical operation, in that he takes the natural or synthetic fiber, knits the fabric (usually a combination of rayon or acrylic fiber combined with cotton), prints it, and manufactures the garment. "From the fiber to the finished article," he said proudly in a recent interview.

In 1950 Ferretti found himself with 140,000 pounds of silk and the machines for silk stockings, a glut on the market.

I didn't know what to do with these circular machines made for stockings but I adapted them and that's how silk jersey fabric was born. I had to

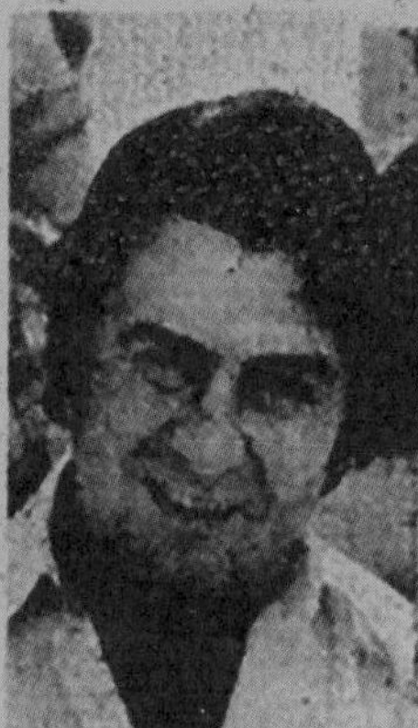

ANGELO FERRETTI

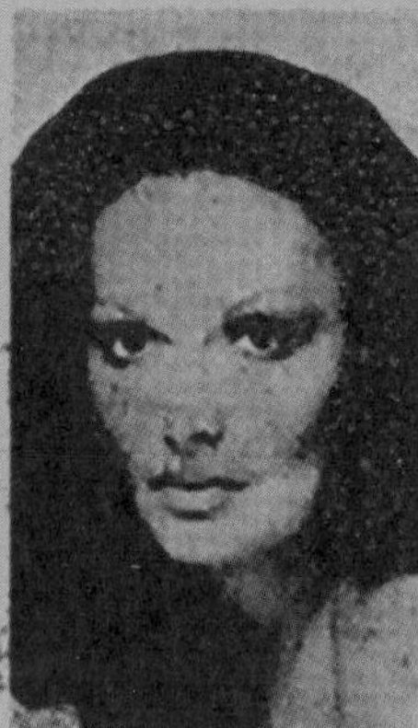

DIANE VON FURSTENBERG

use up all that silk. Then I took some printed designs we had on hand for scarves and printed the fabric with them. For four years I was the only one in Italy to make it," he said.

In 1955 Ferretti started selling to the large department stores, and in the meantime he experimented with flocked velvet and nylon chiffon. He had a factory in Milan to make fabric, one in Como to print it, and a small place near Arezzo to make dresses.

When Diane Halprin married Egon von Furstenberg and planned to move to New York, she told her friend Angelo she wanted to work there.

"Let me take a few of your dresses and see if I can sell them," she pleaded. Ferretti, in an expansive mood, tells the story with great satisfaction: "After a few months she called and asked me to send her 20 more dresses. I told her, 'Diane, I sell dresses by the thousands, I can't afford to do this.'

" 'Trust me,' she said. So, because I like her, I sent them. Then she called and asked for fifty dresses. 'Diane,' I said, 'you are going to ruin me.' But I sent them, and the next thing I found out she had set up a showroom in New York, but her label on them, and the boom began.

"She has a great capacity for work, even 24 hours a day at a stretch. I understood she wanted to succeed and put my factories at her disposition.

"When things really started to take off she came to Milan and told me she wanted to spend a month with me to learn. She was with me all the time and really prepared herself. She learned all about fabrics, printing, manufacturing.

"It's not true she was lucky because her name is von Furstenberg; she worked her head off, and has a lot of perseverance. She will do three fashion shows in three different cities if she has to."

It is a great fairy tale, but there is more to it than that. What, exactly, is responsible for the incredible success story of the von Furstenberg dresses?

"Several things," explains Ferretti.

"For one thing, my hobby has always been to carry high fashion to the masses. And this is easier to do in the United States. I make fabrics for haute couture houses like Louis Feraud and Valention, and I make Banlon in Italy for Dupont, but I have always tried to use the best designs even in inexpensive dresses.

"Then we developed the fabric for Diane's dresses especially for the American market. America is very demanding, and the American woman expects the dress she buys to hold up, be comfortable, and not lose its shape after washing.

"Our fabrics have two important qualities: dimensional stability, which means the fabric does not shrink or distort after washing, and 'imbibleyra,' which means that the synthetic mixed with cotton breathes, so you don't feel clammy when you wear the dress.

"I love the United States. I go there often, and I love the American client. Apart from her appreciation for Italian things she looks, understands, and comes back to buy again.

"Canadians are also crazy about our dresses, and also the Australians, Japanese, and English."

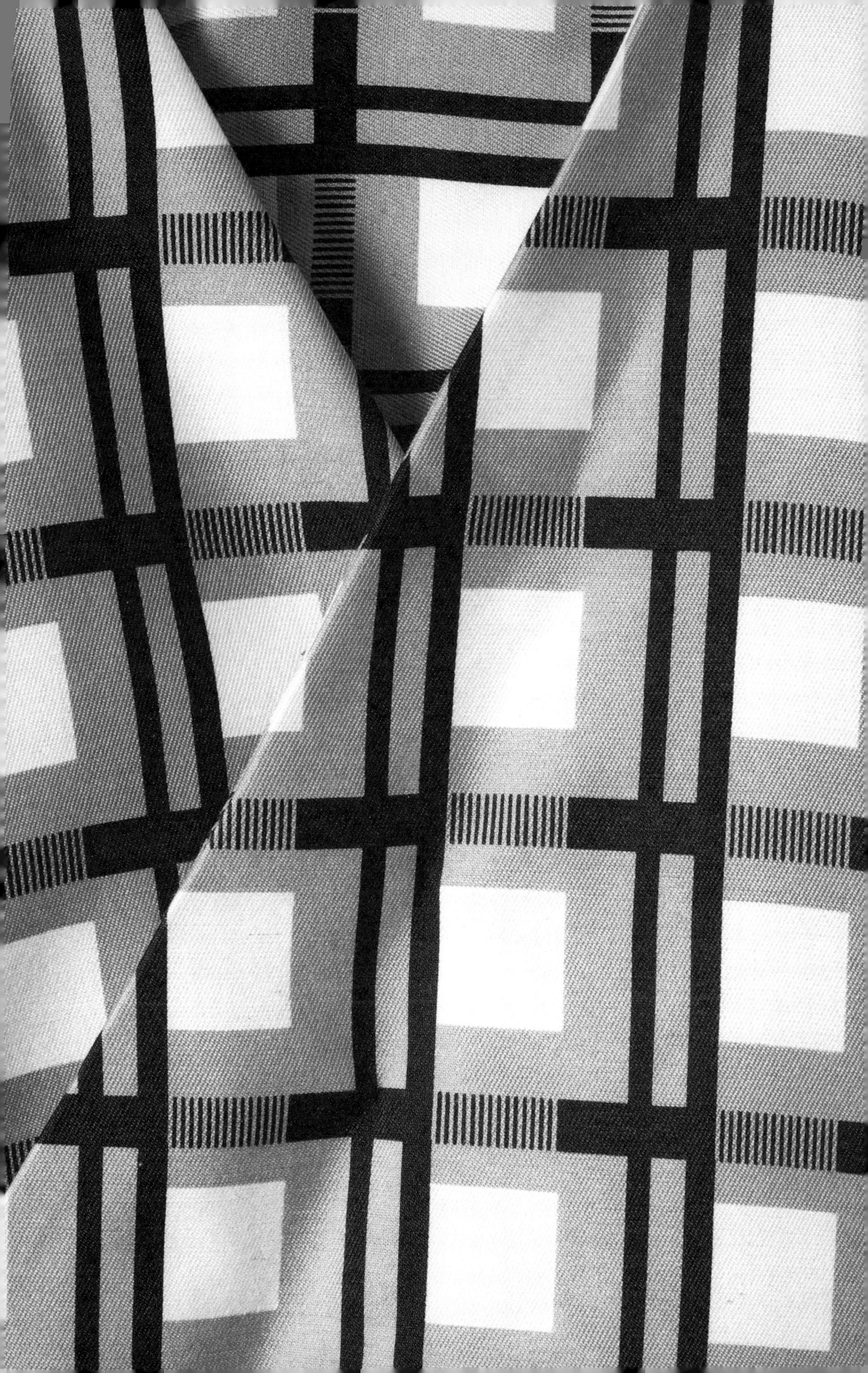

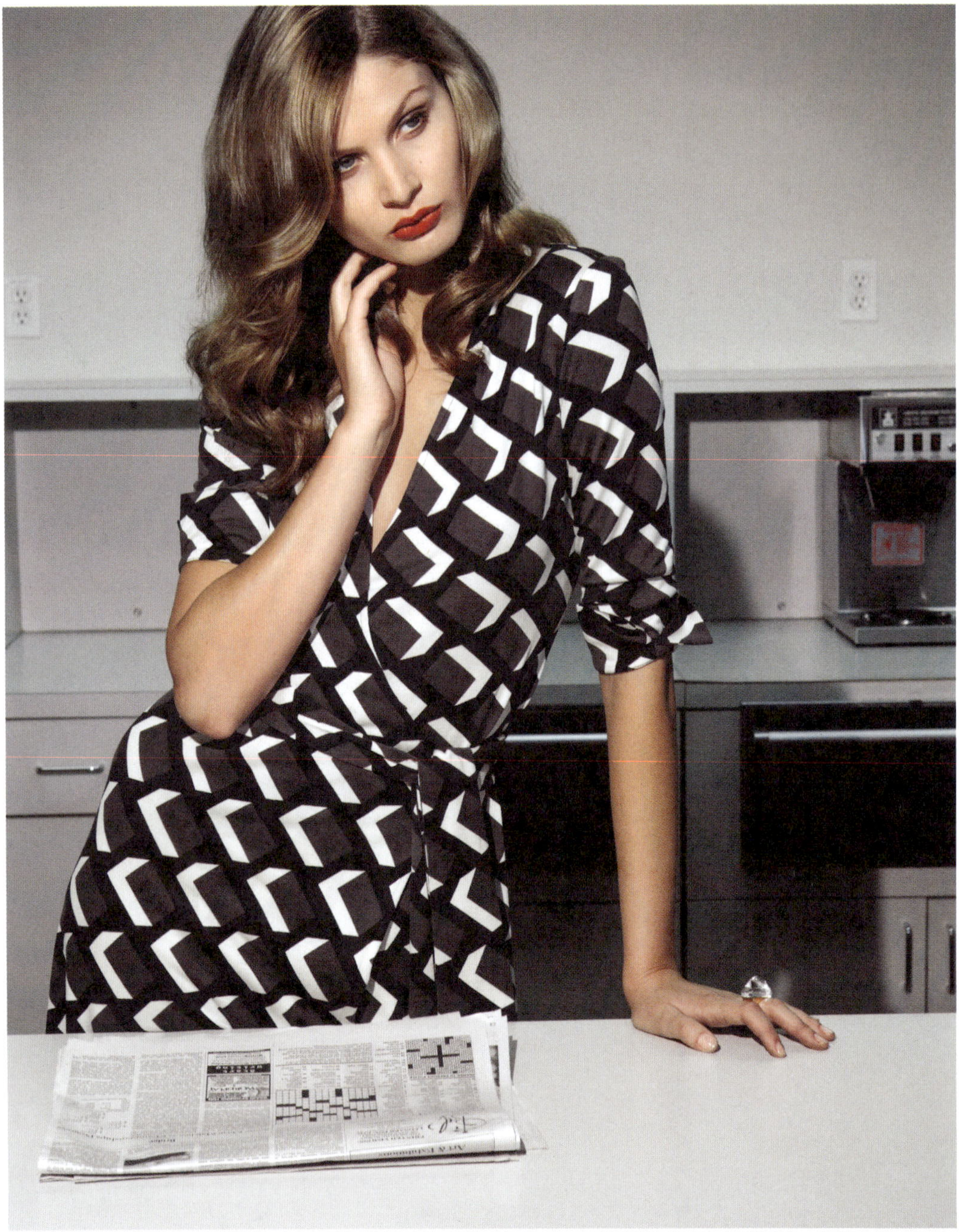

“

Every woman tends to have her own uniform according to her taste, her style, and her body type. I am very proud to say that DVF is the

UNIFORM for the woman INCHARGE.

The wrap dress can be dressed up or down for any occasion.”

”

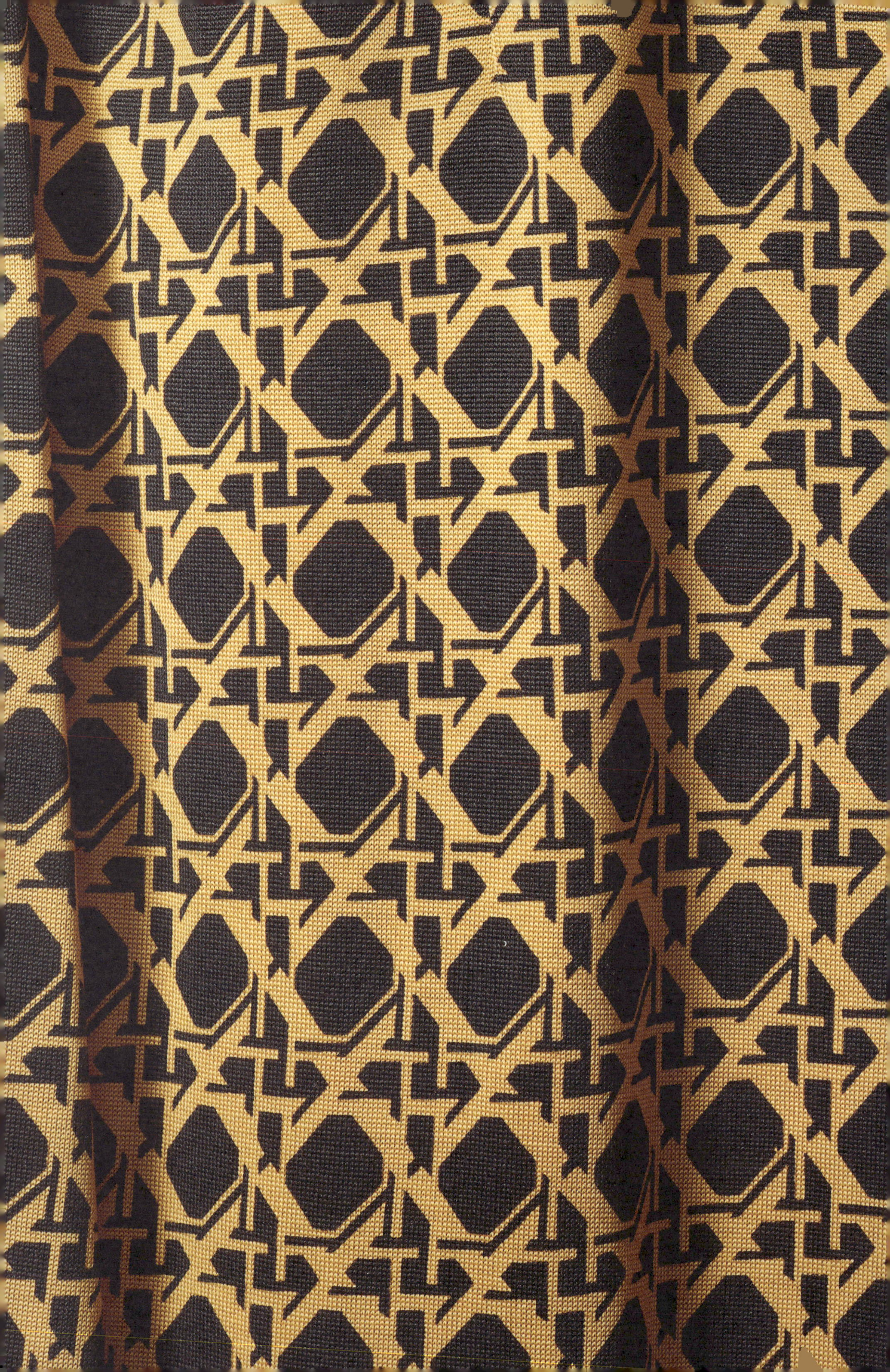

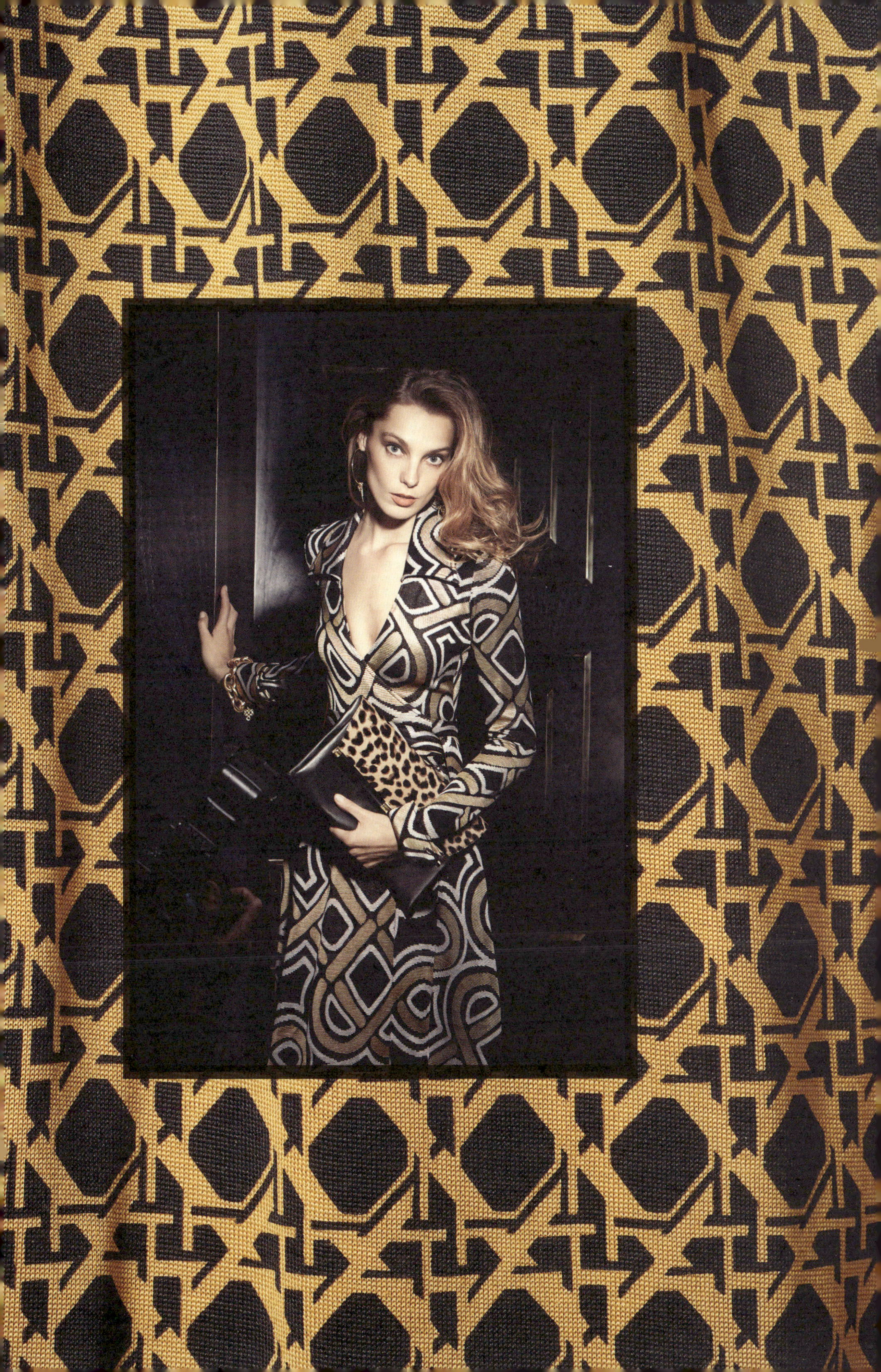

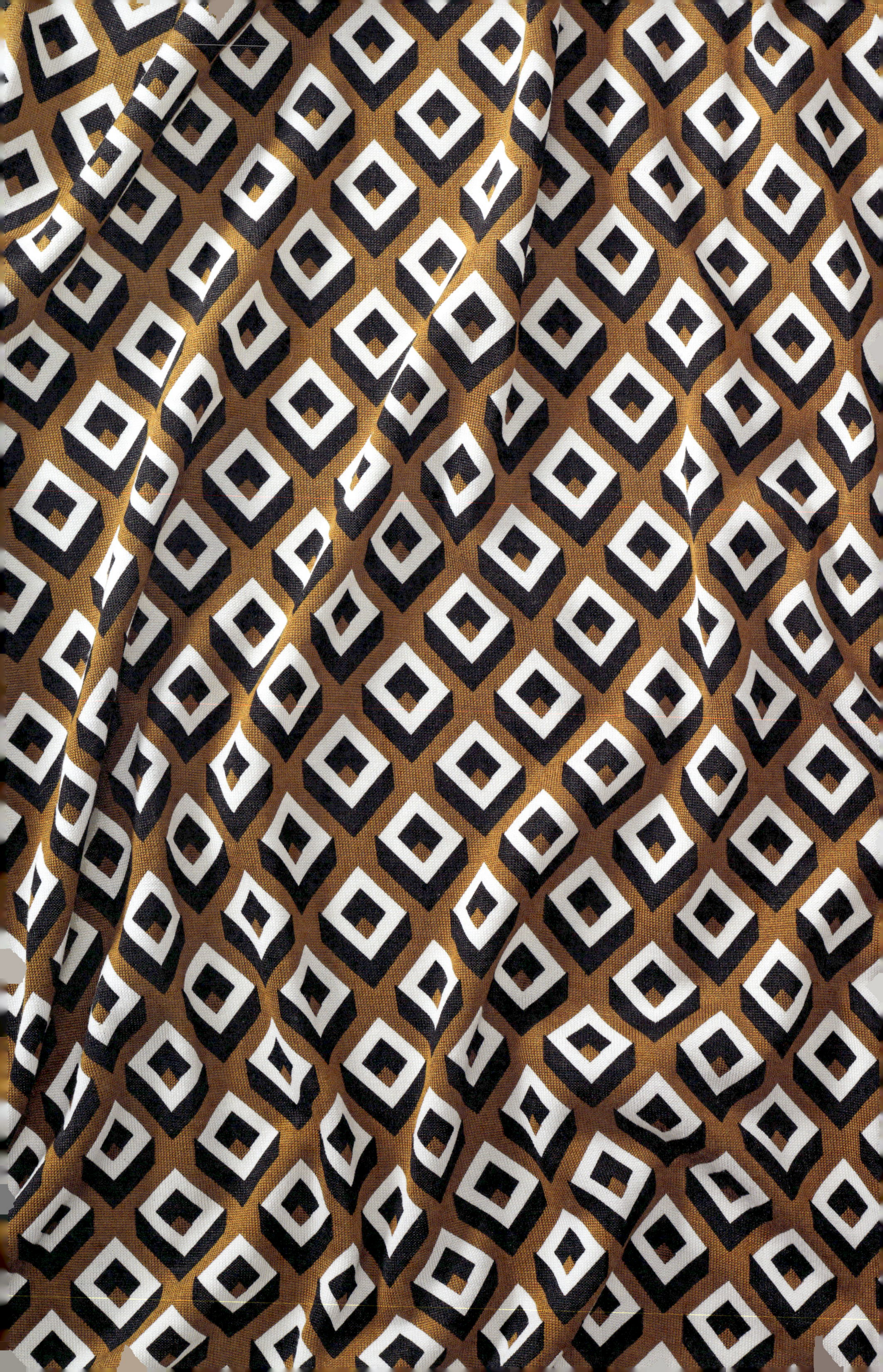

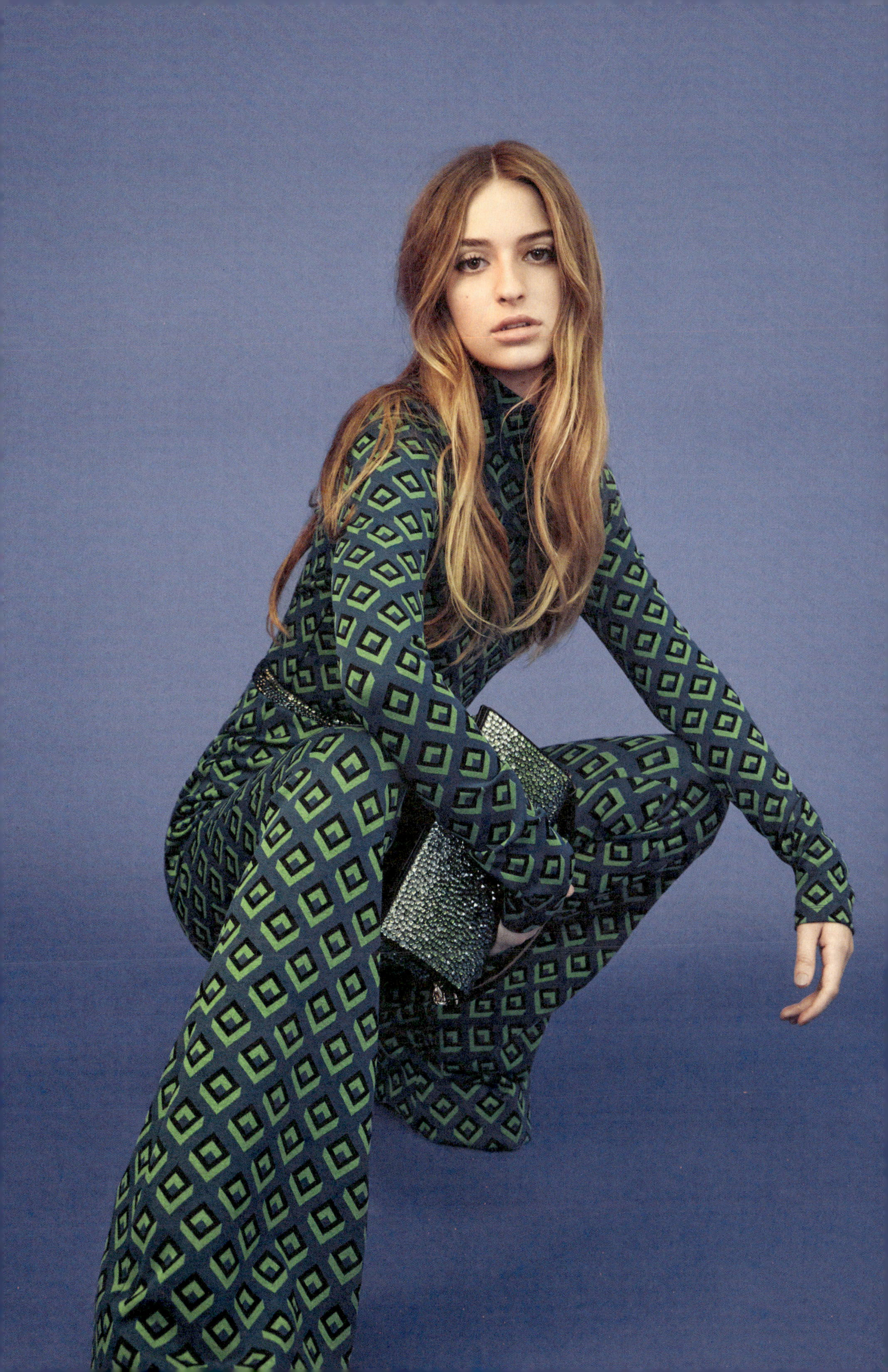

“The wrap dress is a natural form of dressing, like a kimono or a toga, that doesn’t require buttons or zippers. What made my wrap dress different was the printed jersey fabric that moved with the body and became like a second skin, so it was all about body language. It was effortless and practical, but also sexy. The prints were fun, but the cuffs and collar made it feel sophisticated, too.”

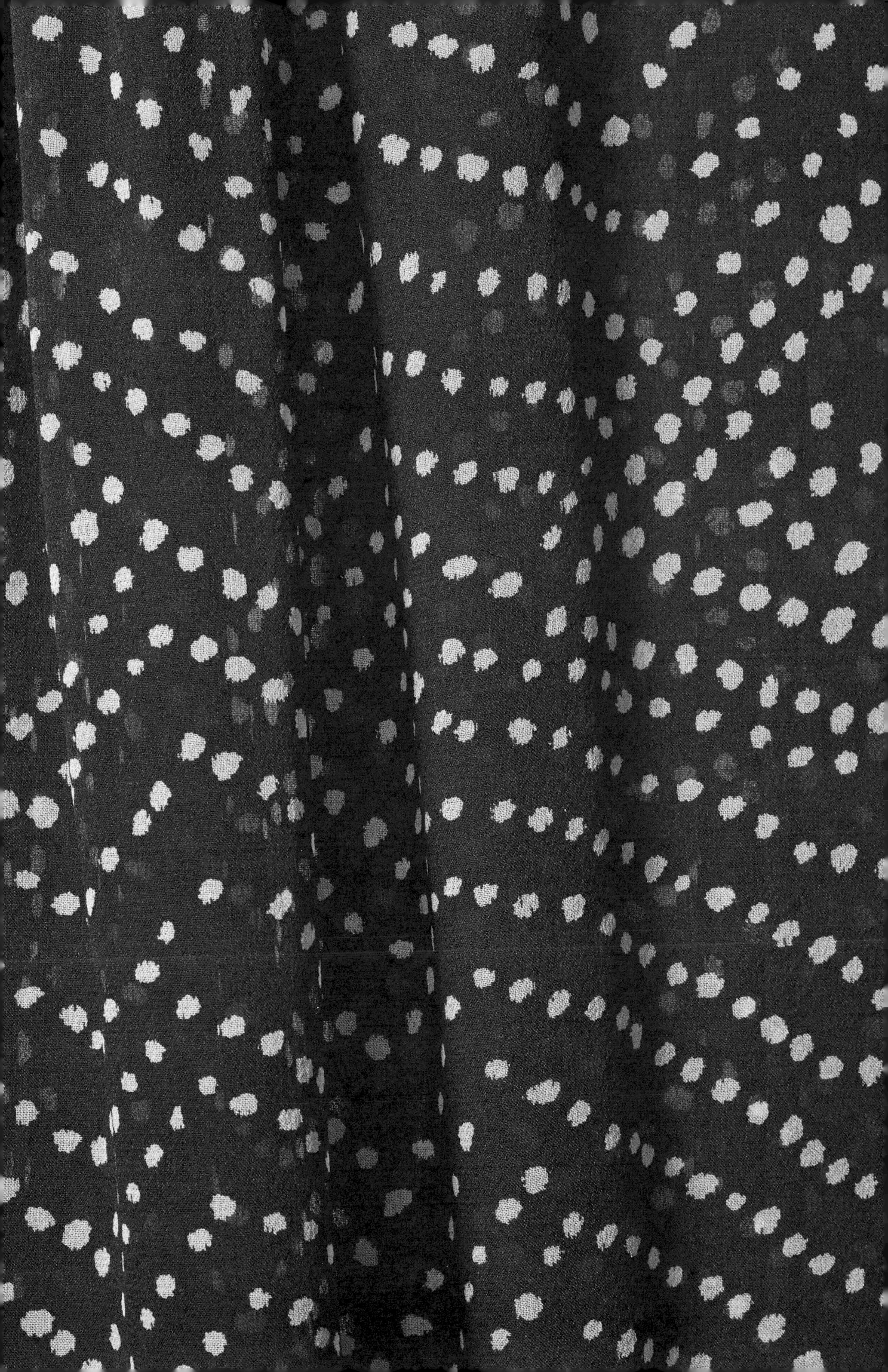

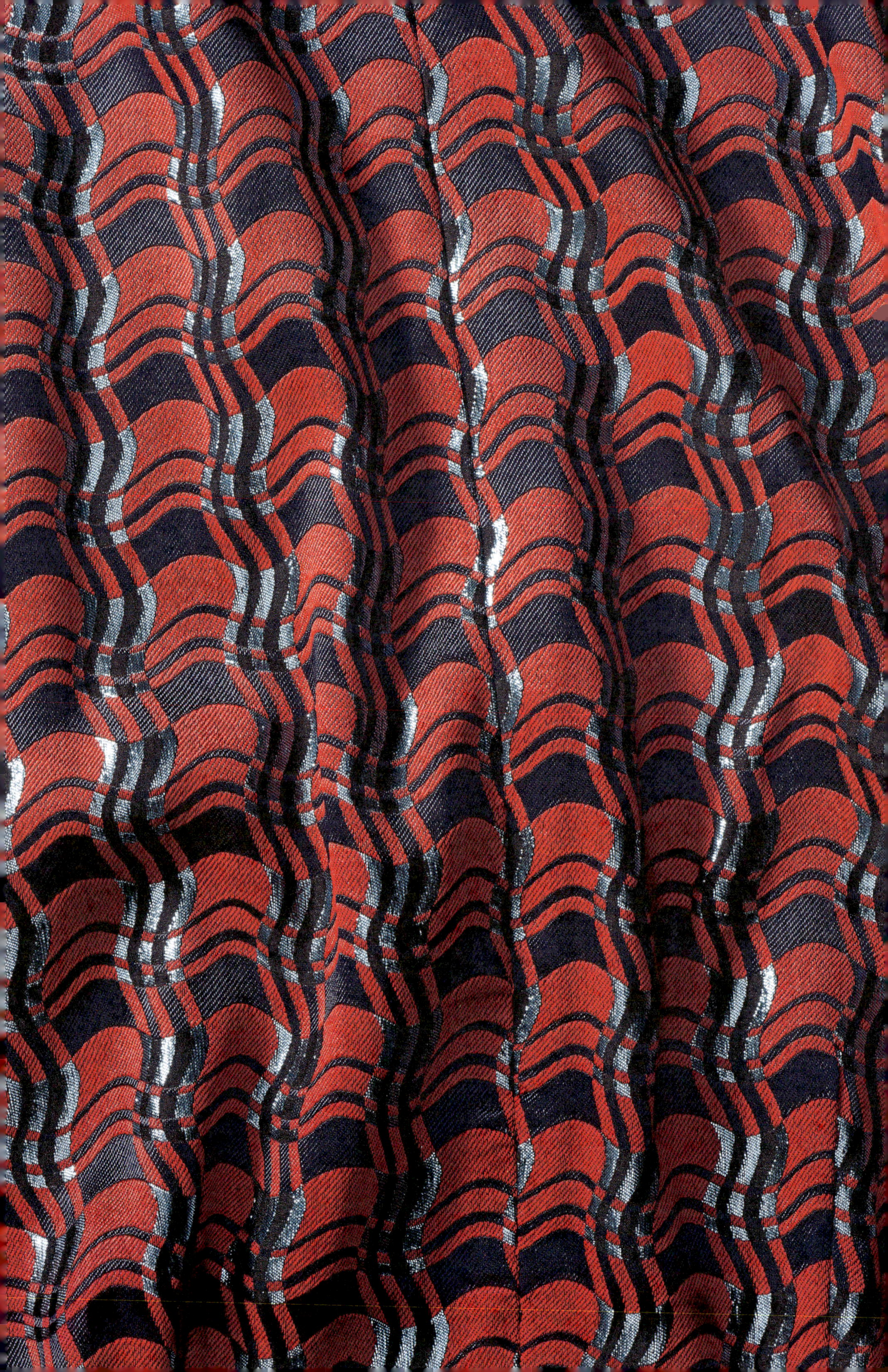

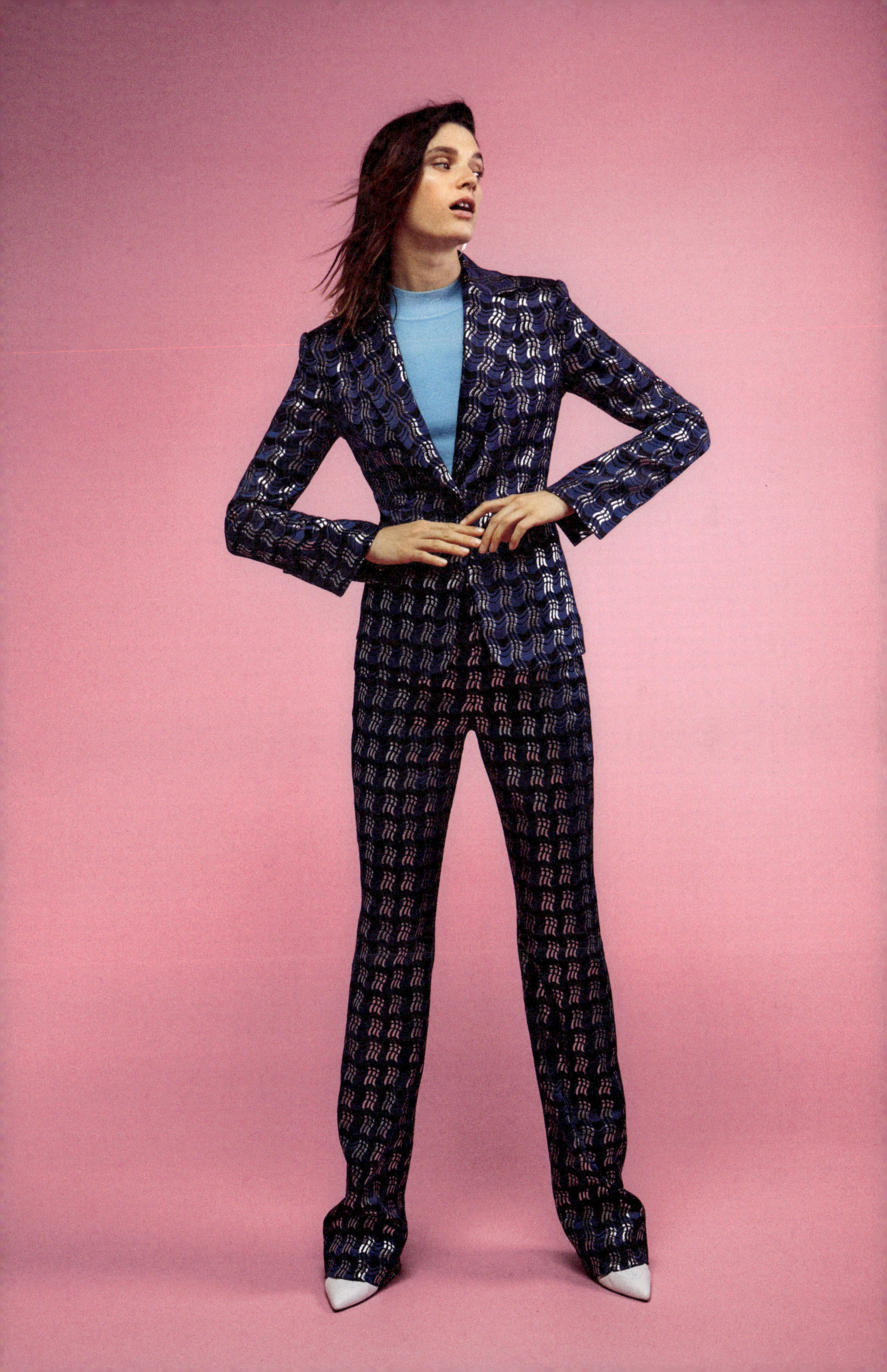

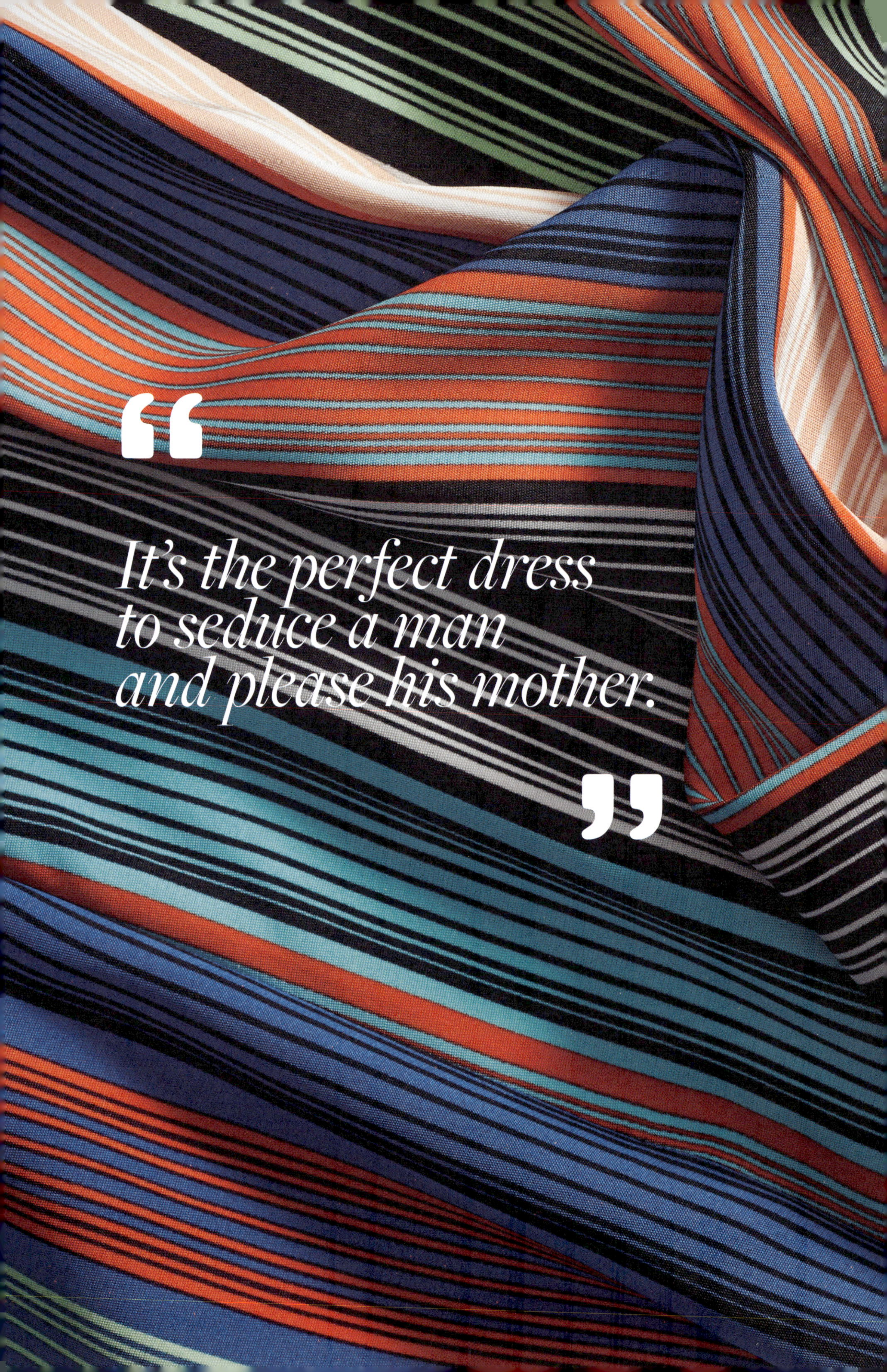

“It’s the perfect dress to seduce a man and please his mother.”

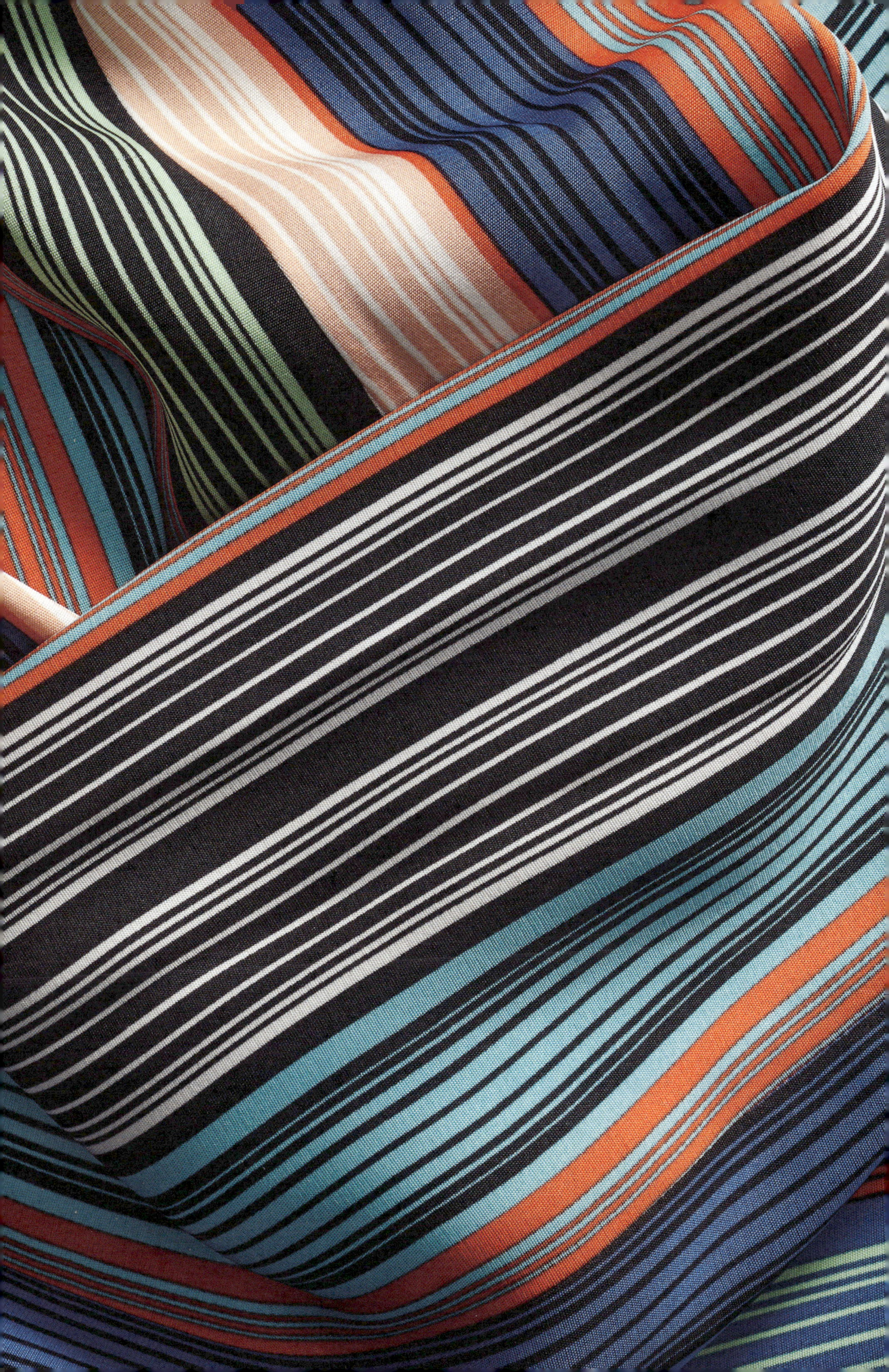

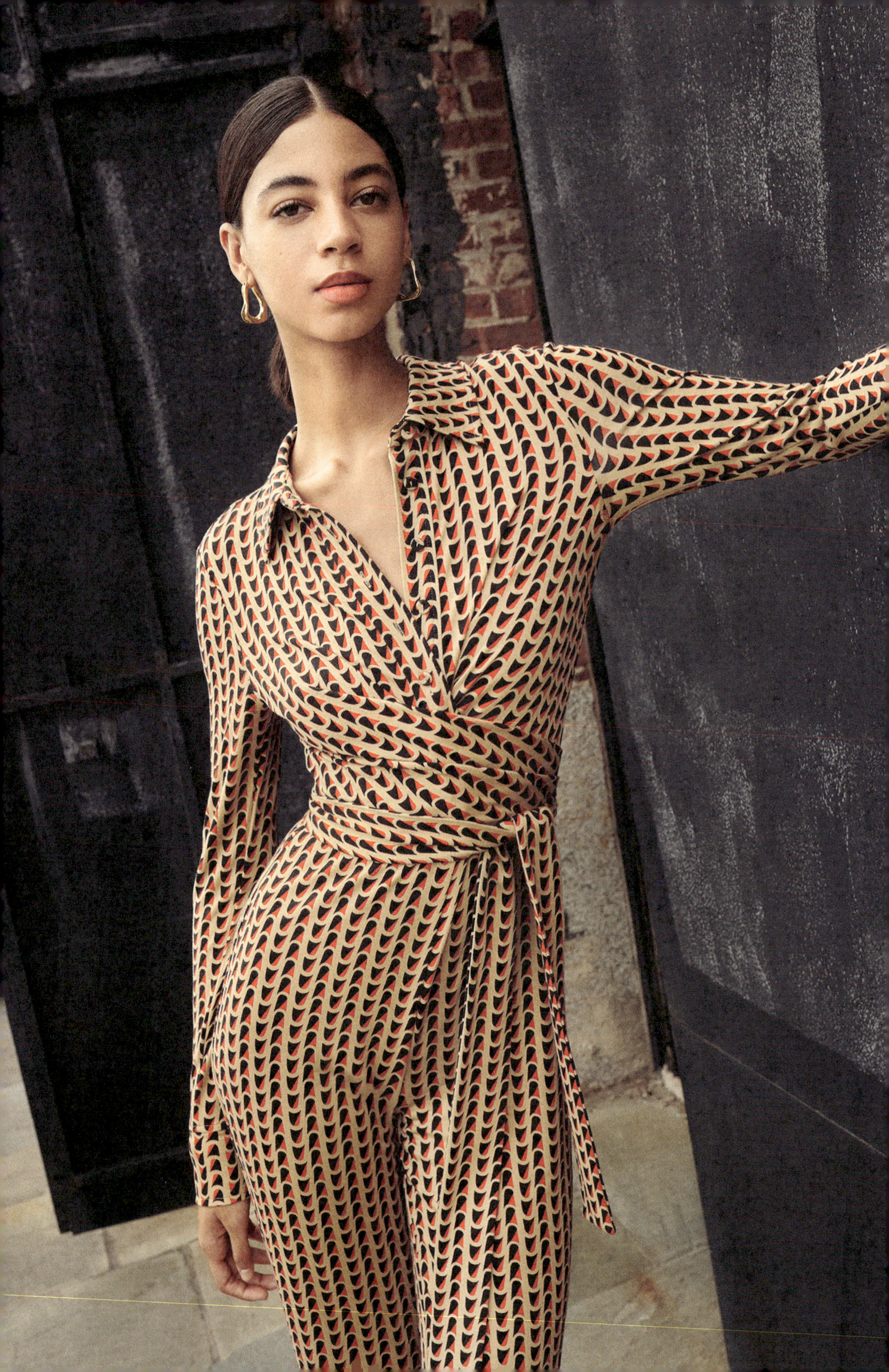

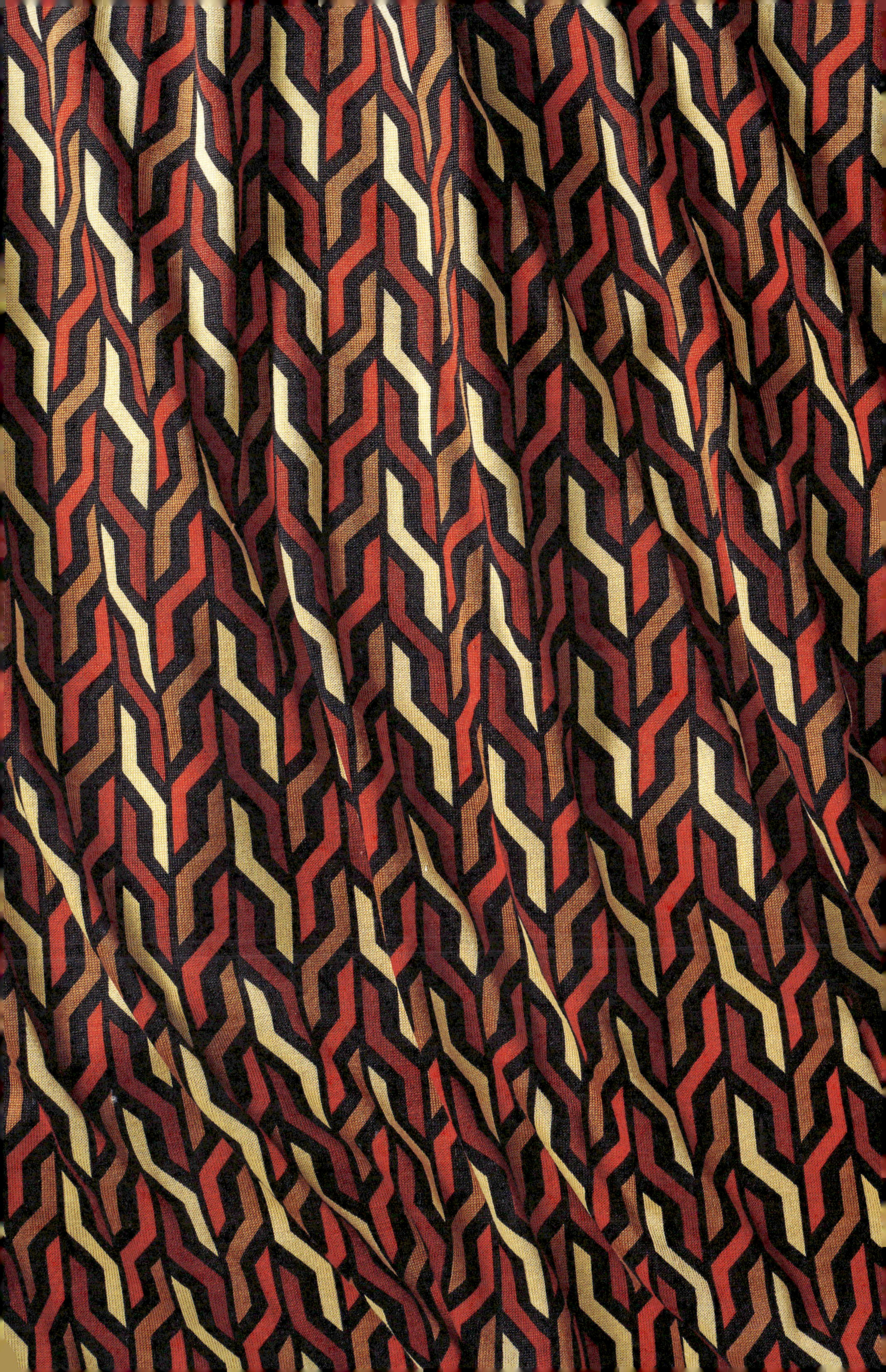

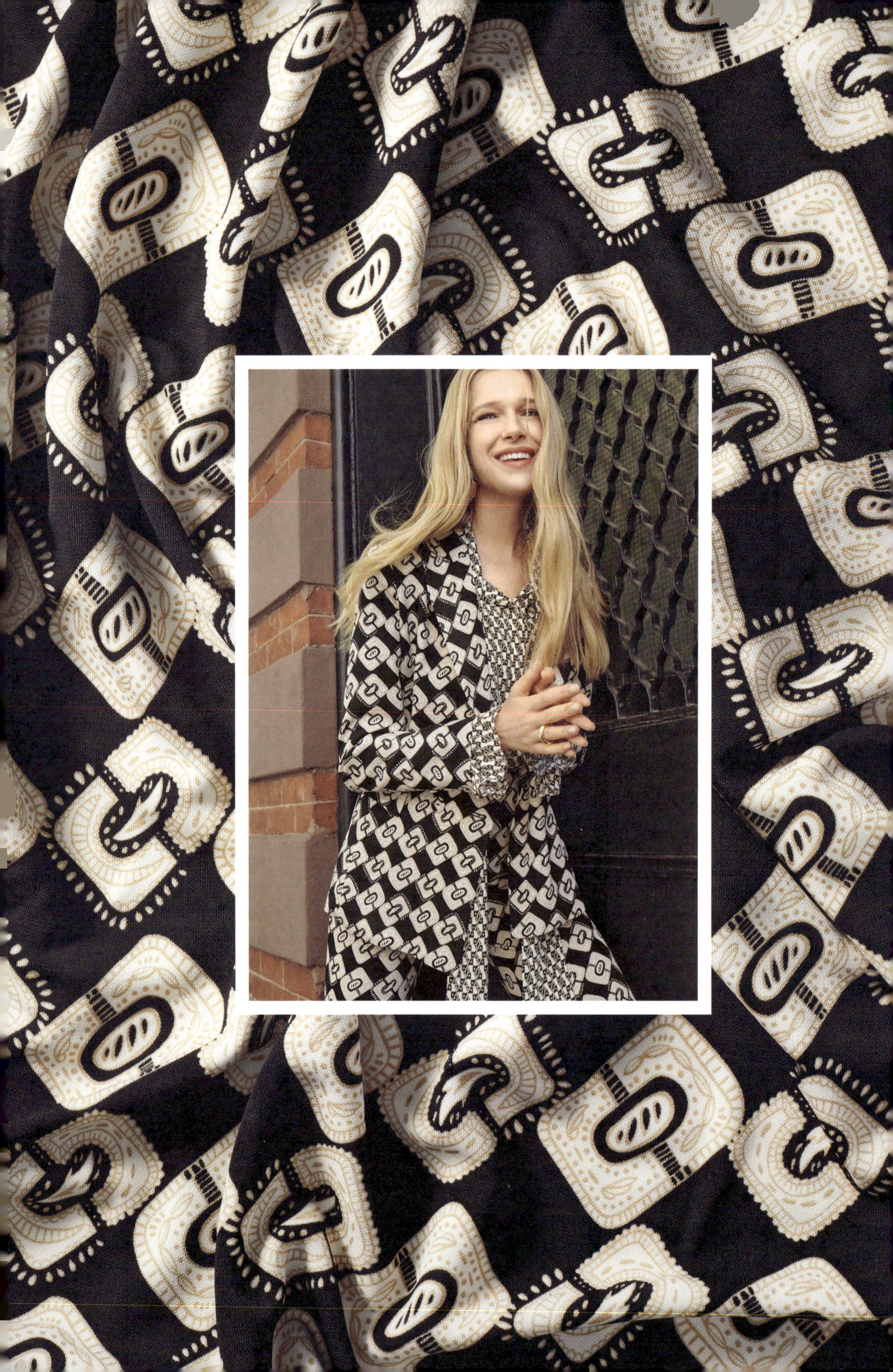

Dress Is a Dress Is a Dress

WRITTEN BY
Lydia Kanitsis

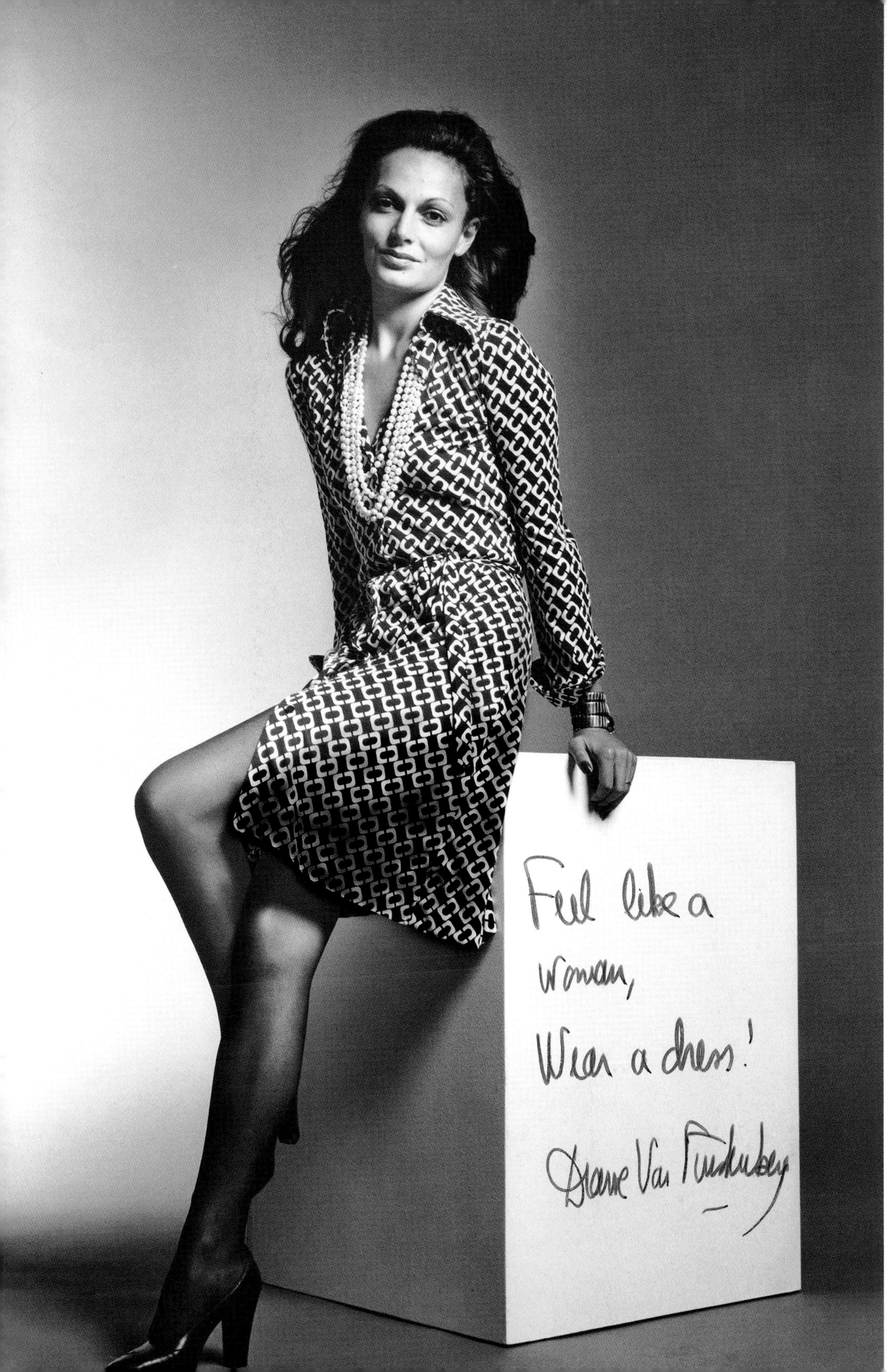

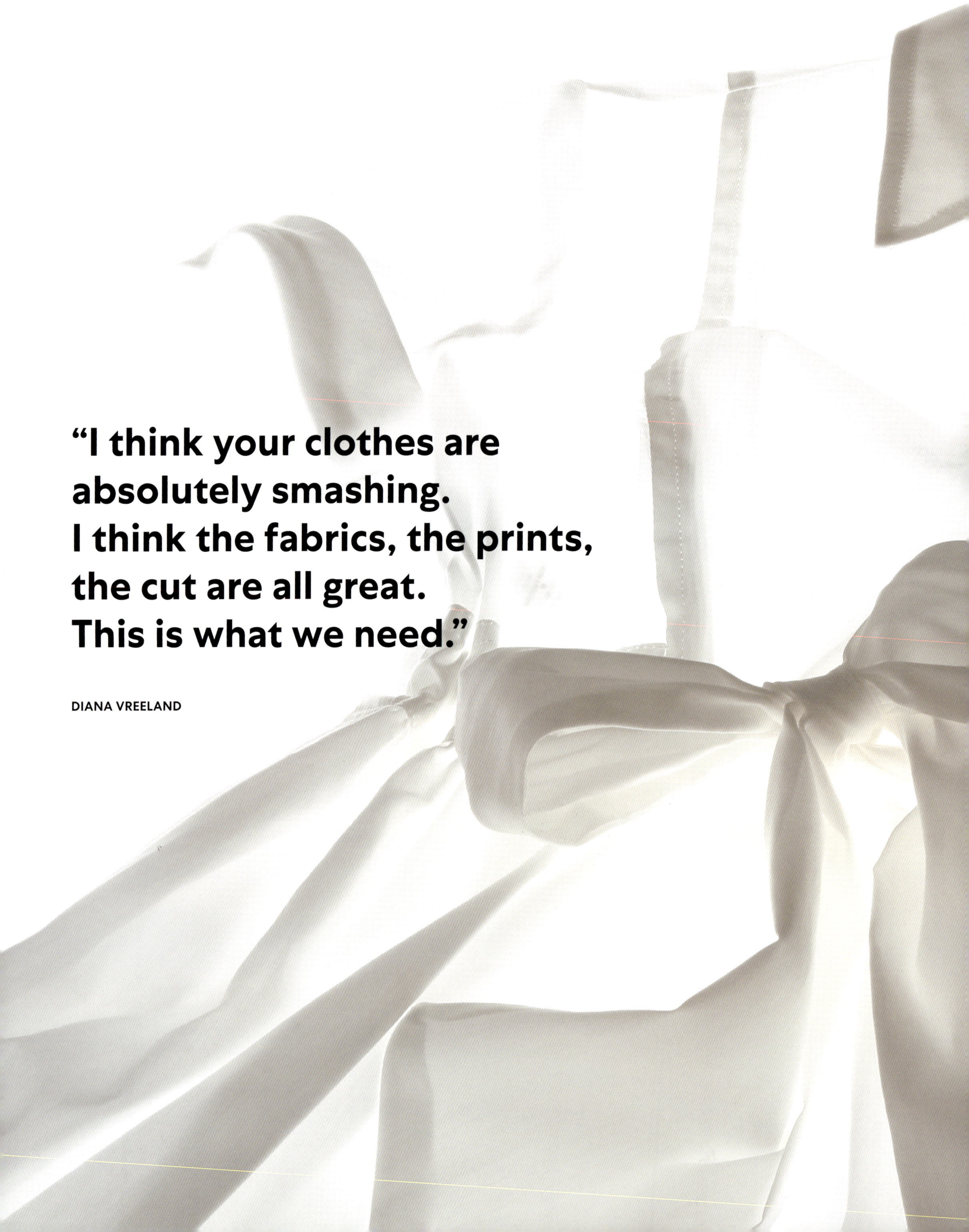

"I think your clothes are absolutely smashing. I think the fabrics, the prints, the cut are all great. This is what we need."

DIANA VREELAND

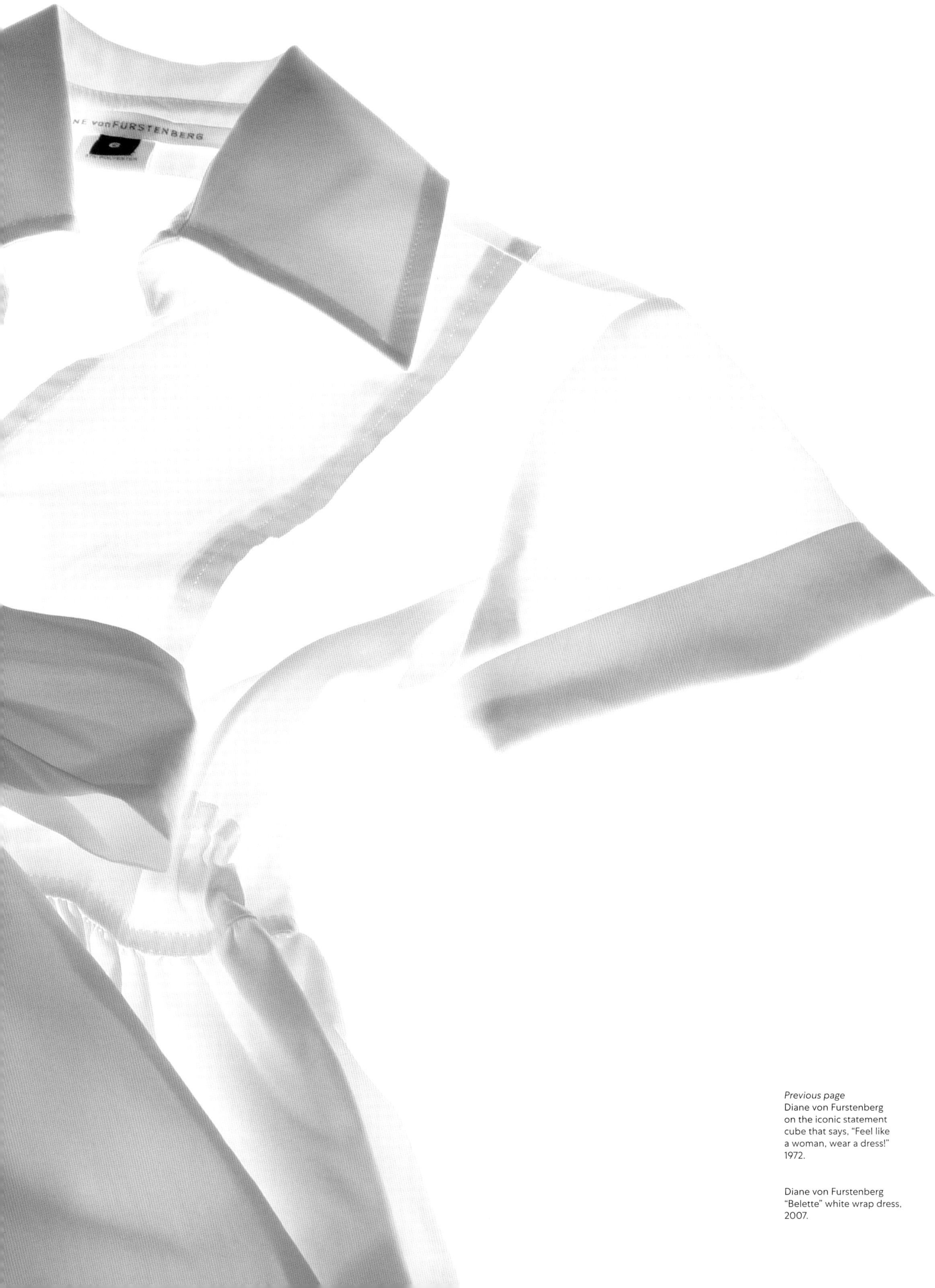

Previous page
Diane von Furstenberg on the iconic statement cube that says, "Feel like a woman, wear a dress!" 1972.

Diane von Furstenberg "Belette" white wrap dress, 2007.

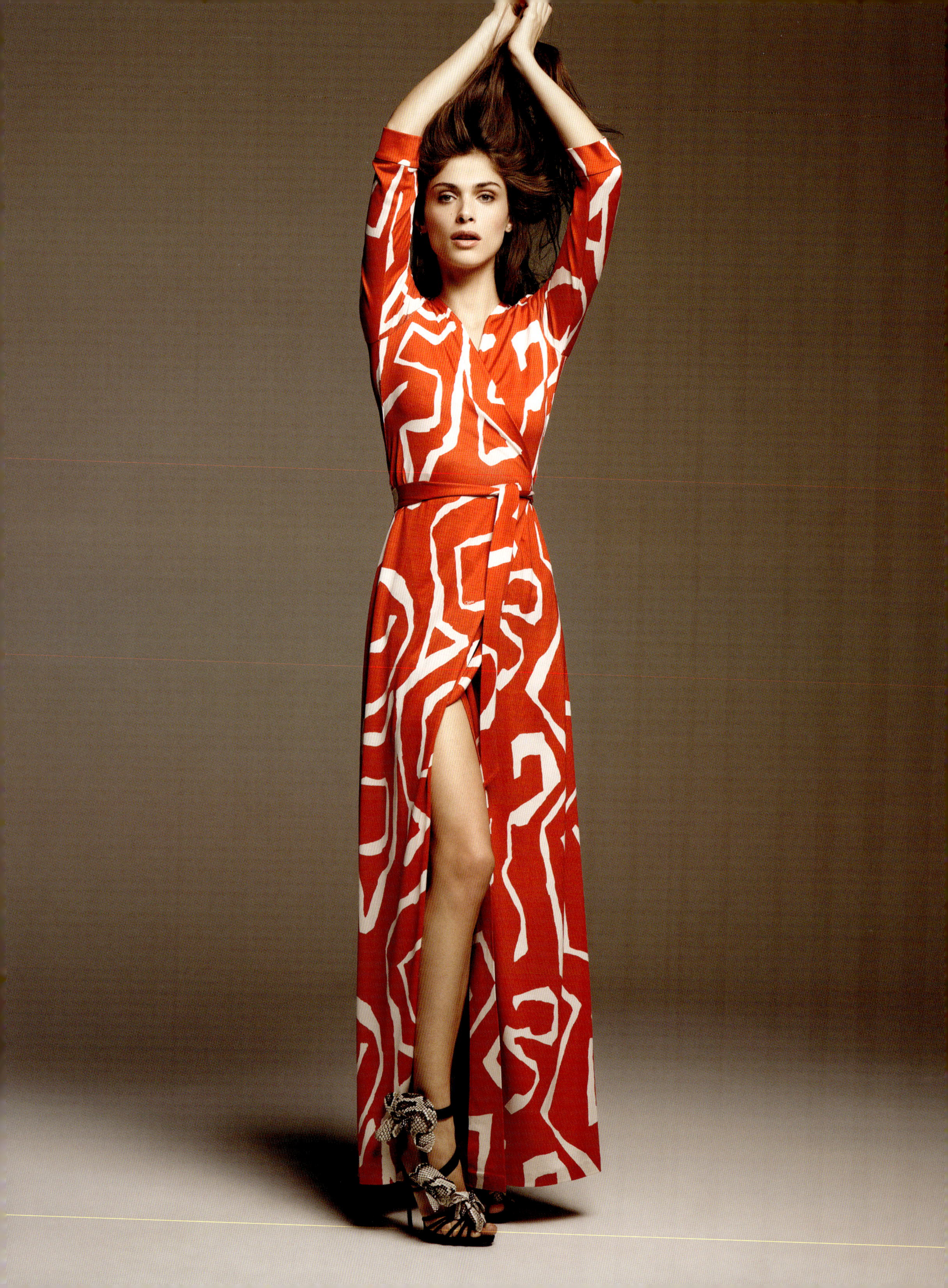

Dress Is a Dress Is a Dress

Opposite
Model Elisa Sednaoui poses in a Diane von Furstenberg long wrap dress, 2015.

A seemingly simple wraparound dress, sold in millions of units, has successfully defied trends and transcended time for what is now close to half a century. It may seem that everything has already been said about this famous wrap dress and the singular adventure that brought its visionary instigator, Diane von Furstenberg, to create it in 1973. Her serendipitous emergence into the world of fashion, motivated by a keen desire for financial independence from her young and aristocratic husband, would shape her experience of the American Dream. Her acquaintance with the Italian textile manufacturer Ferretti, a pioneer in printed jersey fabrics, provided her with the tools for its creation, but it was her vision of an item of clothing that is easy to wear and pack, and accessible and yet infused with the glamour that attended her standing as a European princess and young entrepreneur who undeniably transformed the wrap dress into an object of desire and propelled it to the firmament of the decade's best sellers.

Inextricably linked to the name Diane von Furstenberg, the wrap dress, contrary to a common trope in the media, was not invented by her. In fact, the model has not been copyrighted, and no formal legal protection secures its design. Its tremendous and sudden commercial success and the fame it acquired over the years have given it a "legal" existence—at least, symbolically—as, like any phenomenal success, it has not been spared the curse of copycats.

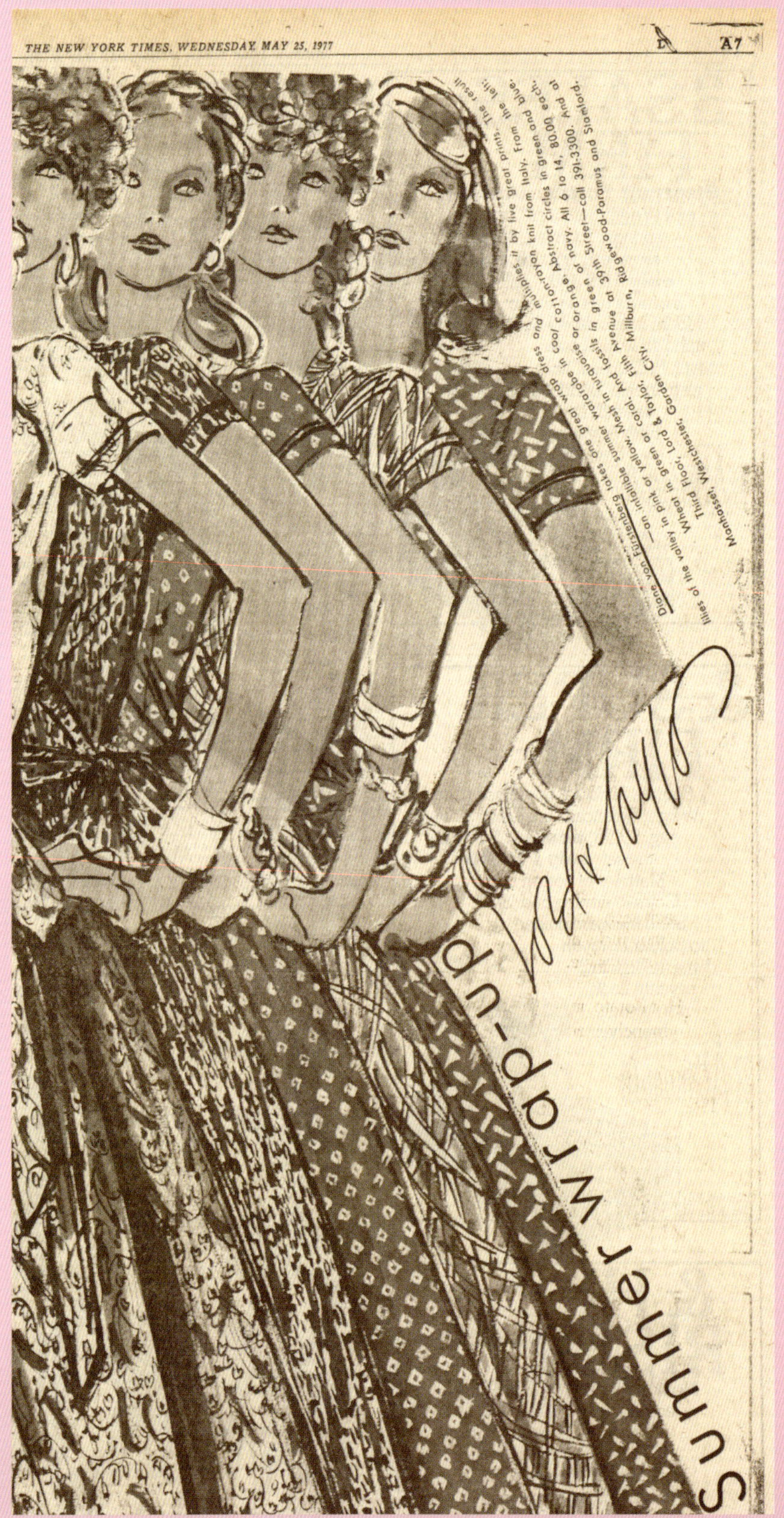

Above
A Lord & Taylor advertisement for Diane von Furstenberg, showing five different prints for Summer 1977.

Opposite
Talita von Furstenberg wearing a Diane von Furstenberg wrap dress, with a print inspired by Venetian tile, in Venice, 2022.

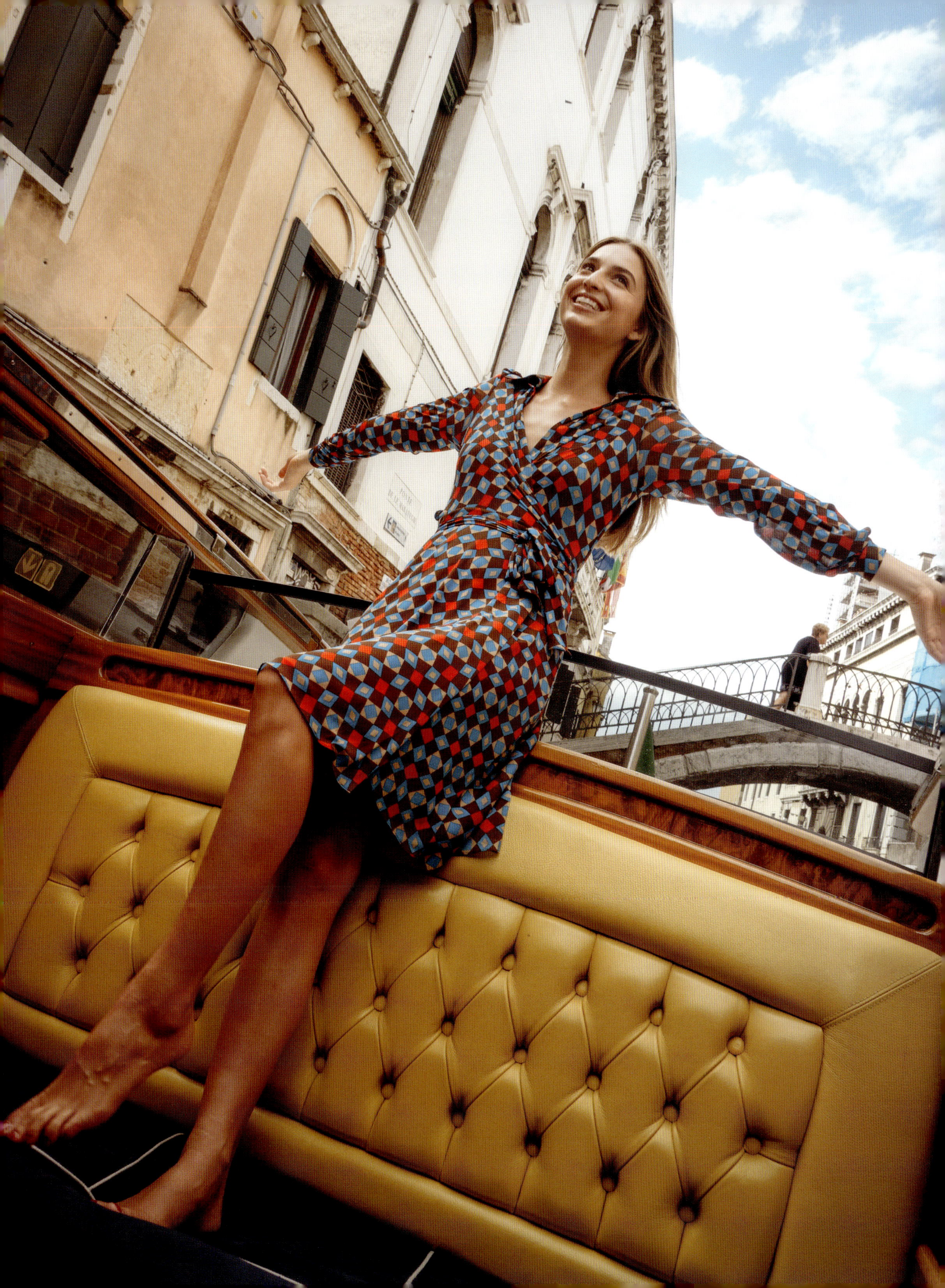

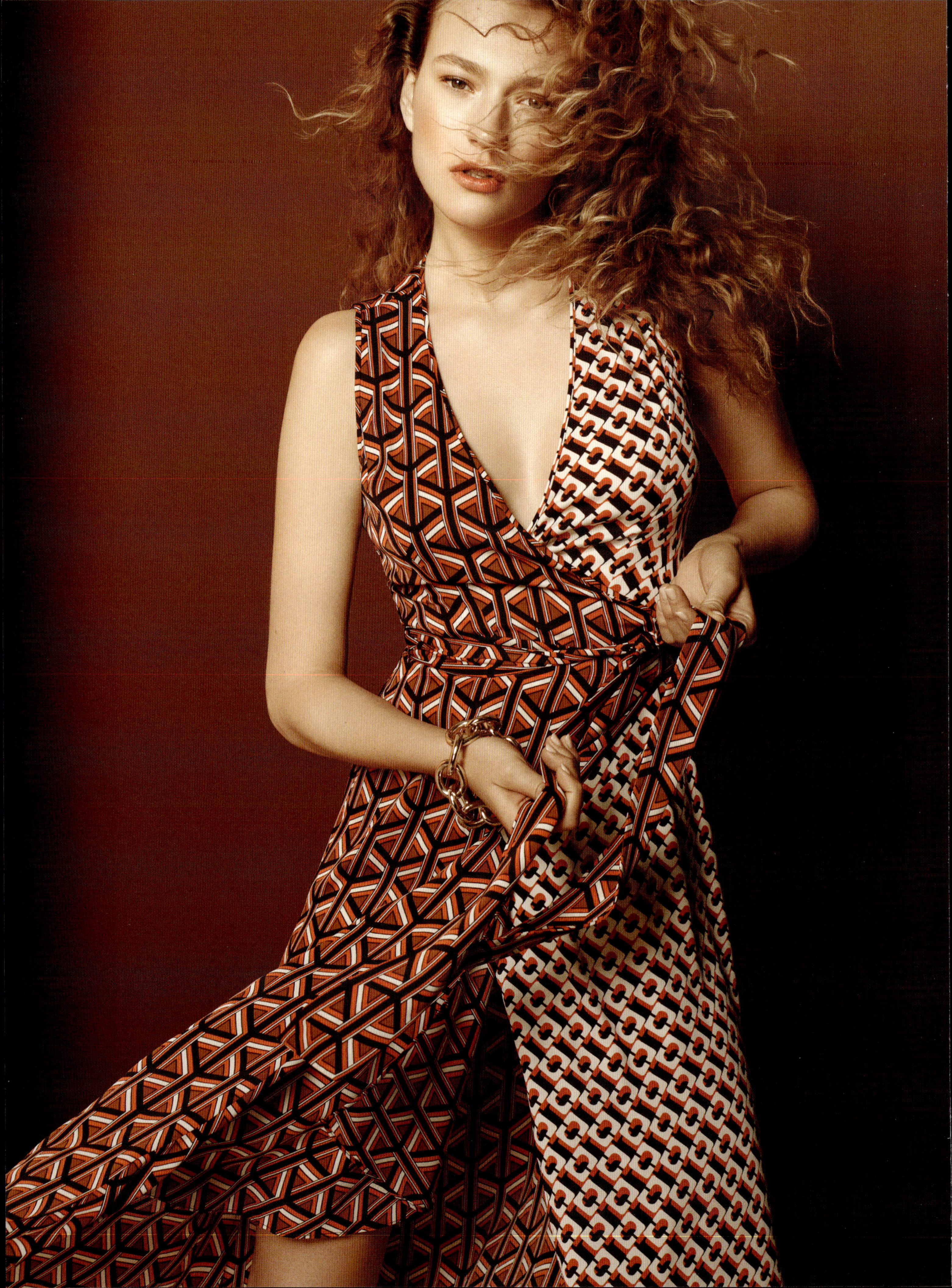

Opposite
Diane von Furstenberg Spring 2020 collection.

Next spread
Diane von Furstenberg white and blue floral wrap dress.

The dress's genesis is well known, as Diane von Furstenberg herself has explained that the inspiration for her wrap dress was sparked by the wraparound tops worn by ballerinas she spotted in the Repetto boutique on the rue de la Paix in Paris, nestled between tutus and pointe shoes, the house's iconic articles. The wrap's first appearance in 1970 was, in fact, in the form of a top, as part of her collection of jersey dresses, which she would come to combine with a skirt, after seeing one of her customers wear them together. To this original wrap top converted into a dress, she would later add a collar, cuffs, and a partially sewn belt with loose ends to add shape and structure to a fabric considered somewhat limp.

The dress wraps across the body with neither a button nor any other formal fastening—its principle, by definition, opposes that of a closed, sheathlike item of clothing. It reveals its distinctive essence in the specific gesture of putting it on. From this point of view, the wrap dress is akin to two major historical clothing archetypes: the Japanese kimono and the Greek peplos and it appears to us as a modern avatar of a garment steeped in multiple significations.

A paragon of traditional dress in Japan, the kimono has been a source of constant fascination in the West since the nineteenth century, as seen in the art of the Impressionists as well as the enthusiasm stoked by the 1900 Paris Exposition, which led to the adoption of the kimono that the elegant women of the Belle Époque would wear at home. Appreciated for its comfort, looseness, and freedom of movement that it allowed, the kimono was duly examined and soon expanded the lexicon of fashion with its hitherto unprecedented aesthetics. French couturier Paul Poiret was to be a passionate interpreter and prolific propagator of a thoroughly revolutionary and disruptive item of clothing with regards to the principles of western fashions. A straight-cut, open-structured garment whose panels cross over the front of the body and are held in place by a separate belt, a kimono is neither sized nor gendered. Like a blank canvas, its flatness lends itself to a wide array of woven, embroidered, or painted decors featuring an infinite repertoire of nature-inspired shapes and symbols. A direct formal connection may be drawn between the wrap dress and the kimono, in the motions of wrapping and tying the belt, and in the ease with which they are constantly updated by new patterns, without ever changing shape.

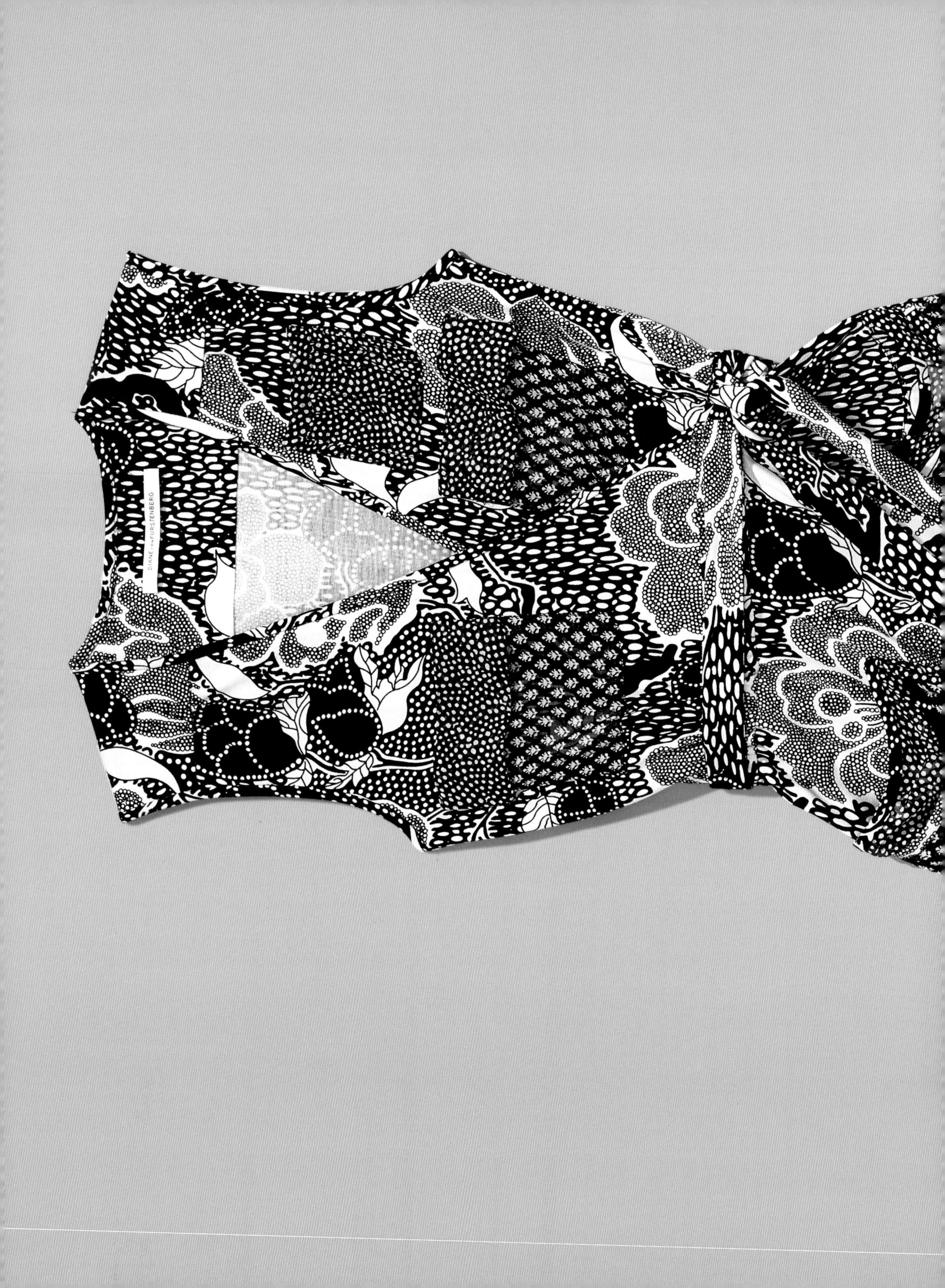
DIANE von FURSTENBERG

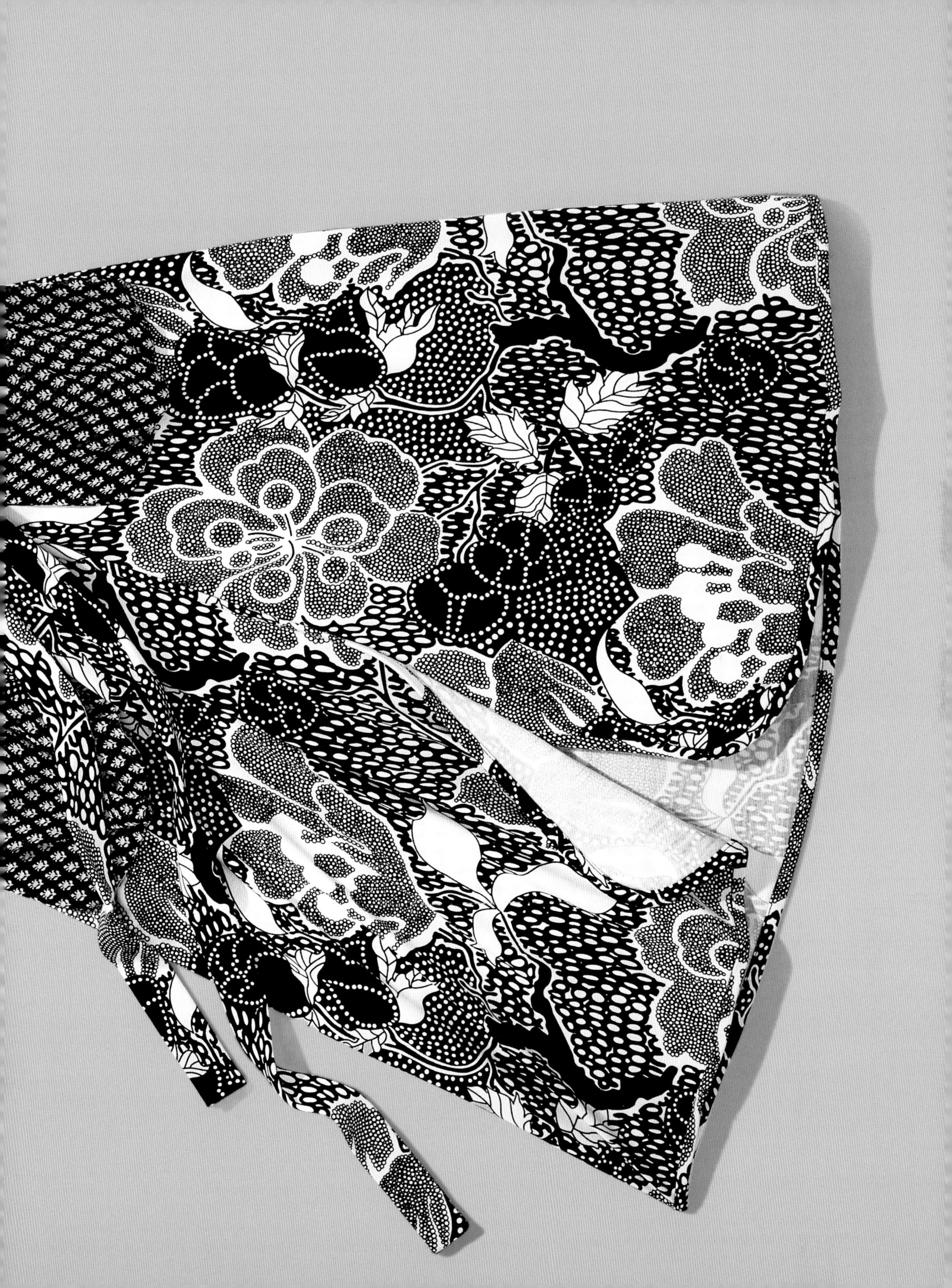

Although from a structural point of view, it may be further removed, the antique peplos of Greece can nonetheless be legitimately considered another key archetype that underlies and inspires the spirit of the wrap dress. A simple rectangle of cloth that is fastened at the shoulders and tied at the waist, falling in soft, graceful folds, the peplos offers both total freedom of movement and a total absence of constraint. In the dynamics of how a body moves, it may reveal an arm or a leg, exposing different parts of the body depending on how the fabric rises and falls and the gestures of the person wearing it.

French master of Couture Madeleine Vionnet, for whom the principle of simplicity was the cornerstone of a large part of her work, incorporated the peplos in the logo that she created in 1919. It inspired the clothing she designed throughout the 1920s and 30s. "I proved that a fabric floating freely over a body freed of any underlying structure was beautiful in and of itself," said Vionnet. "I strove to infuse a fabric with a sense of balance that was in no way altered but rather magnified by movement."[1]

For this prominent fashion figure, who approached the body as a subject rather than a pretext to deploy her pattern-making skills, the Greek peplos, like the Japanese kimono, were key references that guided her creativity. "When a woman smiles, her dress must also smile," said Vionnet.[2] von Furstenberg echoes this same vision when she says, "I have always believed that a woman's clothes should feel like her, be part of her, and an extension of her personality."[3]

The peplos is an item of clothing that invests a body and a personality —by definition, unique—and distinguishes and accompanies each individual's singular expression. The fundamental shapelessness and great plasticity of the peplos embodies an intimate choreography and adaptability that, in today's rationale, makes it a paragon of a consummate harmony between body and fabric. The innately expressive liberty that this versatile and open garment offers clearly connects it with the spirit of the wrap dress.

Despite their distinctly different aesthetics, history, and respective structures, the kimono and peplos share a number of common elements that makes them remarkably relevant to contemporary gender issues: they differentiate neither between sexes nor body shapes, and both draw their shape and essence from the body that inhabits them. Like the so aptly named wrap dress, they also envelop the body and call on the same intuitive gesture to put them on.

Finally, the three garments, of which the wrap dress is the latest avatar, share an oblique line whose magical power writer Oscar Wilde detected in his 1885 essay titled "The Philosophy of Dress": "The oblique line, which one gets by a cloak falling from the shoulder across the body, or by a gown looped up at the side, is suitable to almost all figures. It is a line which corresponds to the direction of motion and conveys an impression of dignity as well as of freedom."[4]

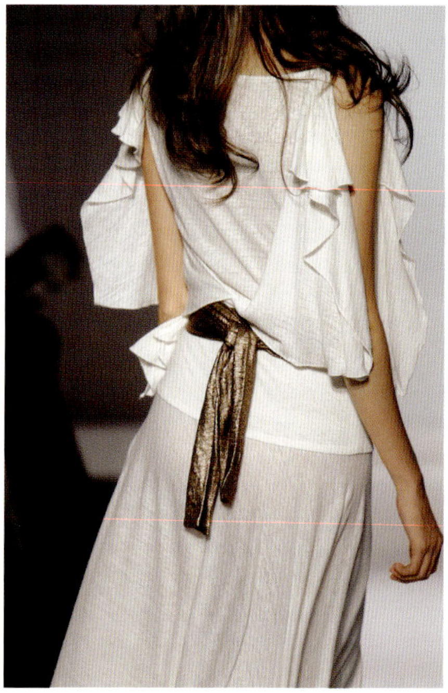

Above
An antiquity-inspired dress on the Diane von Furstenberg Spring 2005 runway.

Opposite
A model walks the Diane von Furstenberg Spring 2011 runway in a flowing dress.

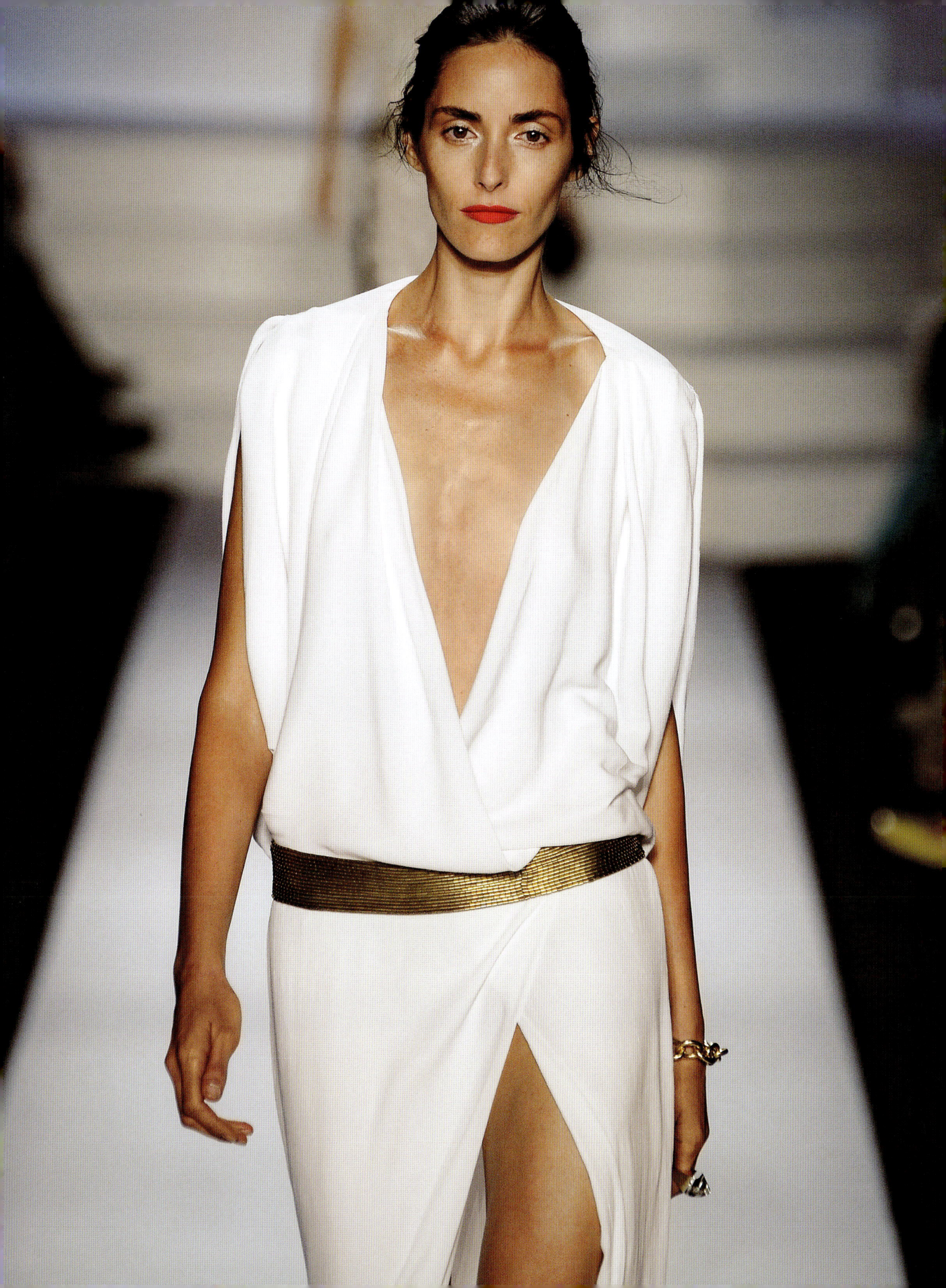

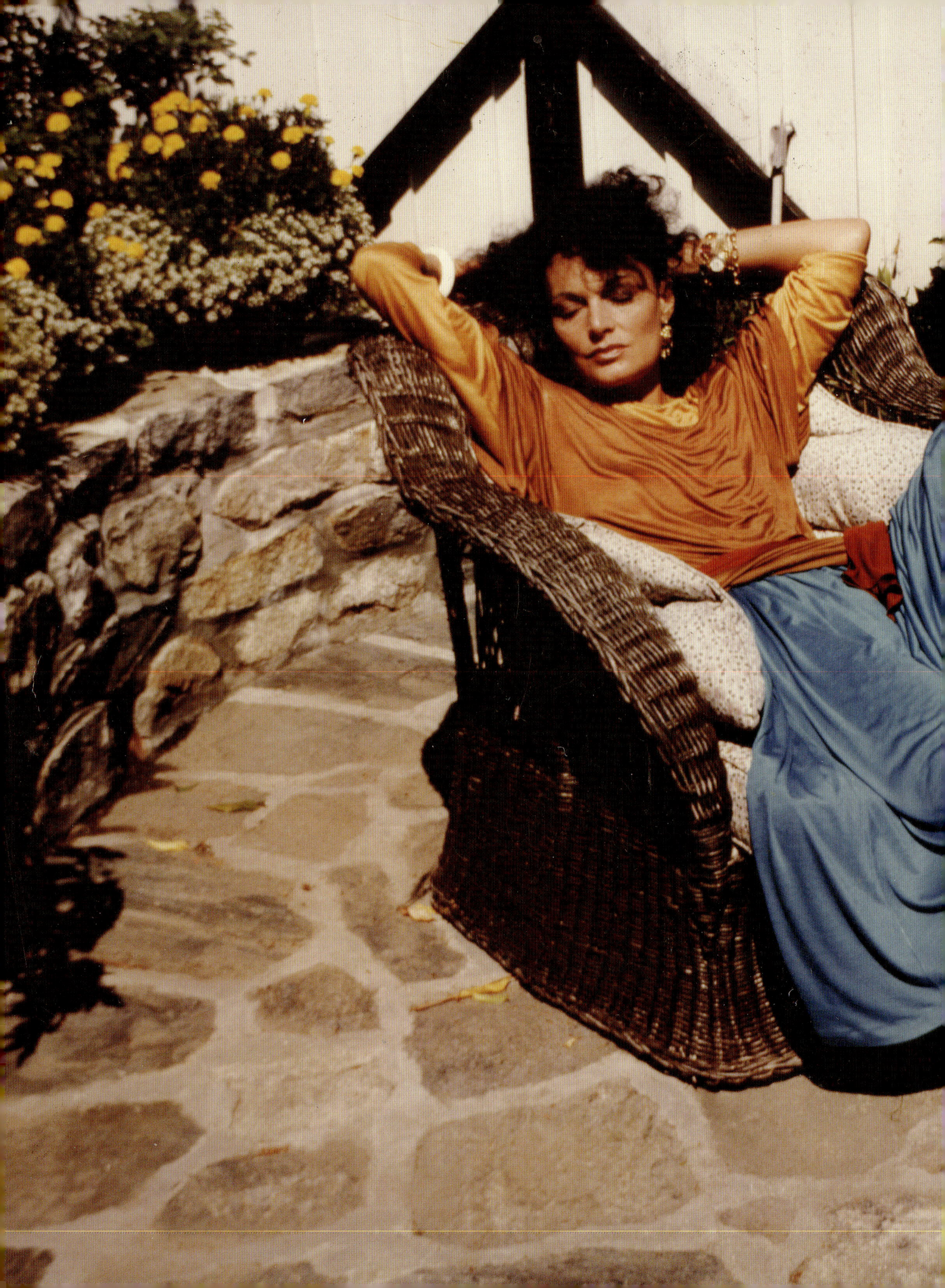

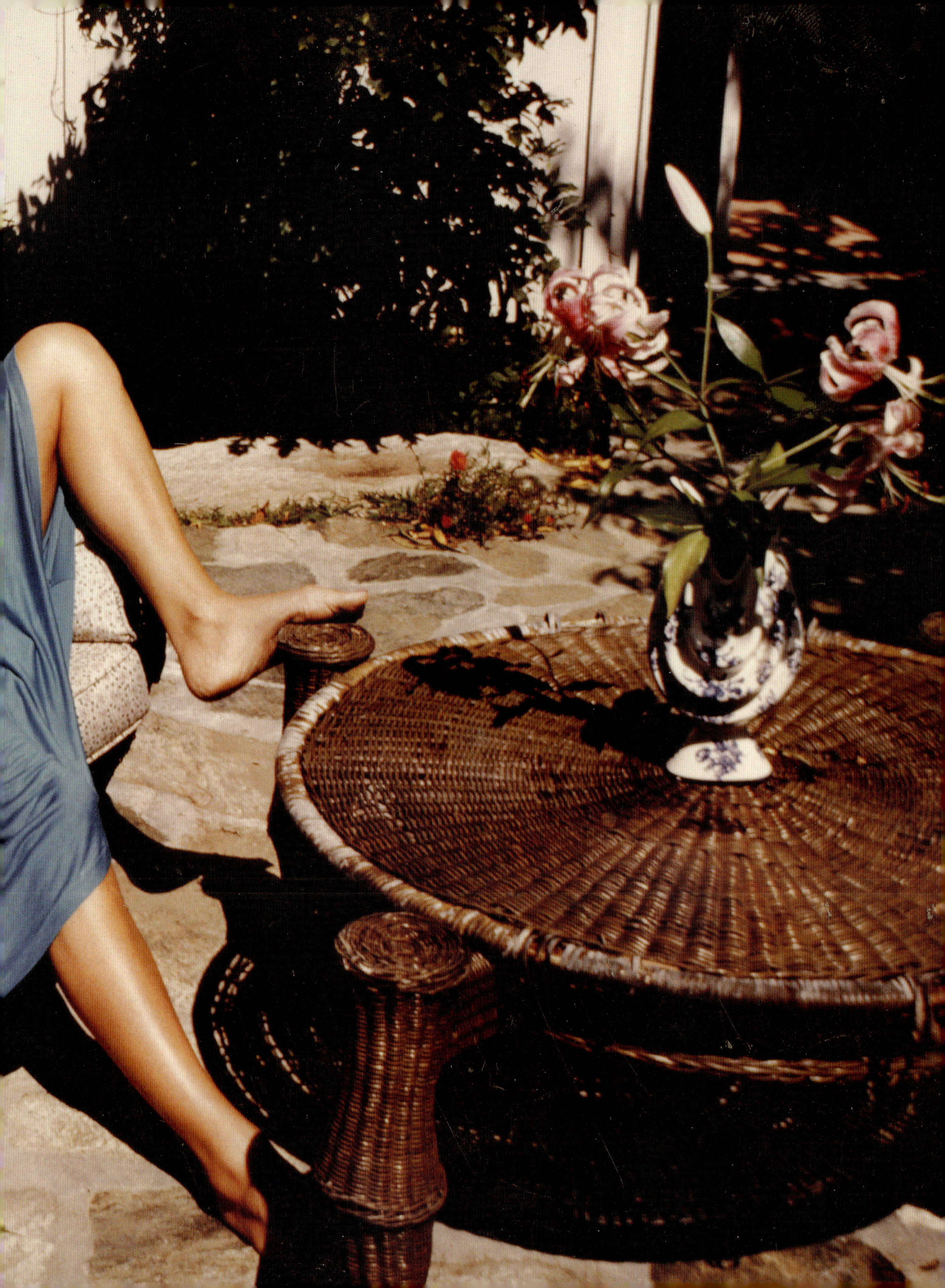

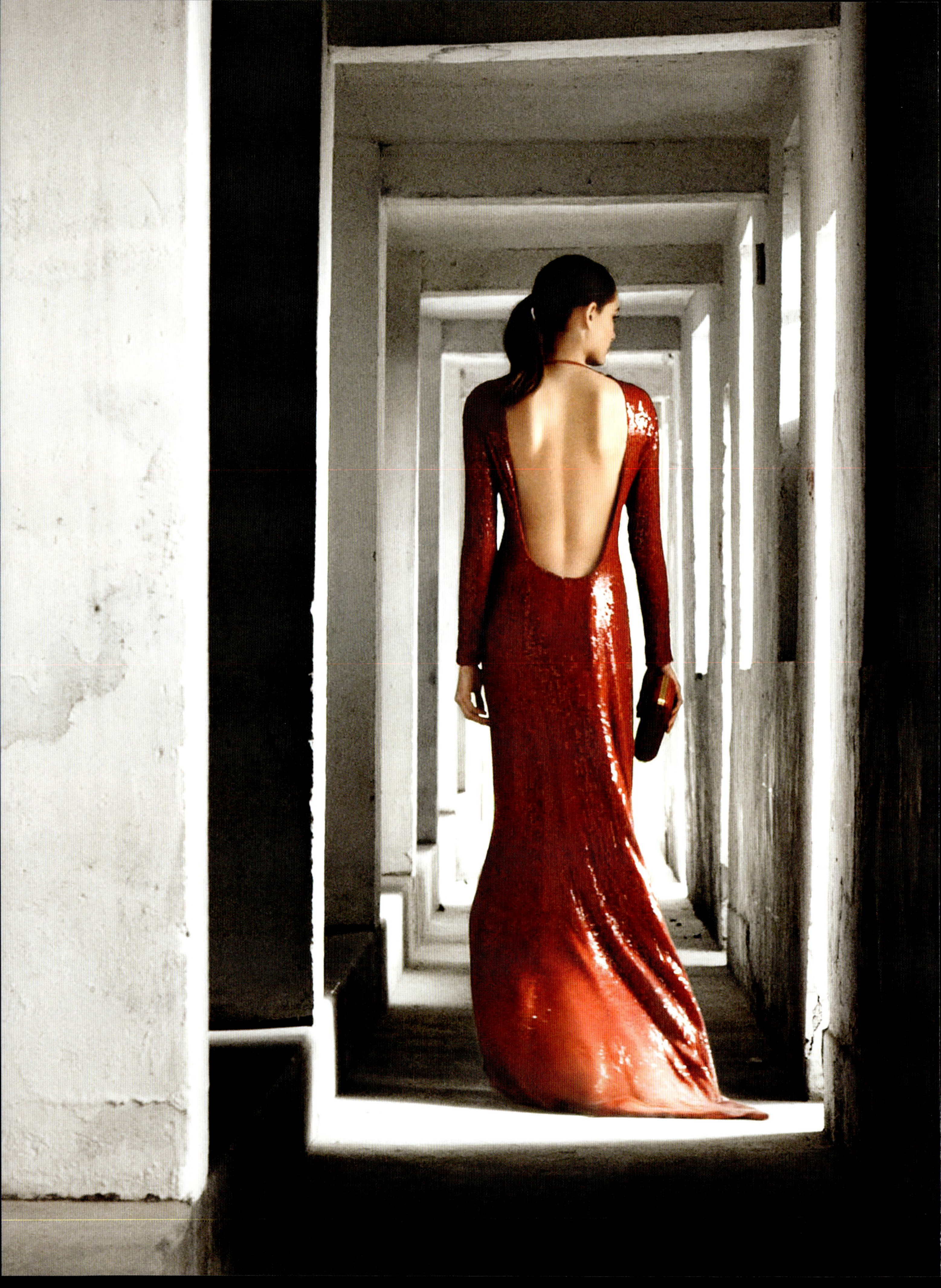

FEEL LIKE A WOMAN, WEAR A DRESS

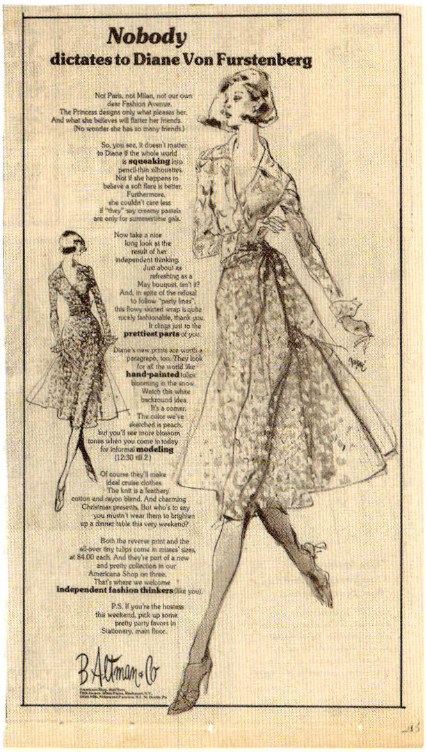

In 1972, Diane von Furstenberg placed her first advertisement in *Women's Wear Daily* to announce the opening of her showroom. The young, self-taught entrepreneur had neither a press agent nor a communications consultant, so she had to improvise a photo shoot. She asked a photographer friend, Roger Prigent, to take some photos and modeled the dresses herself. Wearing one of her favorite shirt dresses with a blue and white geometric pattern, three rows of pearls, a Bulgari watch, and high heels, von Furstenberg posed sitting on a white cube.[5] After the photo was developed, she found that the white mass of the cube was too prominent in the photo. She intuitively picked up a pen and wrote the phrase "Feel like a woman, wear a dress" on top of the white cube and added her signature. This photo with its portrait, handwritten inscription, dress, and designer signature became the stamp of every dress that would be commercialized during the decade. It ultimately became her registered trademark. The precise meaning of this improvised catchphrase, destined to be spectacularly successful, eludes its author to this day, which makes it no less intriguing. The phrase, akin to an injunction, rings oddly at a time of great social upheaval with the rise of the women's liberation movement and demands egalitarian rights.

Previous spread
Diane von Furstenberg wears her Liquid Assets designs, ca. 1982.

Above
A 1976 "Nobody dictates to Diane von Furstenberg" advertisement for B. Altman & Co.

Opposite
A red sequin gown from the Diane von Furstenberg Fall 2011 collection.

In a context that openly questioned established values, the symbols of male domination and the confinement of women to predefined roles took on a new dimension. And clothing, as is often the case, was instrumental in revealing the underlying issues. In the early 1970s, the idea of connecting the notion of womanhood with wearing a dress was at the very least paradoxical, not to say counterintuitive, coming from a woman like von Furstenberg, who espoused freedom and independence.

Admittedly, the gendered differentiation of clothing, though secular and present across all civilizations, and which, in the Western world since the Middle Ages, focused on items as strikingly opposed as the dress (for women) and pants (for men), created a taboo and a symbolism whose substance is clearly spelled out in the expression "Who wears the pants?"

The quarrel over who wears the pants within a couple, and its inverted corollary when women assume what are considered male attributes, are often represented in popular "war of the sexes" iconography that flourished between the fifteenth and nineteenth centuries, ultimately rigidifying the contours of each gender's privileges.

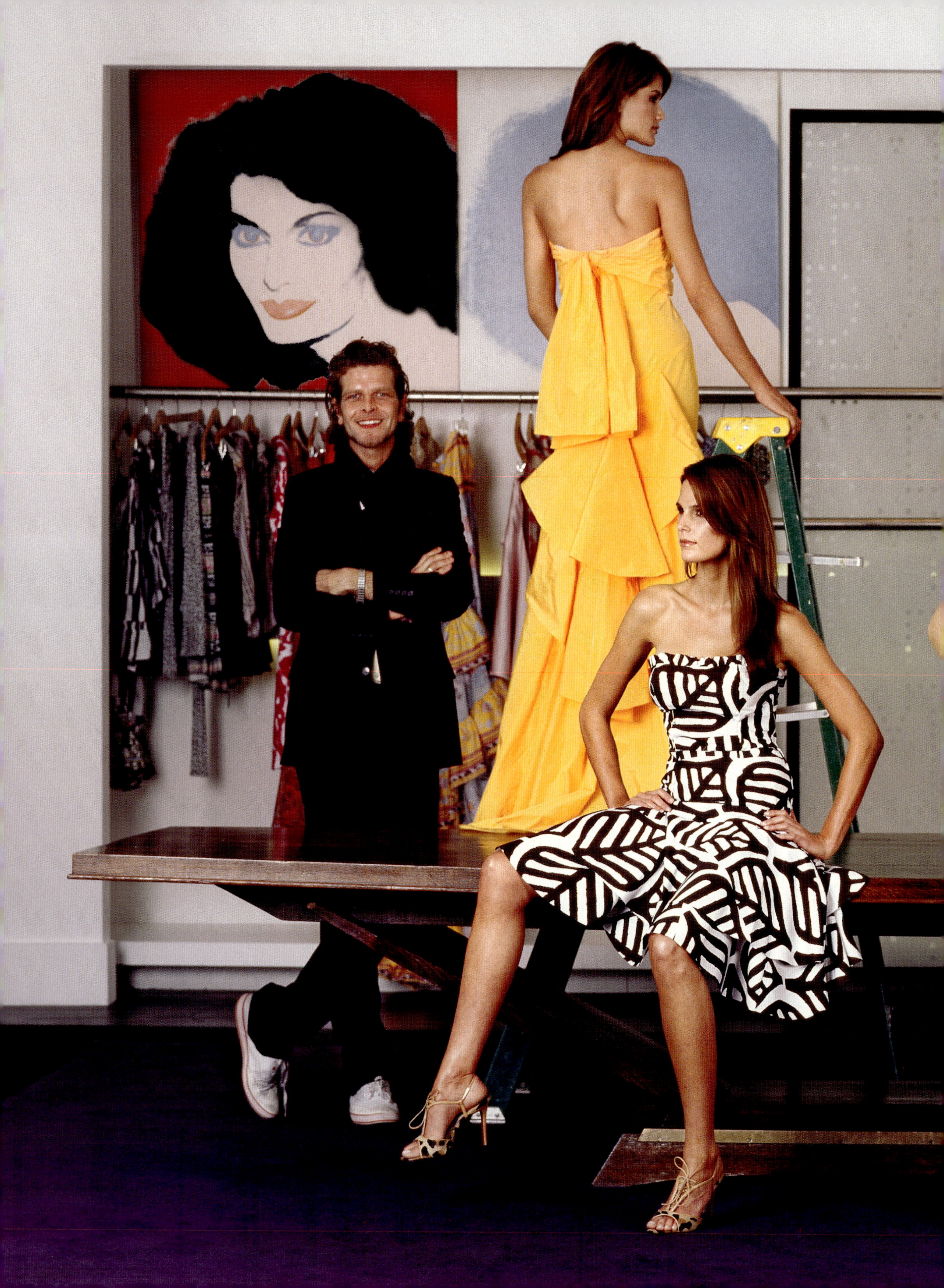

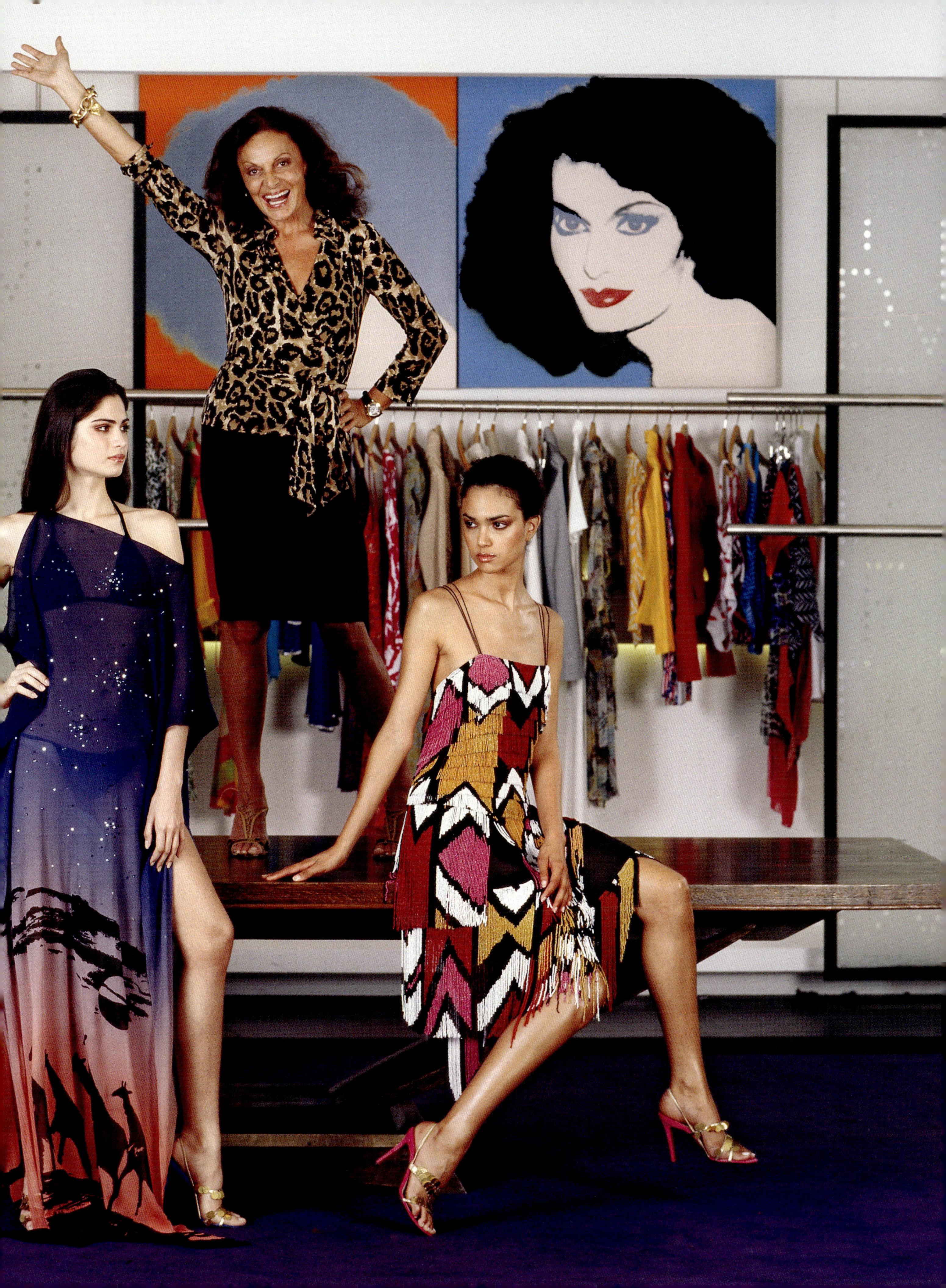

In the collective imagination, shaped by countless legislative, religious, and secular texts, wearing the clothes of the other sex is strictly regulated—its transgression punished by significant disciplinary measures. Not the least of these decrees, considering its longevity and the extent of its audience, appears in the Bible (Deuteronomy, 22:5): "A woman shall not wear anything that pertains to a man, nor shall a man put on a woman's garment, for all who do so are an abomination to the Lord your God." This explains why the wearing of pants of any generic type (whatever its form or origin), de facto erected as a phallic symbol in the Western world since the Middle Ages, was forbidden to women, with rare exceptions.

In the second half of the nineteenth century, on the pretext of preserving female modesty, women were allowed to wear pants for a few emerging sports and leisure activities such as cycling, sea bathing, or gymnastics, which were considered incompatible with the fashionable dresses of the day that were either too tight or voluminous. For exceptional circumstances, during World War II, pants were tolerated because raw materials were lacking, and later, more widely accepted as ski and summer resort wear. It was, however, out of the question to wear pants for every day and beware those who dared!

Previous spread
Nathan Jenden and Diane von Furstenberg with models, ca. 2000s.

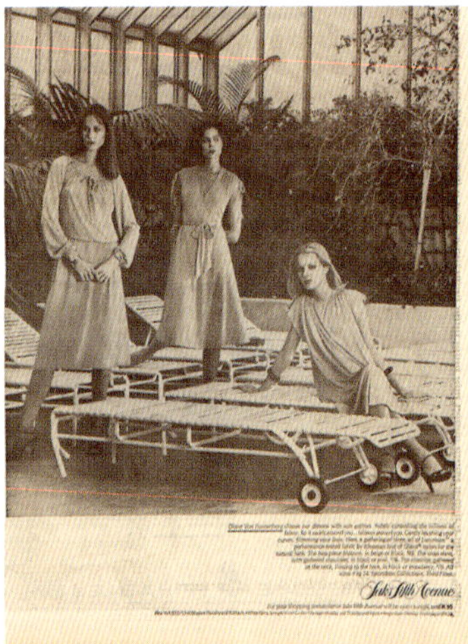

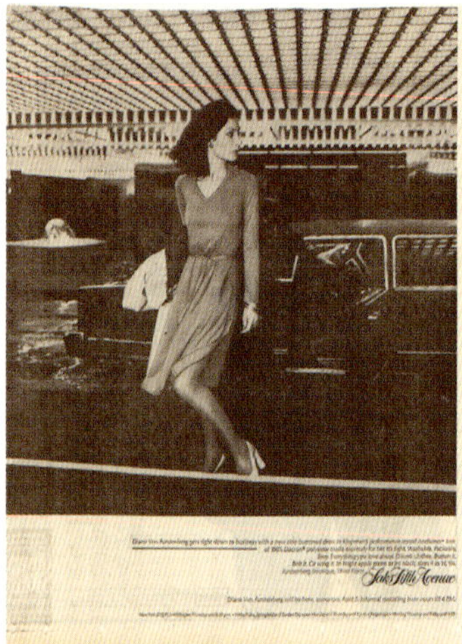

Above
Saks Fifth Avenue advertisements from the 1970s.

Opposite
"Real Style Is Knowing What to Show Off—And What to Keep Under Wraps" Diane von Furstenberg advertisement, ca. 1988.

Writer George Sand's unconventional apparel led to the cutting images and remarks of the day's caricaturists and pamphleteers, delighted to thus discredit her literary work. In 1850, the American women's rights activist Amelia Bloomer promoted a reform that she considered a more practical alternative to the voluminous dresses of the day, consisting of loose pants worn under a short dress. The new costume met with such violent controversy that, despite its success among a growing circle of women who found the proposition attractive, she was forced to abandon her project.[6]

A century later, in a domain where image is everything, the extremely influential icons of the seventh art, actresses Marlene Dietrich, Greta Garbo, and Katharine Hepburn were some of the rare active and independent personalities to brave the taboo, affirming through their dress their determination to behave like men. The image of a woman wearing pants thus remained exceptional in society and was often perceived as scandalous, if not transgressive. In the 1960s, a new guard of young designers, led by André Courrèges and Yves Saint Laurent, presented pant suits in their collections. They were responding to the aspirations of a new generation yearning for freedom. In reality, however, wearing pants in professional and private life was the result of a long women's battle.

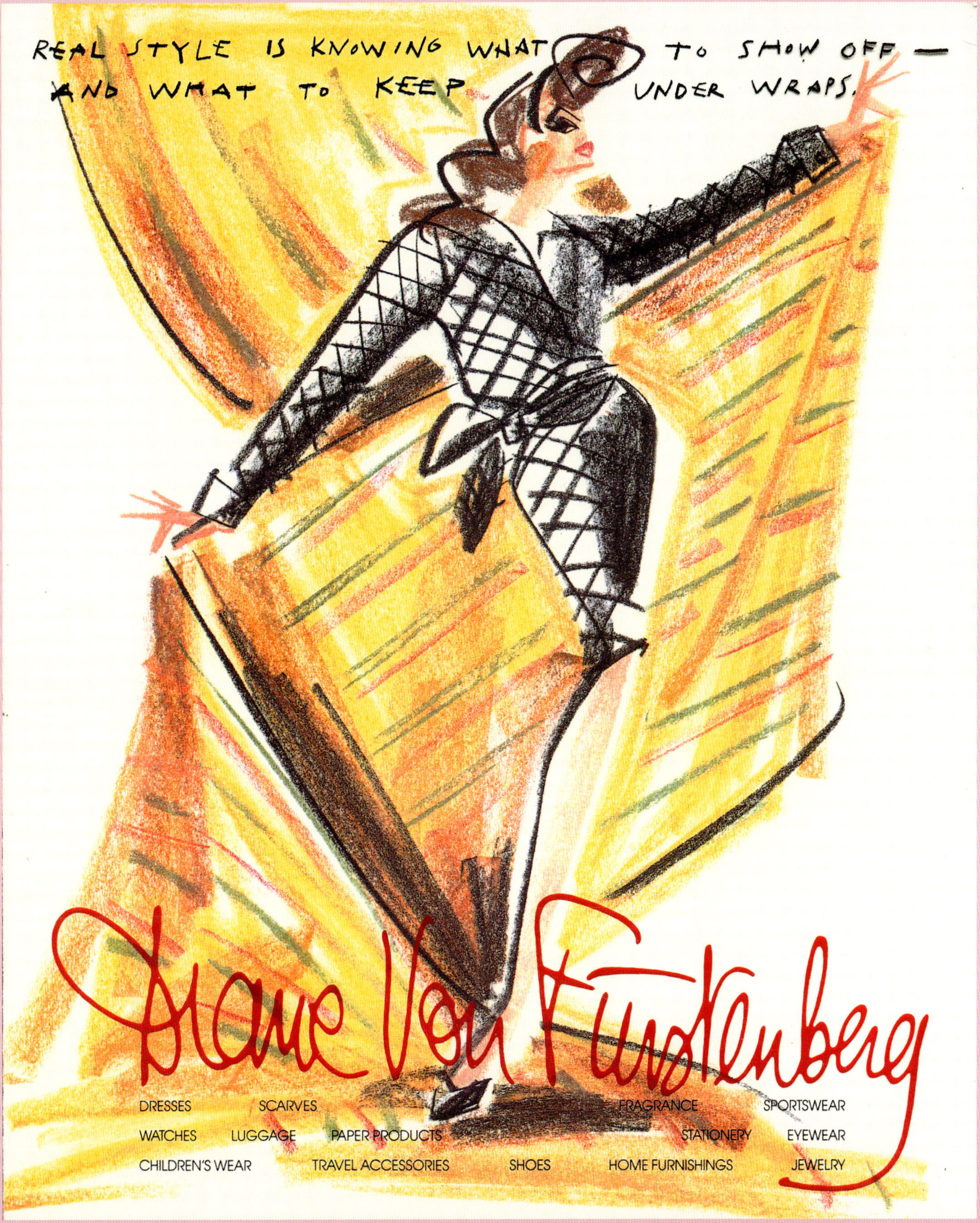
REAL STYLE IS KNOWING WHAT TO SHOW OFF —
AND WHAT TO KEEP UNDER WRAPS.
Diane Von Furstenberg
DRESSES
SCARVES
FRAGRANCE
SPORTSWEAR
WATCHES
LUGGAGE
PAPER PRODUCTS
STATIONERY
EYEWEAR
CHILDREN'S WEAR
TRAVEL ACCESSORIES
SHOES
HOME FURNISHINGS
JEWELRY

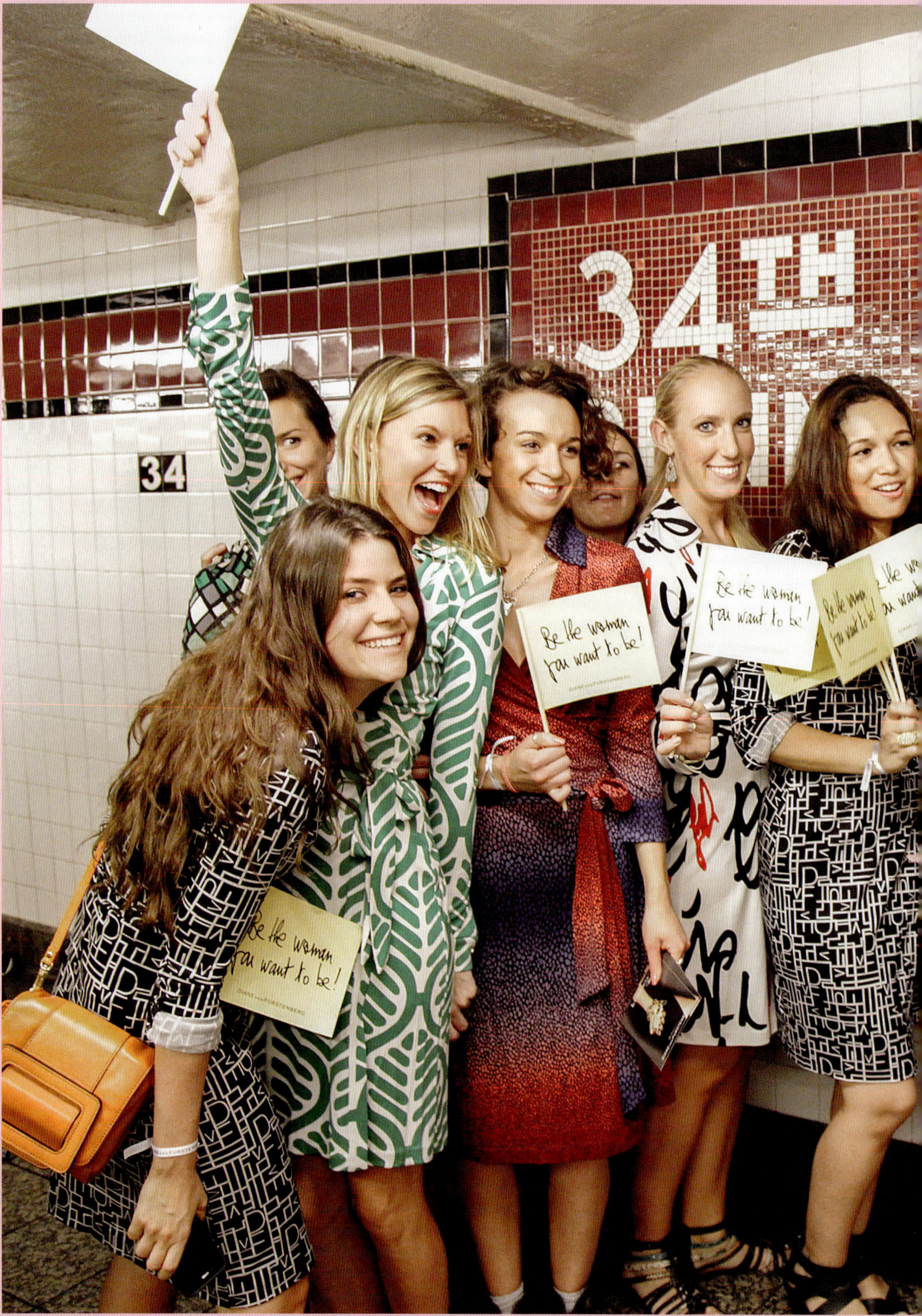
34TH
34
Be the woman you want to be!
Be the woman you want to be!
Be the woman you want to be!

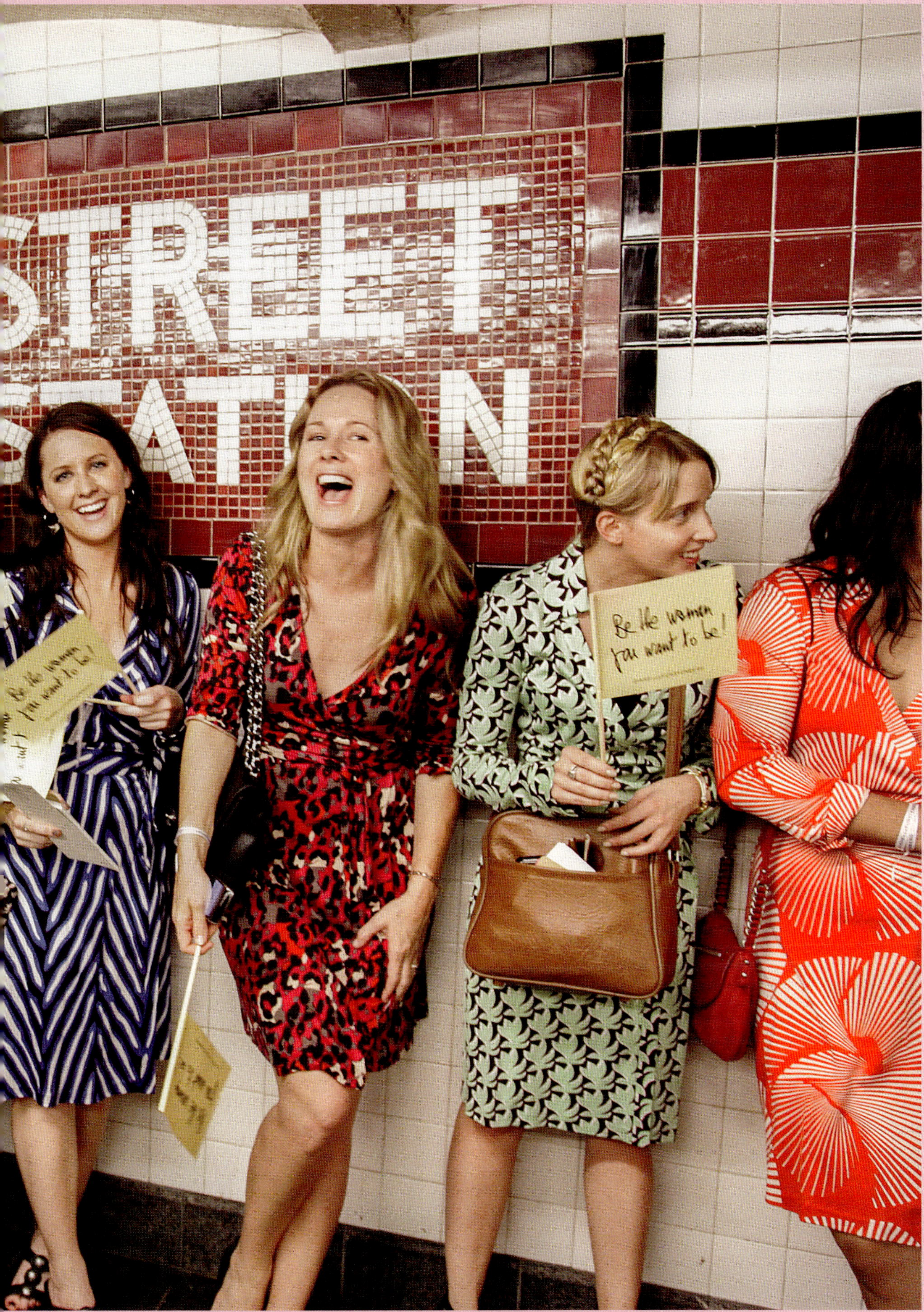
STREET
Be the women you want to be!

At a time when the memory of this battle was still very fresh in mind, von Furstenberg's slogan must have seemed puzzling, especially as she herself wore pants, as testified by many photos of the period.

Retrospectively, speaking of her beginnings, and analyzing the American fashion landscape of the time, she offers a partial explanation when she said, "All I had was an instinct that women wanted a fashion option besides hippie clothes, bell-bottoms, and stiff pant suits that hid their femininity. Though the unisex look was hot in the seventies, I was sure there was a need for simple little sexy dresses that made women feel like a woman. And the dresses made sense. They were sexy and practical, washable and wrinkle proof."[7]

Previous spread
Women flashmob in Diane von Furstenberg wrap dresses in the New York City subway, 2011.

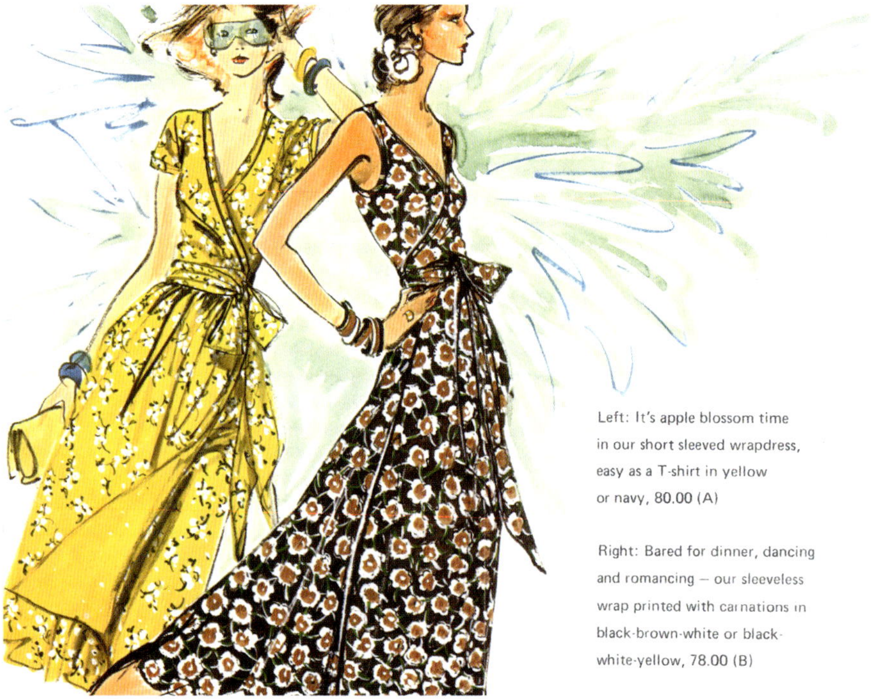

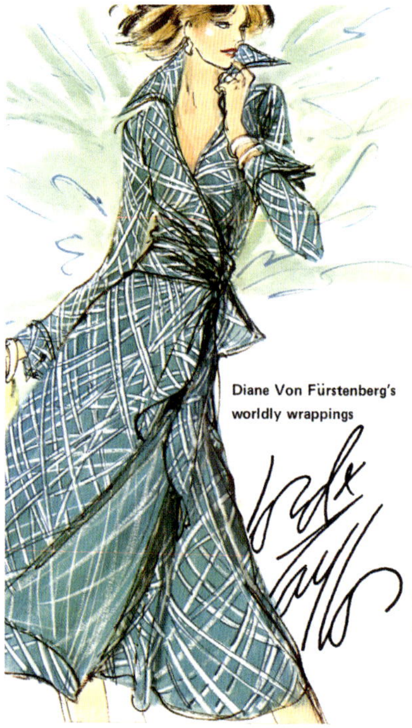

The hedonistic and pragmatic von Furstenberg, who asserted that she had always dreamed of living a man's life in a woman's body, appears to see no contradiction in the desire to wear sexy little dresses to feel like a woman. Could this be a subconscious appropriation of the male gaze on femininity? Or more subtly, given her feminist outlook, a way to suggest a new paradigm? Could it be that one can assume an unapologetically archaic vision of womanhood and at the same time promote progress by recognizing that women are free to wear pants or dresses as they please, to feel fully feminine and be recognized as such? If this is the case, it may then be that the paradoxical injunction "Feel like a woman, wear a dress" prematurely, or prophetically, heralded an end to the hostilities linked to dress code conventions.

Above
1977 Lord & Taylor advertisements for Diane von Furstenberg.

Opposite
Actress Monica Bellucci poses in a Diane von Furstenberg trench coat, 2012.

Her statement can then be understood as an encouragement to explore femininity, arbitrarily embodied by a dress, as an experience of life open to all, regardless of gender. "One is not born a woman, but becomes one," as Simone de Beauvoir so rightly said.[8]

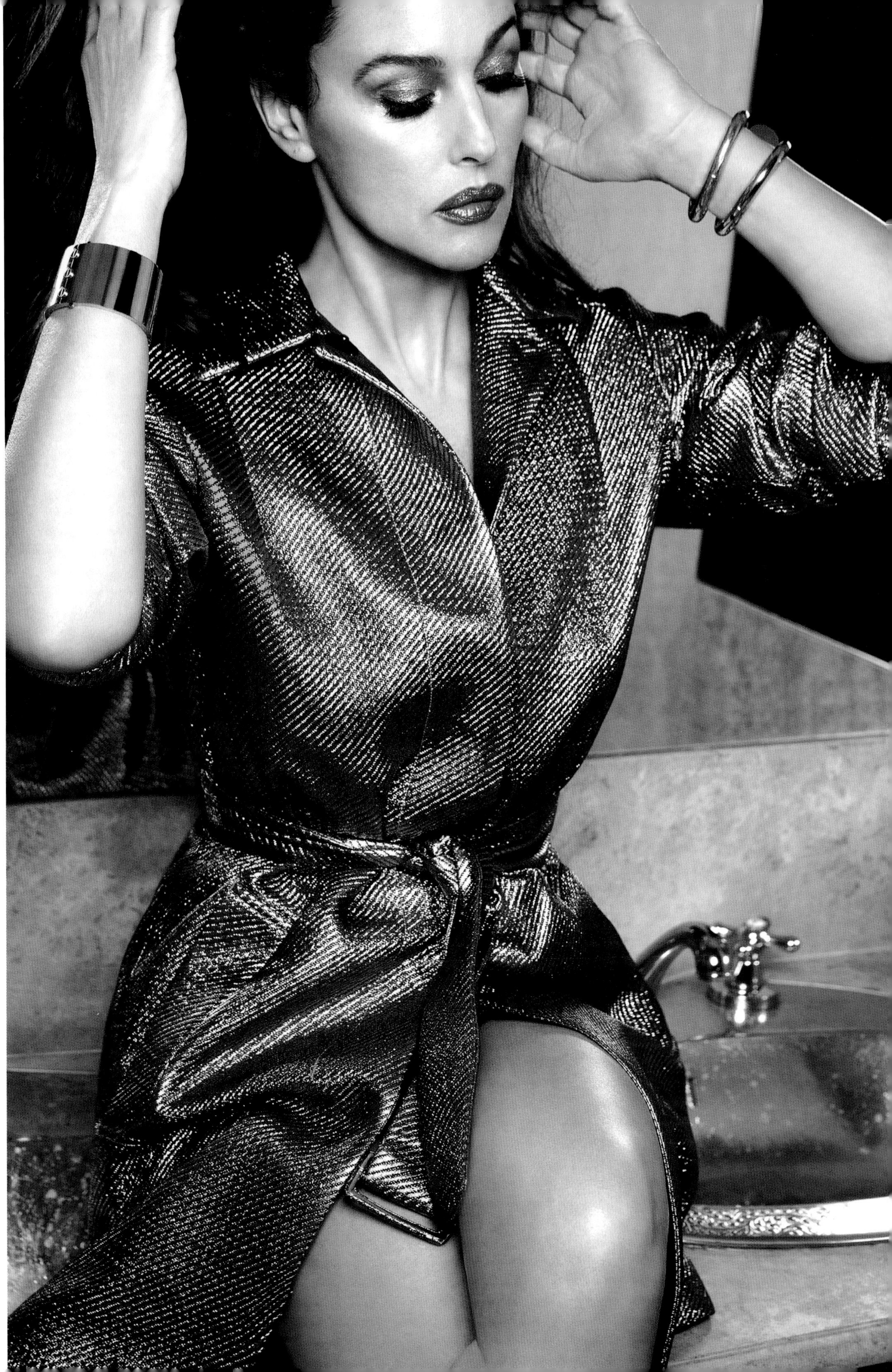

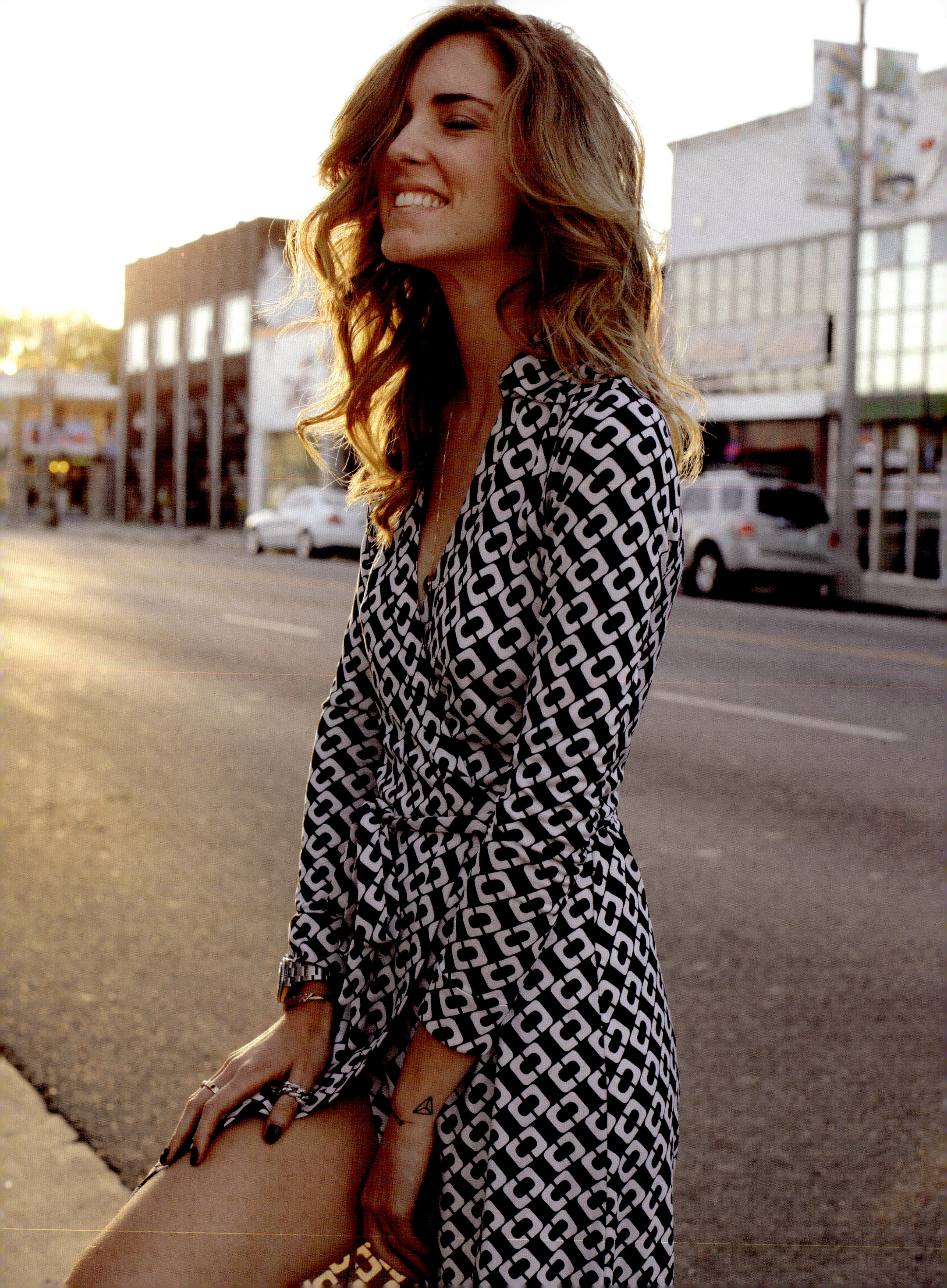

Despite its apparent simplicity, the wraparound dress, as von Furstenberg imagined it, is nonetheless rigorously designed. Far from any academicism or complex formal research, and not subject to any ephemeral fashion trend, von Furstenberg created this dress from her own acute sense of observation, from basic but thoroughly analyzed expectations, carefully collecting any information that, as a self-taught designer, fueled her insatiable curiosity. Practical, lightweight, machine washable, and wrinkle-proof, a von Furstenberg dress meets the needs of women who lead active and busy lives.

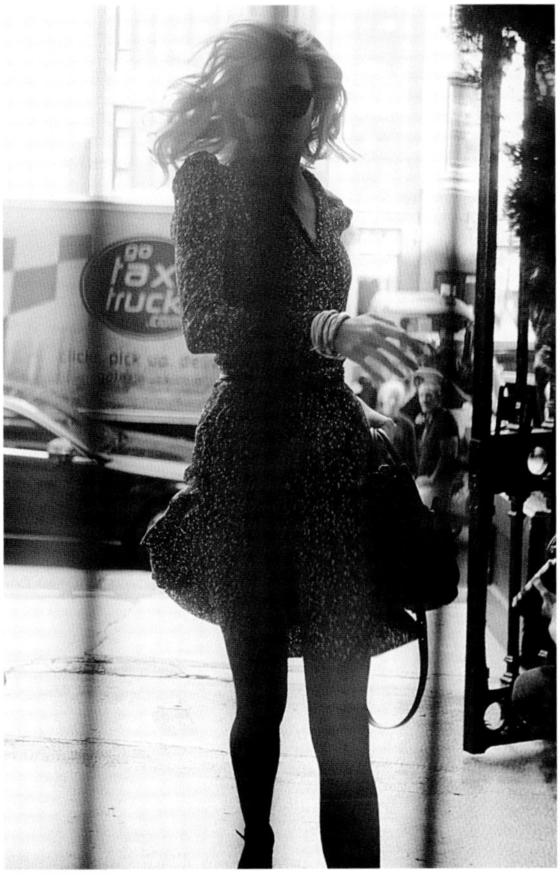

Opposite
Fashion blogger Chiara Ferragni in a chainlink wrap dress, 2014.

Above
Diane von Furstenberg Fall 2015 campaign BTS.

T-shirt dress, A-line dress, shirt dress, wrap dress: the typology of the main models she created, which are now permanent items in each collection, is the result of a smart selection of near-universal styles that are easy to wear and adapted to all body types. They form a series of uniform-like garments that can be worn at any time of the day and adapt to all circumstances. Chameleon dresses, they can be transformed by an accessory or item of jewelry, and they can change status, from casual to sophisticated, depending on the creativity and mood of those who wear them. As for its material of choice—jersey—which instigated its creation, it comes in all colors and shades and is adorned with myriad eclectic prints in an infinite and infinitely updated range of patterns, some of which have lasted for decades.

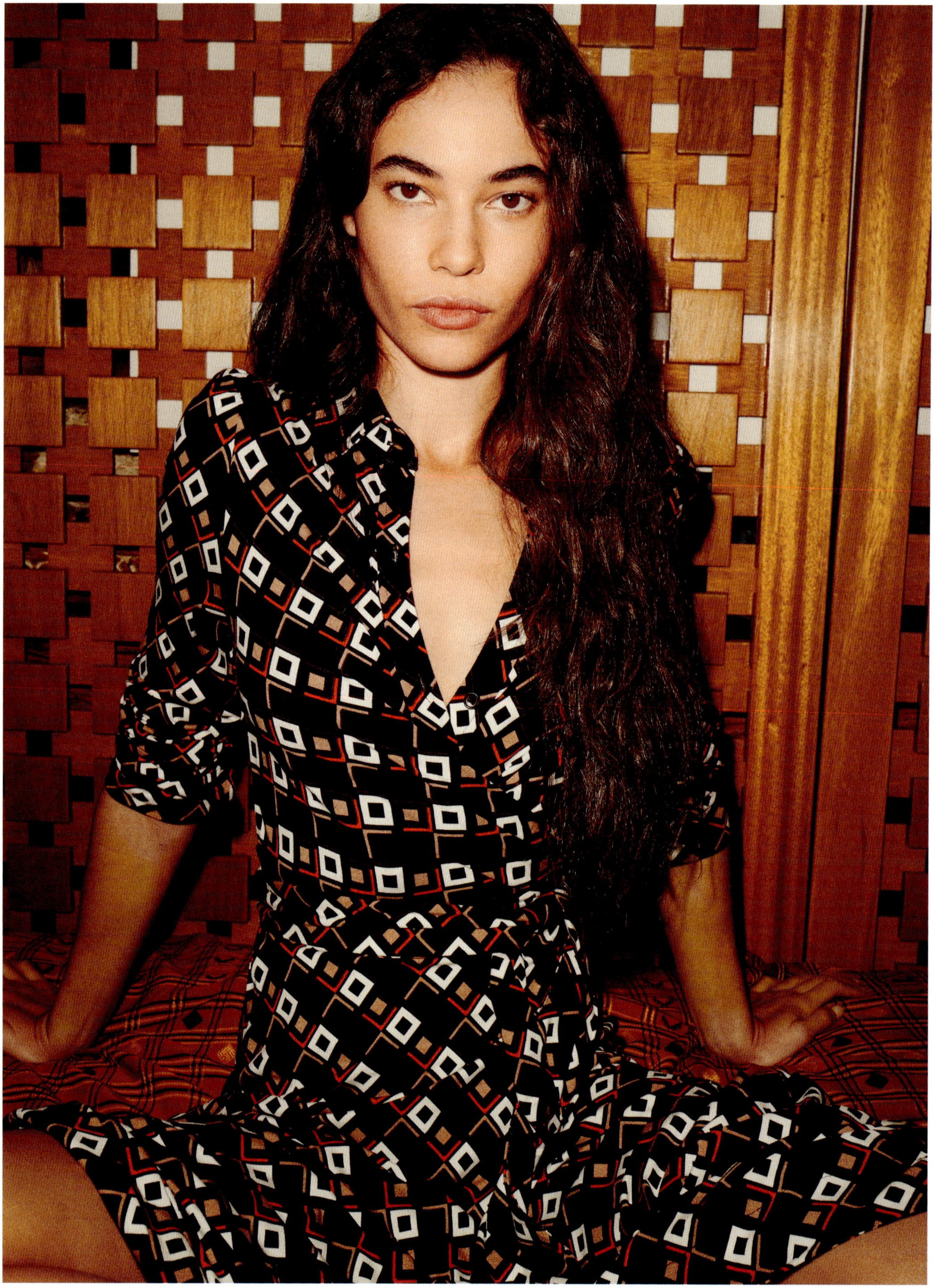

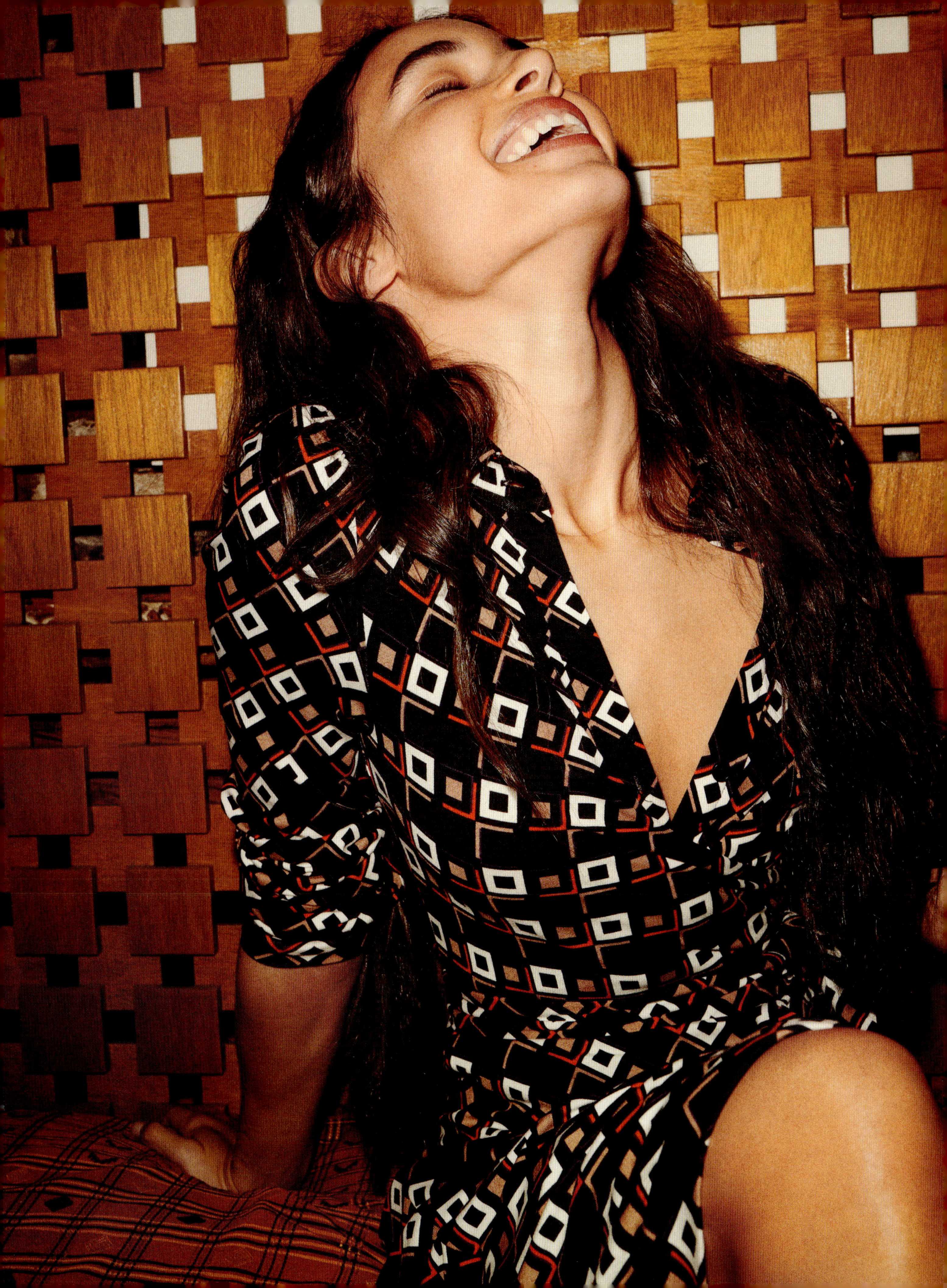

Previous spread
Diane von Furstenberg Fall 2020 collection.

Opposite
Diane von Furstenberg, 2010.

Next page
Diane von Furstenberg Winter 2020 collection.

These simple dresses, which are loved by women of all ages and conditions, undeniably bear von Furstenberg's very personal touch and her talent for storytelling, which is very much inspired by nature and women. There is also a very real and tangible duality, which instills a measure of doubt and disbelief—a tension between its blatant sensuality and something more conventional. von Furstenberg seems to be fully aware of this when she declares: "Perhaps the little dresses I was designing were a bridge between the radical side of me, which wore the shortest, tiniest hot pants, a printed Saint Laurent Rive Gauche blazer, and the highest platform shoes at night, and the more conservative side, which wore little dresses during the day."[9]

"A woman who makes clothes for women" is how von Furstenberg defines her work, and her dresses undeniably reflect this both literally and figuratively. One might be tempted to say they are just simple little dresses if their creator's personality and authentic intelligence did not call for a more subtle analysis and a more conscientious examination of their inherent characteristics and put them in perspective so as to reconsider her opus from a new angle.

Aware of her place in the history of fashion, von Furstenberg does, at times, question her own legacy as she reminisces on a long and brilliantly led adventure. Although she may not have a place in the pantheon of great couturiers and fashion designers, she clearly contributed to making her wraparound dress, her most famous model, a fashion equivalent of the Biro pen. What better tribute for this compulsive diarist, who always has any number of notebooks at hand to jot down her passing thoughts, ideas, and sources of inspiration?

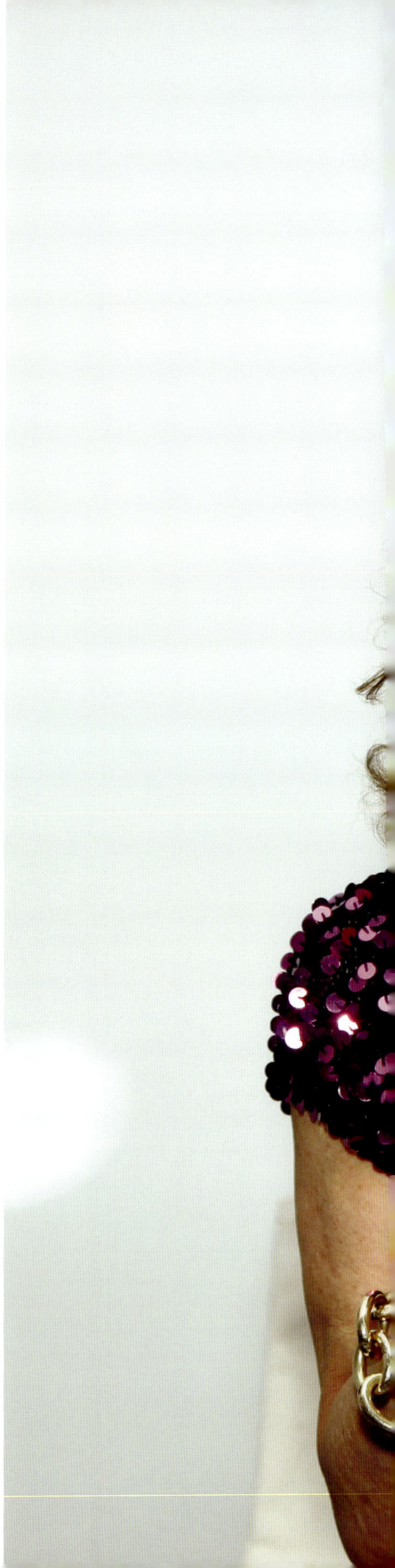

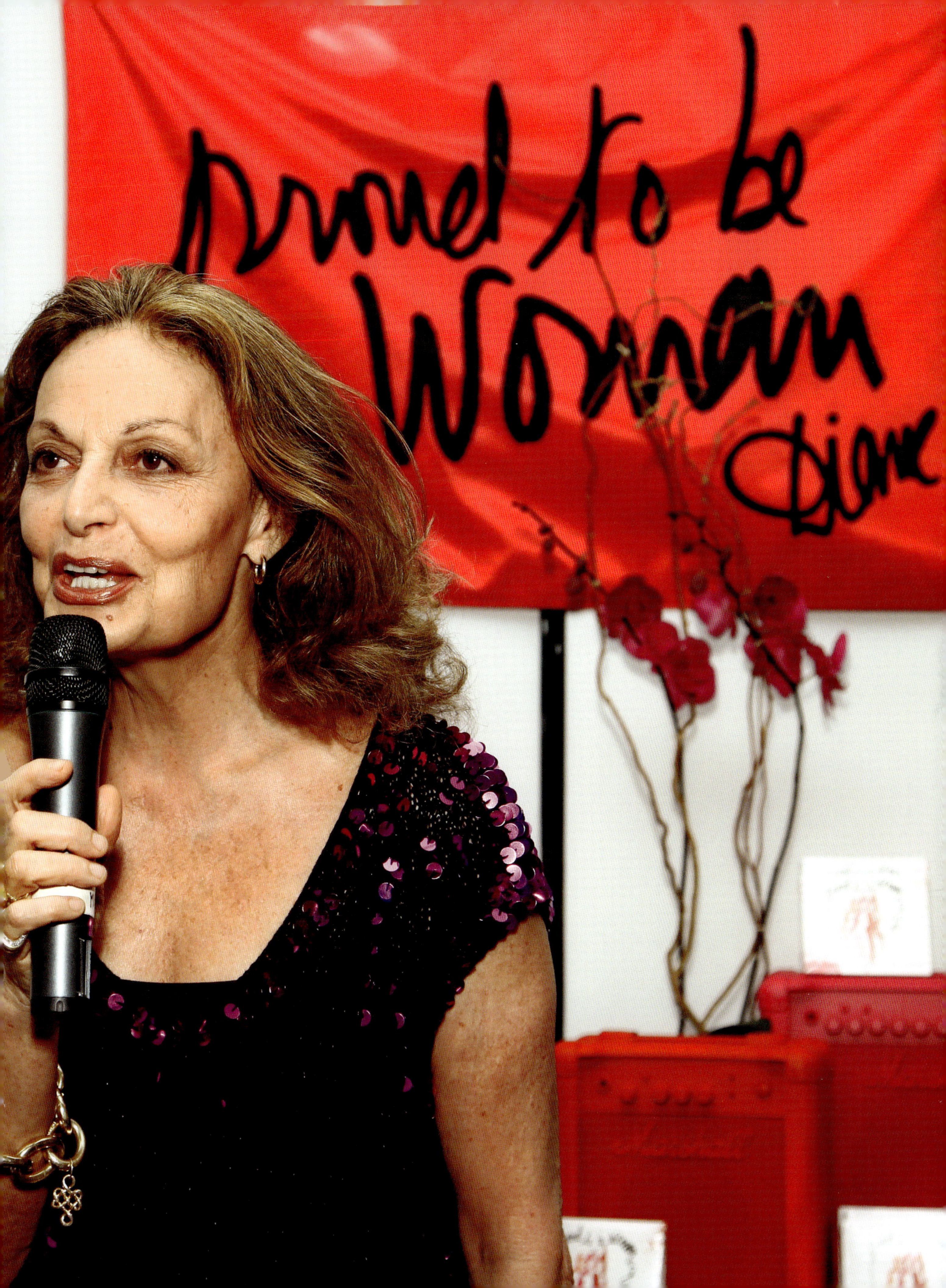
Proud to be
Woman
Diane

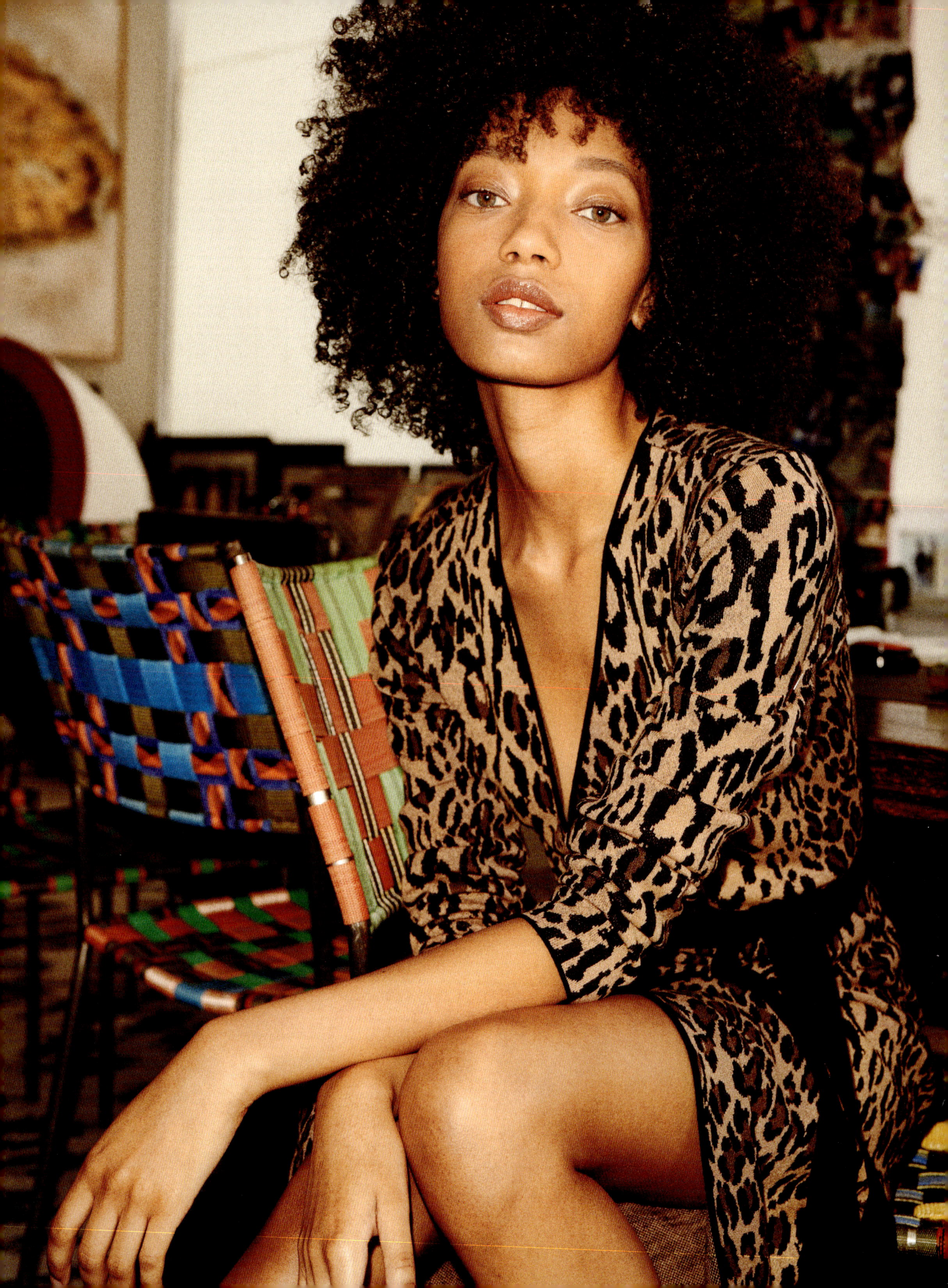

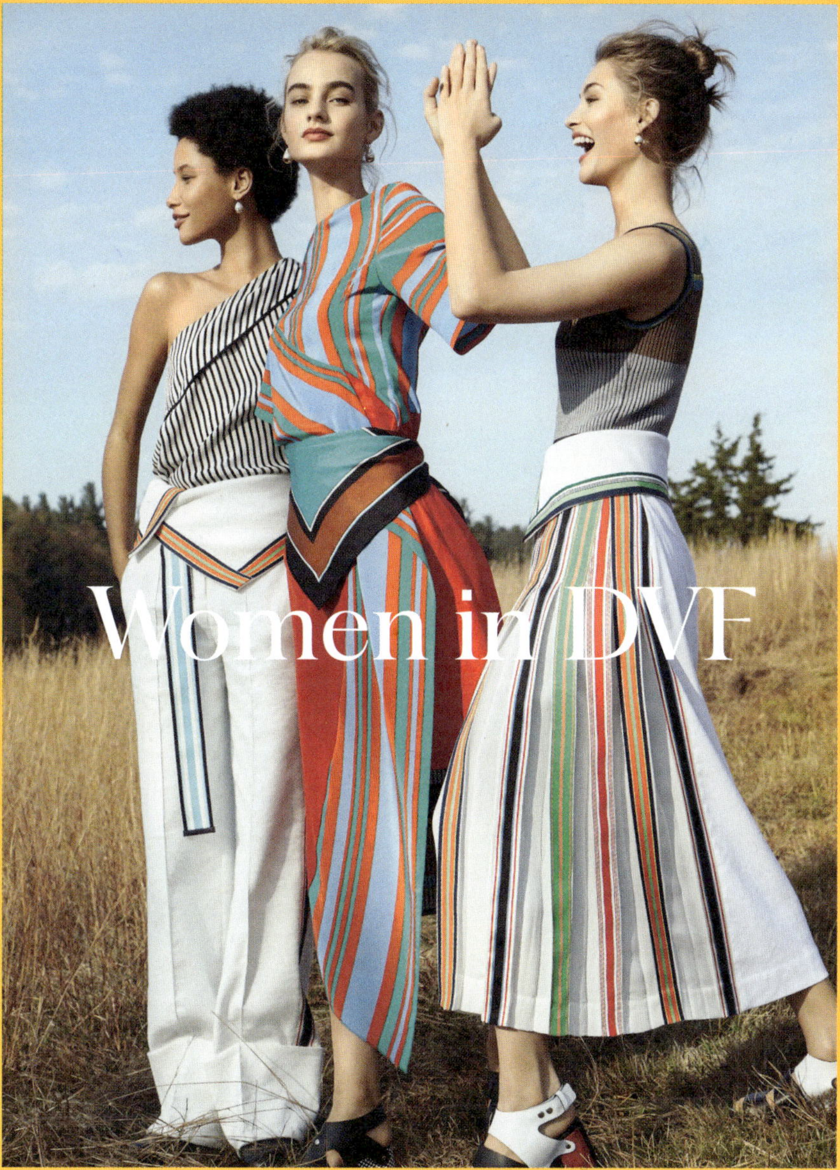

CHAPTER 02

Women in DVF

INTERVIEWS BY

Nicolas Lor

Cindy Crawford

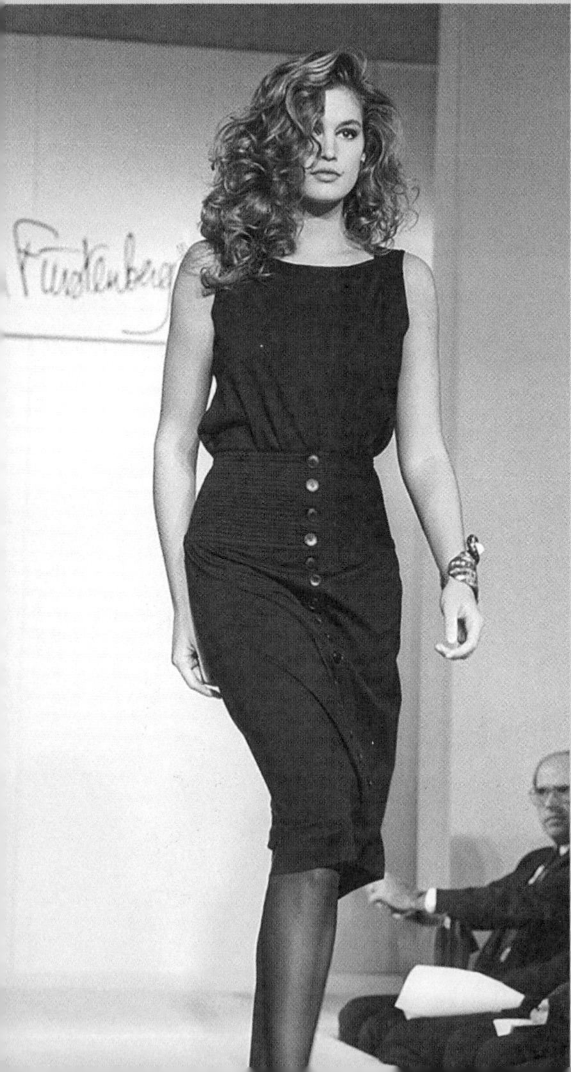

"It's impossible to think separately about Diane as a woman and her brand. Diane is the perfect role model of the strong, powerful woman who is also not afraid to be feminine and fun. Her ability to stay relevant while at the same time remain true to herself shows us all how to celebrate our own authenticity."

Previous page
Vogue editorial,
February 2017.

Cindy Crawford
in a sleeveless
Diane von Furstenberg
black dress, ca. 1988.

"I love Diane! I met her when she was married to Prince Egon and I was with Mick Jagger. She was always so glamorous, beautiful, vivacious, and fun. She still is. I love her clothes and have many that I still wear for years. I loved doing her fashion shows and think her wrap dress is so flattering and genius. She is a triumph in everything she does."

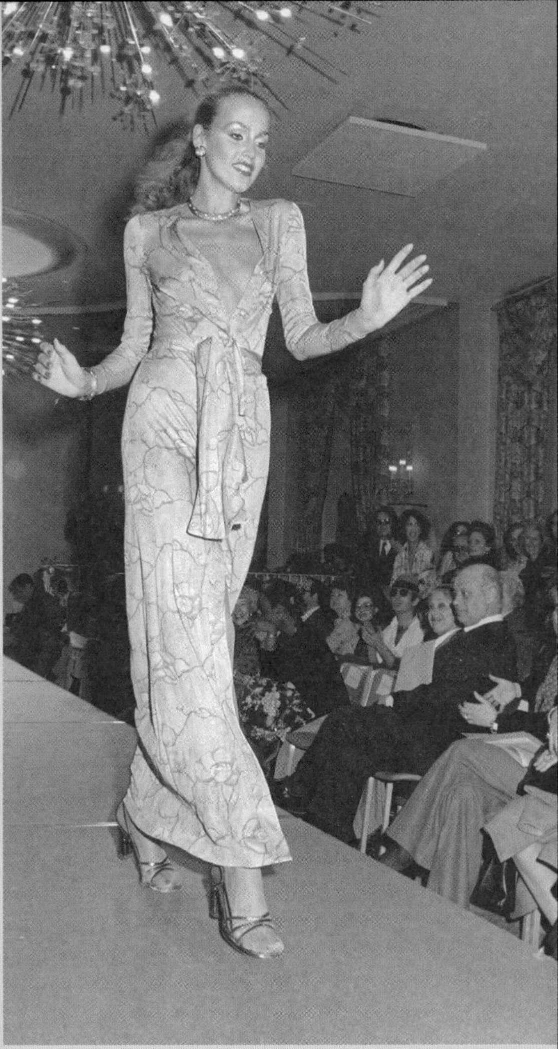

Jerry Hall in a Diane von Furstenberg long wrap gown, 1975.

Jerry Hall

Naomi Campbell

Naomi Campbell walks the Diane von Furstenberg Spring 2014 show.

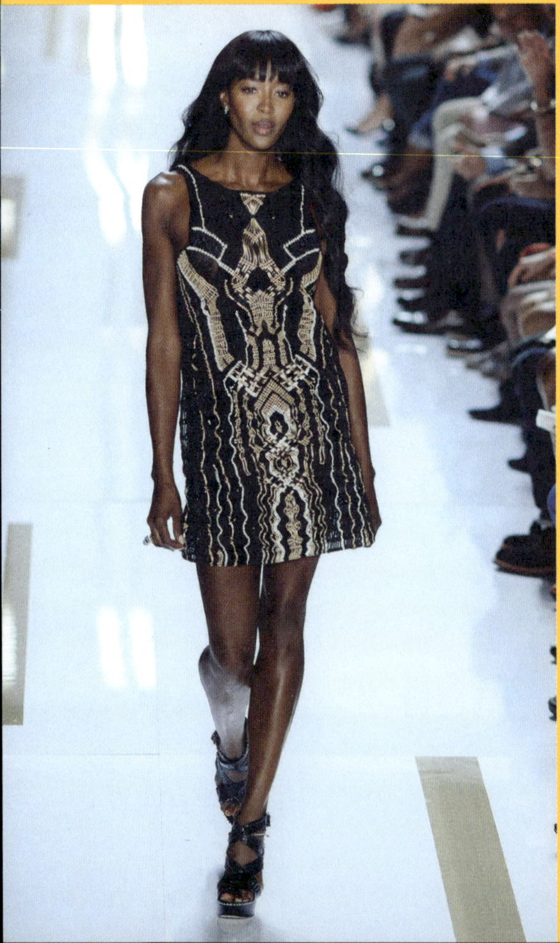

"To me, Diane is a woman epitome of great elegance and intelligence. I first met Diane when I was 17 years old. I've always thought her encouragement and support is limitless. She is always there and tells you the things you need to hear at that time. She is like a fairy godmother. Her energy and thirst for life are truly inspiring as well. She is not only a designer but also a supporter—a force of nature who did so many wonderful things to bring those without a voice to the forefront. The DVF brand is for the everyday working woman—a woman who is independent and successful, and has strong confidence in herself."

"DVF is a perfect example of how fashion is more than a dress, more than style, and more than image. It's an attitude to life, a message of hope, and a new standard set. Diane didn't just create a dress; she freed women from their own stereotypes. She said, 'You can wear a dress and be successful like a man, and you can have fun and enjoy yourself, be feminine, and build an empire.' She empowered so many women—me included—by simply saying, 'You can do anything.'"

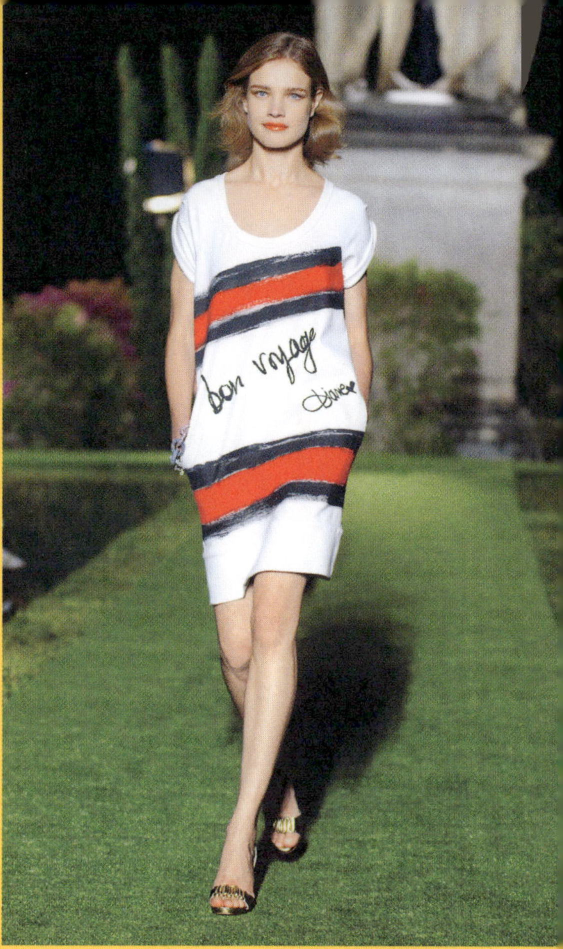

Natalia Vodianova walks the Diane von Furstenberg Resort 2008 show.

Natalia Vodianova

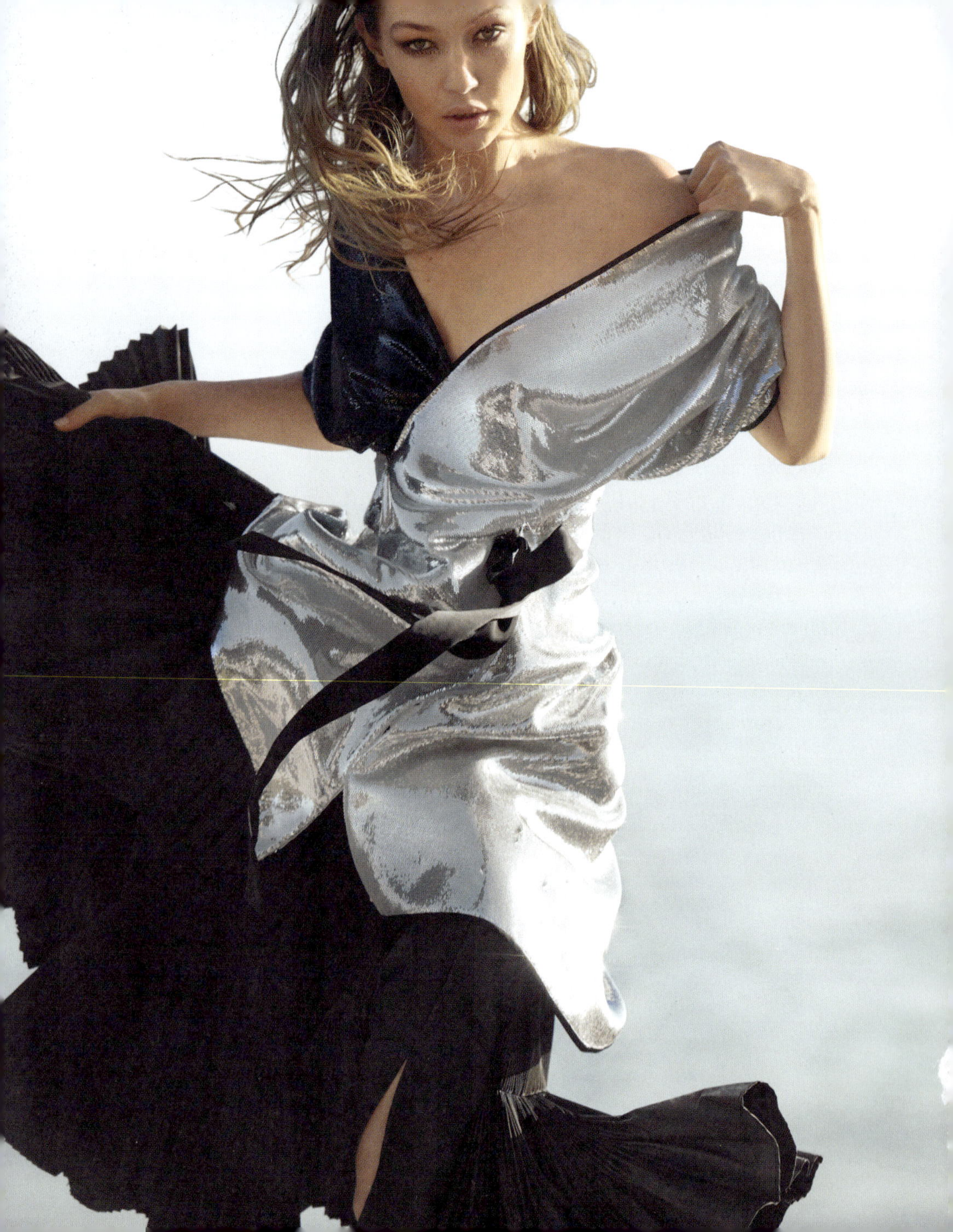

"Diane wants you to bring yourself and not be anything you're not. She says if you feel sexy today, be sexy. If you feel powerful today, be powerful. That's what I love about her."

Opposite
Gigi Hadid in DVF, 2017.

Gigi Hadid

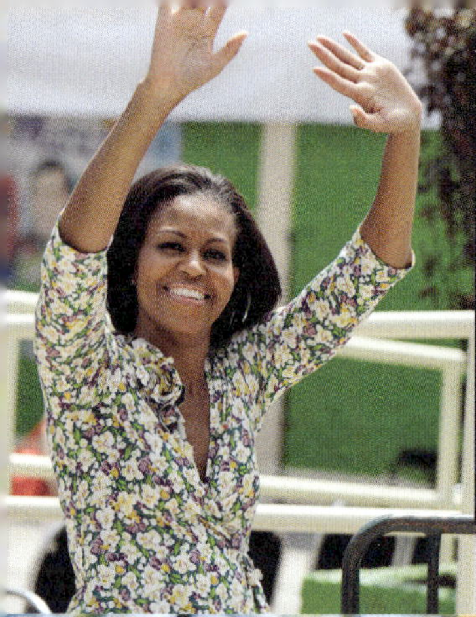
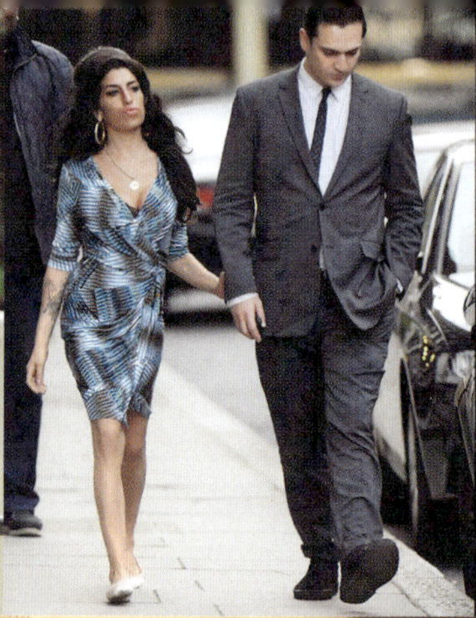
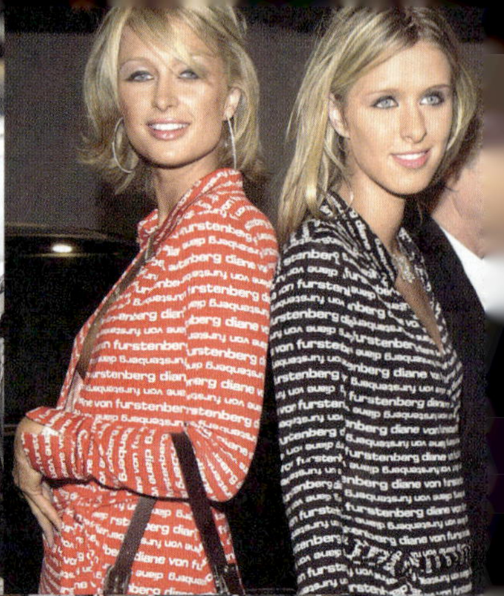
diane von furstenberg
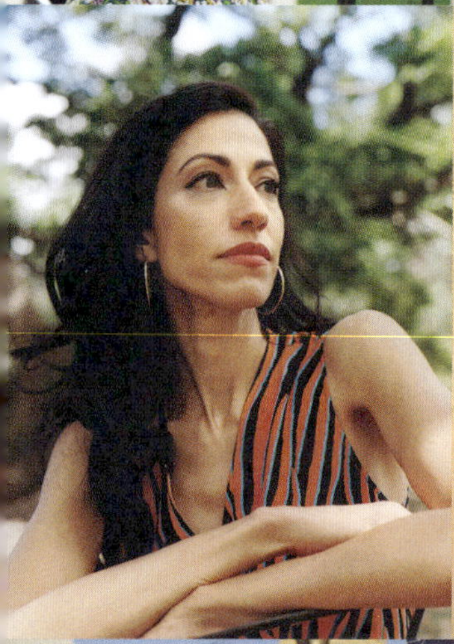
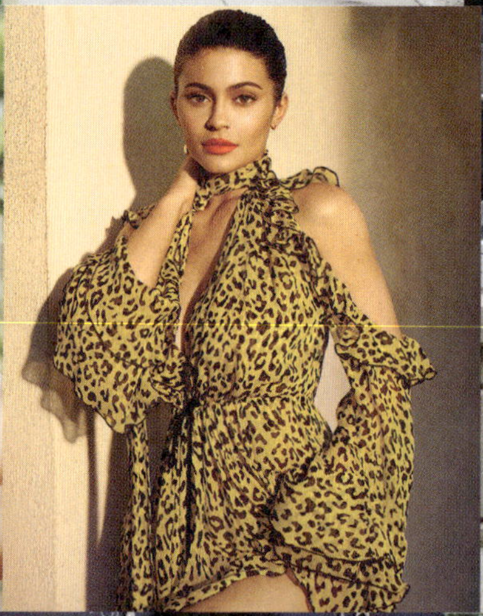
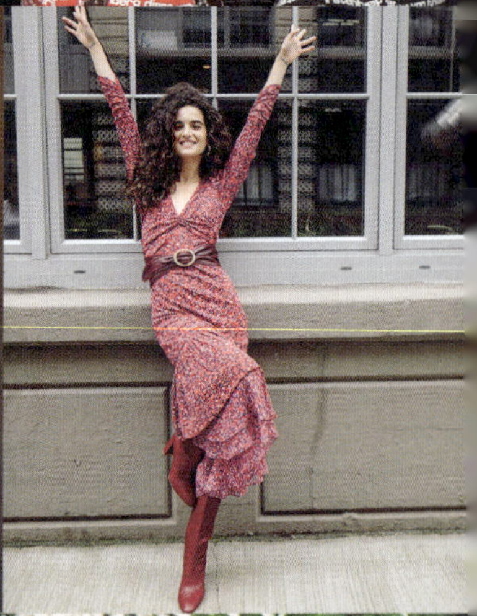
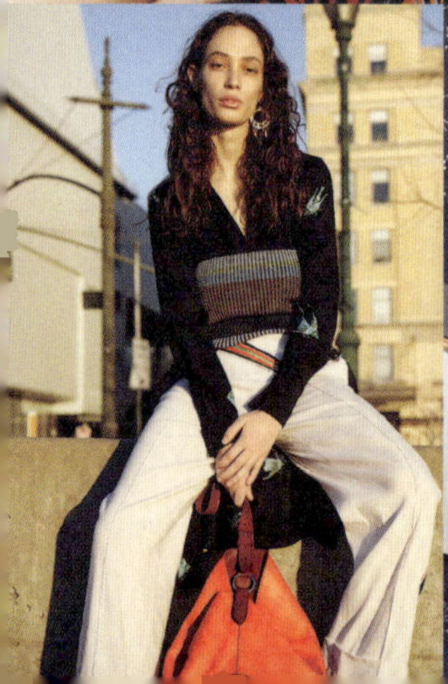
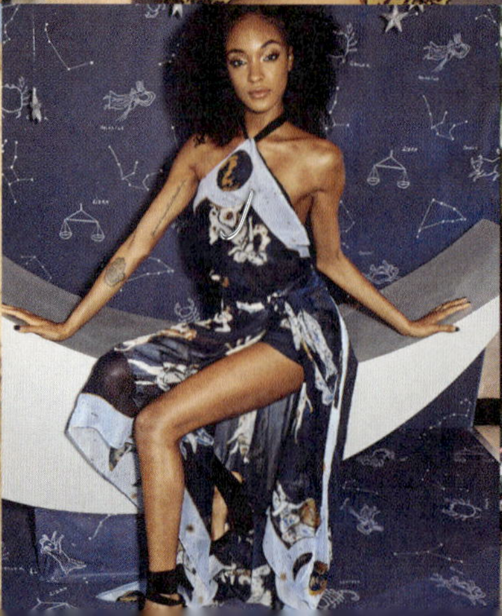
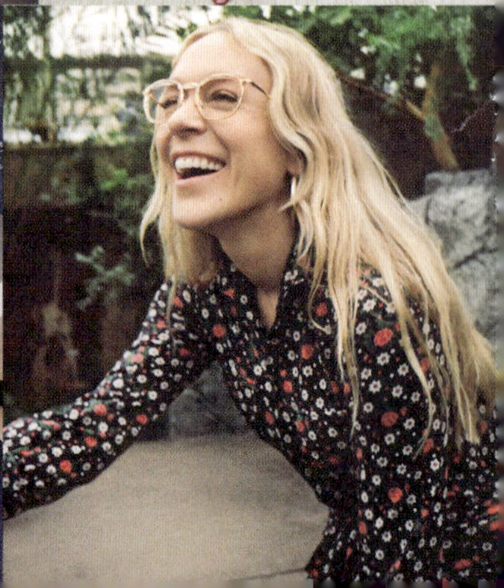

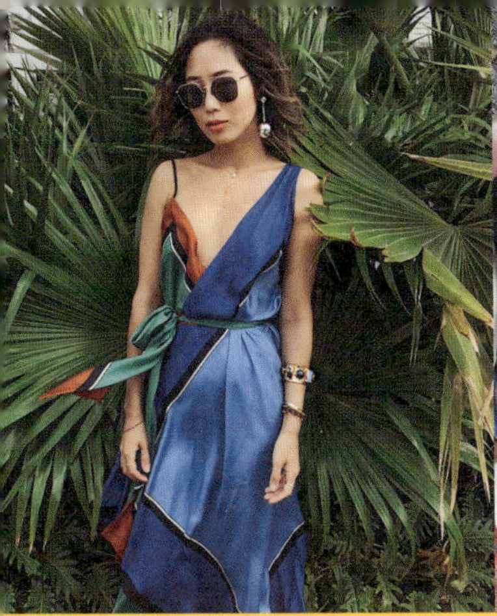
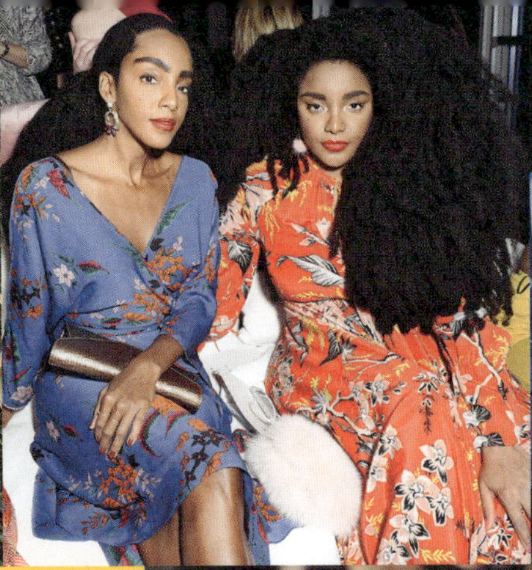
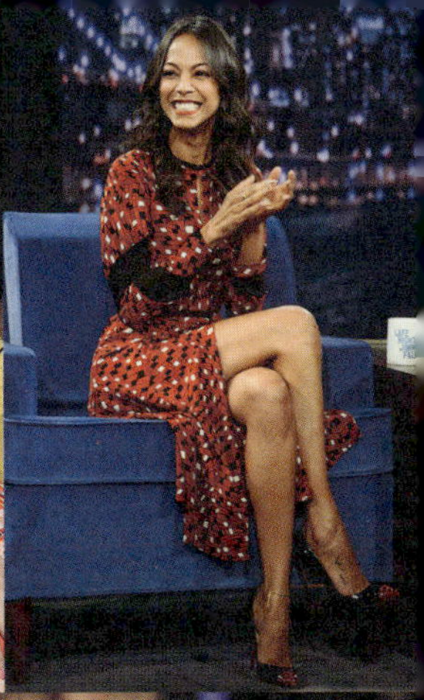

People of note
wearing DVF

Opposite page:

(top)
Michelle Obama, 2010;
Amy Winehouse, 2011;
Paris and Nicky Hilton, 2001;

(middle)
Huma Abedin, 2022;
Kylie Jenner, 2018;
Chiara Scelsi, 2019;

(bottom)
Sophie Koella, 2017;
Jourdan Dunn, 2018; Chloe Sevigny, 2019.

This page:

(top)
Aimee Song, 2017;
TK Wonder and Cipriana Quann, 2018;
Zoe Saldana, 2013;

(middle)
Allison Williams, 2016;

(bottom)
Oprah Winfrey, 2012;
Priyanka Chopra, 2019;
Adwoa Aboah, 2019.

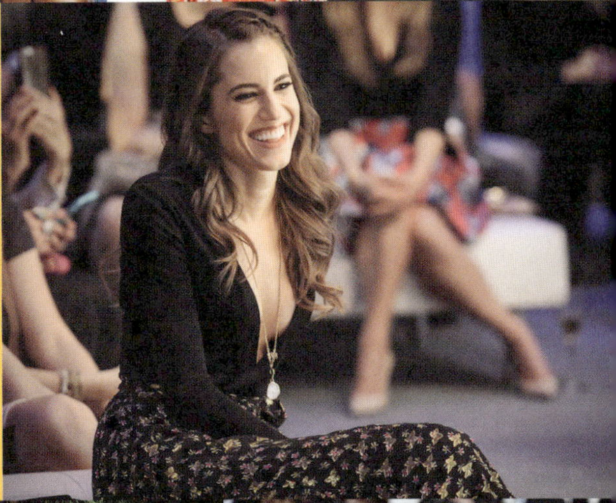
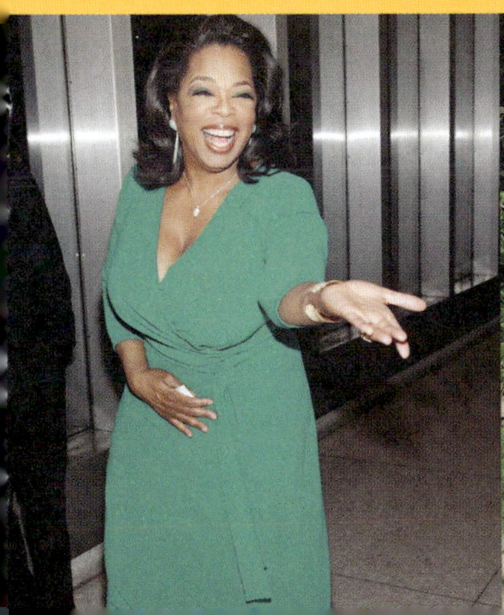
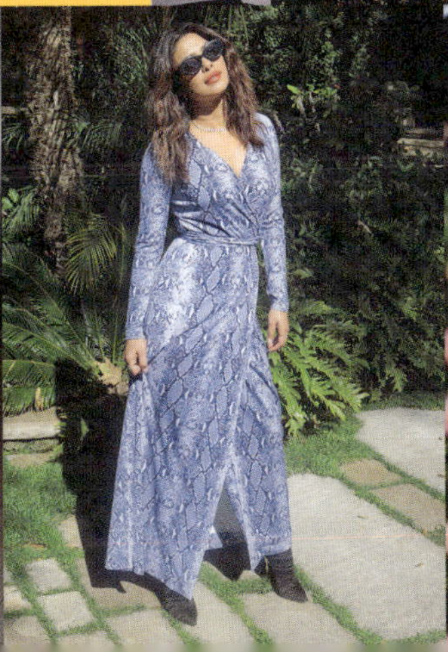
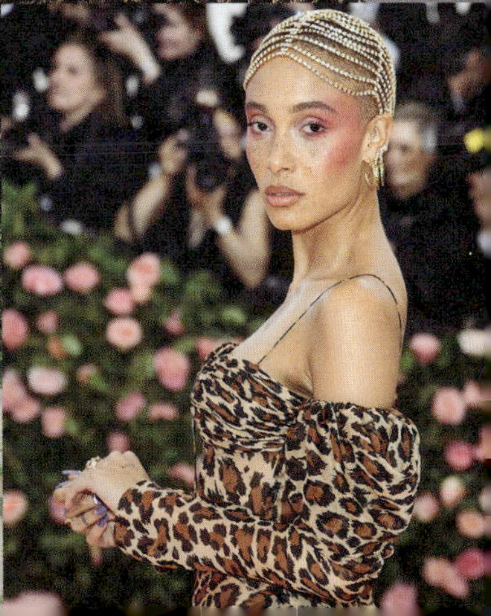

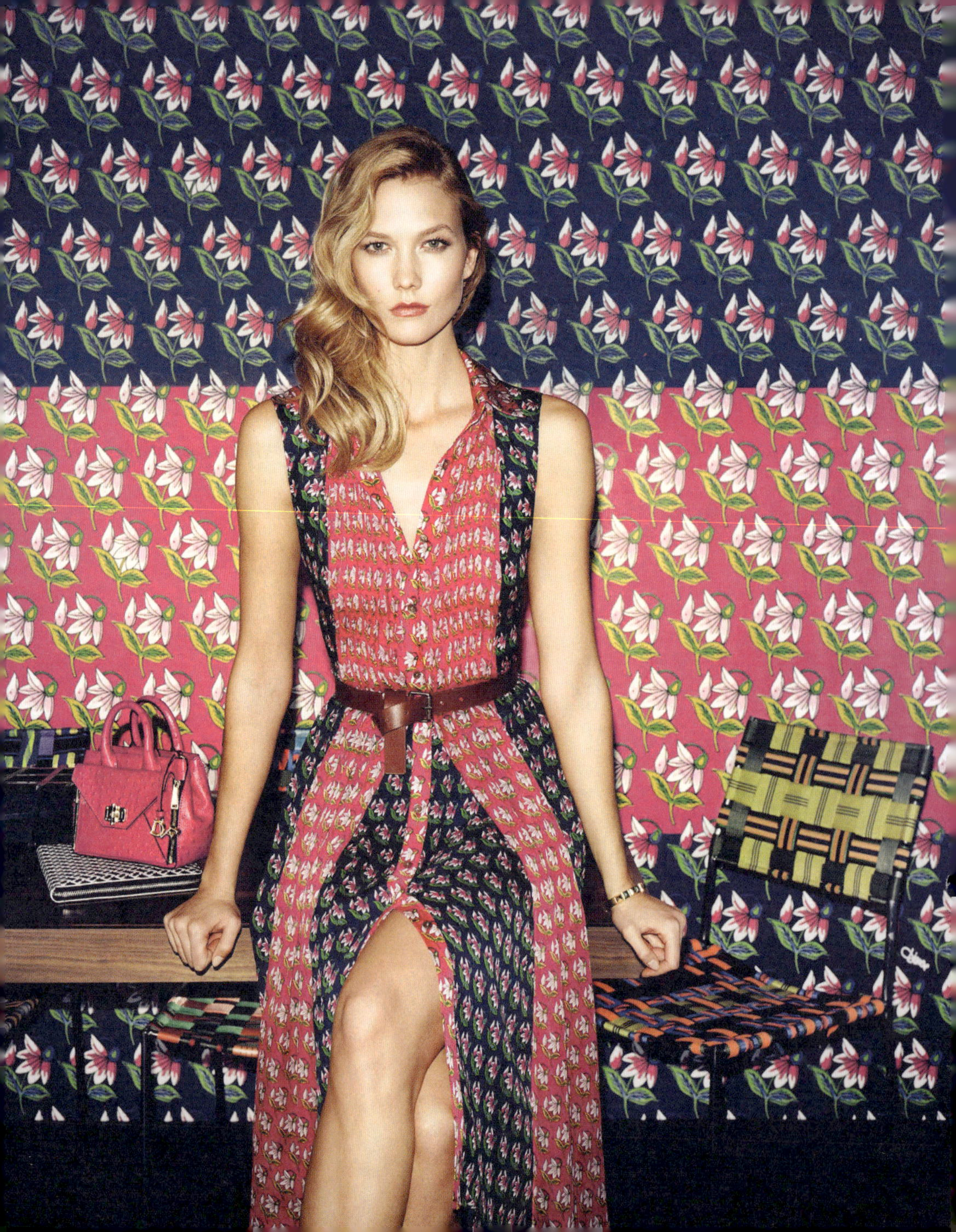

KARLIE KLOSS

Karlie Kloss (b. 1992, United States) is a fashion model. In 2016, she started the charity organization Kode with Klossy, a coding camp and career scholarship program. In 2019, she became the host of the reality competition television series "Project Runway."

How and when did you begin working with Diane?

Opposite
Karlie Kloss in a floral print dress from the Diane von Furstenberg Spring 2016 collection.

I met Diane very early in my career. I was 15 years old when we met at her New York City atelier. From the first moment, we connected. I have been in awe of her magnetism, energy, and creativity. I knew instantly that she was someone I wanted and needed in not only my career but in my personal life. I have been lucky enough to walk in her show for many years, join her in some very memorable campaigns, travel the world together, and share some of my most important career and life moments with Diane. She has been one of the most influential people in my life.

How would you describe your first DVF fashion show?

Opposite
Karlie Kloss walks the Diane von Furstenberg Spring 2014 show.

I remember being backstage at DVF's shows at Bryant Park through the early years of my career. From the moment you walked into her show, the energy was electric. Before we walked the runway, she would give the models the most incredible pep talks that made us feel so strong and sexy. She made all of the models feel so powerful and inspired as they stepped foot onto the catwalk. It is the same power that her clothes have to help make women feel their most confident every day they wear a DVF piece in a board room, classroom, or down the street.

Diane proposes feminine collections that make you feel strong and invincible.

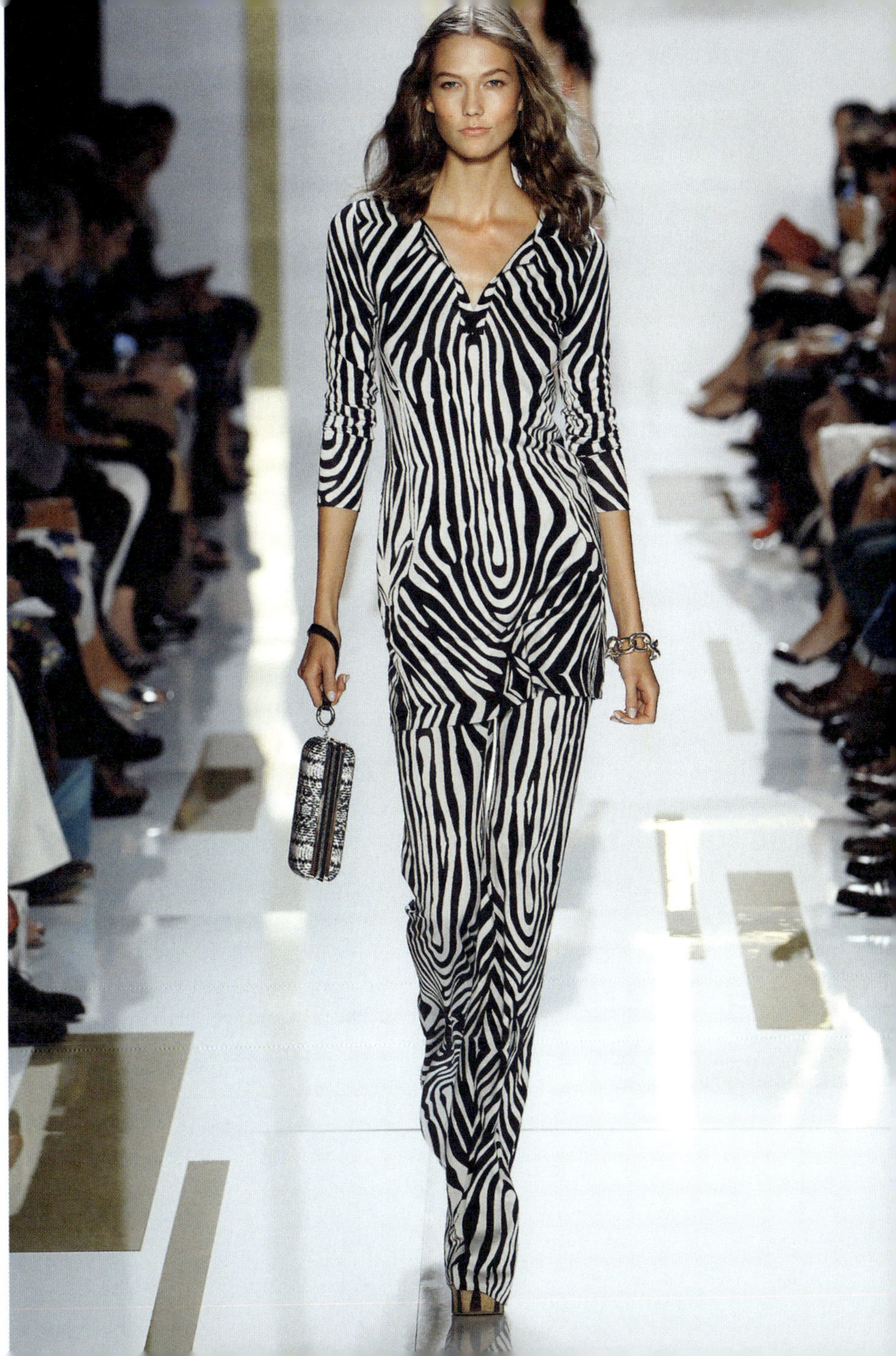

What is your relationship to clothing?

Opposite
Karlie Kloss and Irina Shayk at the Diane von Furstenberg Fall 2016 show.

Next page, from left to right
Karlie Kloss, Diane von Furstenberg, and Kate Bosworth at the DVF Awards, 2017.

Fashion and clothing have always been a huge part of my life. The clothing that I wear on set inspires the characters whom I become in front of the camera. In my personal life, I get dressed in the morning to feel my best as a mom and a model, leading Kode with Klossy and working on my partnership with Roblox. Clothing empowers me to put my best foot forward every day. Clothing allows women to experiment creatively and show off their personality. Clothing can leave them feeling energized, inspired, and confident.

I love to wear DVF when I am looking to feel feminine and strong. DVF fits into so many parts of my life: walking a red carpet, hosting friends for a dinner party, or giving a speech. Versatility is what makes Diane's designs so timeless.

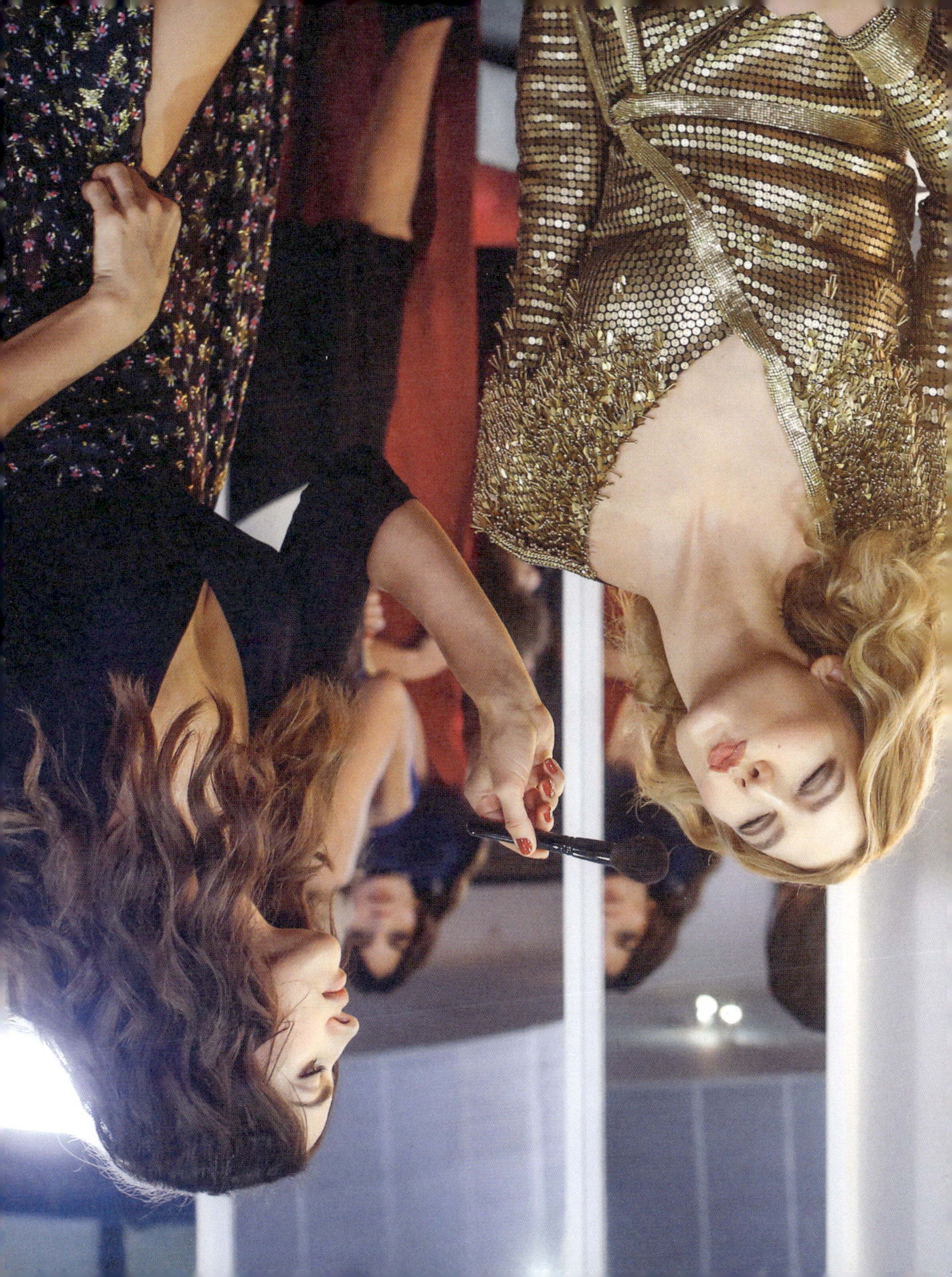

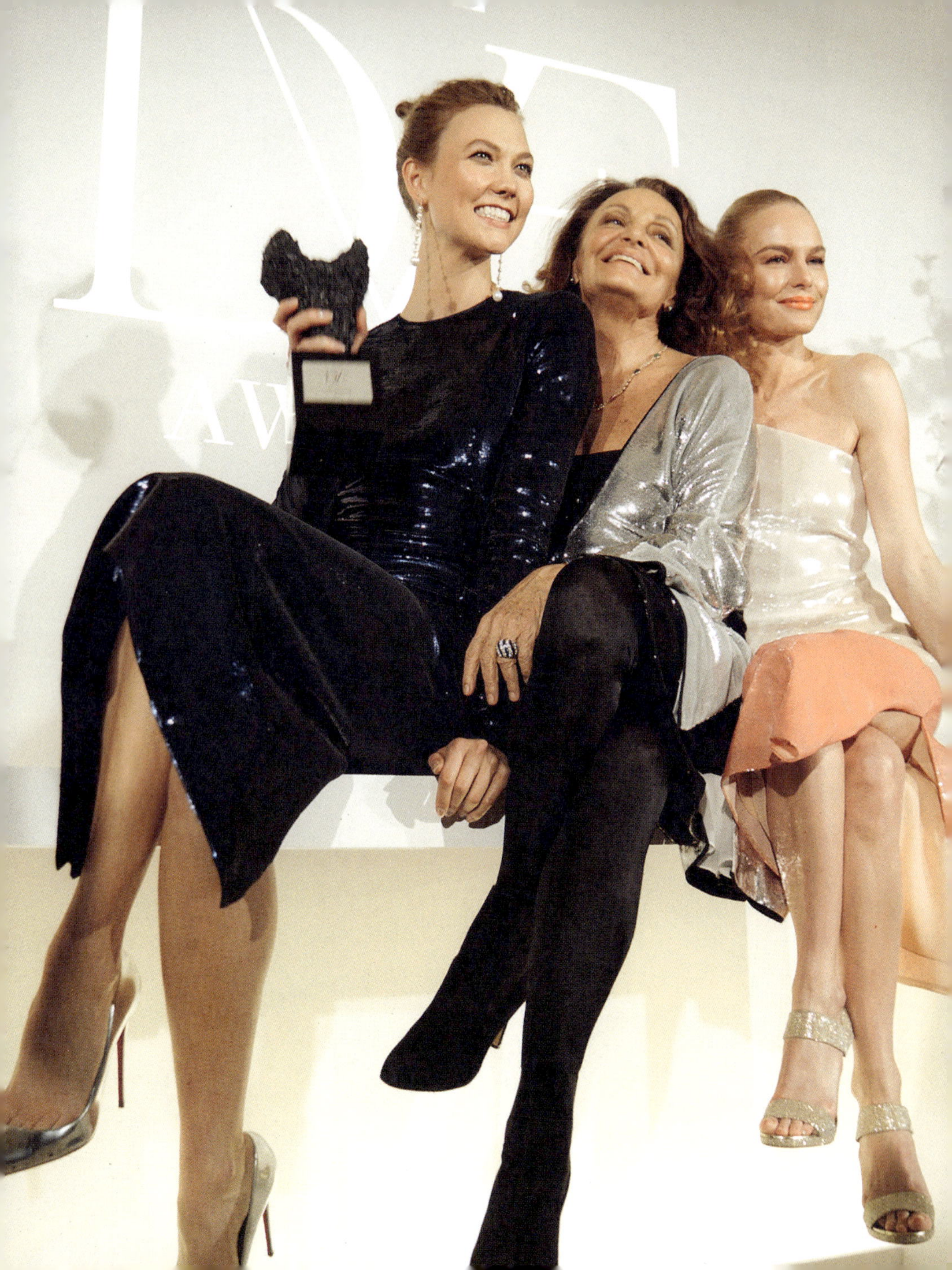

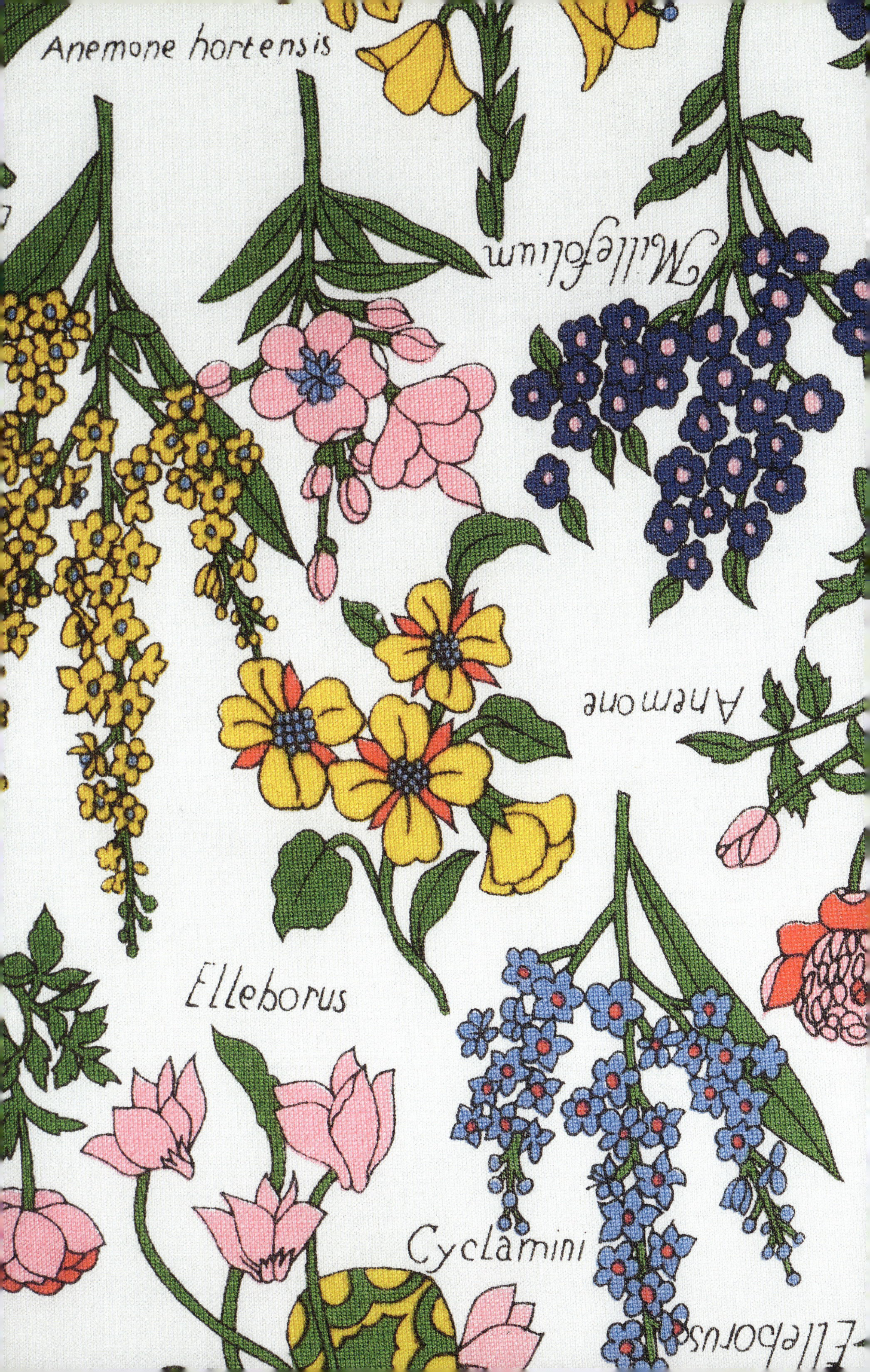
Anemone hortensis
Millefolium
Anemone
Elleborus
Cyclamini
Elleborus

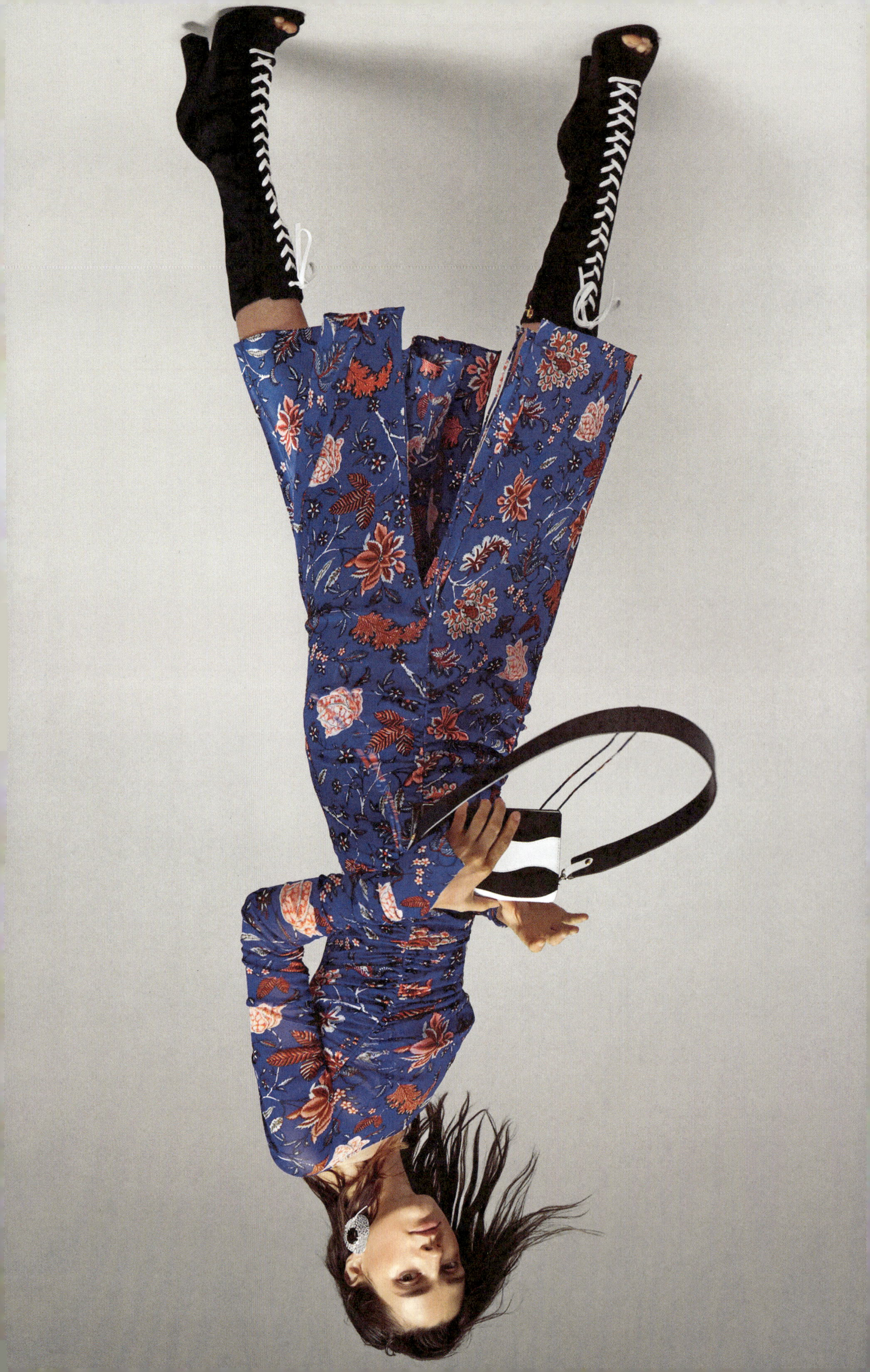

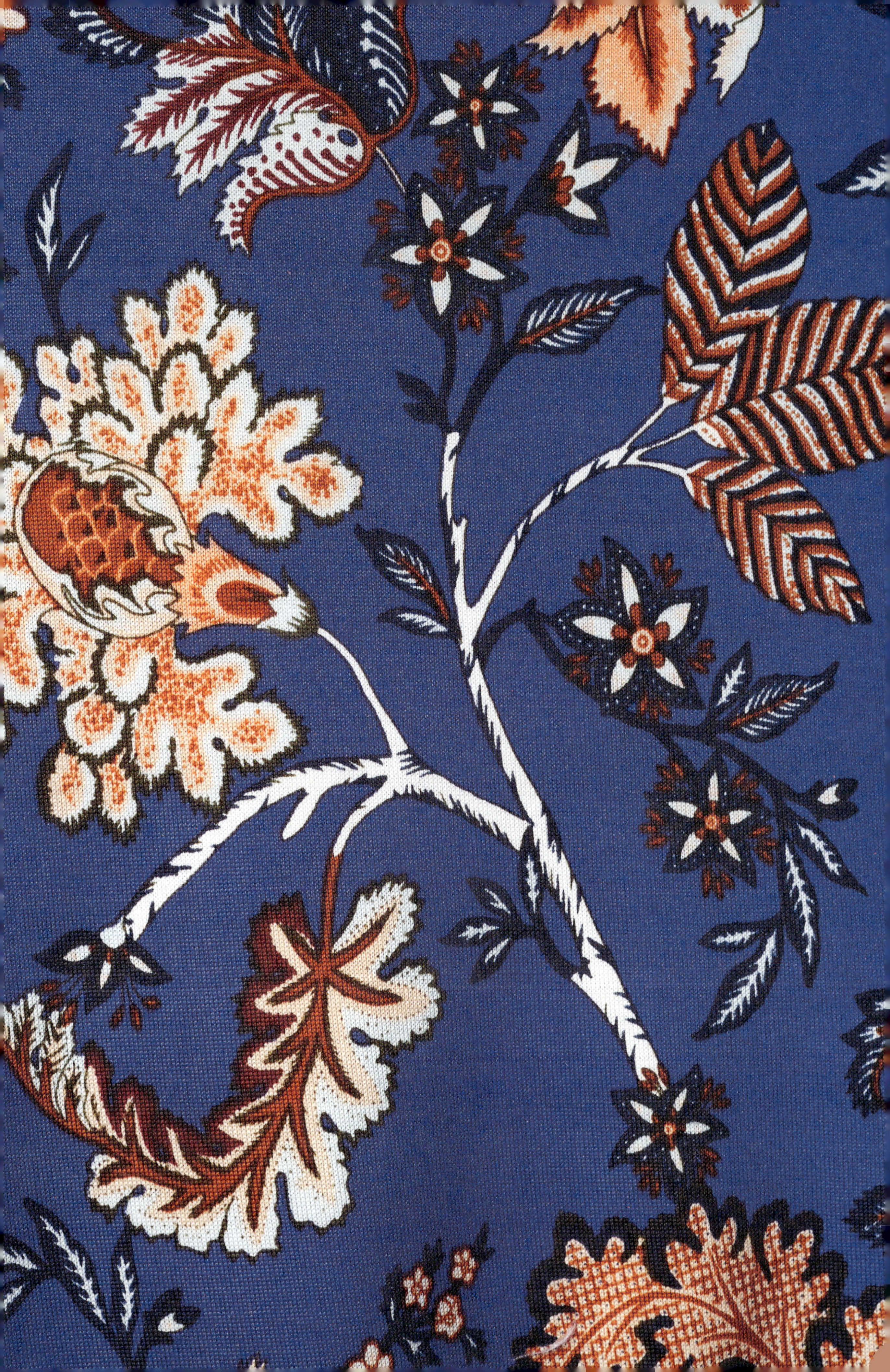

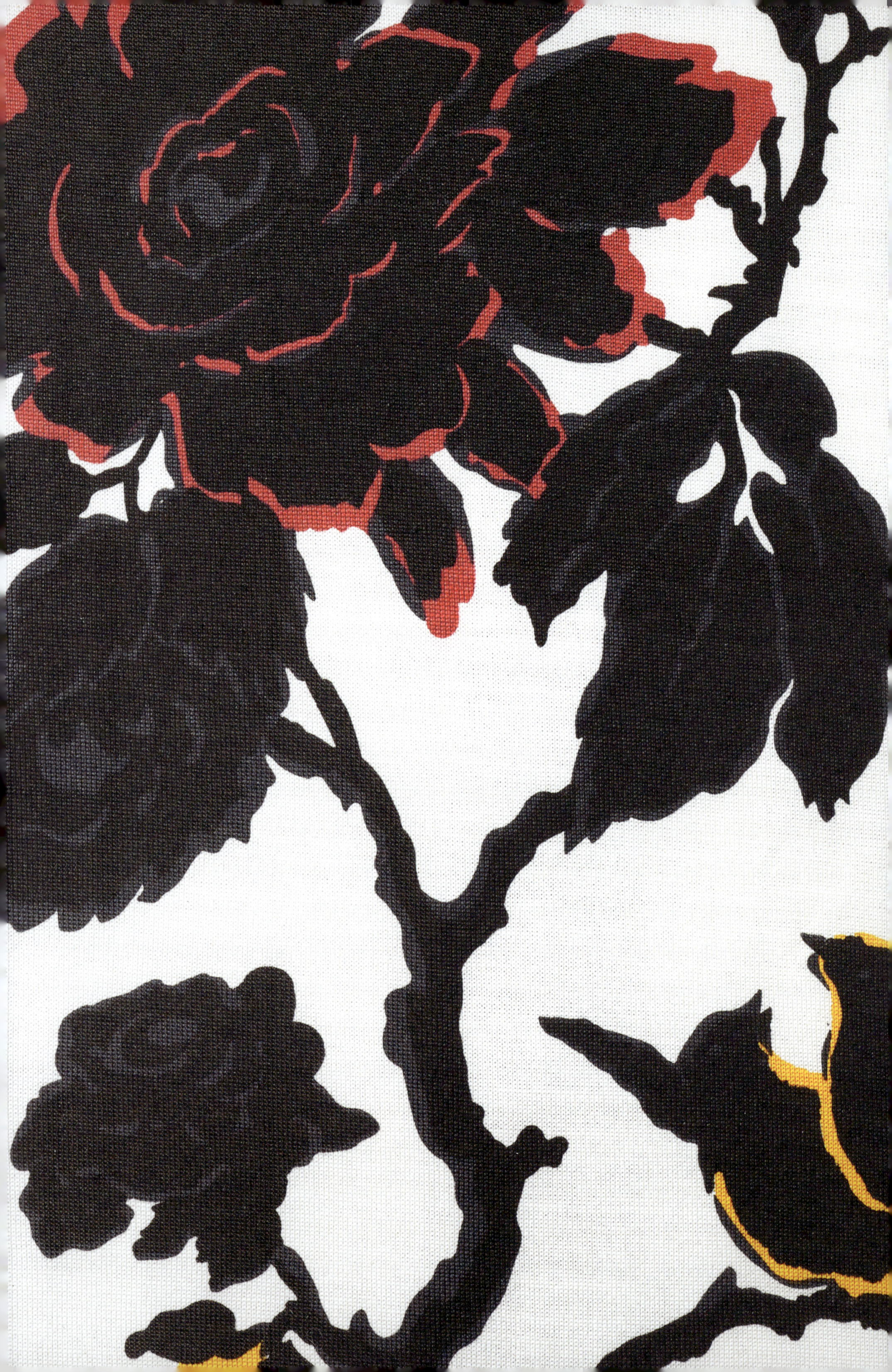

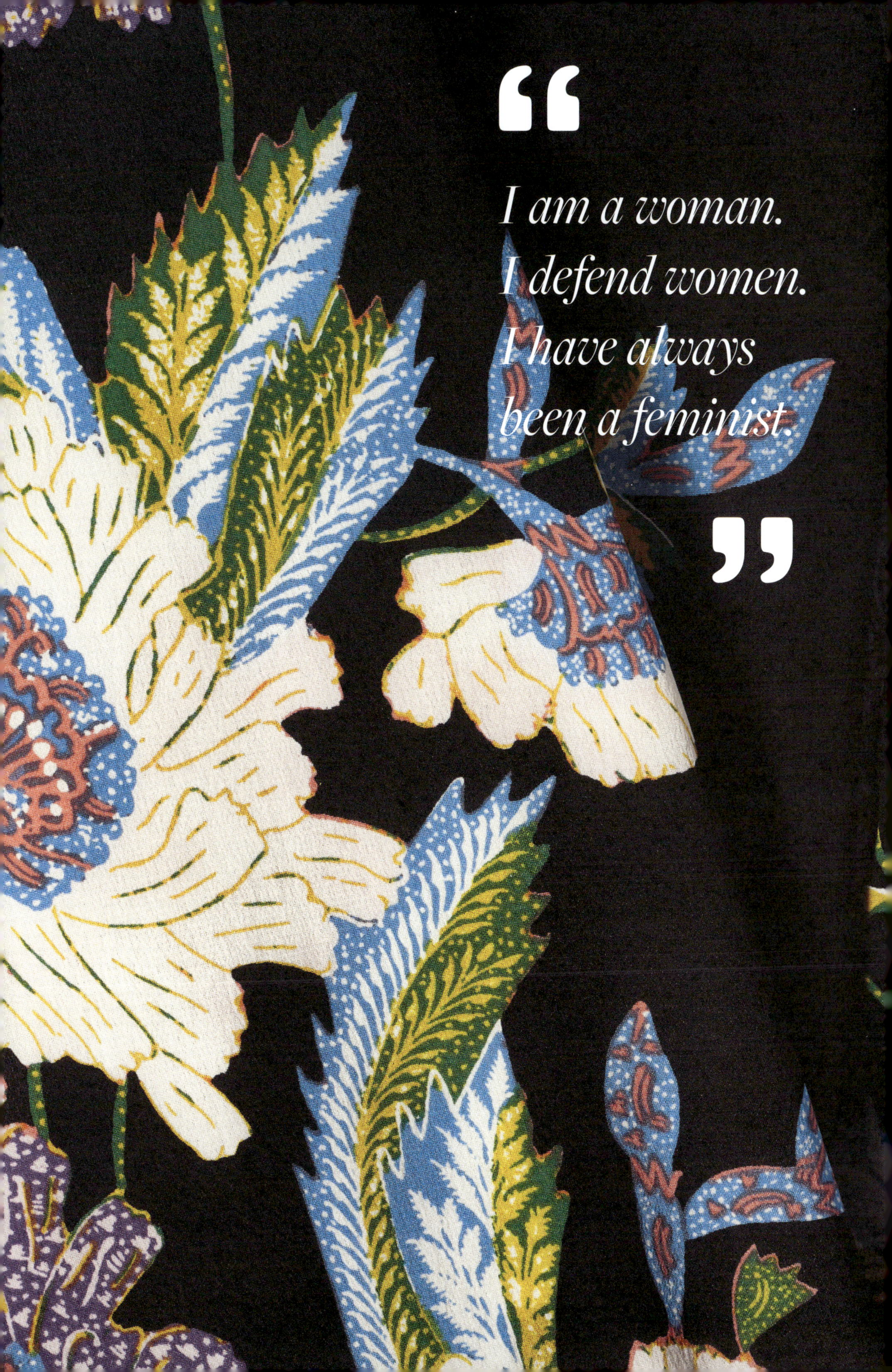

*“I am a woman.
I defend women.
I have always
been a feminist.”*

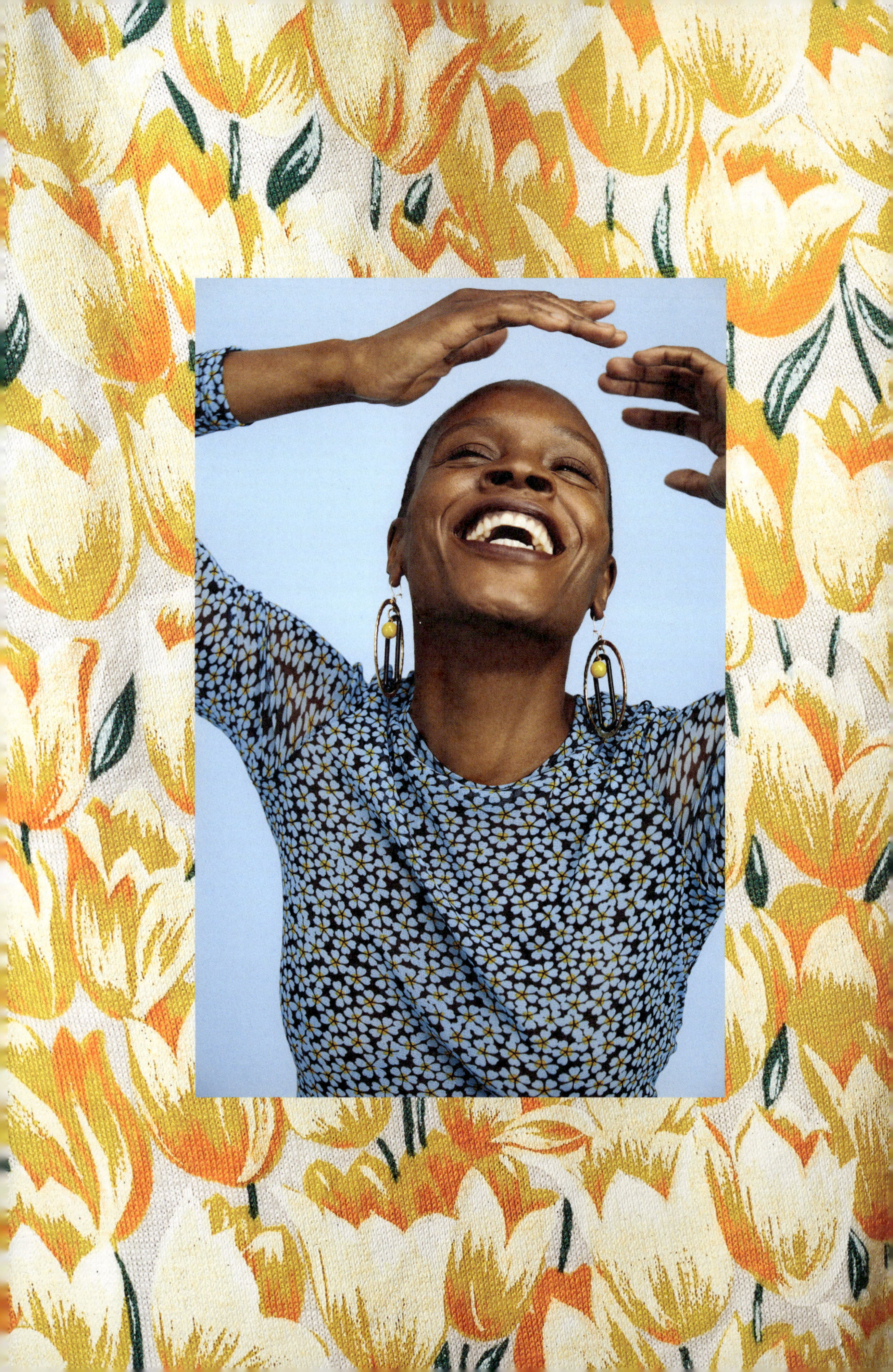

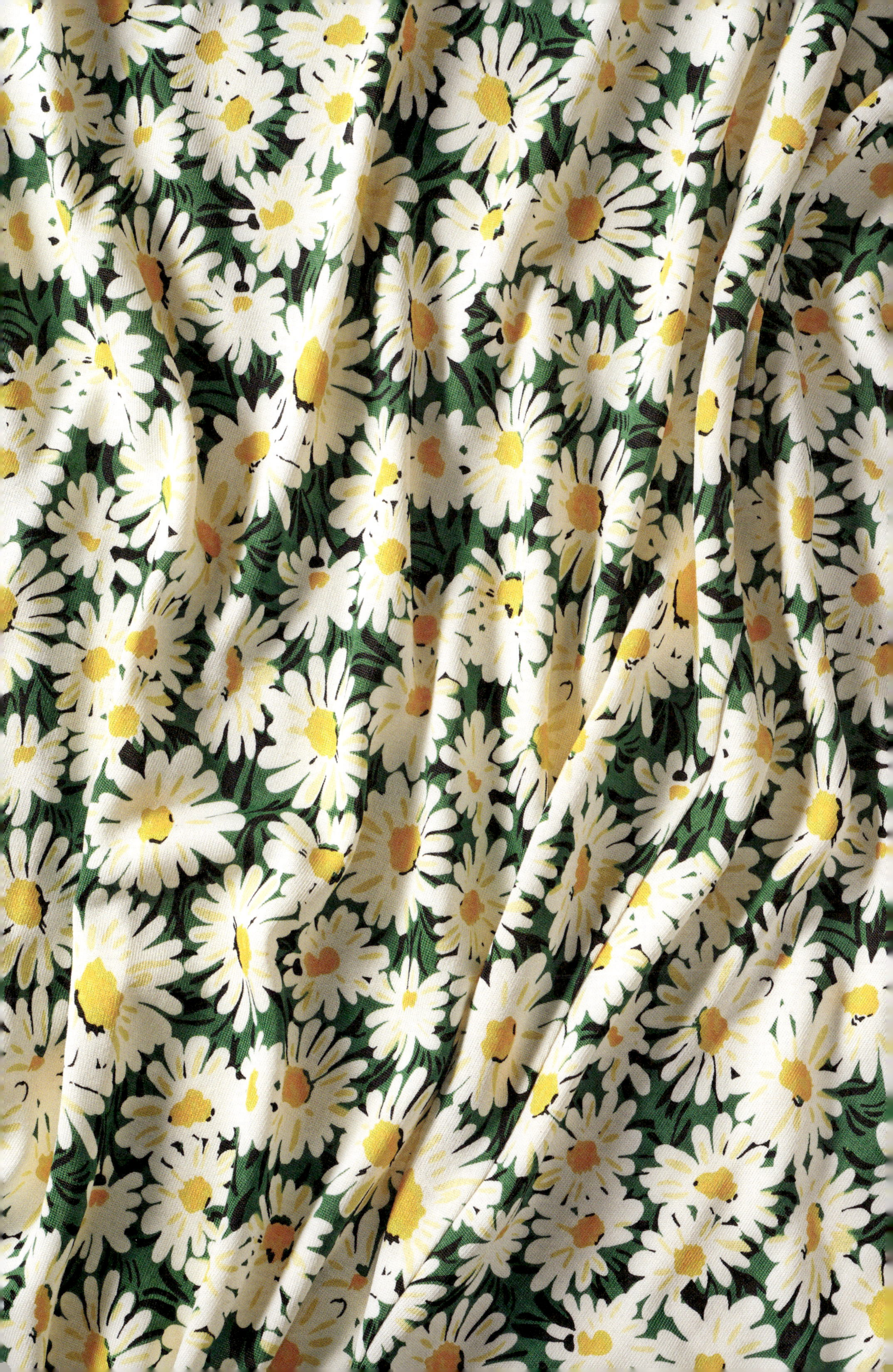

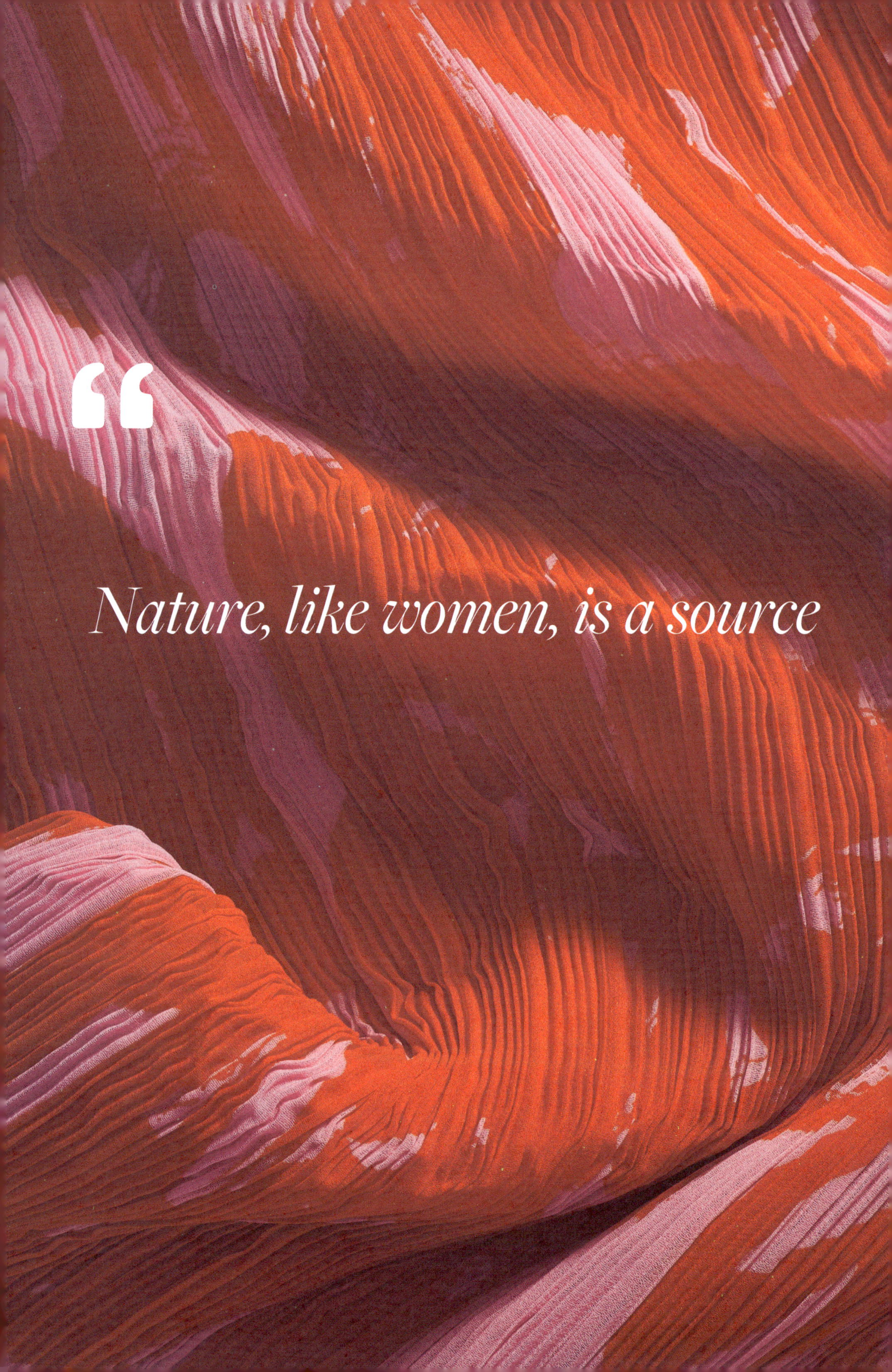

“

Nature, like women, is a source

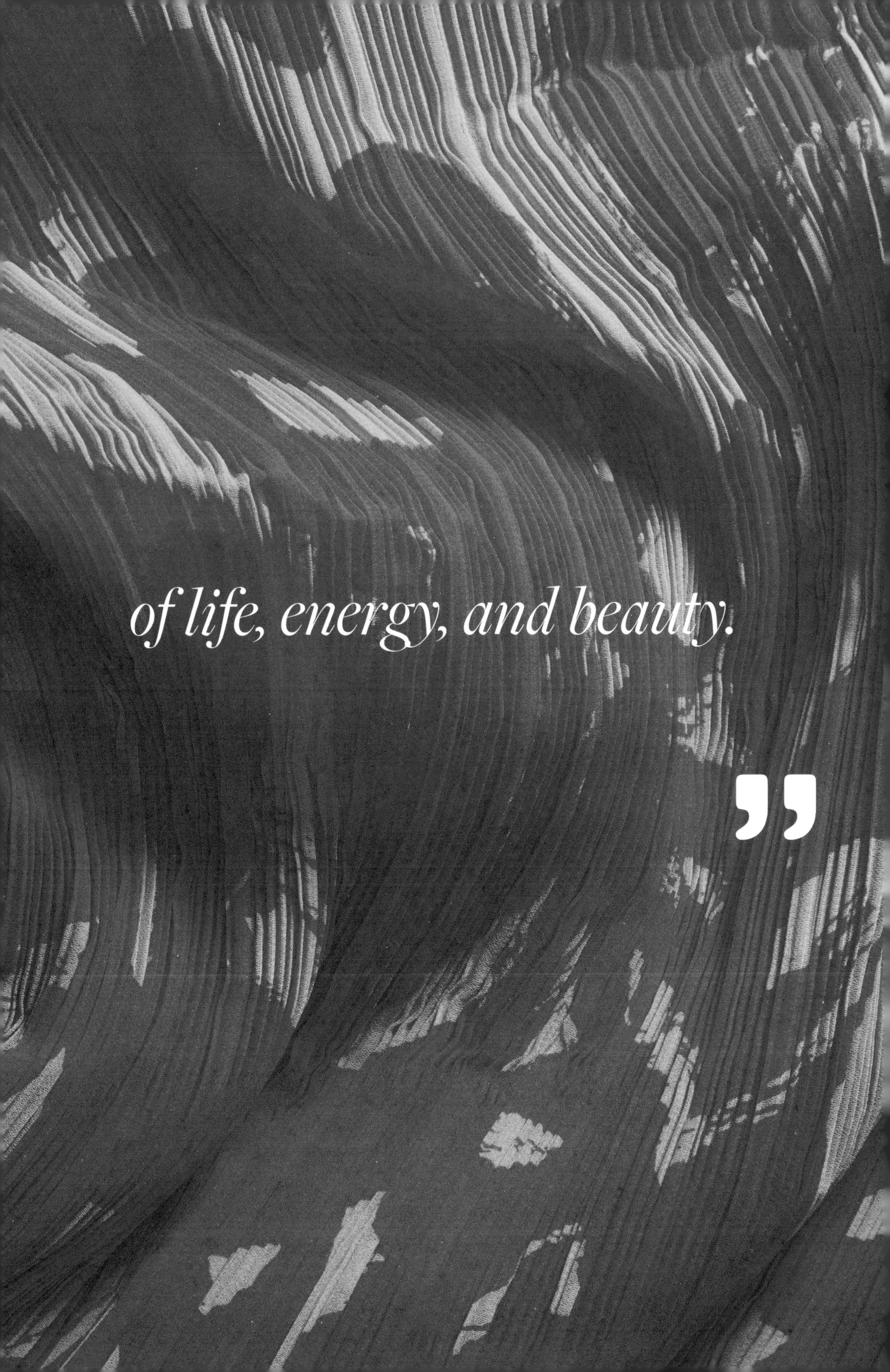

of life, energy, and beauty.

”

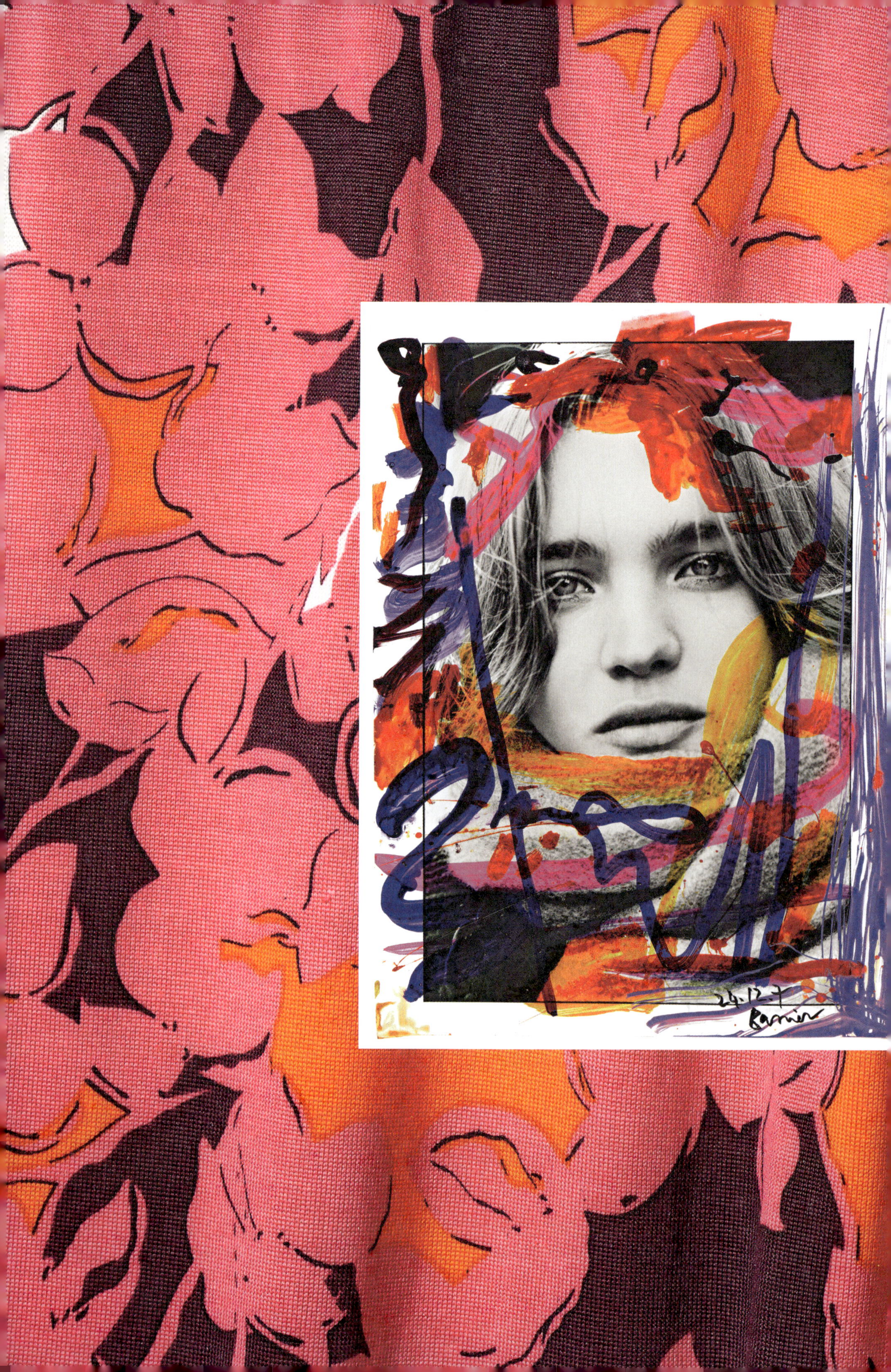
24.12.7

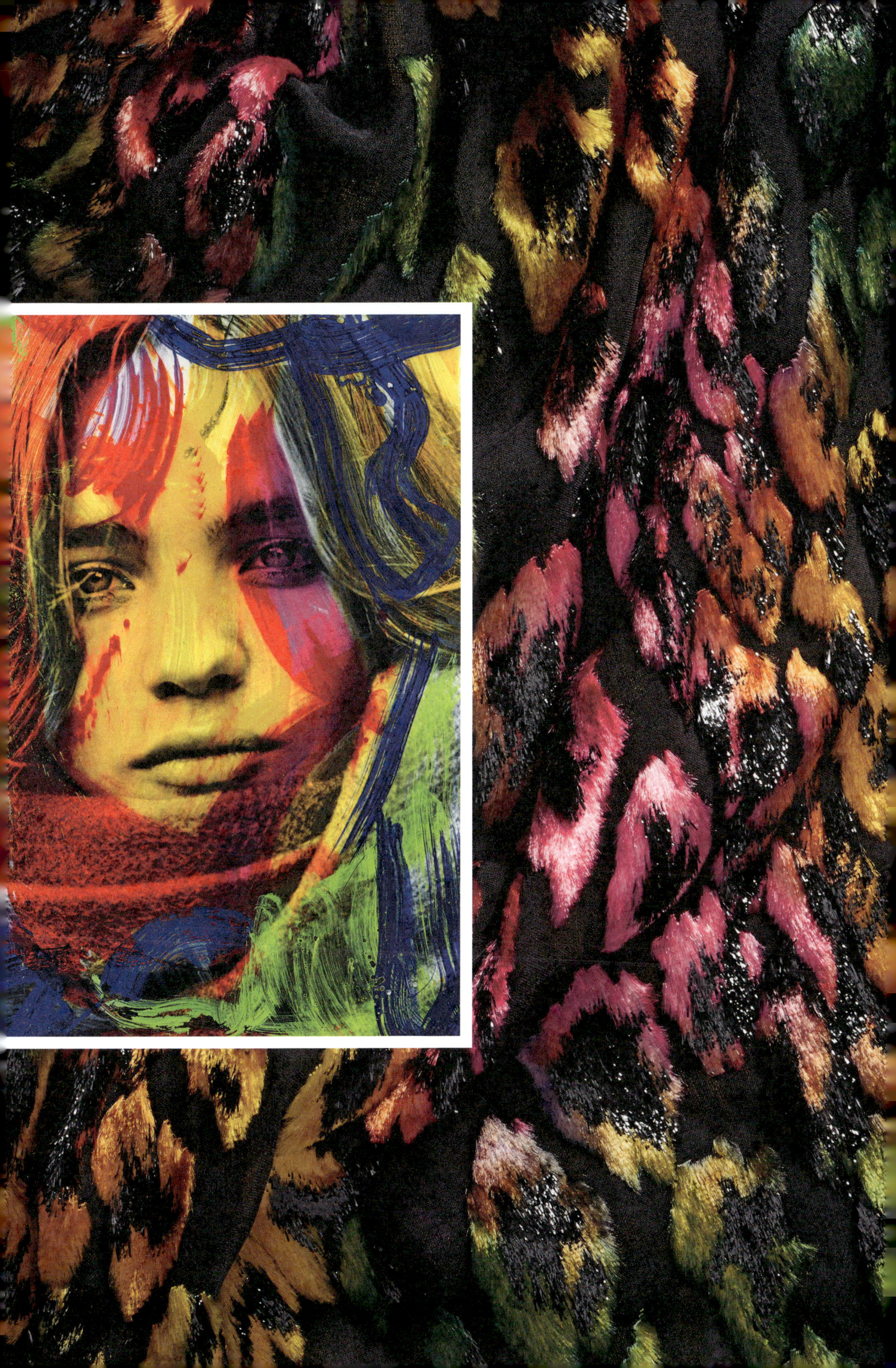

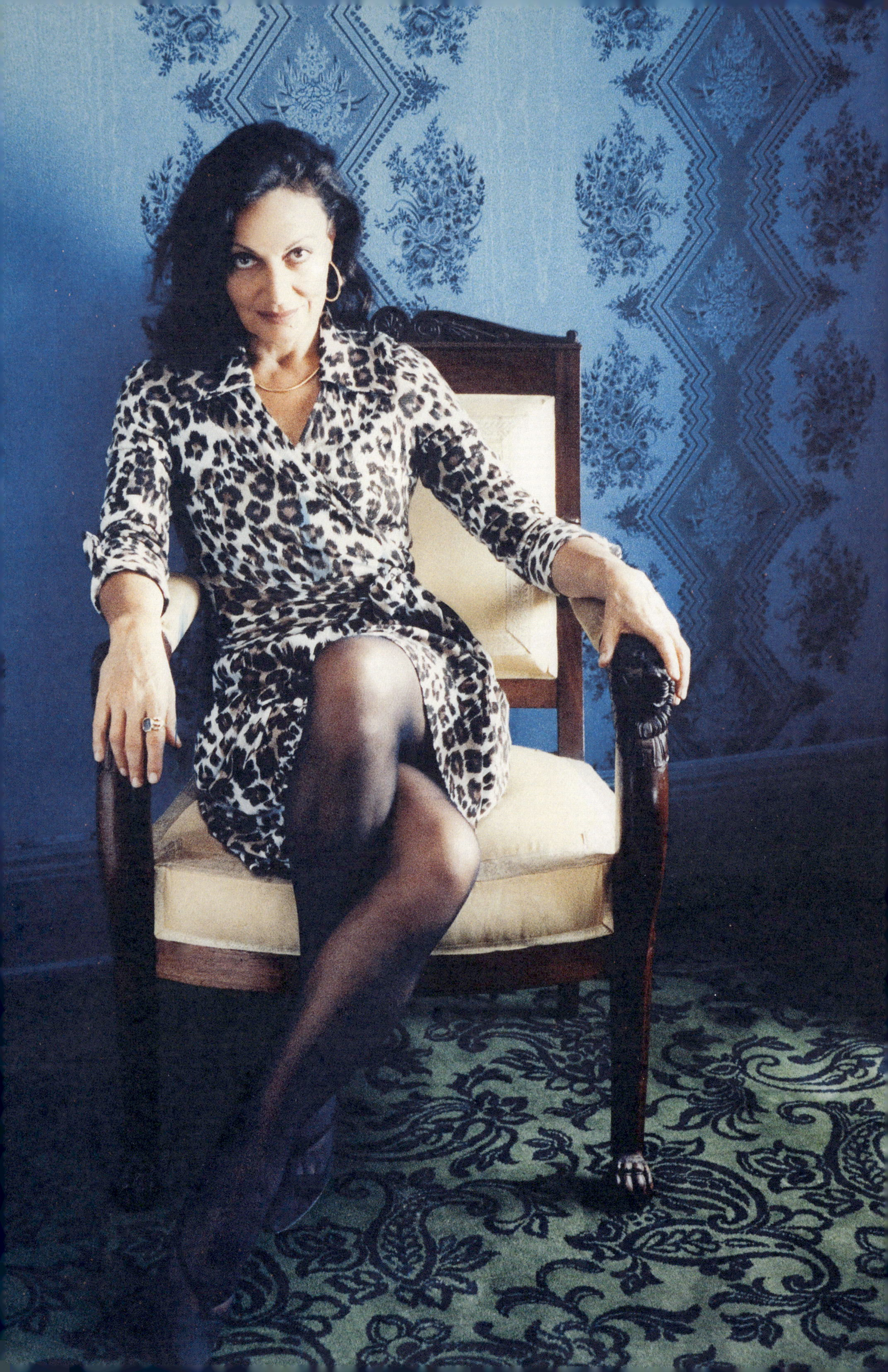

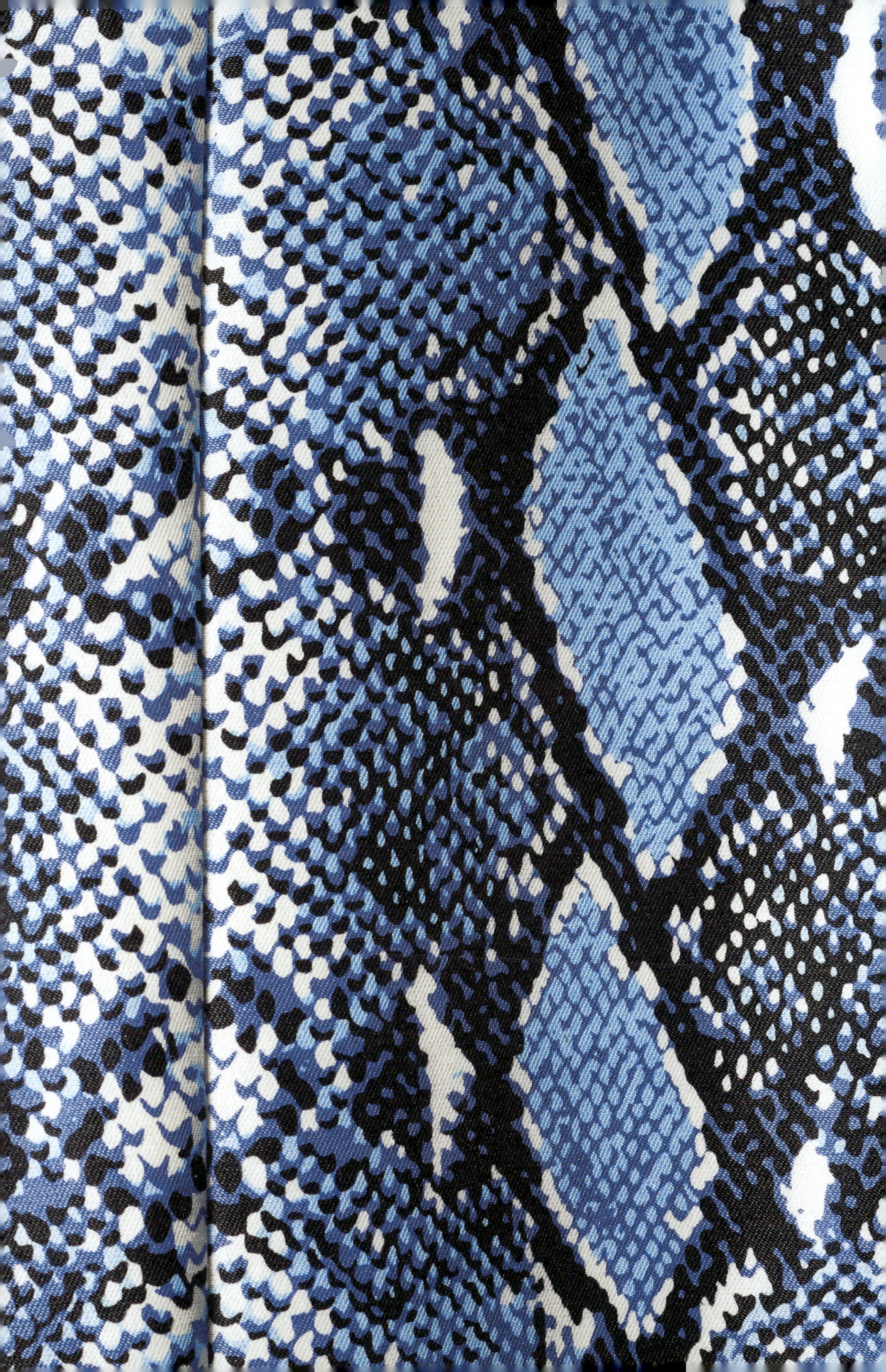

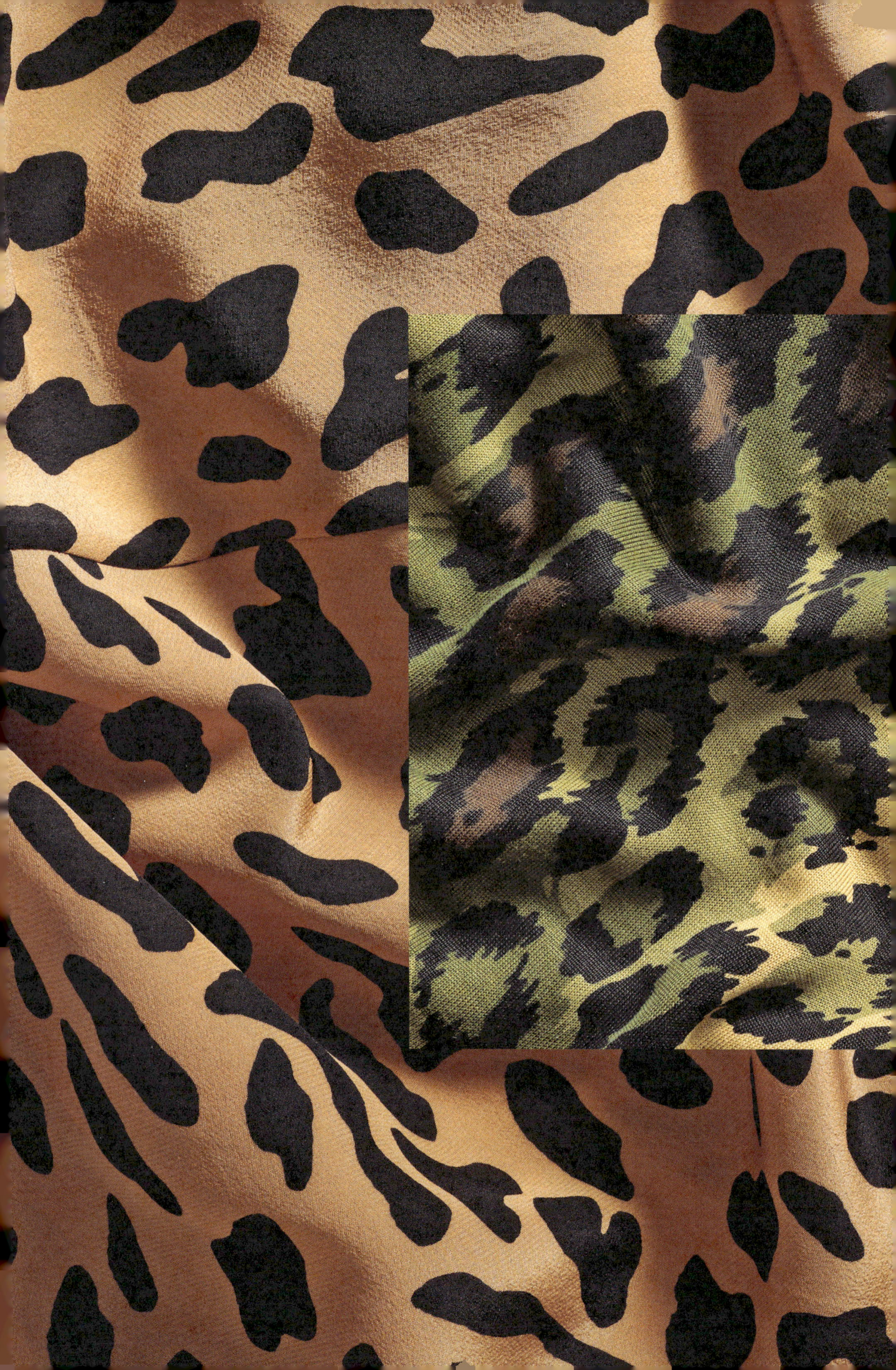

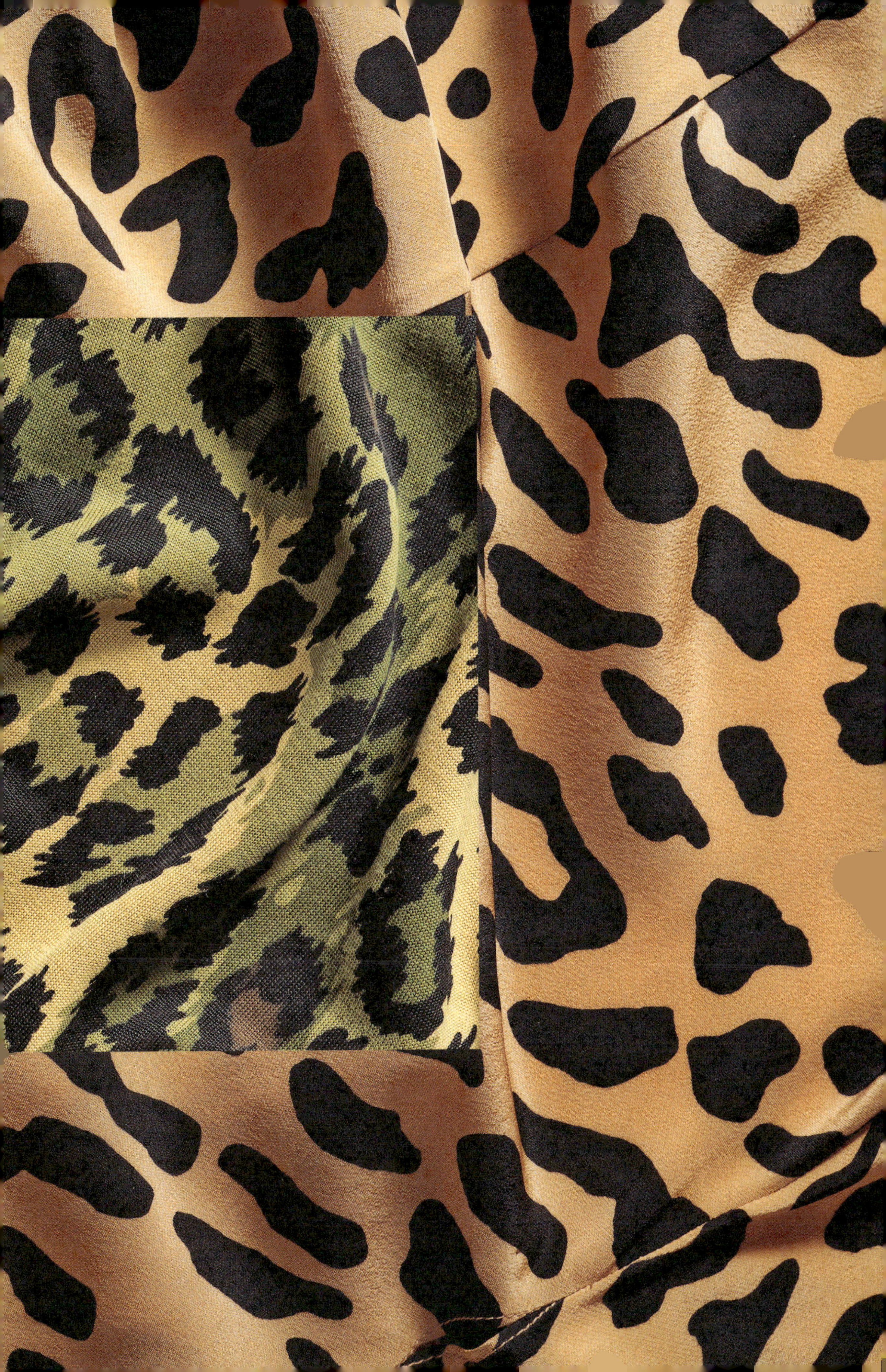

“

WOMEN
inspire me.
I DESIGN TO
inspire them
AND MAKE THEM
feel confident.

”

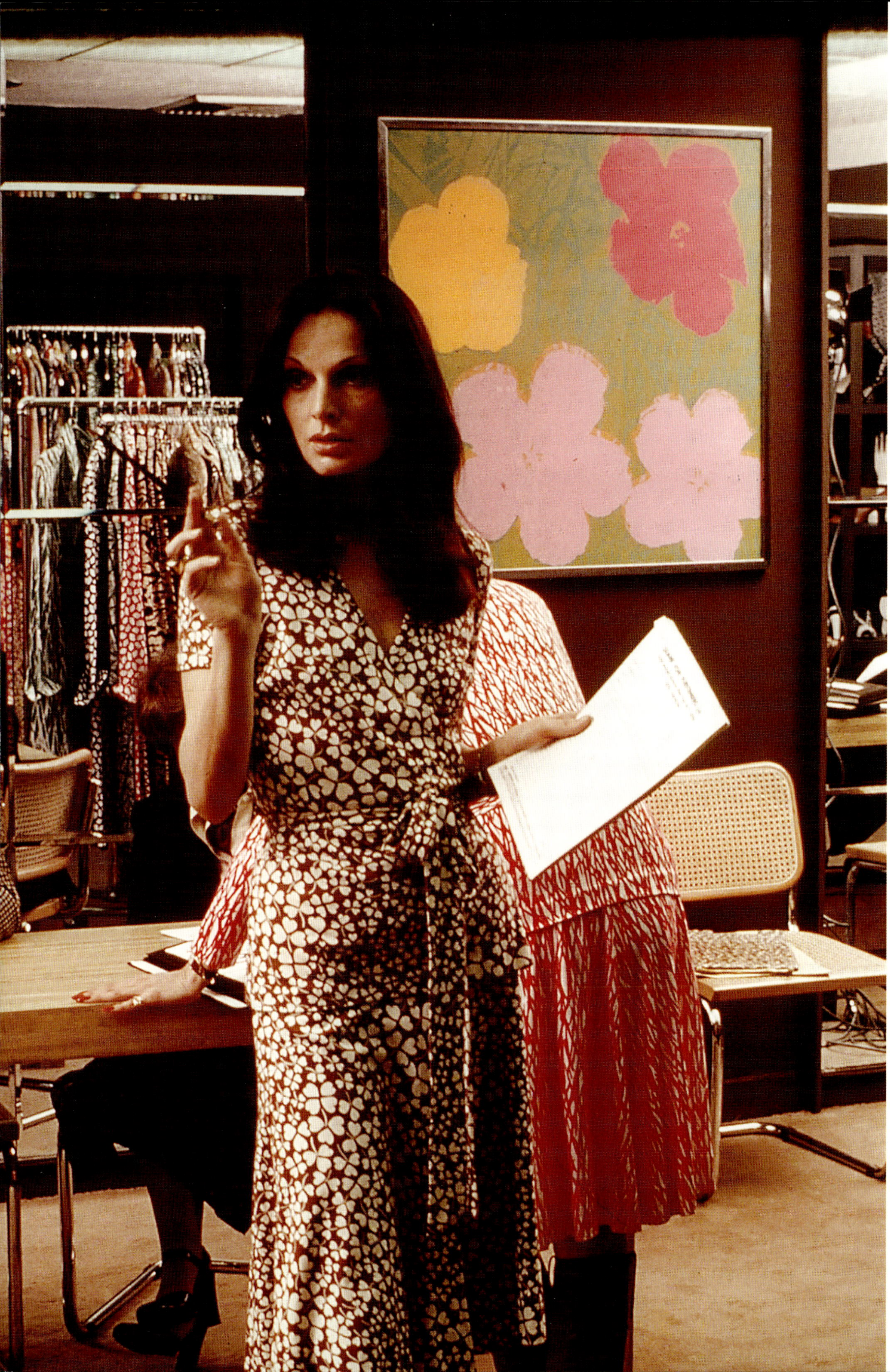

The Dress Makes the Woman

WRITTEN BY
Karen Van Godtsenhoven

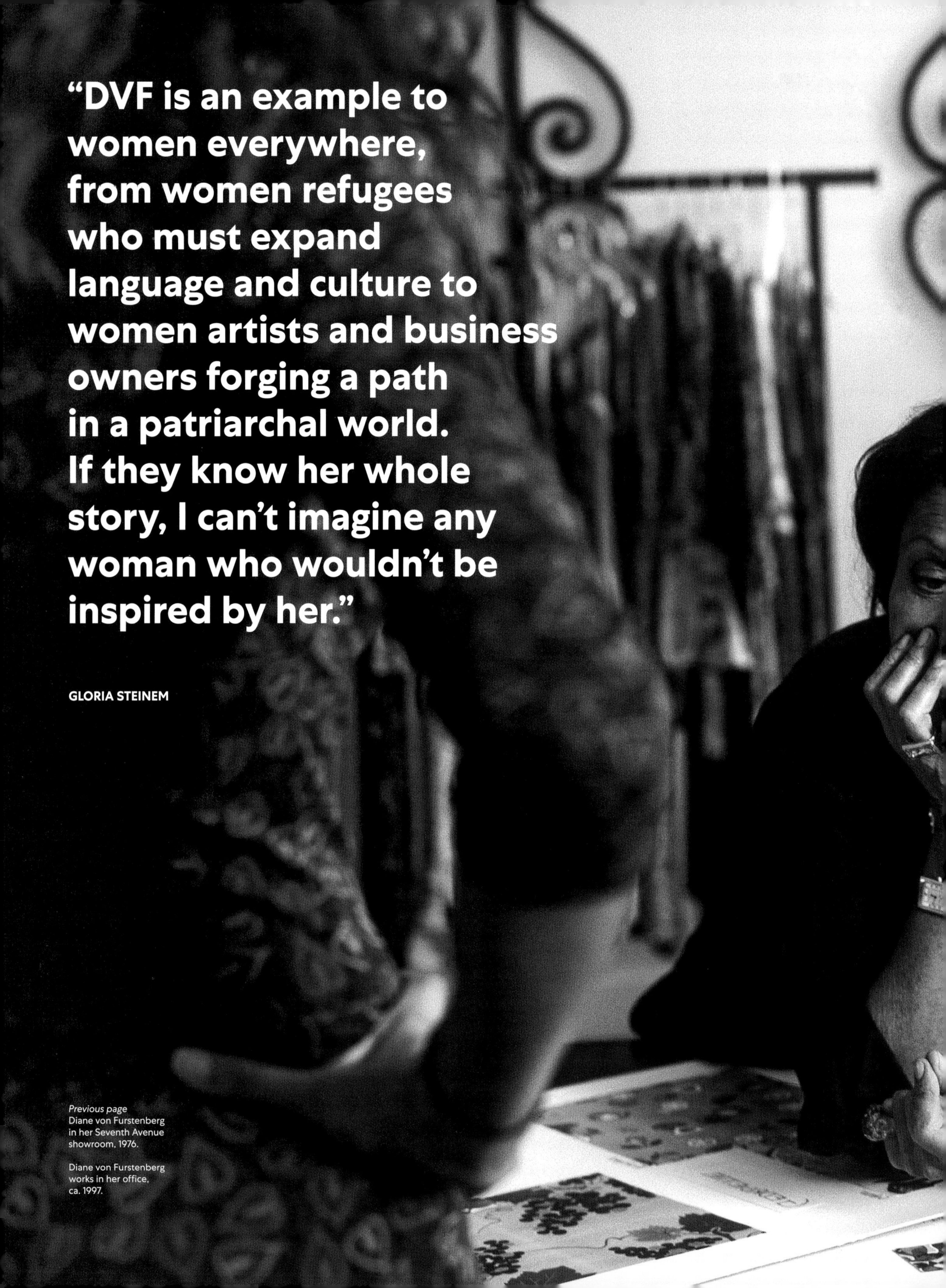

"DVF is an example to women everywhere, from women refugees who must expand language and culture to women artists and business owners forging a path in a patriarchal world. If they know her whole story, I can't imagine any woman who wouldn't be inspired by her."

GLORIA STEINEM

Previous page
Diane von Furstenberg in her Seventh Avenue showroom, 1976.

Diane von Furstenberg works in her office, ca. 1997.

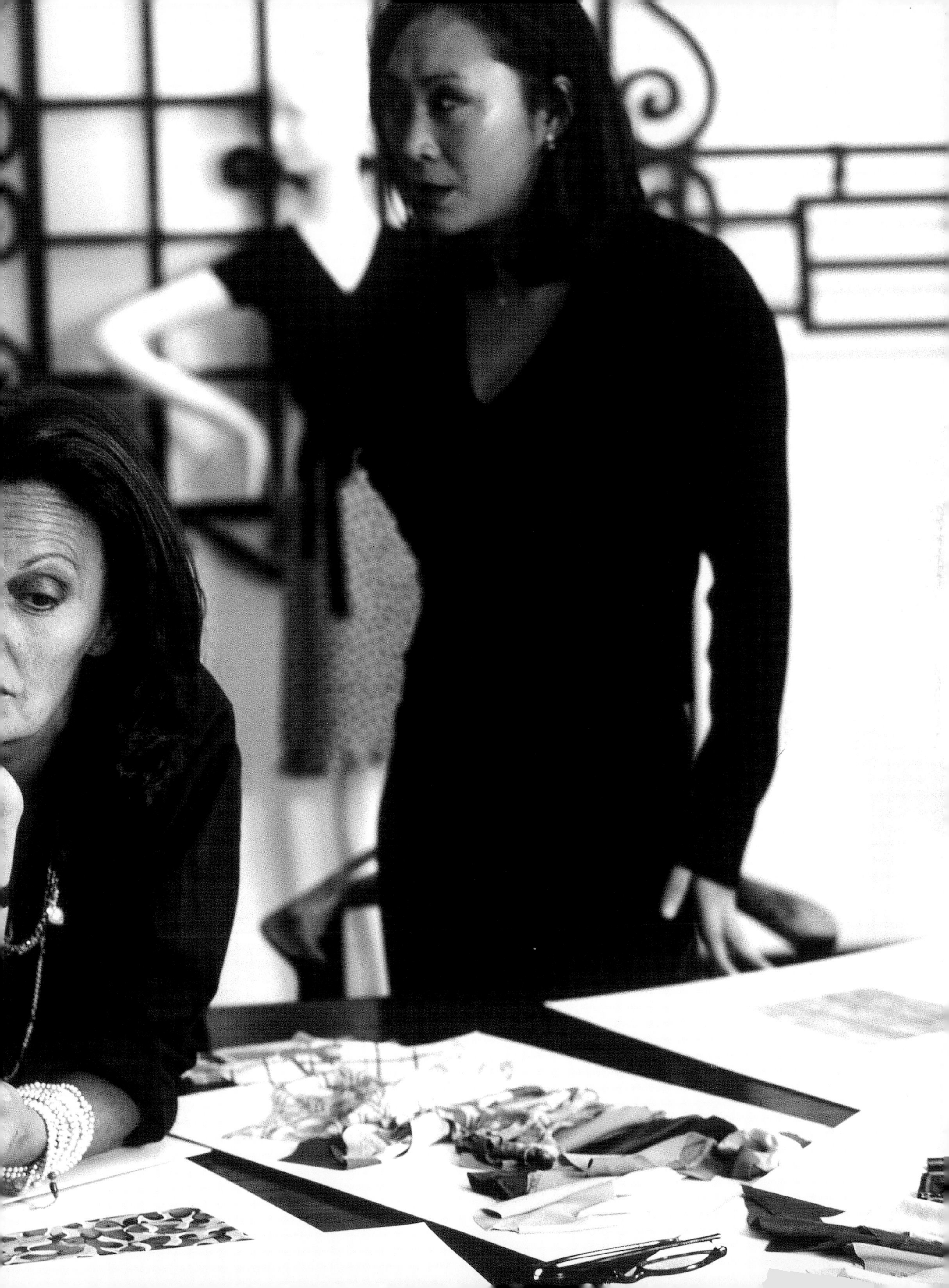

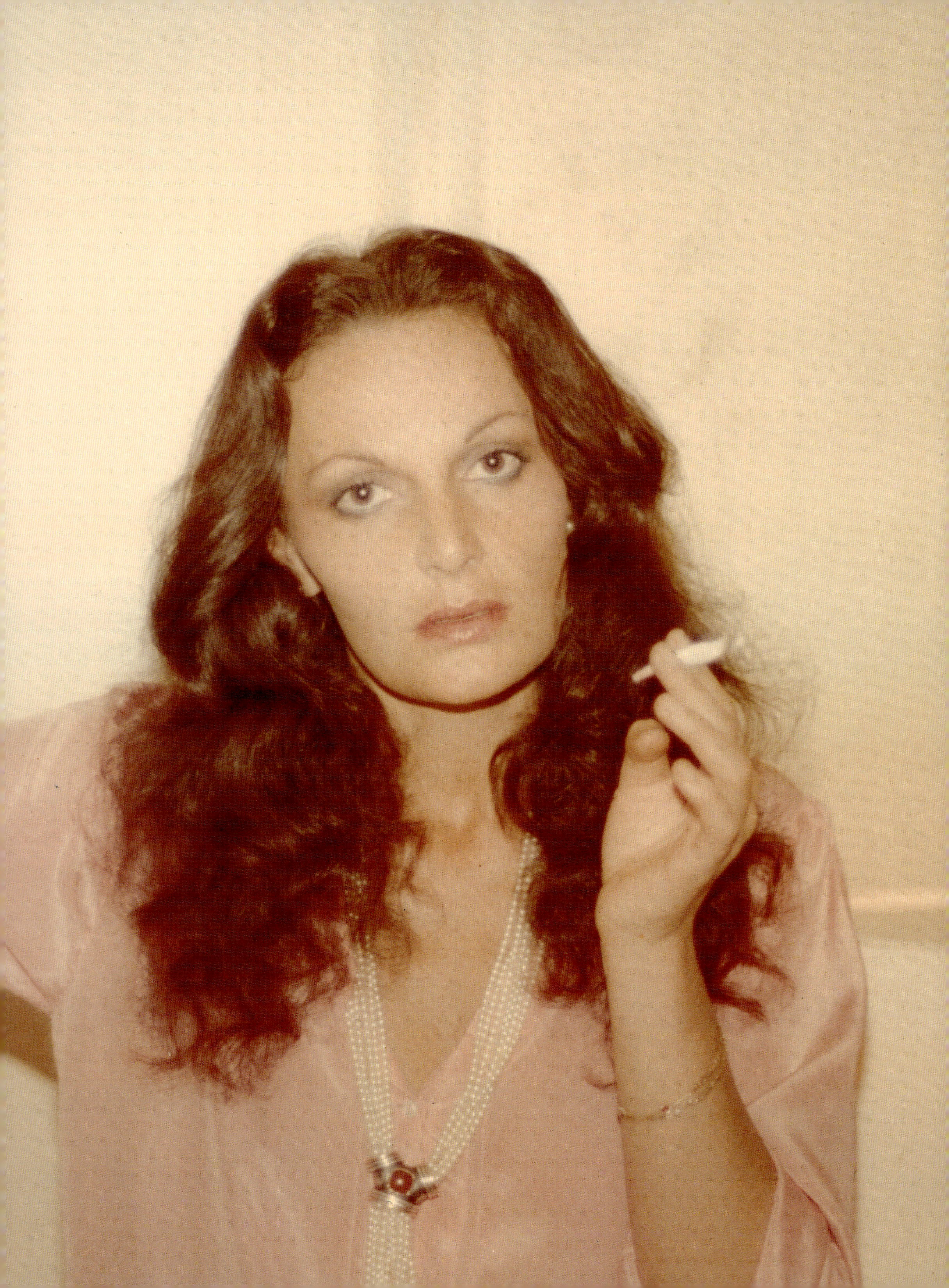

The Dress Makes the Woman: Diane von Furstenberg's Feminism, Fashion, and Politics

Opposite
Diane von Furstenberg in the 1970s.

A close examination of the life and work of Diane von Furstenberg over five decades reveals that she embodies the second-wave feminists' motto that "the personal is political."[10] Her transformation from a fashion designer with feminist values to a global feminist icon and political powerhouse demonstrates that a single woman's decisions, both in her private and professional life, can serve as torchbearers for a wider political movement pertaining to all women. By weaving fashion, feminism, love, motherhood, business, activism, and creativity into the fabric of her prolific life, she has mirrored the global pulse of women's lives and their evolving position over the last five decades, starting with a dress.

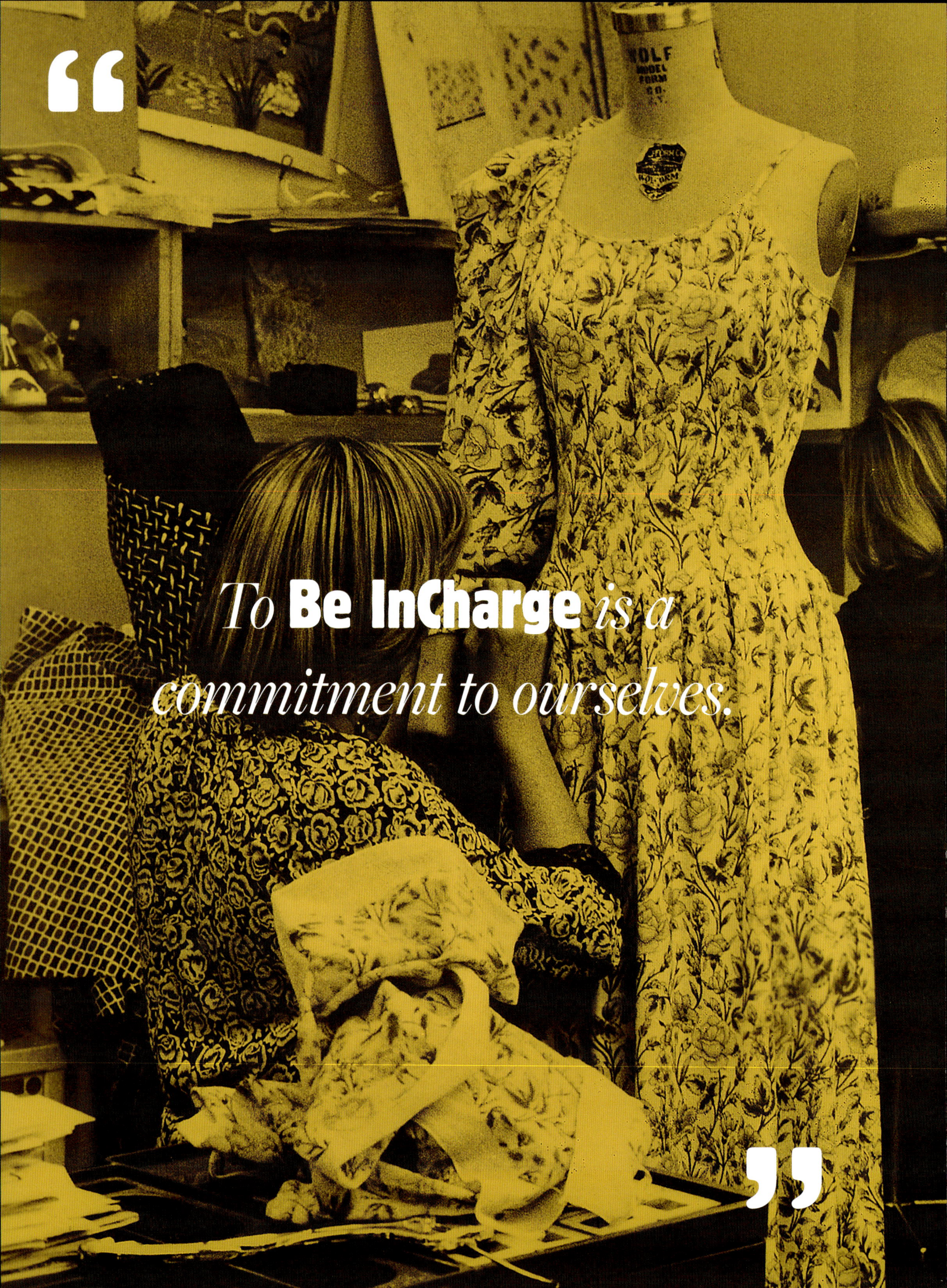

“*To* **Be InCharge** *is a commitment to ourselves.*”

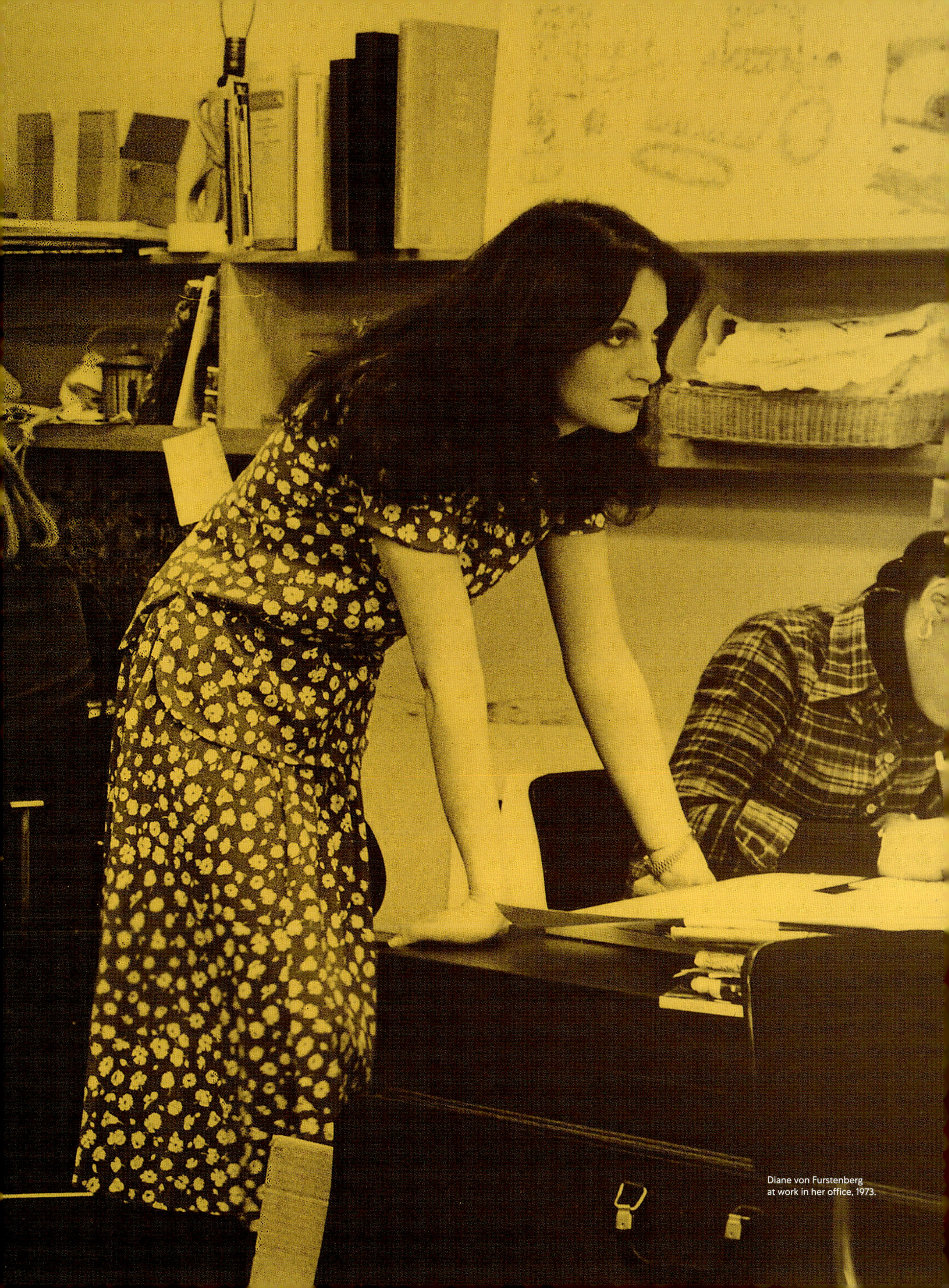

Diane von Furstenberg
at work in her office, 1973.

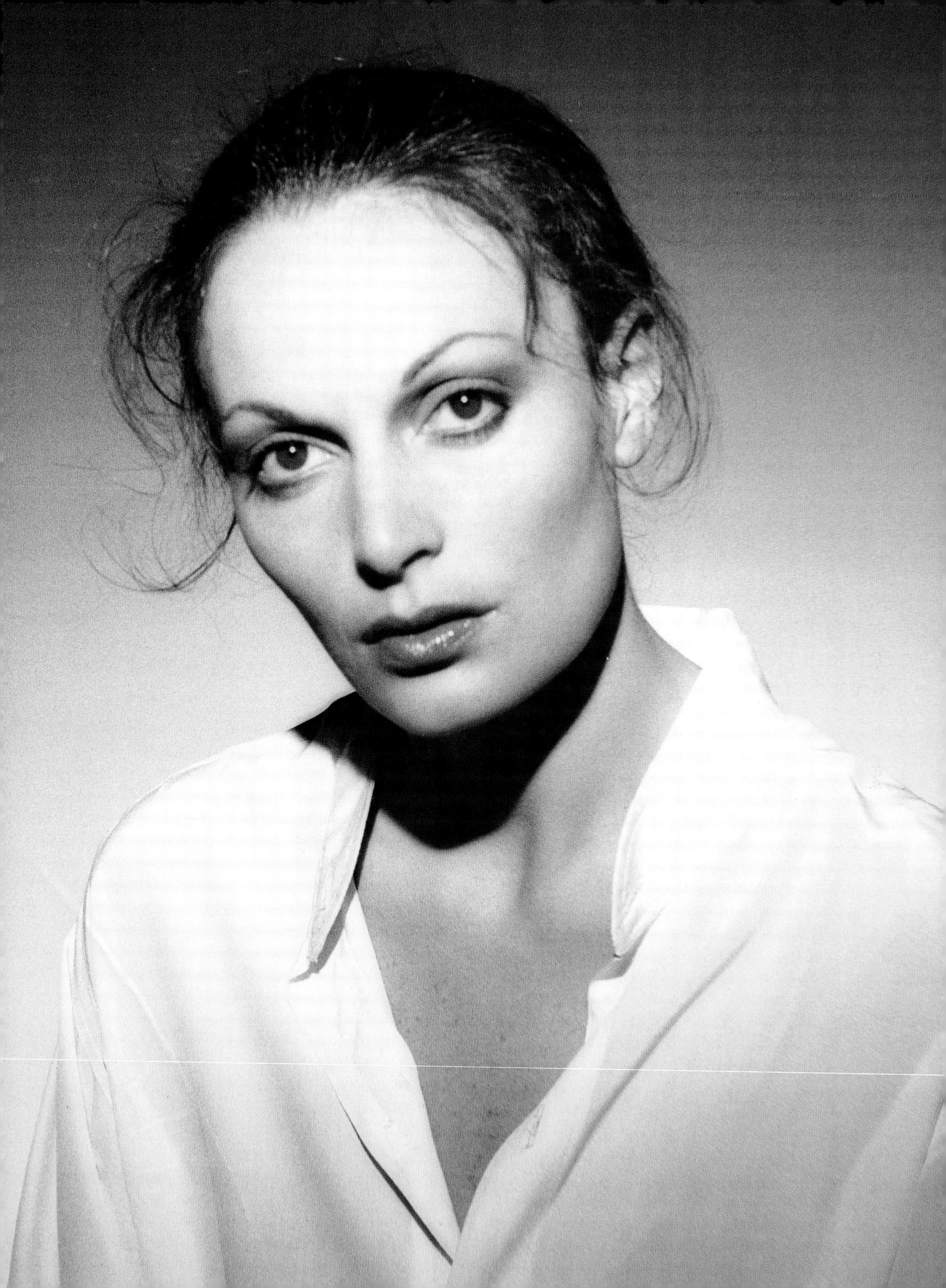

SARTORIAL REVOLUTIONS AND FEMINISMS BETWEEN EUROPE AND AMERICA: THE RECEPTION OF THE WRAP DRESS

> **"I like to see women feeling comfortable and being comfortable with themselves."[2]**

An important key to understanding von Furstenberg's life is recognizing her hybrid position between Europe and America, geographically as well as culturally, which resulted in different feminist and commercial receptions of her work over the years. Born in Belgium to Jewish parents with Greek and Bessarabian roots, whose families were both active in the textile industry and commerce, she "got the taste for knitted fabrics at the elegant boutique of her aunt Mathilde at rue de la Boétie in Paris."[3] Later, as an expatriate to the United States, von Furstenberg fused an American pragmatic and utilitarian attitude to fashion (i.e., the wrap dress as an "easy-to-go" uniform for working women) with the French flair of *la petite robe* and its sensual *jouissance*, reflected in her attention to the haptic pleasures of the fabric. Her conviction that women did not have to do away with sensuality while being in charge, both at home and at work, is exemplified in the wrap dress.

von Furstenberg believed that "You should wear a dress that moves with your body, clings a little, and makes you feel sensual."[4]

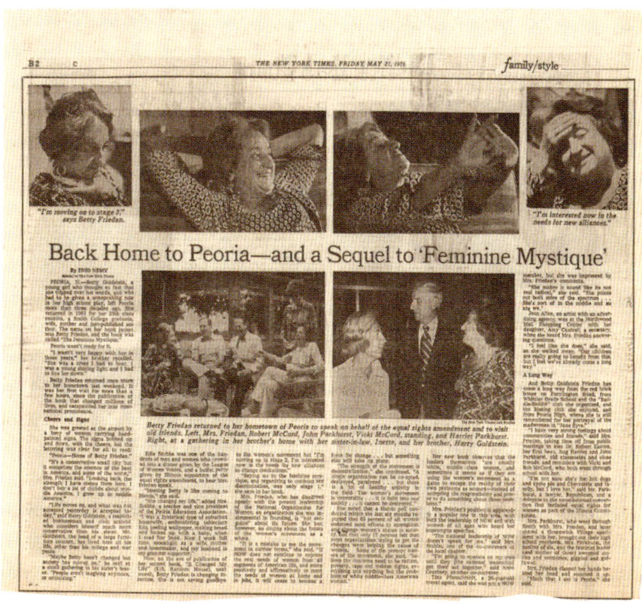
B2 C THE NEW YORK TIMES, FRIDAY MAY 21, 1976 family/style

"I'm moving on to stage 2," says Betty Friedan.

"I'm interested now in the needs for new alliances."

Back Home to Peoria—and a Sequel to 'Feminine Mystique'

By ENID NEMY

Betty Friedan returned to her hometown of Peoria to speak on behalf of the equal rights amendment and to visit old friends. Left, Mrs. Friedan, Robert McCord, John Parkhurst, Vicki McCord, standing, and Harriet Parkhurst. Right, at a gathering in her brother's home with her sister-in-law, Inette, and her brother, Harry Goldstein.

Above
An article about Betty Friedan, titled "Back Home to Peoria—and a Sequel to 'Feminine Mystic,'" published in *The New York Times*, 1976.

Opposite
Diane von Furstenberg, 1976.

In the 1970s, Anglosaxon "second-wave"[5] (1960s to mid-1980s) feminists like Gloria Steinem, Betty Friedan, and Germaine Greer were not a fan of seductive dress because of their view of beauty and fashion as superficial and oppressive to women's bodies and minds. They loathed society's emphasis on women's physical allure, criticizing the fashion and beauty industry for setting impossible standards and making a profit out of women's insecurities. To these pants-wearing equality feminists, dressing sexy was a form of heterosexist, 1950s "wife dressing," or a way of succumbing to the male gaze and desire, or—even worse—a form of female narcissism, a kind of work or servitude women had taken on themselves to compensate for their lack of real-world agency.

The attitude against "the woman of fashion" had been vehemently expressed by French feminist Simone de Beauvoir in her 1949 anthem *The Second Sex*: "When she has accepted her vocation as a sexual object, then she gladly adorns herself...she costumes herself to the pleasure of all men, and to the pride of her owner."[6] However, on the personal level, it has to be noted that both de Beauvoir and Steinem showed a certain pleasure in dressing well—even seductively—and de Beauvoir admitted to believing in the transformative power of fashion and the intimate pleasures of wearing silks. These private attitudes to fashion actually prefigure the perspective of "third wave" (mid-1980s to 2000) feminists, who embraced fashion as a source of personal agency, creativity, and pleasure.

In von Furstenberg's view, adhering to beauty standards does not make one less feminist because it gives women self-confidence. "We weren't just selling cosmetics, we were selling feminism," explains von Furstenberg. "You should not spend more than seven minutes on makeup because you have more important work to do."[7]

Below (left)
An article titled "Whither Ms. Steinem?'" by Beverly Stephen, published in *The San Francisco Chronicle*, 1974.

Below (right)
Diane von Furstenberg and Gloria Steinem, 2019.

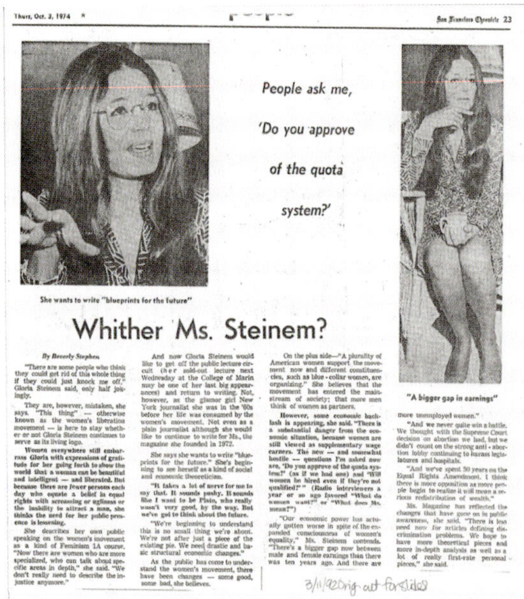

Thurs., Oct. 3, 1974 — San Francisco Chronicle 23

People ask me, 'Do you approve of the quota system?'

She wants to write "blueprints for the future"

Whither Ms. Steinem?

By Beverly Stephen

"There are some people who think they could get rid of this whole thing if they could just knock me off," Gloria Steinem said, only half jokingly.

They are, however, mistaken, she says. "This thing" — otherwise known as the women's liberation movement — is here to stay whether or not Gloria Steinem continues to serve as its living logo.

Women everywhere still embarrass Gloria with expressions of gratitude for her going forth to show the world that a woman can be beautiful and intelligent — and liberated. But because there are fewer persons each day who equate a belief in equal rights with screaming or ugliness or the inability to attract a man, she thinks the need for her public presence is lessening.

She describes her own public speaking on the women's movement as a kind of Feminism 1A course. "Now there are women who are more specialized, who can talk about specific areas in depth," she said. "We don't really need to describe the injustice anymore."

And now Gloria Steinem would like to get off the public lecture circuit (her sold-out lecture next Wednesday at the College of Marin may be one of her last big appearances) and return to writing. Not, however, as the glamor girl New York journalist she was in the '60s before her life was consumed by the women's movement. Not even as a plain journalist although she would like to continue to write for Ms., the magazine she founded in 1972.

She says she wants to write "blueprints for the future." She's beginning to see herself as a kind of social and economic theoretician.

"It takes a lot of nerve for me to say that. It sounds pushy. It sounds like I want to be Plato, who really wasn't very good, by the way. But we've got to think about the future.

"We're beginning to understand this is no small thing we're about. We're not after just a piece of the existing pie. We need drastic and basic structural economic changes."

As the public has come to understand the women's movement, there have been changes — some good, some bad, she believes.

On the plus side—"A plurality of American women support the movement now and different constituencies, such as blue-collar women, are organizing." She believes that the movement has entered the mainstream of society; that more men think of women as partners.

However, some economic backlash is appearing, she said. "There is a substantial danger from the economic situation, because women are still viewed as supplementary wage earners. The new — and somewhat hostile — questions I'm asked now are, 'Do you approve of the quota system?' (as if we had one) and 'Will women be hired even if they're not qualified?'" (Radio interviewers a year or so ago favored "What do women want?" or "What does Ms. mean?")

"Our economic power has actually gotten worse in spite of the expanded consciousness of women's equality," Ms. Steinem contends. "There's a bigger gap now between male and female earnings than there was ten years ago. And there are more unemployed women."

"A bigger gap in earnings"

"And we never quite win a battle. We thought with the Supreme Court decision on abortion we had, but we didn't count on the strong anti-abortion lobby continuing to harass legislatures and hospitals.

"And we've spent 50 years on the Equal Rights Amendment. I think there is more opposition as more people begin to realize it will mean a serious redistribution of wealth."

Ms. Magazine has reflected the changes that have gone on in public awareness, she said. "There is less need now for articles defining discrimination problems. We hope to have more theoretical pieces and more in-depth analysis as well as a lot of really first-rate personal pieces," she said.

3/11/92 Orig out for slides

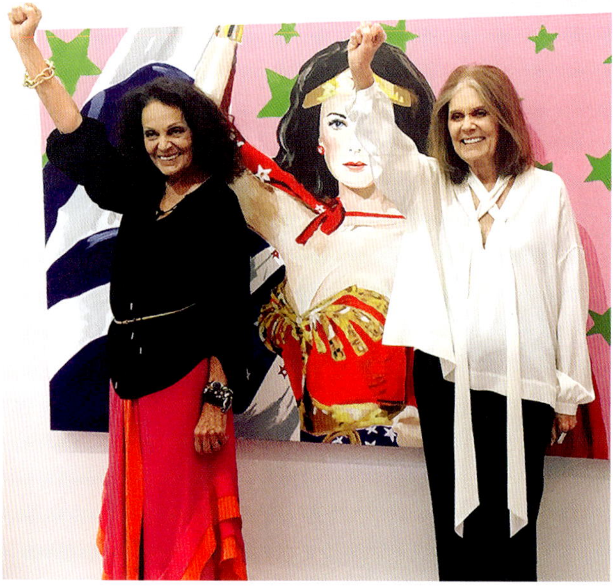

In the early 1970s, during the heyday of the sportswear trend, the mainstream feminist attitude—especially in the United States—was to wear unisex looks, jeans, and no bras. Separates were popular since their introduction in the 1930s, and the midi length, which was introduced by designers in the late 1960s, was rejected by American women, who wanted to make their own choices. Whereas there was a cultural anti-fashion sentiment in the United States, in Europe, beauty and sensuality were not necessarily in opposition with traditionally masculine ideals like intellectual rigor. In France, feminists like Luce Irigaray and Hélène Cixous wrote about female difference and the female body with its capacity for unbound pleasure and touching itself, as a site for a new type of women's writing that is outside of patriarchal structures.[8,9]

Opposite
Diane von Furstenberg (center) and friends in the streets of New York City, 1971.

The *écriture féminine* of which these feminists wrote claimed that women's writing and creativity were tied to the female body. In the same vein, von Furstenberg speaks of her own creations as a type of language that is tied to the female body: "To me, colors are the letters, prints are words, fabric and silhouette make the sentences," says von Furstenberg. "The fabric is the basic structure, made with color and print, but it is enhanced by silhouette, body language, smiles, and behavior."[10]

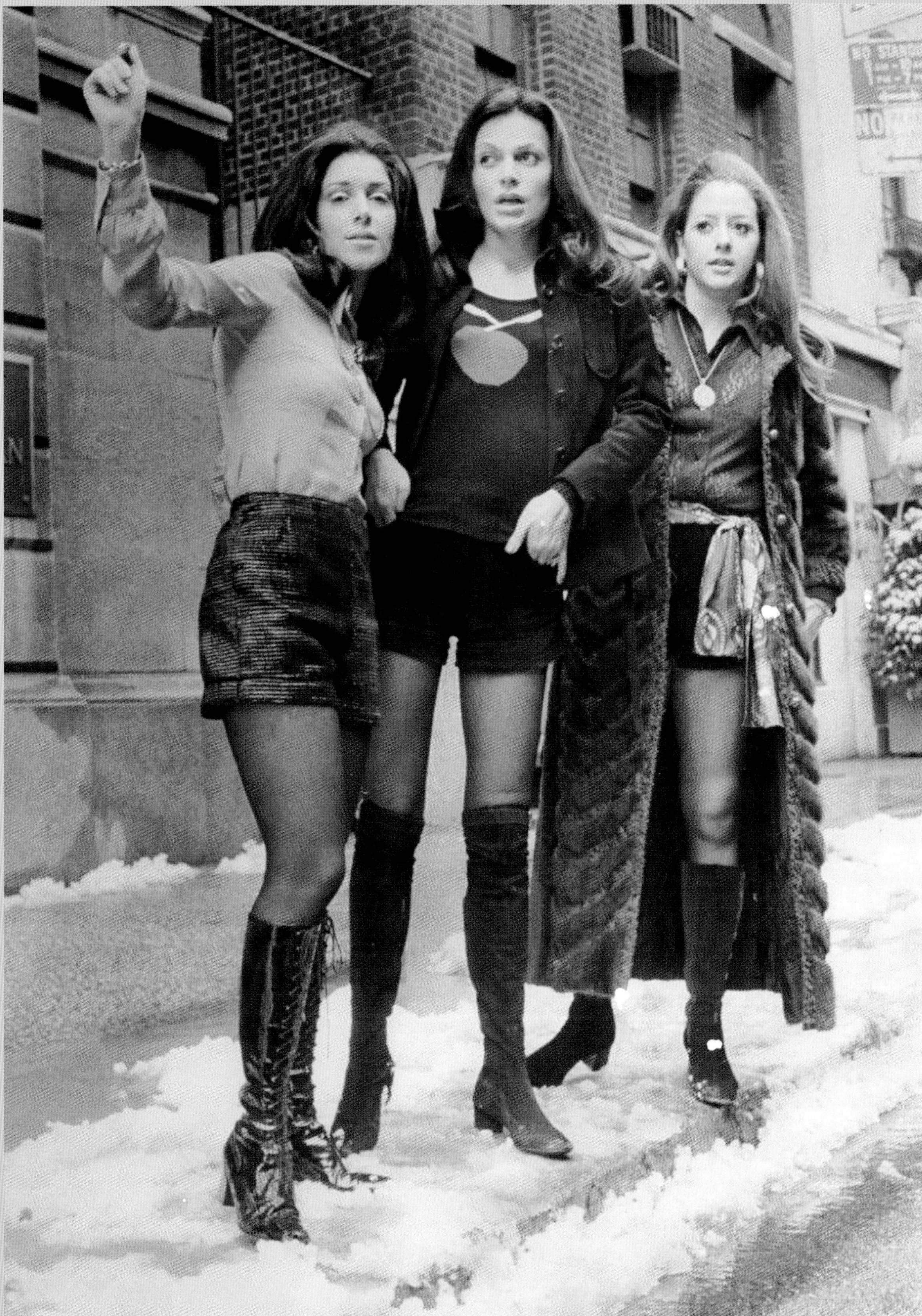

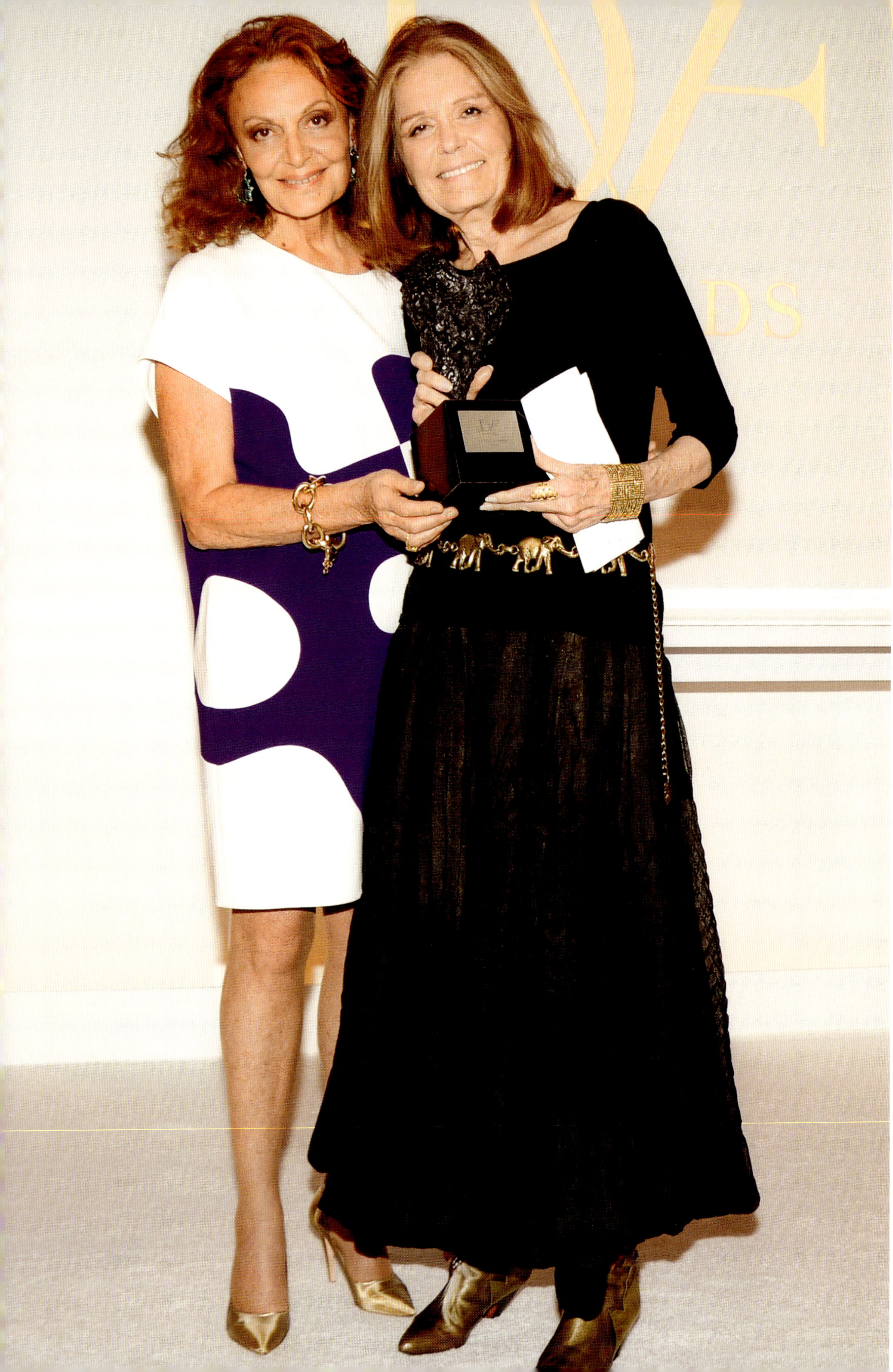

This European flavor of difference feminism was more in tune with von Furstenberg's taste for bodily effect and physical pleasure, which the American press—specifically, John Fairchild for *Women's Wear Daily*—commented on in passing: "Her clothes had that naughty European look."[11] The wrap even enabled "naughty behavior" because you can be in and out of it without a sound in less than a minute. Indeed, in a changing world, the wrap dress "joined feminist ideals of independence and achievement to old world beauty standards, sex, and femininity."[12]

As a work uniform, the wrap dress exemplifies what Annemarie Strassel refers to as the "labor aesthetic"[13],[14] of American fashion, which had its origins in the 1930s under the auspices of designers Claire McCardell and Elizabeth Hawes, whose functional designs empowered women to go to work both at the office and in the service and defense industries.

"To some, the wrap became a manifesto for the liberated woman of the 1970s," says von Furstenberg. "The dress fits in with the woman's revolution by allowing the millions of women off to work to be well dressed and out the door a minute without worrying about wrinkles, buttons, zippers, hooks, and eyes. The wrap also fits in with the sexual revolution; a woman who chose to could be out of it in less than a minute."[24]

With regards to von Furstenberg's reception in the United States, fashion doyenne Diana Vreeland was an early supporter of the wrap dress because of its body-celebratory qualities and dynamic character, which she continued to feature in *Vogue* editorials.[15] Even though Gloria Steinem's *Ms* magazine, the first magazine run by and owned by women, did not cover von Furstenberg at first because of its editorial anti-fashion stance, Steinem and Friedan themselves wore a wrap for press interviews. Hence, at least personally, these feminists endorsed von Furstenberg's creations, and von Furstenberg in turn admired Steinem. "Gloria had given 'a key to freedom' to many women and I had always admired her," says von Furstenberg.[16] It took until 1986 (the onset of the so-called "third wave" of feminism) for von Furstenberg to get a write-up in *Ms* magazine alongside Donna Karan, Katherine Hamnett, and Liz Claiborne as empowered female leaders of the fashion industry.

In the context of 1980s power dressing, the wrap dress prefigured the easy-to-work, easy-to-go-out philosophy, as exemplified by Donna Karan's "Seven Easy Pieces," launched in 1985. The collection helped the career woman go from day to night with a modular wardrobe. In this context of third-wave feminism, when feminist and queer thinkers like Judith Butler stated that gender is performative and not based on biological or "essential" qualities in men and women,[17] there was more room for feminists to appreciate von Furstenberg's motto, "Feel like a Woman, Wear a Dress," which expressed the effect and performativity of womanhood, which was to be slipped on and off almost like a dress; that is, you "feel" like a woman, you "are" not a woman as an essential category.

Opposite
Diane von Furstenberg and Gloria Steinem at the DVF Awards, 2014.

Next page
Diane von Furstenberg and her children Alexandre and Tatiana, ca. 1980s.

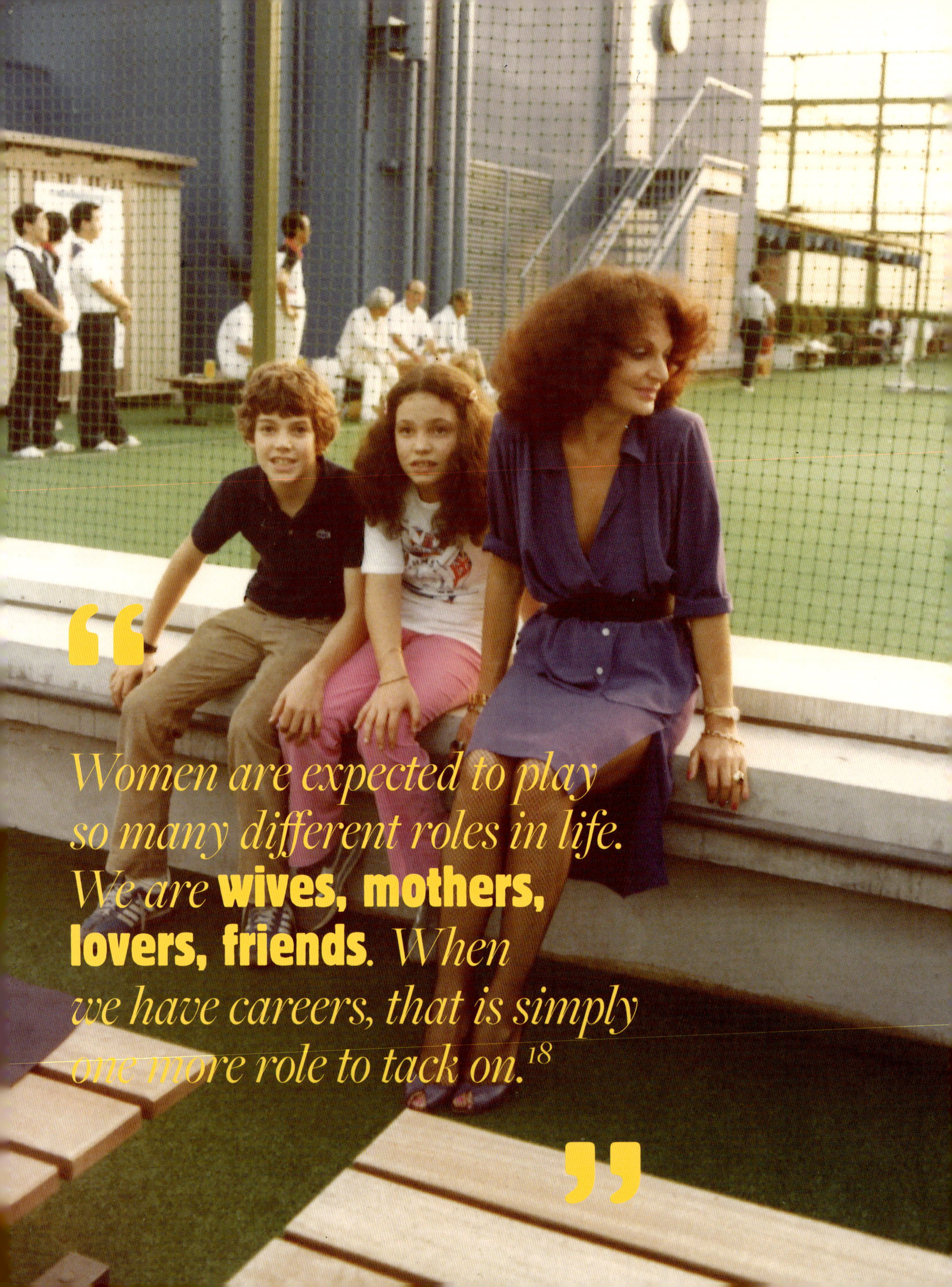

Women are expected to play so many different roles in life. We are **wives, mothers, lovers, friends**. *When we have careers, that is simply one more role to tack on.*[18]

A BALANCING ACT

von Furstenberg has always spoken openly about the challenge of being a career woman, fashion designer, partner, and mother of two. Her private status evolved from being a married princess to a single mom, to a remarried political and activist icon with a fashion business. She famously quipped, "I gave up the princess title so I could use the Ms title."[18] Press often foregrounded her princess status in their headlines. For example, in 1976, *The Detroit Free Press*[19] profiled her as "Diane: Princess, Mom, Dressmaker, Feminist." She used her own experience juggling these different roles and expectations in order to emphatically understand what her customers needed.

Her entwined family and business life with Prince Egon von Furstenberg, with whom she had shared a fashion label titled "His and Hers," came to an end when he suggested that she give him her business, which she refused.[20] Even though she stayed emotionally connected to him as the father of her children until his death, she was feminist enough not to concede her life's work to him. In a few accounts, she testified of how giving up too much of her own identity for her partners has at times endangered her sense of self:

"Like the leopard who wanted to change their skin in Kipling's novel, it seems to me that most women change their personality or at least adapt themselves to their love affairs, especially during the delicious period of seduction. From one day to another, they become football or sailing fans, interested in politics, before letting their own personality take over again when the relationship is solid or finished."[21]

In her autobiography, von Furstenberg describes her sartorial transformations from high glamour seductress to sarongs to existentialist garb as expressions of her intense adulation of the men in her life. Luckily, she never completely changed her spots because of her strong sense of self: "I was seeing too many of my friends give up their own identities to please their husbands of lovers, only to be lost when the relationship ended... By comparison, my life was my own and I cherished it."[22]

Below (left)
"Mother Knows Best," a 1983 advertisement campaign for DVF Kids.

Below (right)
An article titled "Diane: Princess, Mom, Dressmaker, Feminist" by Marji Kunz, published in *Detroit Free Press*, May 19, 1976.

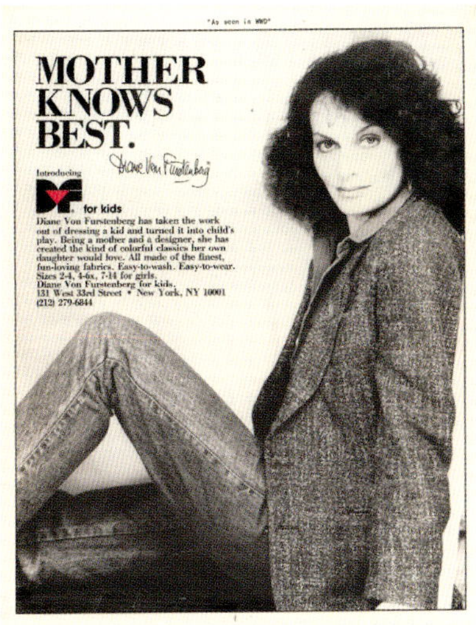

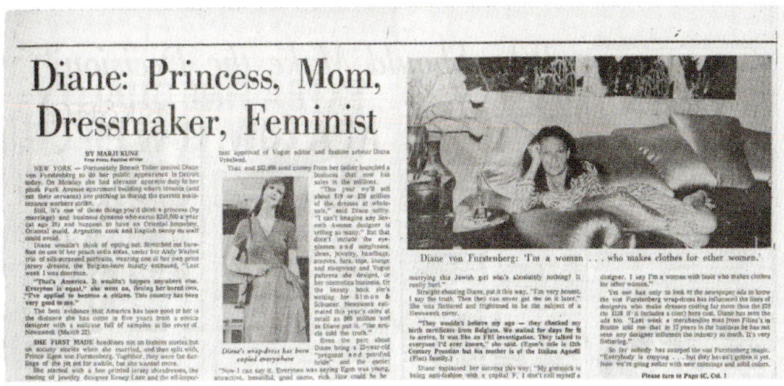

Diane: Princess, Mom, Dressmaker, Feminist

BY MARJI KUNZ

Diane's wrap-dress has been copied everywhere

Diane von Furstenberg: 'I'm a woman . . . who makes clothes for other women.'

Next spread (left)
Diane von Furstenberg works on products with her staff at her New York City office, ca. 1976.

Next spread (right)
Diane von Furstenberg applies a woman's make-up, 1976.

In her *Book of Beauty*, which embraces the principles of the male gaze, she warns against becoming too entwined with the man in your life: "Every woman should have an identity of her own that is separate from the man in her life... You do it because it is your choice."[23] She explains how she kept a balance between her life as a hard-powered, traveling businesswoman and her family life and romantic involvements by working in the city four long days every week and spending Fridays and the weekend in her Cloudwalk residence in Connecticut.

Even though von Furstenberg's position has been privileged and her specific situation cannot be transposed to other women's lives, her candid testimony of the struggles that she has faced in her career and personal life remains a powerful example of women's advances and setbacks since the sexual and social revolution of the 1960s.

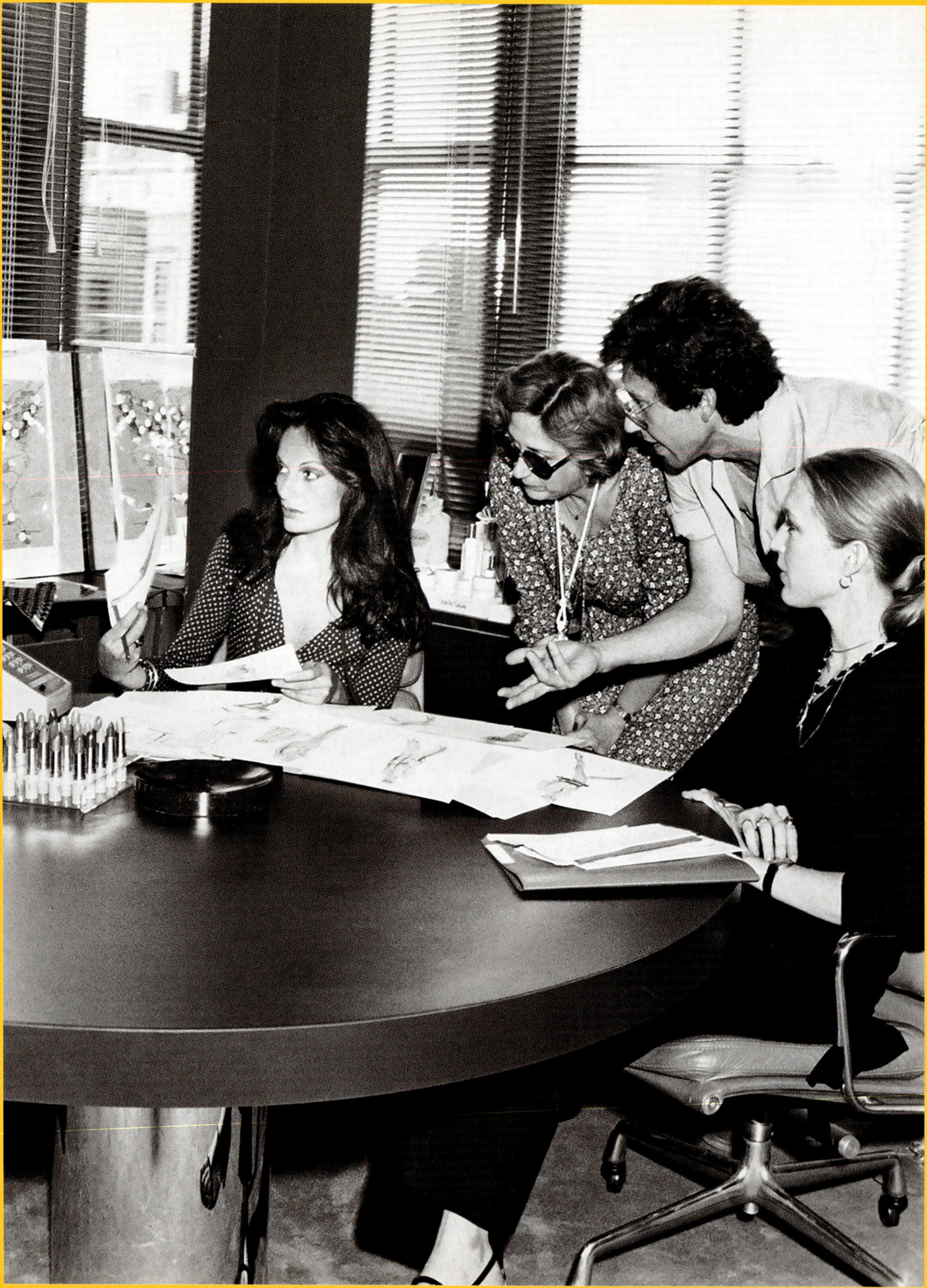

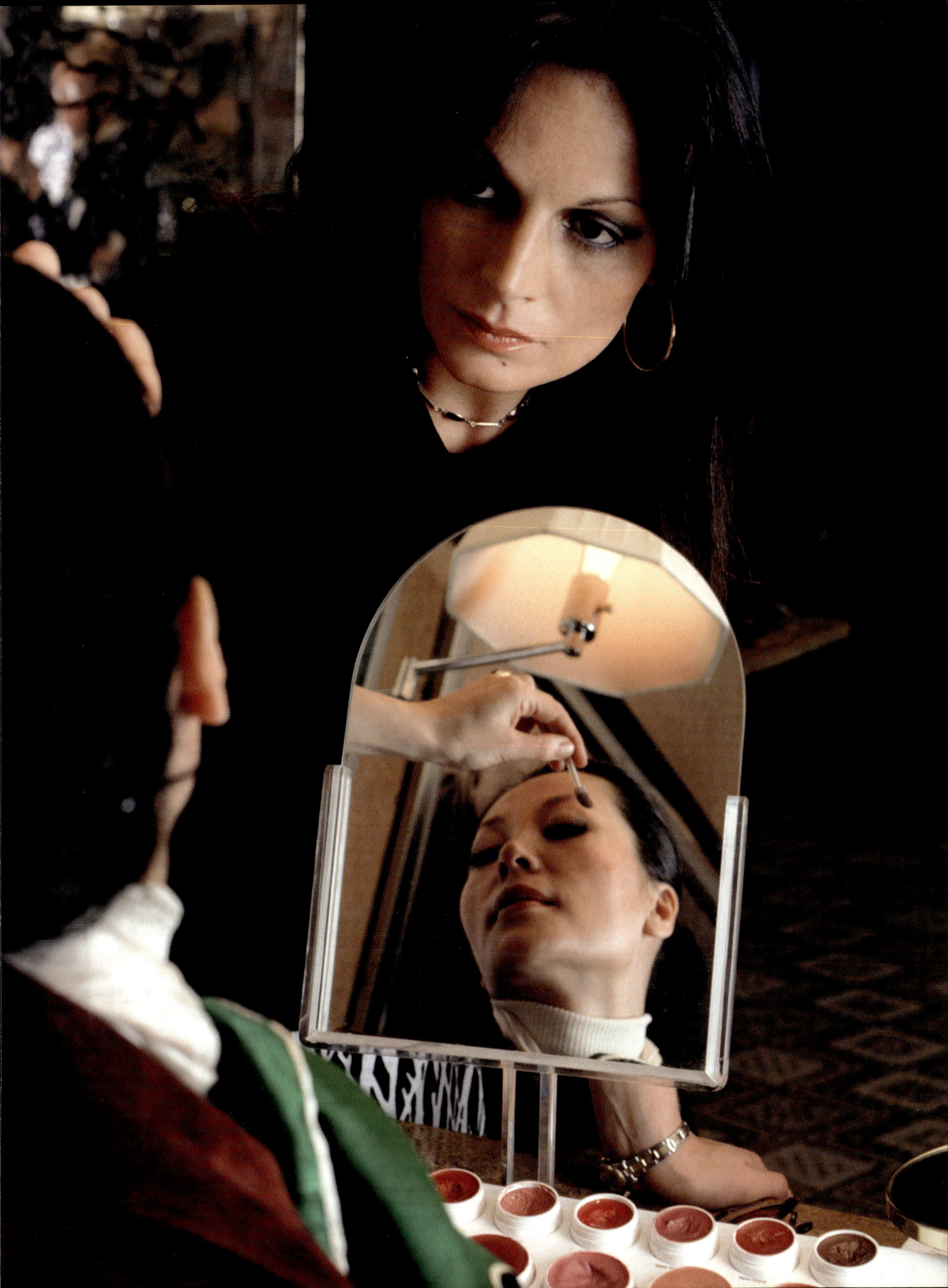

ANTI-FASHION SENTIMENTS

"To be blunt, I think women are often ridiculed by the fashion industry through constant change, new looks, new lengths, new 'attitudes.' I've never believed in drastic fashion changes because they don't last. There are always trends but they shouldn't be taken all that seriously."[24]

In the body-liberatory lineage of couturières Madeleine Vionnet and Gabrielle "Coco" Chanel, von Furstenberg wrapped the female body in timeless garments because she saw changing fashion trends as a form of misogyny.[25] In Women's Wear Daily, she states, "I'm pro-women, and I want them to look nice. Most designers want women to look like fools."[26] This statement echoed Chanel's comment about the introduction of the corseted New Look post–World War II, which she felt made women look "like fools." For von Furstenberg too, women need to be liberated from the tyranny of male decorative fantasies, of being dressed as a *femme-objet*: "My clothes were flattering to women and not overwhelming. Many designers were men, whose clothes may have shown their creativity but were not always designed to enhance a woman. It was and is so much more important for a woman to be able to express herself rather than expressing a designer's ego."[27]

In 1977, *The New York Times* covered feminism's positive liberatory effect on fashion. It stated that "Before feminism, women were uncomfortable, cold, obedient to trends. Since the movement, they wear what they want."[28] Whereas Chanel introduced her suit as a timeless, pragmatic uniform equivalent to the masculine suit, von Furstenberg went against the unisex look of the day. "All I had was an instinct that women wanted a fashion option besides hippie clothes, bell-bottoms, and stiff pantsuits that hid their femininity," says von Furstenberg. "Though the unisex look was hot in the seventies, I was sure there was a need for simple little sexy dresses that made women feel like women."[29]

von Furstenberg also mirrors Chanel's marketing genius and modern sensibility. "I got started because I thought there was a need for the new woman. I'm very much in favor of every woman feeling free and looking terrific," says von Furstenberg.[30] Her ability to fuse a progressive cultural attitude with the garments women wanted made her one of the most commercially successful female designers since Chanel. Methodologically, von Furstenberg sits in the lineage of female designers like Madeleine Vionnet, Madame Grès, and Claire McCardell, who used bias cut, drape, and wrapping as an embodied, intuitive, and adaptive approach to the female body, as opposed to patterned designs.

In interviews, von Furstenberg firmly places herself in the female-gendered dressmaking tradition. Nevertheless, she also quotes male designers like Giorgio di Sant'Angelo, Emilio Pucci, Stephen Burrows, and Halston as influences—all of whom had a liberatory and sports-influenced approach toward the body in comparison to their couturier predecessors like Charles James. It is between these intergenerational constellations in fashion—between Europe and the United States—that we can situate the success of the wrap dress.

Below
An article by Mildred Istona, published in *Chatelaine* magazine, April 1978.

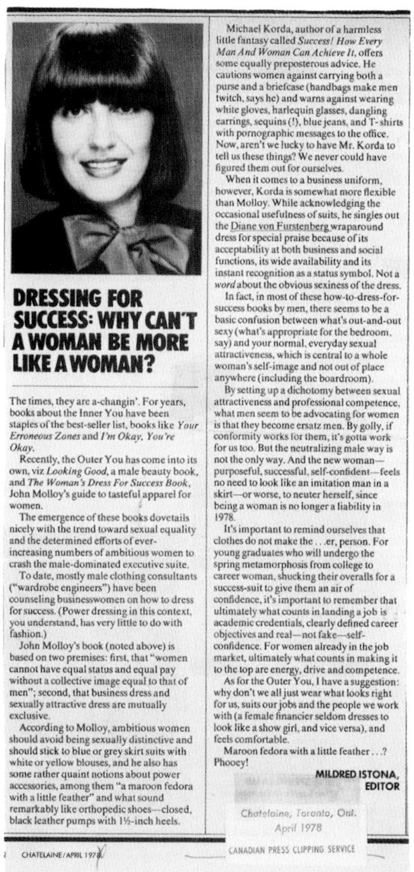

DRESSING FOR SUCCESS: WHY CAN'T A WOMAN BE MORE LIKE A WOMAN?

The times, they are a-changin'. For years, books about the Inner You have been staples of the best-seller list, books like *Your Erroneous Zones* and *I'm Okay, You're Okay*.

Recently, the Outer You has come into its own, viz *Looking Good*, a male beauty book, and *The Woman's Dress For Success Book*, John Molloy's guide to tasteful apparel for women.

The emergence of these books dovetails nicely with the trend toward sexual equality and the determined efforts of ever-increasing numbers of ambitious women to crash the male-dominated executive suite.

To date, mostly male clothing consultants ("wardrobe engineers") have been counseling businesswomen on how to dress for success. (Power dressing in this context, you understand, has very little to do with fashion.)

John Molloy's book (noted above) is based on two premises: first, that "women cannot have equal status and equal pay without a collective image equal to that of men"; second, that business dress and sexually attractive dress are mutually exclusive.

According to Molloy, ambitious women should avoid being sexually distinctive and should stick to blue or grey skirt suits with white or yellow blouses, and he also has some rather quaint notions about power accessories, among them "a maroon fedora with a little feather" and what sound remarkably like orthopedic shoes—closed, black leather pumps with 1½-inch heels.

Michael Korda, author of a harmless little fantasy called *Success! How Every Man And Woman Can Achieve It*, offers some equally preposterous advice. He cautions women against carrying both a purse and a briefcase (handbags make men twitch, says he) and warns against wearing white gloves, harlequin glasses, dangling earrings, sequins (!), blue jeans, and T-shirts with pornographic messages to the office. Now, aren't we lucky to have Mr. Korda to tell us these things? We never could have figured them out for ourselves.

When it comes to a business uniform, however, Korda is somewhat more flexible than Molloy. While acknowledging the occasional usefulness of suits, he singles out the Diane von Furstenberg wraparound dress for special praise because of its acceptability at both business and social functions, its wide availability and its instant recognition as a status symbol. Not a *word* about the obvious sexiness of the dress.

In fact, in most of these how-to-dress-for-success books by men, there seems to be a basic confusion between what's out-and-out sexy (what's appropriate for the bedroom, say) and your normal, everyday sexual attractiveness, which is central to a whole woman's self-image and not out of place anywhere (including the boardroom).

By setting up a dichotomy between sexual attractiveness and professional competence, what men seem to be advocating for women is that they become ersatz men. By golly, if conformity works for them, it's gotta work for us too. But the neutralizing male way is not the only way. And the new woman—purposeful, successful, self-confident—feels no need to look like an imitation man in a skirt—or worse, to neuter herself, since being a woman is no longer a liability in 1978.

It's important to remind ourselves that clothes do not make the . . .er, person. For young graduates who will undergo the spring metamorphosis from college to career woman, shucking their overalls for a success-suit to give them an air of confidence, it's important to remember that ultimately what counts in landing a job is academic credentials, clearly defined career objectives and real—not fake—self-confidence. For women already in the job market, ultimately what counts in making it to the top are energy, drive and competence.

As for the Outer You, I have a suggestion: why don't we all just wear what looks right for us, suits our jobs and the people we work with (a female financier seldom dresses to look like a show girl, and vice versa), and feels comfortable.

Maroon fedora with a little feather . . .? Phooey!

MILDRED ISTONA, EDITOR

Chatelaine, Toronto, Ont.
April 1978
CANADIAN PRESS CLIPPING SERVICE

CHATELAINE/APRIL 1978

A MAN'S LIFE IN A WOMAN'S BODY

"Instead of feeling sorry for myself, I was playing the games men play. And reversing traditional gender roles turned out to be fun."[31]

In the course of her career, von Furstenberg has expressed how her own "masculine" traits helped her to succeed in business while struggling to uphold the traditionally female role of nurturer and lover at home. A sense of personal agency and satisfaction comes from her sense of "leading a man's life" while feeling and dressing as a woman, like when she walked into Studio 54 by herself or when she traveled around the country. "My business was skyrocketing. I loved feeling like the tycooness as I strode through airports wearing fishnet stockings and impossibly high heels with my dresses in a shoulder bag," recalls von Furstenberg. "I was very pleased that I could live a man's life and still be a sexy young woman."[32] However, she also points out the loneliness and hardships, and the ways in which her life is not equal to that of a businessman. "The difference is most men have wives at home to take care of them," says von Furstenberg.

Below (left)
Diane von Furstenberg walks with a colleague, 1975.

Below (right)
Diane von Furstenberg with colleagues in her office, 1976.

She relates her need for independence to her mother's survival in the concentration camps of Auschwitz and her participation in the resistance. In terms of fashion, her credo is that independence and femininity go together, and they are actually the key to success for women in business, rather than equality dressing. "There were very few businesswomen at the time, and the few in management tended to play down their gender by dressing more like men than like women," says von Furstenberg. "For me, however, flaunting my femininity had always given me an advantage, even a weapon. It gave me the opportunity to charm, to be light and fun, and seductive."[33]

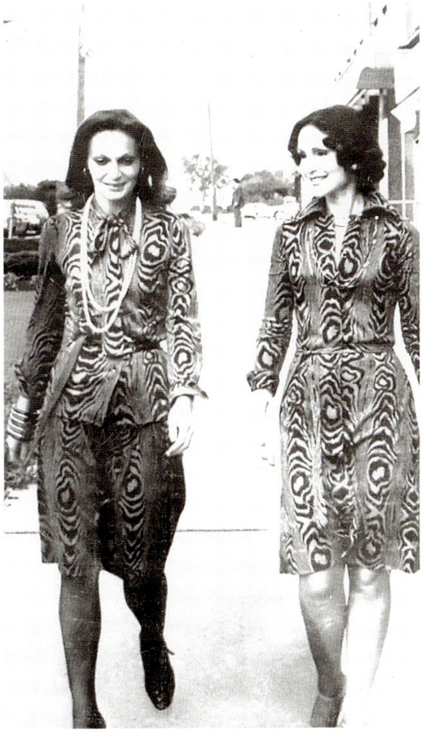

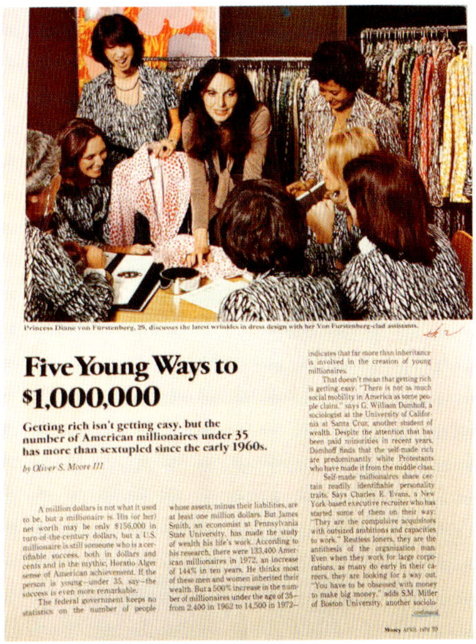

Princess Diane von Fürstenberg, 29, discusses the latest wrinkles in dress design with her Von Furstenberg-clad assistants.

Five Young Ways to $1,000,000

Getting rich isn't getting easy, but the number of American millionaires under 35 has more than sextupled since the early 1960s.

by Oliver S. Moore III

A million dollars is not what it used to be, but a millionaire is. His (or her) net worth may be only $156,000 in turn-of-the-century dollars, but a U.S. millionaire is still someone who is a certifiable success, both in dollars and cents and in the mythic, Horatio Alger sense of American achievement. If the person is young—under 35, say—the success is even more remarkable.

The federal government keeps no statistics on the number of people whose assets, minus their liabilities, are at least one million dollars. But James Smith, an economist at Pennsylvania State University, has made the study of wealth his life's work. According to his research, there were 133,400 American millionaires in 1972, an increase of 144% in ten years. He thinks most of these men and women inherited their wealth. But a 500% increase in the number of millionaires under the age of 35—from 2,400 in 1962 to 14,500 in 1972—indicates that far more than inheritance is involved in the creation of young millionaires.

That doesn't mean that getting rich is getting easy. "There is not as much social mobility in America as some people claim," says G. William Domhoff, a sociologist at the University of California at Santa Cruz, another student of wealth. Despite the attention that has been paid minorities in recent years, Domhoff finds that the self-made rich are predominantly white Protestants who have made it from the middle class.

Self-made millionaires share certain readily identifiable personality traits. Says Charles E. Evans, a New York-based executive recruiter who has started some of them on their way: "They are the compulsive acquisitors with outsized ambitions and capacities to work." Restless loners, they are the antithesis of the organization man. Even when they work for large corporations, as many do early in their careers, they are looking for a way out. "You have to be obsessed with money to make big money," adds S.M. Miller of Boston University, another sociolo-

continued

Money APRIL

Von Furstenberg criticizes John Molloy's 1977 book *The Woman's Dress for Success* book, which advocates a conservative business uniform for women. "Women should wear whatever they want to work," responds von Furstenberg. "The only important piece of apparel a woman should have is her brain, and she will be promoted on that and that only. In the meantime, why should she play herself down? Why can't she look like a woman on the job?"[34] From her own experience and perspective, to dress for success means to wear a dress.

CORPOREAL COMPLICITY

"I never thought of myself as a true fashion designer. I was a woman who made clothes for women."[35]

One of the most central elements in von Furstenberg's commercial success as a fashion designer is her own physical and psychic embodiment of her vision for women. "My work and my designs have always been an expression of me and an extension of my personality," says von Furstenberg.[36] She acknowledges that it is not just her positive image of a successful, sexy career woman but her hardships too that make her a real-life role model. "By confessing my own vulnerabilities and insecurities, I made myself reachable and established a link," says von Furstenberg.[37] She believes that only women understand what women want.[38] Her vendors insisted that Diane herself star as a model in her own ads. "The result would be a total identity of me, the product, and the brand," explains von Furstenberg.[39]

Many of the models von Furstenberg cast in the 1970s looked like her doubles, mirroring the multiple sides of her own personality and style, such as the sexually assertive model Gia Carangi. To further the idea of the "total brand," she even had a mannequin made in her own image, which was used to display her dresses in department stores. "My identity had become so interchangeable with the clothes that Rich's department store in Atlanta advertised one of my personal appearances there by displaying a life-sized mannequin of me wearing a green wrap dress," says von Furstenberg.[40]

The first time Bloomingdale's bought DVF dresses, it used an advertisement with her in it and organized a meet and greet with her fortis customers.[41] In 1975, a Bonwit Teller ad confirmed that "Diane's secret is knowing how you want to look."

Early on, she had conceived of the wrap dress together with Italian pattern maker Bruna Sequalino, who worked at Ferretti, by describing what she wanted: a best friend in a woman's closet, a personal uniform, concealing and revealing different body parts, with sensual qualities. During the process, she adjusted the fit on herself, as she would continue to do with her designs. "I have always believed that a woman's clothes should feel like her, be a part of her, and an extension of her personality. That is what I have always liked for myself, and what I liked for myself, I wanted to make for others," says von Furstenberg.[42] She is literally her own muse, transposing her own image and attitude to thousands of women who wear the wrap in her image. "Just as you sell products, you become a product yourself," says von Furstenberg.[43]

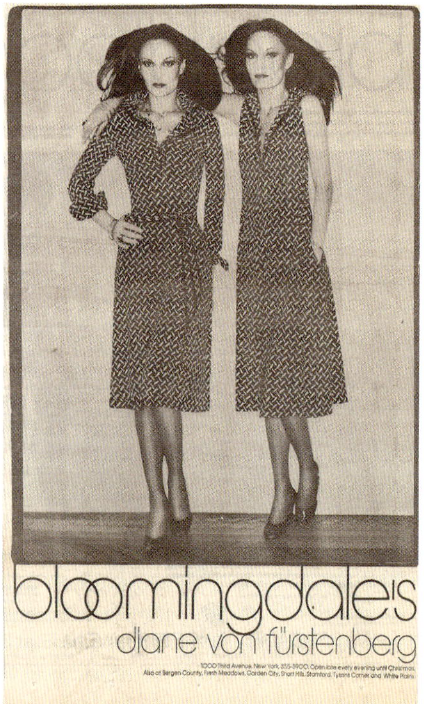

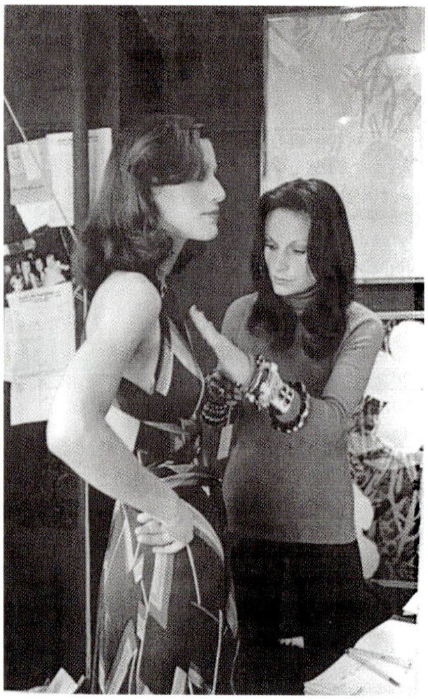

Above
A 1976 Bloomingdale's advertisement, featuring twin Diane von Furstenbergs.

Below
Diane von Furstenberg in a fitting, 1973.

Opposite
Diane von Furstenberg in her office, 1972.

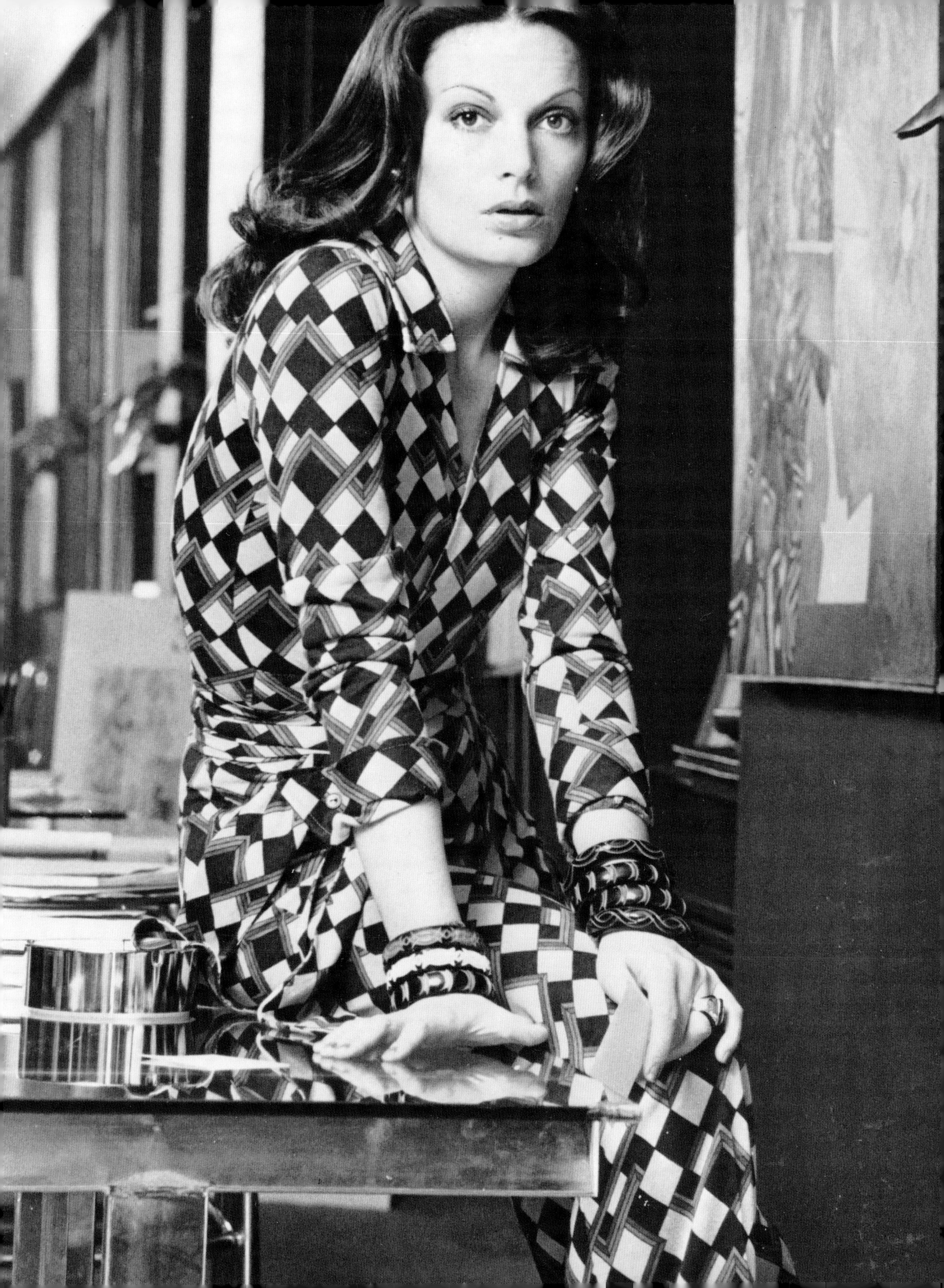

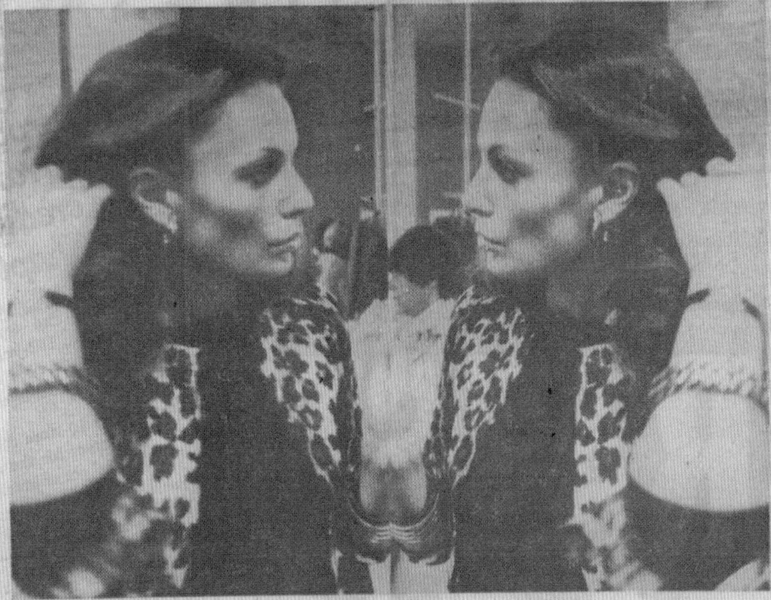

Photographs for The New York Times by JACK MANNING

Princess Diane von Furstenberg, center, checks appearance in mirror during recent personal appearance at Lord & Taylor. A prospective customer, left, and a saleswoman, right, in two of "Diane dresses," mostly in $70-$90 range.

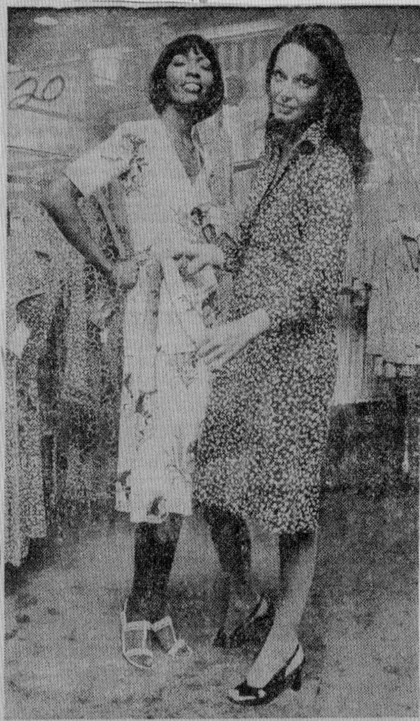

—Staff Photo by Phil Huber

DESIGNER Diane von Furstenberg, right, visited Dallas Wednesday as part of Lord & Taylor's first anniversary activities. She wears one of her newest silhouettes, the smock dress in a popcorn print. Her model shows off the more basic two-piece print dress.

As part of an embodied and even intimate, almost-maternal marketing campaign, she traveled around the United States to help women try on the wrap dress, peering into changing rooms, adjusting dresses, and tying the sash of the dress so it stayed put. Between 1973 and 1976, she traveled across the United States, sometimes visiting up to fourteen cities in thirteen days. "More important to me was that I was meeting the women who were buying my clothes and getting to know America," explains von Furstenberg.[44] Her practice-based approach echoes feminist designer and author Elizabeth Hawes's remark that "by the time you have finished designing and seeing to the fitting and making of a dress for any woman, there is practically nothing you don't know about her, mentally and physically."[45] She thus created real complicity and corporeal intimacy with her customers, empowering them as a mentor, as well as learning about their wants and needs, their bodies, sizes, and insecurities. Her philosophical mission was for women to feel good about themselves and their femininity, all the while also vouching for their independence to support themselves. She loved listening to their anecdotes of what they were going to do or had done in the wrap dress, like asking for a promotion at work.[46]

"I felt very connected to these women and enjoyed making them look and feel good," says von Furstenberg. "Nothing gave me greater pleasure than seeing a woman transformed by the way she looked in one of my dresses. The mirrors in the dressing rooms were too close, and I encouraged women to look at themselves outside on the sales floor. It was wonderful to see the surprise on their faces and the way their body language changed as they looked at themselves in the mirror. I don't think I know any other designer who actually enjoyed going into the stores the way I did then and do now again."[47]

Opposite (left)
Diane von Furstenberg checks her appearance in mirror during a public appearance at Lord & Taylor, 1974.

(right)
Diane von Furstenberg wraps the top of a two-piece print dress on a model in Dallas, 1975.

Below
Talita von Furstenberg in the TVF for DVF 2020 collection campaign.

"I talked to women, advised women, listened to women during my tours around the country. Whether in Texas, Georgia, Illinois, or Kansas, we women spoke a common language. '*Try this red print or this green print*', I urged those who usually wore only brown or navy blue," recalls von Furstenberg. "I walked through the display racks, helped women with their selections, then often followed them into the changing rooms. '*You have to pull the wrap tight in the front so the V-neck sits smoothly.*' Often I did the pulling myself so the women could see the proper effect. I have thousands of memories of myself looking into changing room mirrors over women's shoulders."[48]

Even though she also had high-profile metropolitan clients like Nan Kempner, Diana Vreeland, and Elsa Perretti, her customers in the more remote American cities were equally important to her. Over the years, the stores kept insisting that she was part of the image and the marketing materials, and this timeless image is still being channeled today, with her granddaughter Talita modeling a sustainable remake of a 1974 wrap ensemble in 2019.

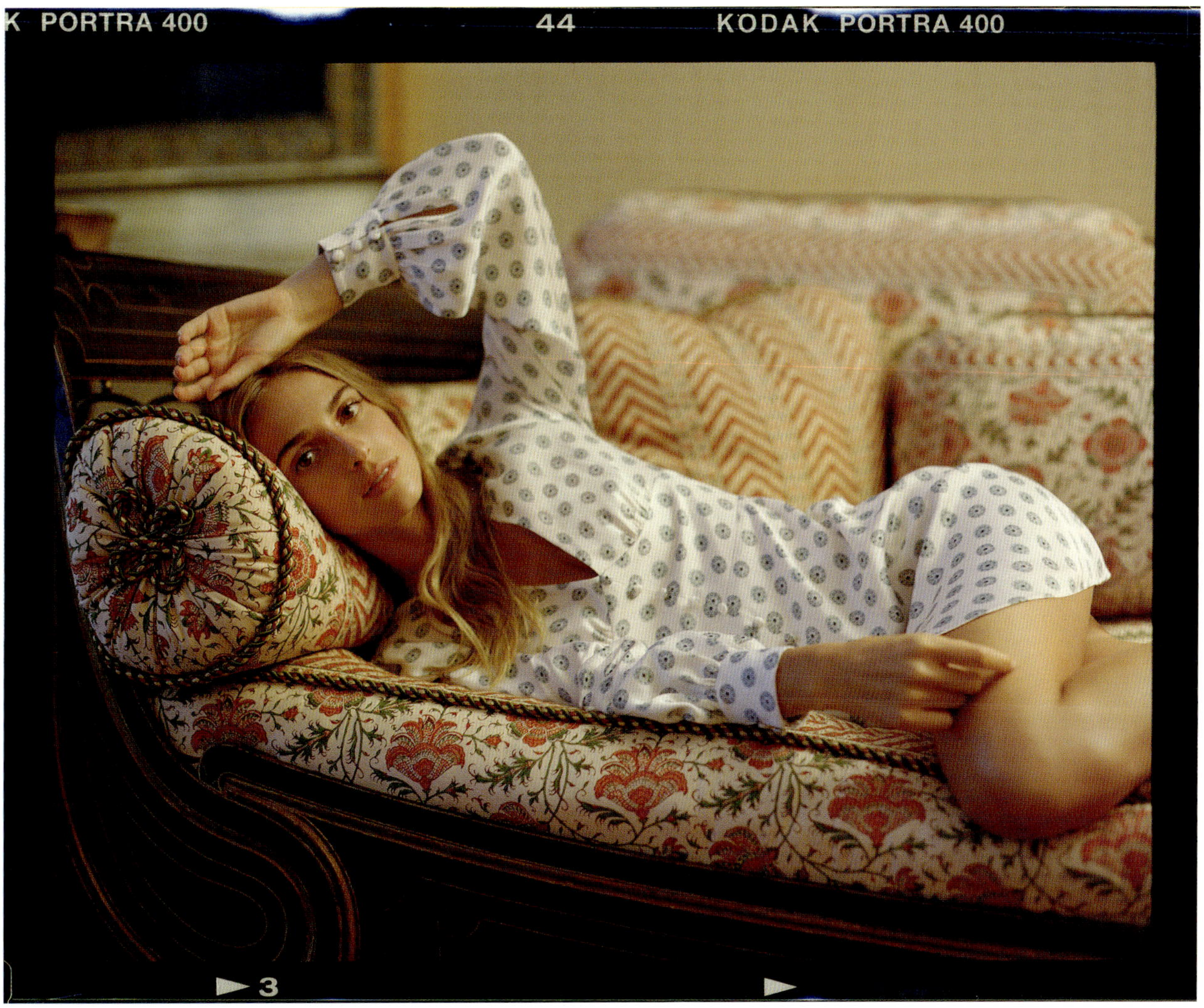

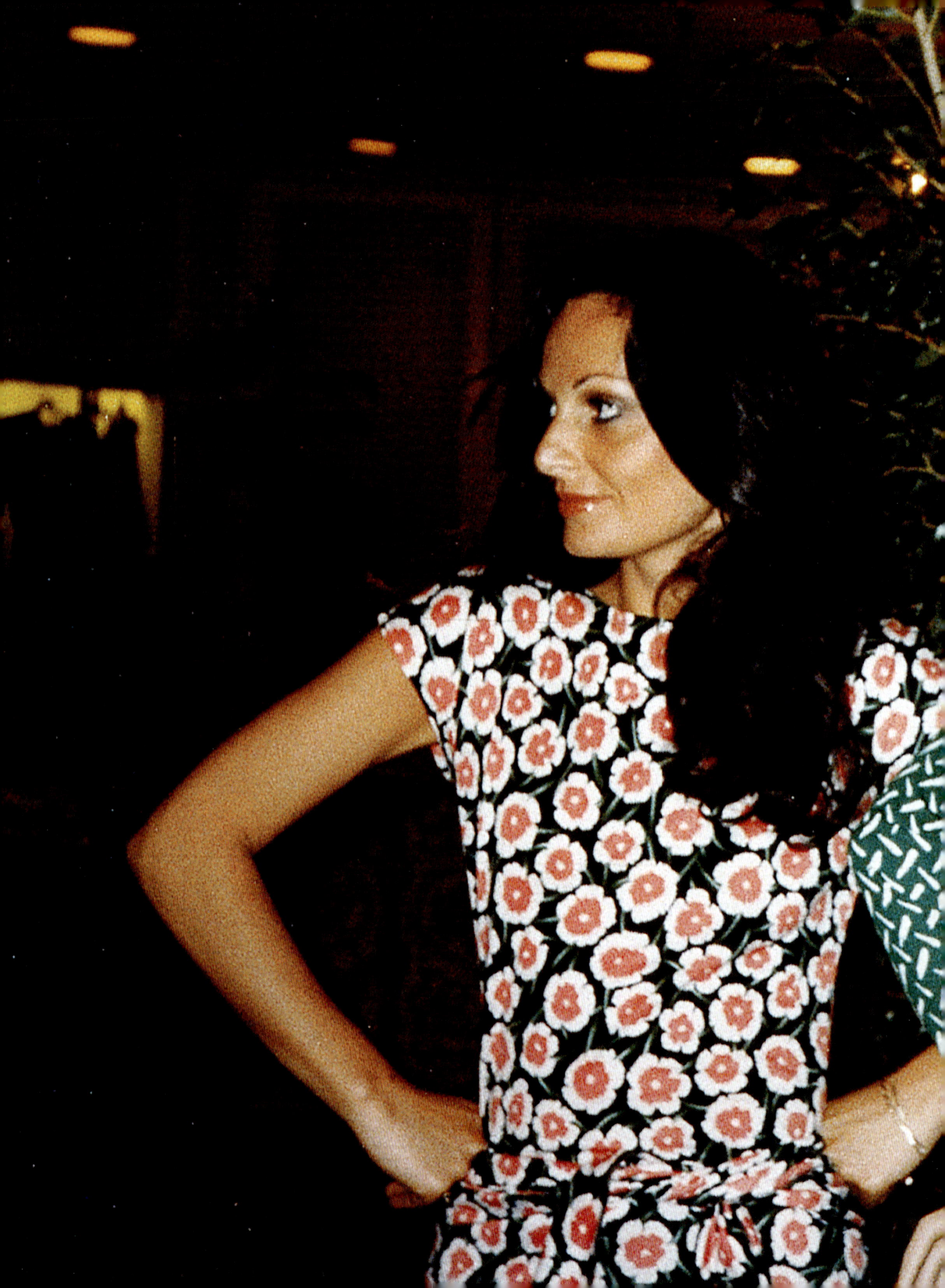

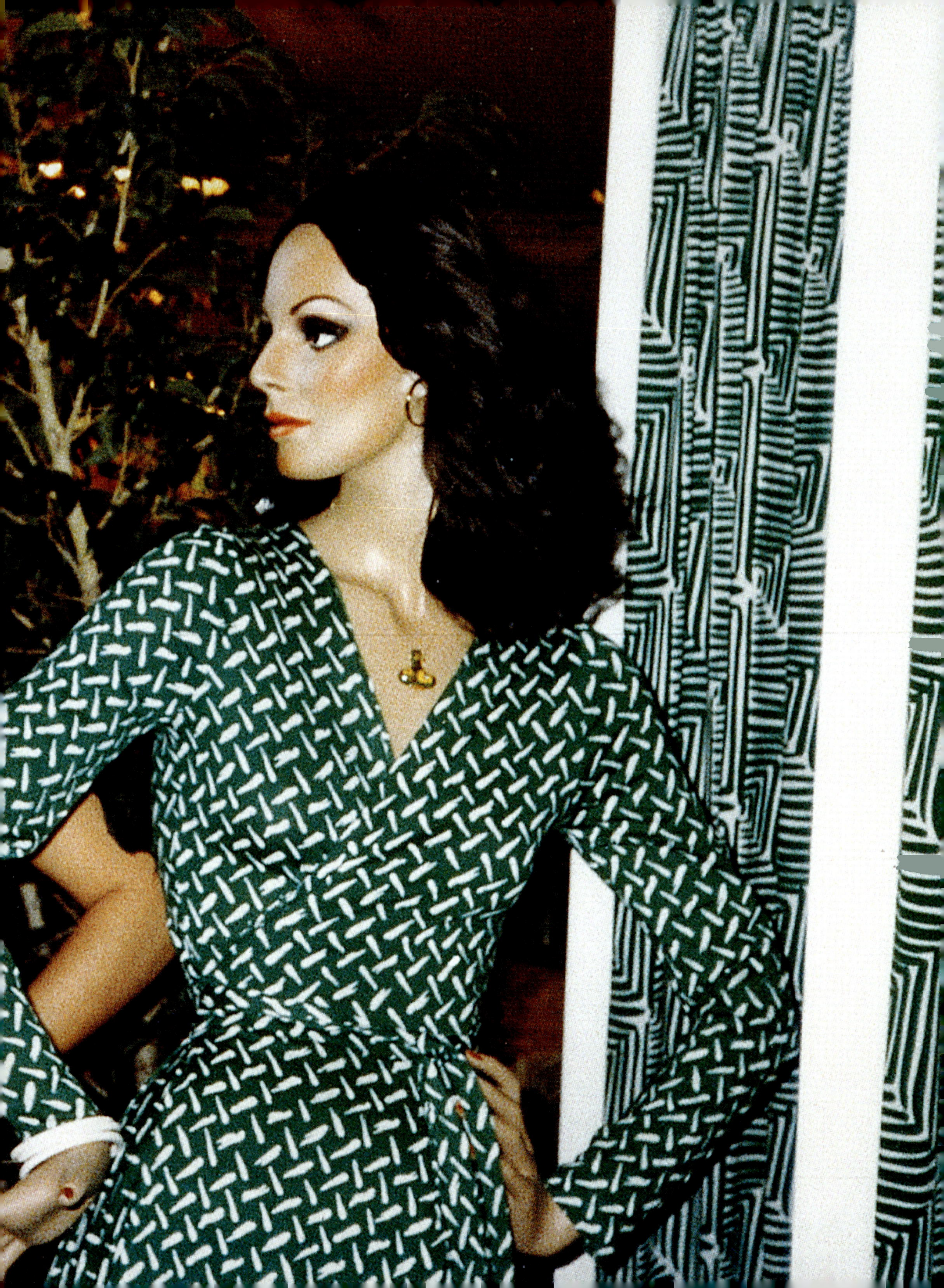

"To be InCharge is first a commitment to ourselves.
It is owning who we are.
It is respecting and trusting our character, knowing
that it is forever the home and the core of our strength."[49]

In her metamorphosis from a fashion designer to a feminist political powerhouse, Diane von Furstenberg has integrated her personal growth and life experience into her convictions, demonstrating at each turn that "the personal is political." While she admits to being sympathetic to the 1968 student protests only superficially in her early days, her business decisions are the best expressions of her political convictions: wanting to make something democratic and accessible for all women, clothes that were not just "easy to go" but also moderately priced, averaging $86 in-store in 1974. This makes her one of the only examples of her generation of female ready-to-wear designers who did not make boutique/high-end designer clothes but tried to erase financial and accessibility obstacles by being distributed in department stores for a customer base that consisted of rich women, aspiring professionals, and budget-conscious housewives. From the suburbanite to the metropolitan career woman, she designs for the everywoman because of her understanding of women's aspirations and insecurities. Apart from the democratic pricing and wide distribution, the "sensibility" of the dresses (i.e., being washable and wrinkle-proof) as well as their casual and supple feel on the body, ensured their appeal with a large demographic. Like lipstick, the wrap was both glamorous and democratic.

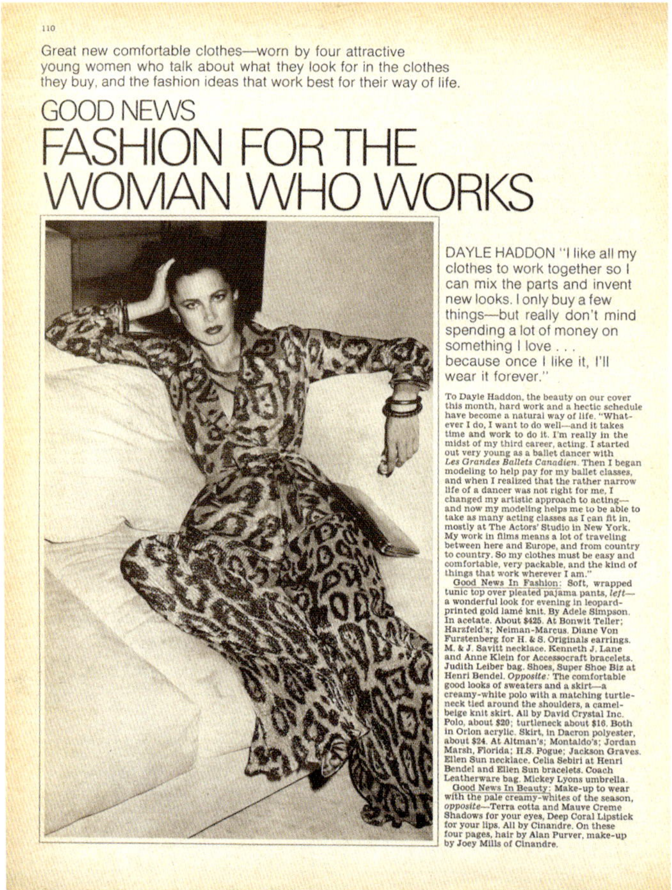

110

Great new comfortable clothes—worn by four attractive young women who talk about what they look for in the clothes they buy, and the fashion ideas that work best for their way of life.

GOOD NEWS
FASHION FOR THE WOMAN WHO WORKS

DAYLE HADDON "I like all my clothes to work together so I can mix the parts and invent new looks. I only buy a few things—but really don't mind spending a lot of money on something I love . . . because once I like it, I'll wear it forever."

To Dayle Haddon, the beauty on our cover this month, hard work and a hectic schedule have become a natural way of life. "Whatever I do, I want to do well—and it takes time and work to do it. I'm really in the midst of my third career, acting. I started out very young as a ballet dancer with *Les Grandes Ballets Canadien*. Then I began modeling to help pay for my ballet classes, and when I realized that the rather narrow life of a dancer was not right for me, I changed my artistic approach to acting—and now my modeling helps me to be able to take as many acting classes as I can fit in, mostly at The Actors' Studio in New York. My work in films means a lot of traveling between here and Europe, and from country to country. So my clothes must be easy and comfortable, very packable, and the kind of things that work wherever I am."

Good News In Fashion: Soft, wrapped tunic top over pleated pajama pants, *left*—a wonderful look for evening in leopard-printed gold lamé knit. By Adele Simpson. In acetate. About $425. At Bonwit Teller; Harzfeld's; Neiman-Marcus. Diane Von Furstenberg for H. & S. Originals earrings. M. & J. Savitt necklace. Kenneth J. Lane and Anne Klein for Accessocraft bracelets. Judith Leiber bag. Shoes, Super Shoe Biz at Henri Bendel. *Opposite:* The comfortable good looks of sweaters and a skirt—a creamy-white polo with a matching turtleneck tied around the shoulders, a camel-beige knit skirt. All by David Crystal Inc. Polo, about $20; turtleneck about $16. Both in Orlon acrylic. Skirt, in Dacron polyester, about $24. At Altman's; Montaldo's; Jordan Marsh, Florida; H.S. Pogue; Jackson Graves. Ellen Sun necklace. Celia Sebiri at Henri Bendel and Ellen Sun bracelets. Coach Leatherware bag. Mickey Lyons umbrella.

Good News In Beauty: Make-up to wear with the pale creamy-whites of the season, *opposite*—Terra cotta and Mauve Creme Shadows for your eyes, Deep Coral Lipstick for your lips. All by Cinandre. On these four pages, hair by Alan Purver, make-up by Joey Mills of Cinandre.

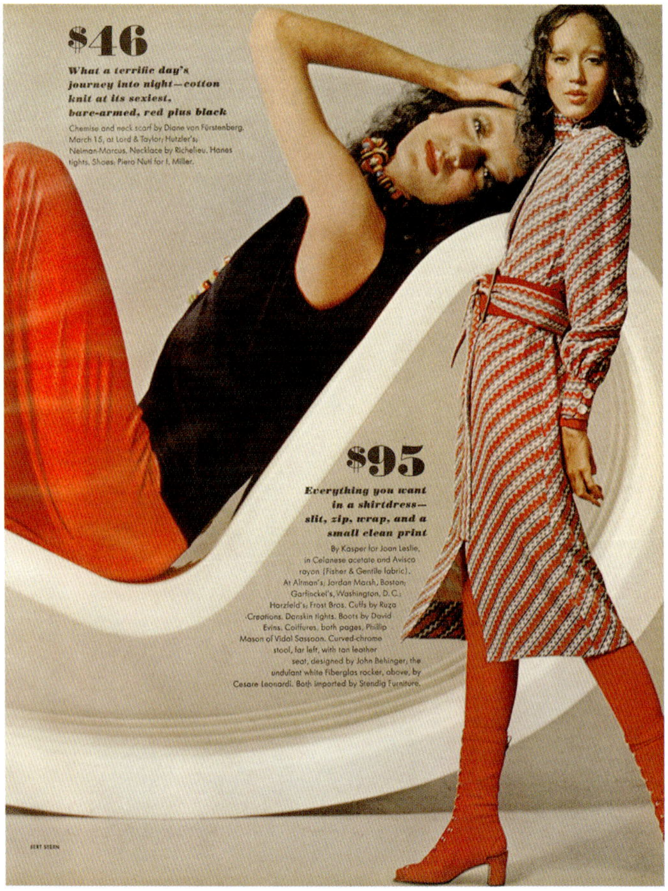

Previous spread
Diane von Furstenberg poses with a look-alike mannequin in Atlanta, 1977.

Opposite (left)
An article titled "Good News: Fashion for the Woman Who Works" featuring Dayle Haddon wearing a Diane von Furstenberg gown, 1975.

Opposite (right)
Pat Cleveland poses in a Diane von Furstenberg dress in a 1971 advertisement.

Next spread
(clockwise from top left)
Ariela Suster, Kakenya Ntaiya, Chouchou Namegabe, Gloria Steinem, Karlie Kloss, and Diane von Furstenberg at DVF's New York City office, 2019.

In her political colors too, von Furstenberg always supported the liberal values espoused by the Democratic Party. As a feminist and self-made woman, she is a working woman for the workers. "The woman I relate to works," says von Furstenberg. "She is busy. She has no time for complicated clothes."[50] Early on, she fundraised for Democratic candidates like New York lawyer and Congresswoman Bella Abzug, who, in 1971, joined leading feminists such as Gloria Steinem, Shirley Chisholm, and Betty Friedan to found the National Women's Political Caucus. An ecofeminist and gay rights activist, Abzug's motto was "This woman's place is in the House—the House of Representatives."[51] DVF's continued support for female Democratic candidates like Hillary Clinton and icons like US Supreme Court Justice Ruth Bader Ginsburg shows her unwavering political belief in equality, democracy, feminism, and justice.

Since 2010, she has organized the DVF Awards, supported by The Diller-von Furstenberg Family Foundation, with the goal of honoring women who have displayed leadership, strength, and courage in their commitment to causes that have a positive impact on other women with a $50,000 grant. Winners have included US Supreme Court Justice Ruth Bader Ginsberg, Oprah Winfrey, the Women of Afghanistan, Christine Lagarde, Robin Roberts, Karlie Kloss (for her girls coding project, "Kode w Klossy"), Hillary Clinton, Jane Goodall, and Ava Duvernay. Each year, two DVF Awards are given to women within The Vital Voices Global Partnership, an organization that supports women leaders and change-makers, for which von Furstenberg sits on the board. Another feminist initiative of hers is the contemporary women leaders platform, podcast, and community, InCharge, which supports and activates leading women to use their personal connections to help all women "be the women they want to be."

A fundraising project close to DVF's heart was the 2019 Statue of Liberty Museum project for which she was honored with the title "the godmother of the Statue of Liberty." Raising $100 million, she did it as a tribute to her own mother, Liliane Nahmias, an Auschwitz survivor, who once said to her, "God has saved my life so that I can give you life. By giving you life, you gave me my life back. You are my torch, my flag of freedom."[52] The symbolism of these words reflects von Furstenberg's drive and passion, which is also expressed in the statue itself. "She has broken chains at her feet, but she is strong and she is the light. The message is important: Women's voices can save humanity," says von Furstenberg.[53] All these myriad examples of von Furstenberg's political and feminist engagements reveal her lifelong project of helping women reach their full potential.

The arc of Diane von Furstenberg's life mirrors a larger global feminist evolution, balancing a private family life with a demanding profession and a powerful role in society. Her openness about her process and growth has inspired many women, not only sartorially. In her autobiography, she describes a moment at the age of six years old when she consciously decided to become her own best friend,[54] and it is this self-confidence and love she has taken, with the help of a dress, to thousands of women around the world, touching their lives and inspiring them to be their own best friend.

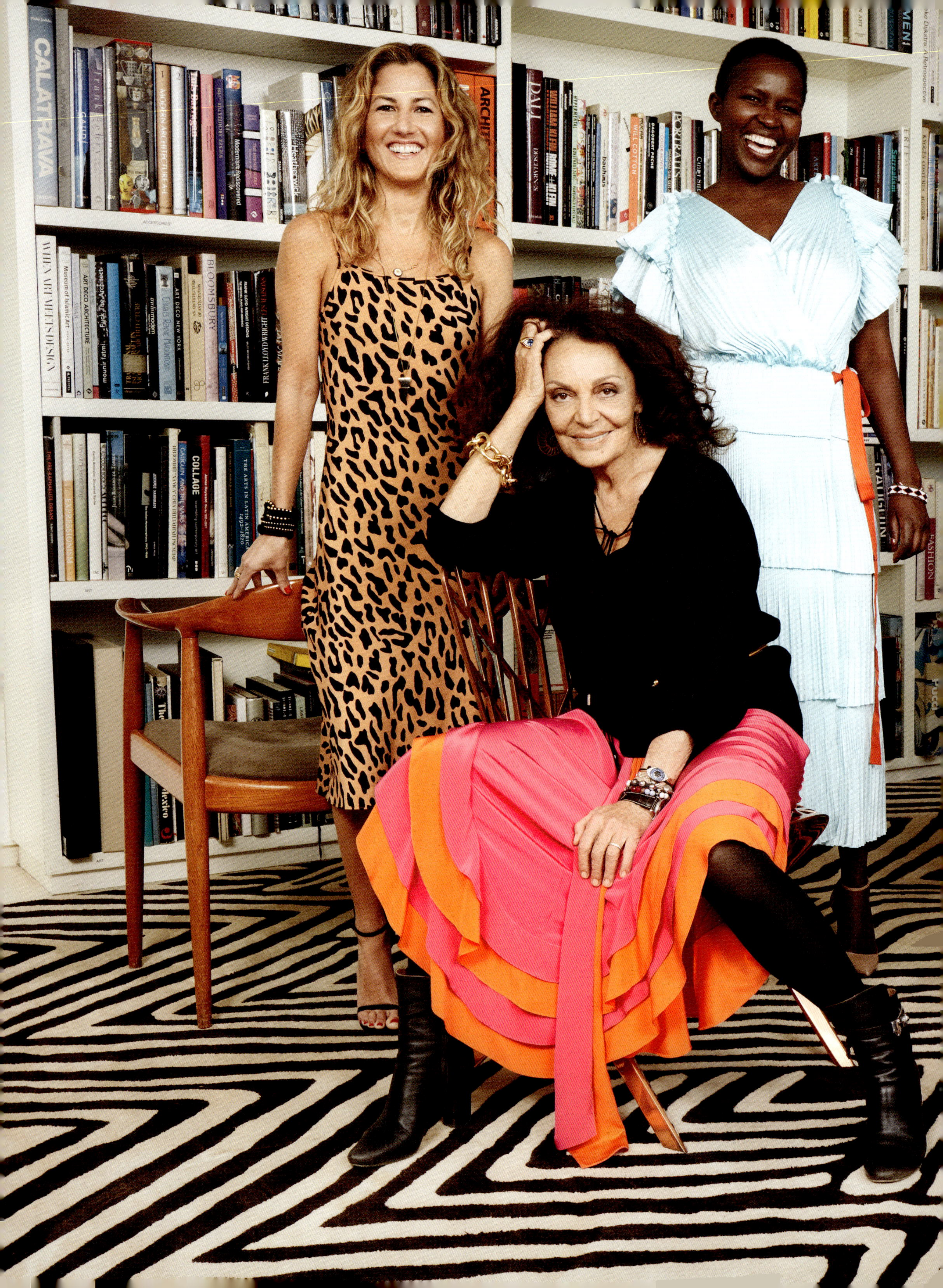
CALATRAVA
MODERN ARCHITECTURE
Modernism Rediscovered
Heatherwick
DALI
bauhaus
WILL COTTON
PORTRAITS
BLOOMSBURY
ART DECO ARCHITECTURE
Museum of Islamic Art
ART DECO NEW YORK
FRANK LLOYD WRIGHT
COLLAGE
EXPRESSIONISM
THE ARTS IN LATIN AMERICA 1492–1820
FASHION

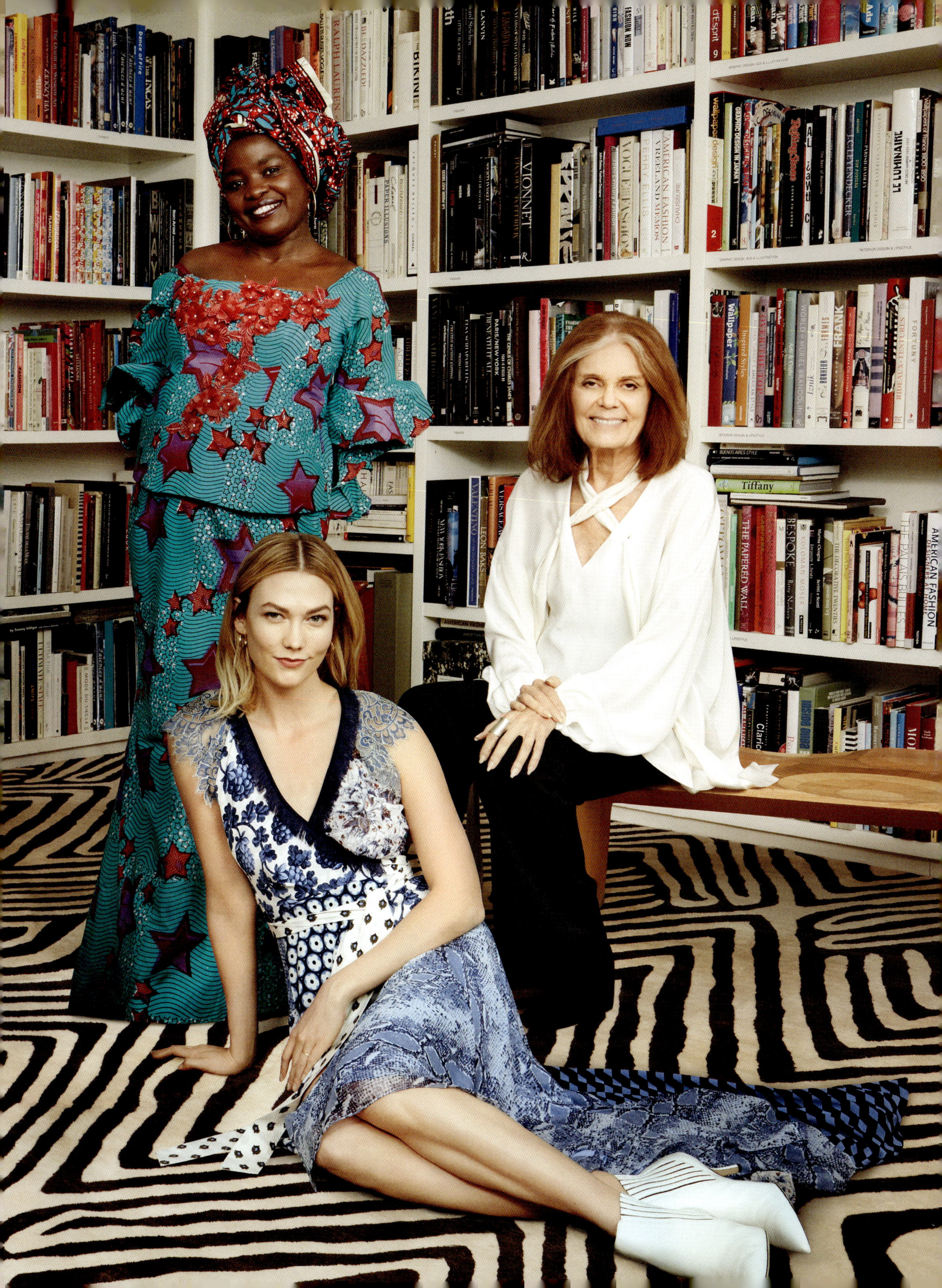
RALPH LAUREN
BIKINI
LANVIN
FASHION NOW
VIONNET
AMERICAN FASHION
PERRY ELLIS
LE LUMINAIRE
J.C. LEYENDECKER
Wallpaper
Tiffany
FRANK
BESPOKE
THE PAPERED WALL
THE DECORATIVE TWENTIES
PARIS/NEW YORK
FORTUNY
AMERICAN FASHION

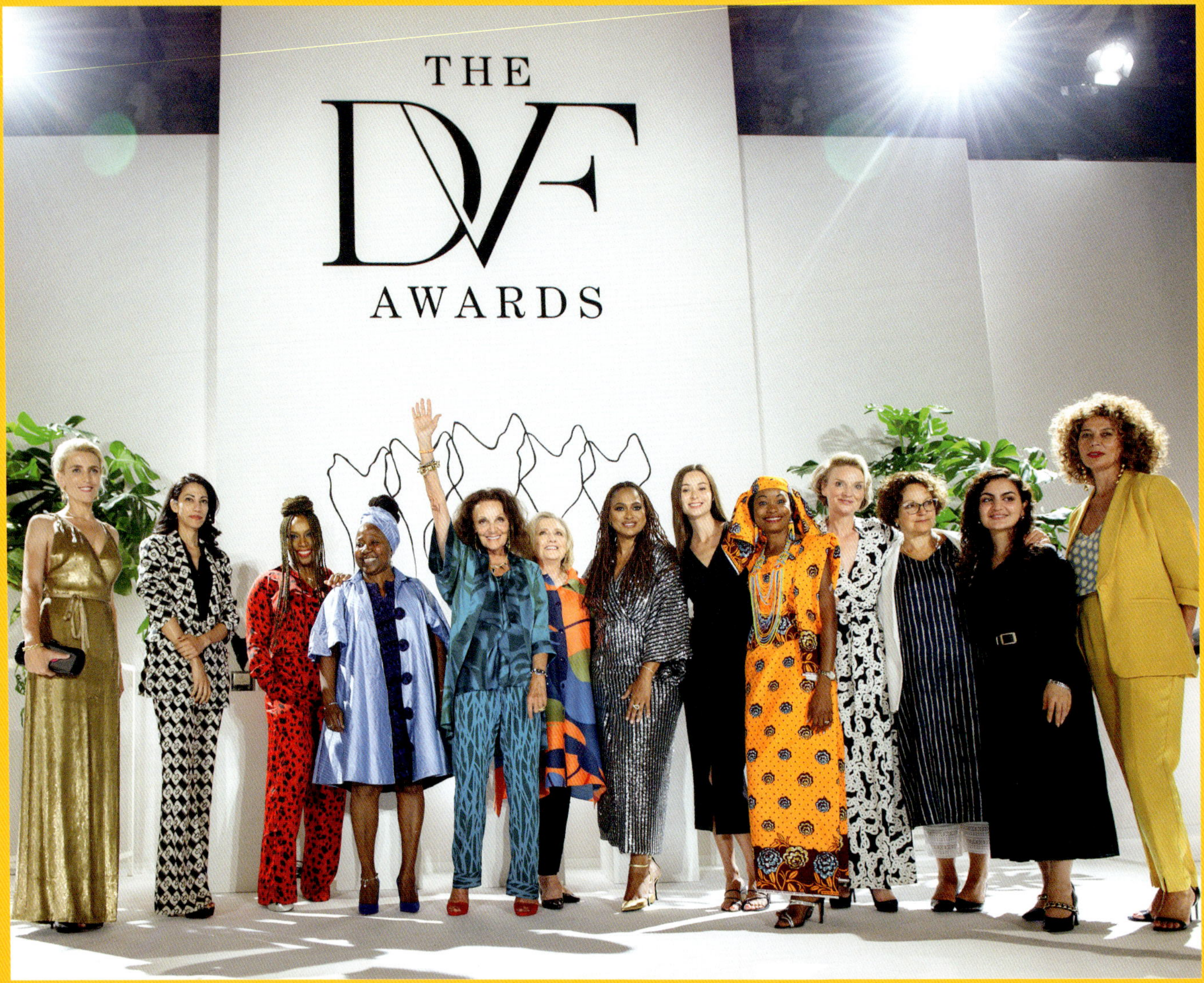

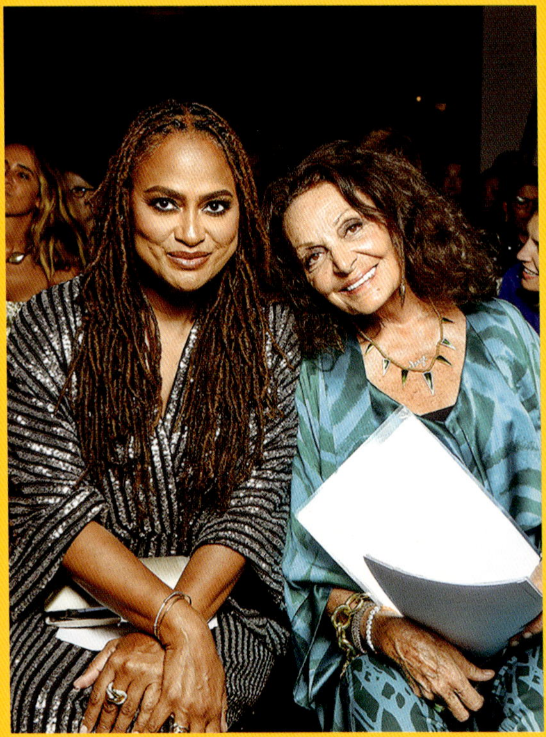

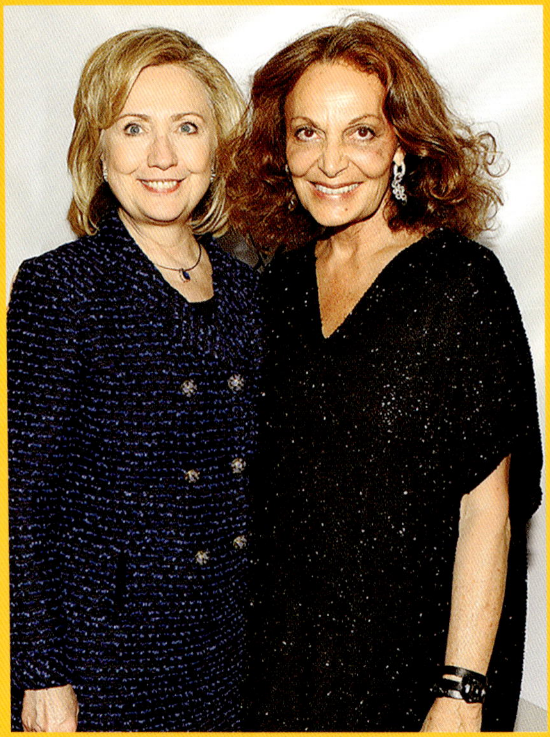

Above
The DVF Awards in Venice, 2022.

Below (left)
Filmmaker Ava DuVernay and Diane von Furstenberg at the DVF Awards, 2022.

Below (right)
Diane von Furstenberg and Hillary Clinton at the DVF Awards, 2011.

Opposite
(clockwise from top left)
Diane von Furstenberg and Malawi Chief Theresa Kachindamoto at the Vital Voices Global Leadership Awards, 2017; Naomi Campbell and Diane von Furstenberg, 2004; Hong Huang and Diane von Furstenberg at the Shanghai Red Ball, 2011; Diane von Furstenberg and Ruth Bader Ginsburg, 2022.

Next page
Diane von Furstenberg in her office, 2014.

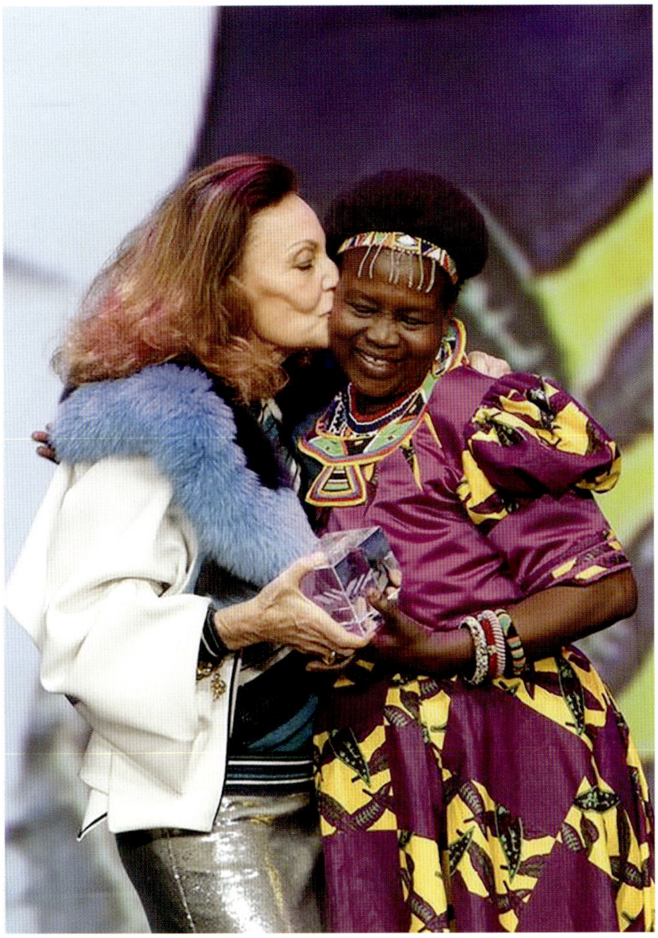
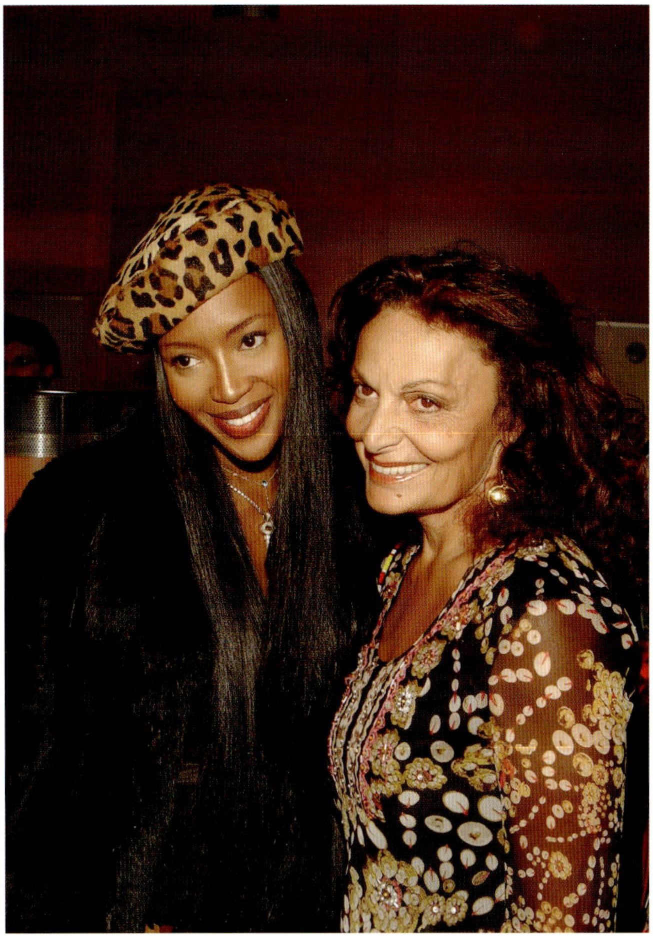
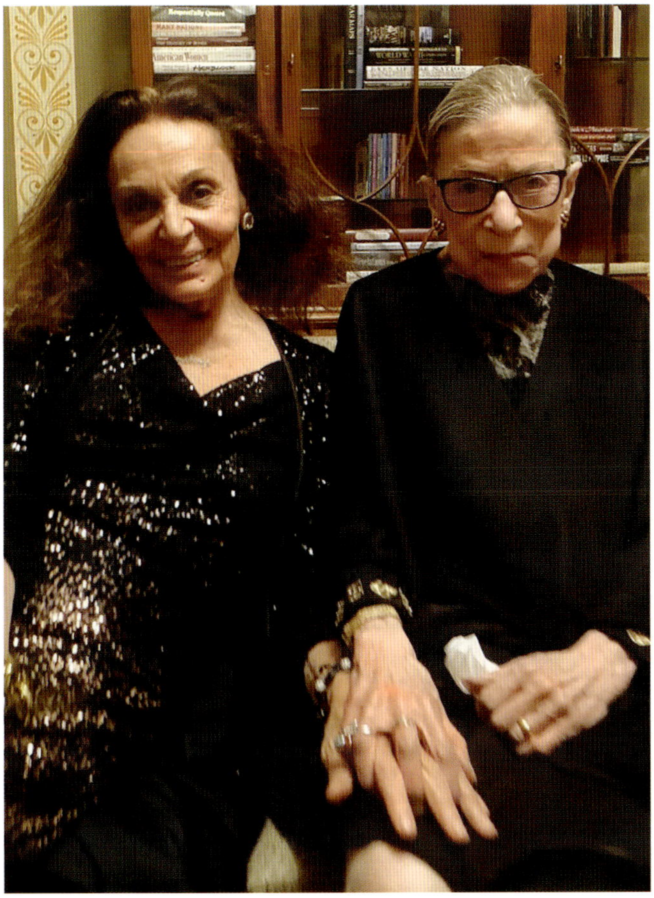
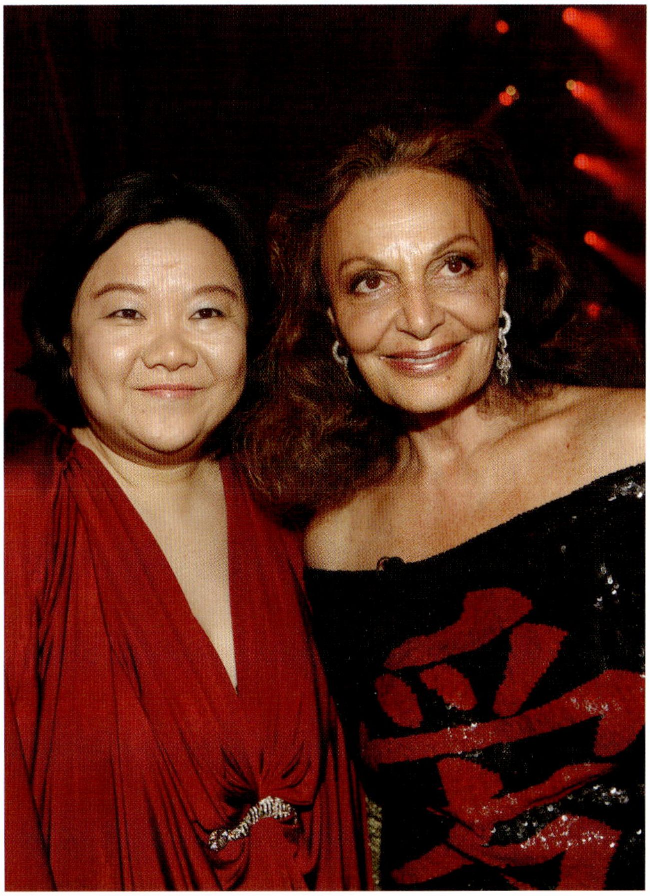

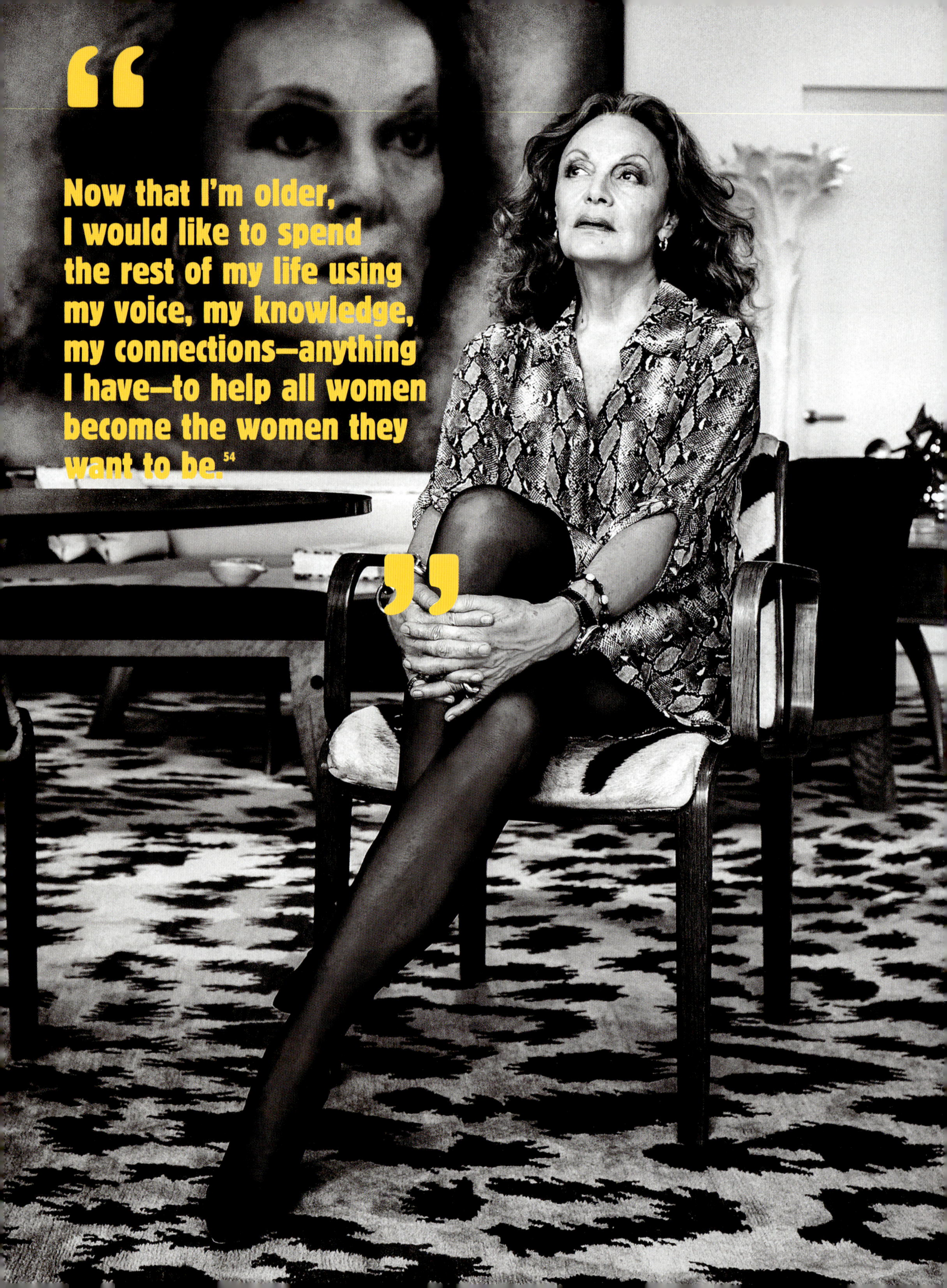

"Now that I'm older, I would like to spend the rest of my life using my voice, my knowledge, my connections—anything I have—to help all women become the women they want to be.[54]"

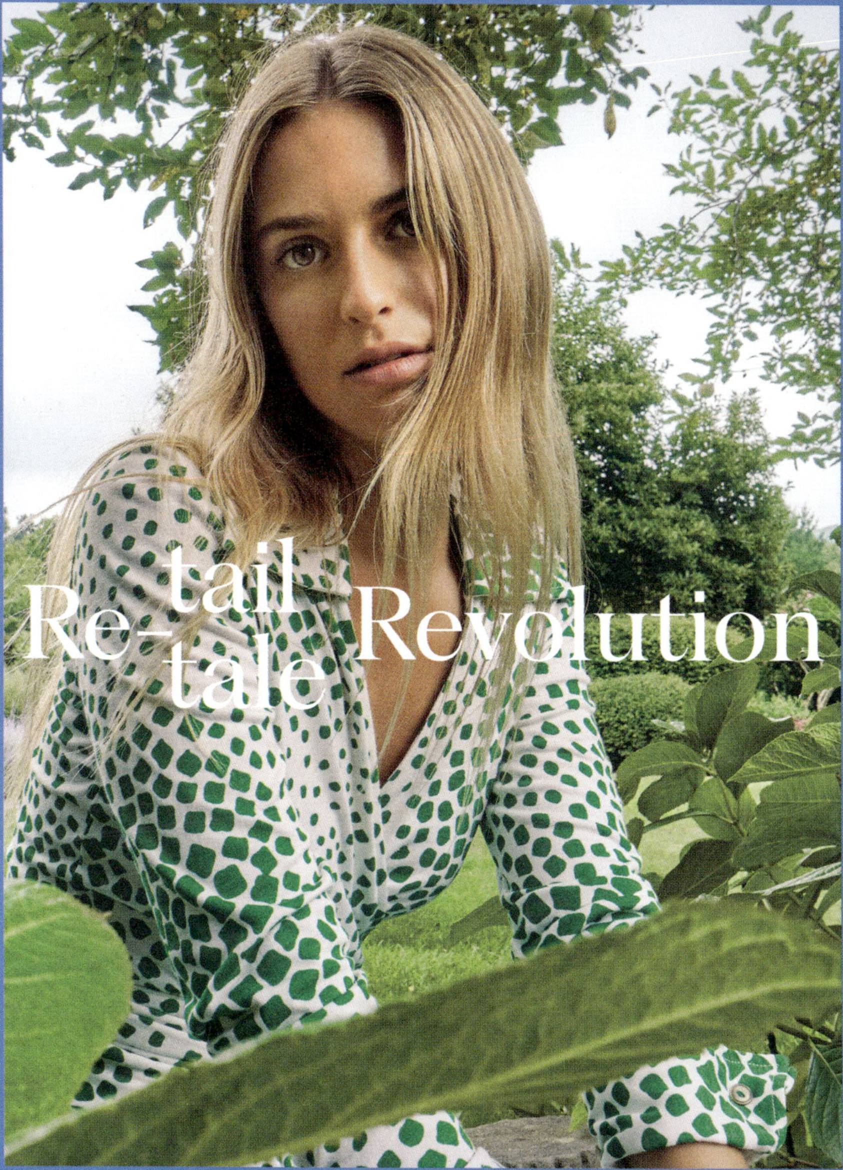

CHAPTER 03

Re– tail tale Revolution

INTERVIEWS BY

Nicolas Lor

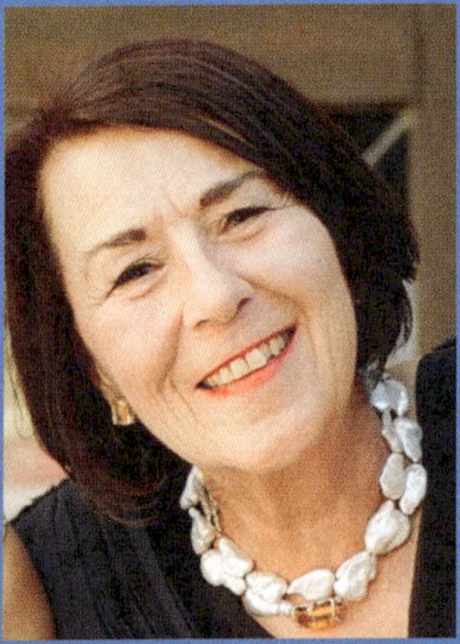

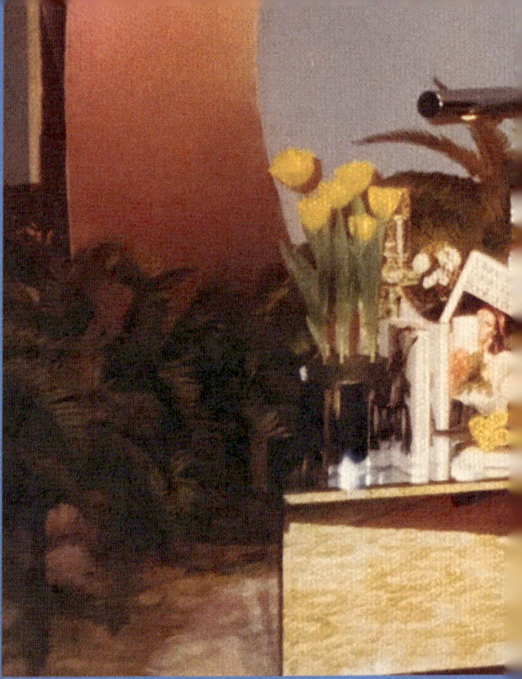

Previous page
Talita von Furstenberg in Diane von Furstenberg 2022 Originals.

Above
Elizabeth McKenzie, 2013.

Opposite
Diane von Furstenberg at an appearance to promote *Book of Beauty*, 1977.

ELIZABETH MCKENZIE

Elizabeth McKenzie (b. 1949, United States) was the buyer for women's contemporary dresses, coats, and suits for Bullock's department store from 1974 to 1978. During this time, she bought Diane von Furstenberg dresses for Bullock's. McKenzie was vice president of public relations and special events for Macy's department store from 1978 to 2009. Her proudest achievement was Macy's Passport Fashion Show, which raised more than $35 million dollars for AIDS/HIV nonprofit organizations.

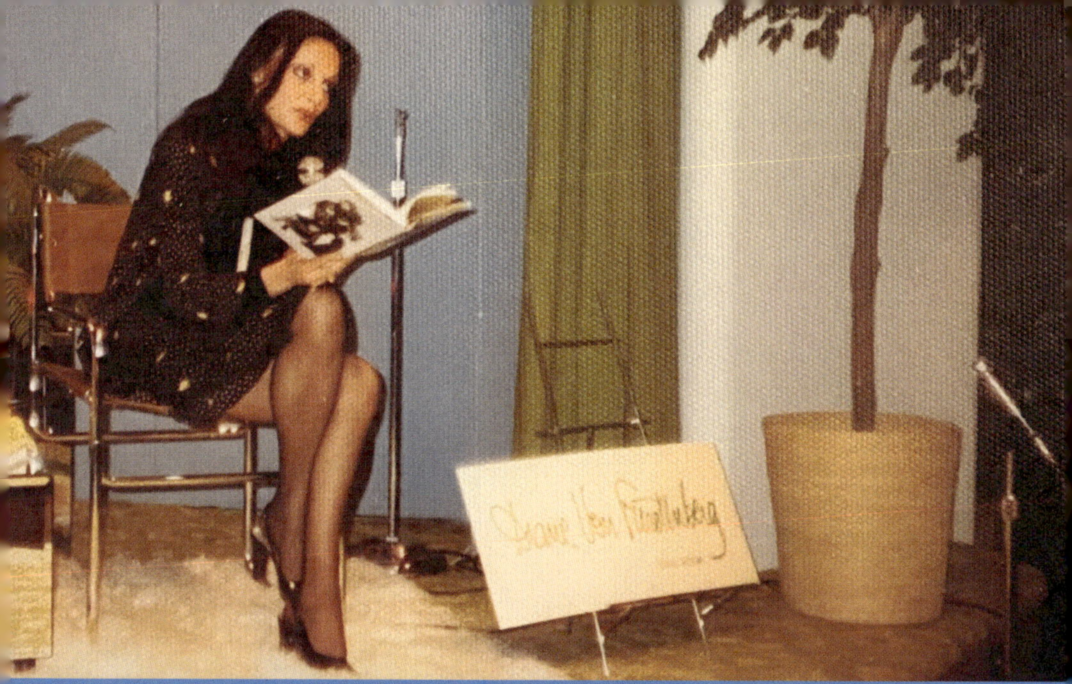

How was the process of buying and selling Diane von Furstenberg dresses in the early 1970s?

The contemporary dress department was not well-developed in the United States at that time. Women's suit was actually the current work dress attire which included very serious looking trouser or skirt ensembles imitating men's work suits. At Bullock's, we developed the contemporary department "Emphasis," which was a new alternative between the junior and women's department. It was created for that group of young women joining the workforce. I was buying dresses in the five branch fork of sizes: 6, 8, 10, 12, and 14. Then, Diane's dress came to market. It changed my buying process. I bought to fill entire fixtures; it was no longer just one piece per size. Merchandising this way made a stronger statement for the wrap dress. I recall that we were selling twenty-five to thirty-five pieces a week in five stores. The dress gave women an emotional lift. There were very few people who would walk out of the fitting room and not buy the dress after trying it on.

What is your personal opinion about the wrap dress?

Diane developed the knit jersey dress, which would conform to your individual body type. The wrap dress could be as sexy as you want or as conservative as you needed by the way you wrapped it around yourself. The dress made women feel very empowered. It had a high level of sophistication and was well-made. Her prints also gave it an unusual but engaging beauty. Most customers gravitated to her bold and colorful prints, but some of them would go back to a black and white pattern, which was less of a statement.

The right clothing can feed your emotions and be a statement of who you are. The right outfit can help get you through the day as much as clothes that have functions. Women can have clothes that fit well and are comfortable wearing, but they don't necessarily take care of their emotions. Moods, meetings, and conference room climates and their audiences are constantly changing; the Diane von Furstenberg wrap dress was the morning-to-evening solution.

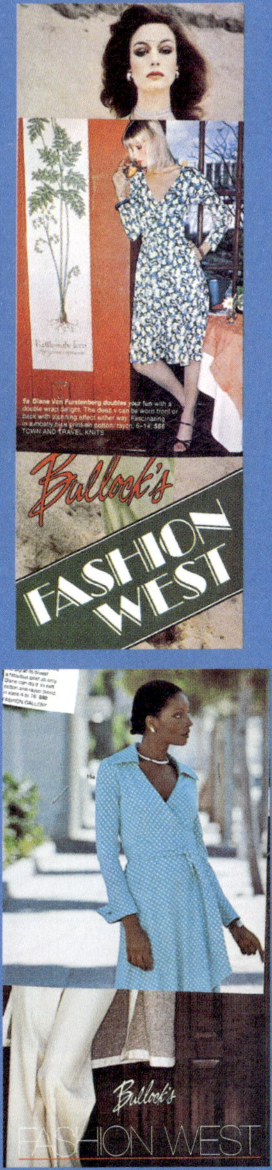

Two pages from a Bullock's department store catalogue, featuring models in Diane von Furstenberg wrap dresses, ca. 1976.

Diane von Furstenberg in her office, 2005.

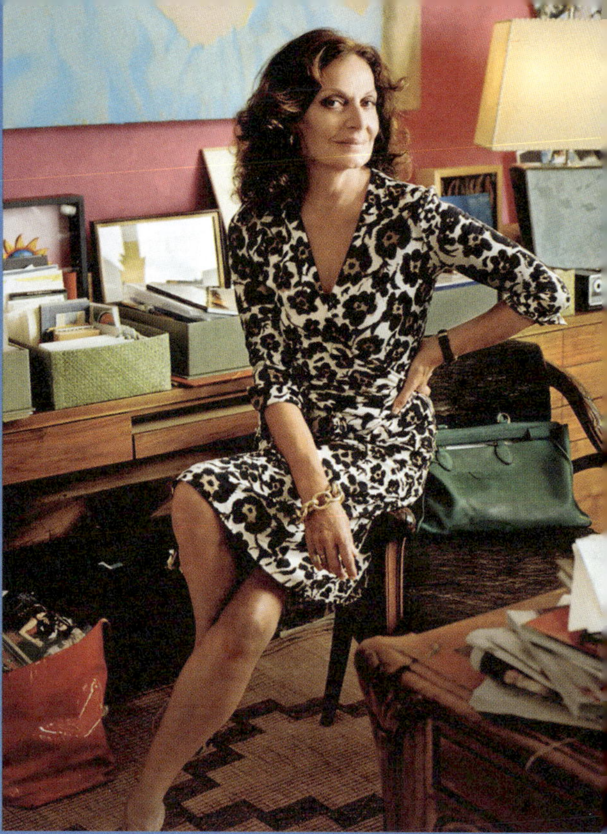

Were you wearing Diane von Furstenberg yourself? How were you feeling in?

I was that working girl—young and out of college going through the 60s sexual revolution. My Diane von Furstenberg dress was the go-to for any and all of my day-to-evening attire.

It always felt like the right thing to wear. It was the most expensive dress that I purchased until my wedding dress. It made me feel accomplished and successful. The Diane von Furstenberg wrap dress was power dressing for me and my customers.

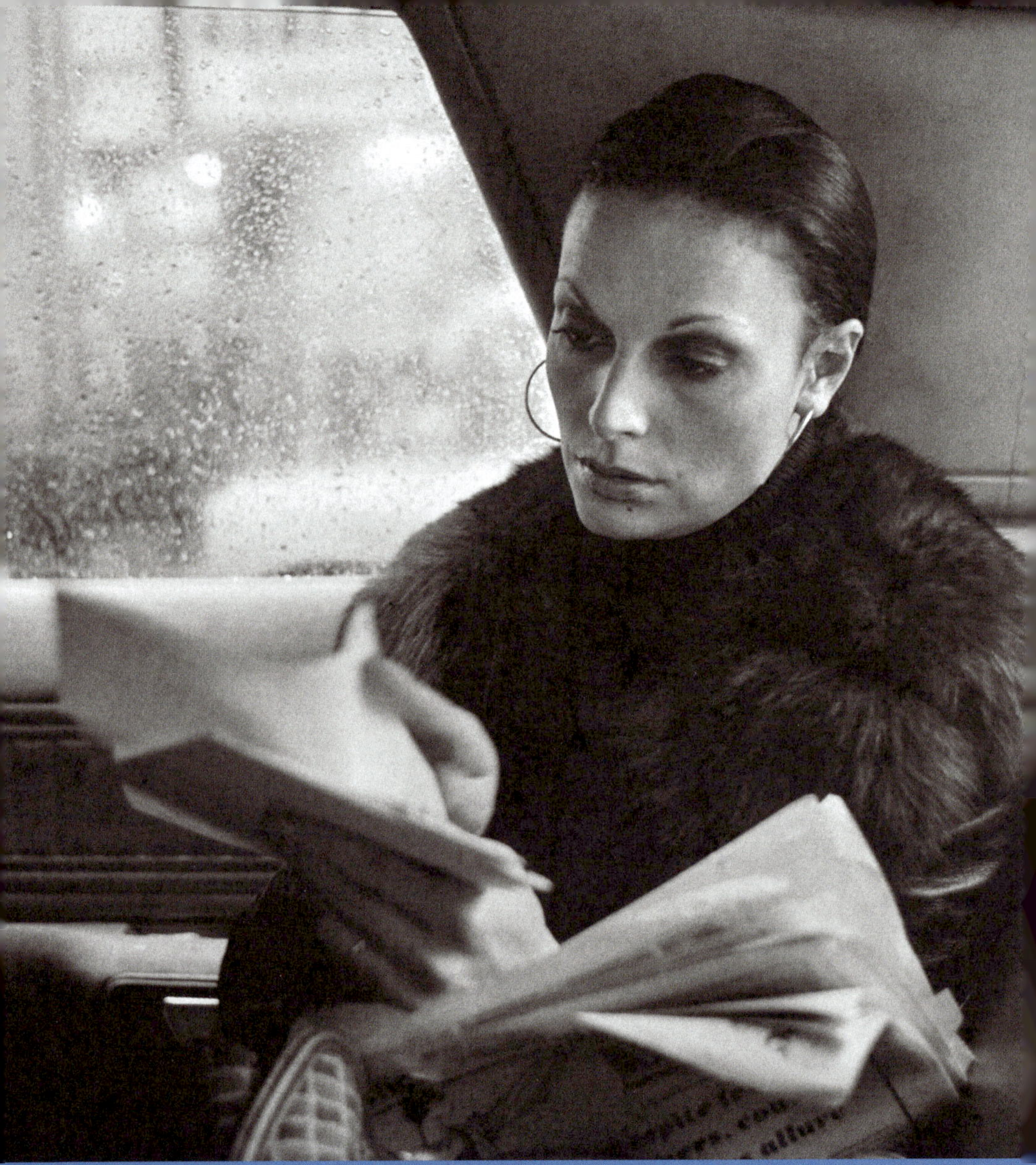

Above
Diane von Furstenberg works in a car, 1976.

Opposite
A Bullock's department store invitation for an informal Diane von Furstenberg fitting, ca. 1976.

How would you explain Diane von Furstenberg's huge commercial success in the United States?

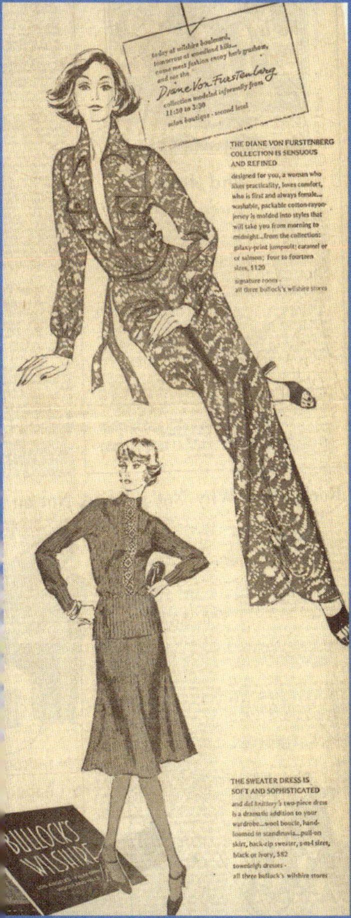

It was the beginning of an educated female workforce. We were the beginning of that generation that was going to break the glass ceiling. We were sexually aware, driven by the potential of our future, and knew that how we felt about ourselves would be a statement of our success. Wearing a Diane von Furstenberg dress empowered women.

At this time, there wasn't street fashion per se. The only place where people considered fashion to be real fashion was in the couture showrooms. Diane's dress began to carve a path toward fashion in an everyday sense for a woman.

You did not have to be a well-known doyenne and go off to the couturier for gowns to go to the opera. Diane made it possible for the woman to think about how she was going to present herself. She opened that door for women. It changed thinking about how fashion was and how people could be fashionable.

We had informal modeling at Bullock's all the time. It was different from the New York catwalks. When Bullock's sold Diane's fragrance, we would have the models walk in the store with testers and share her perfume. Customers could have the full experience: the scent of Diane and the garments of Diane.

Below
Stefani Greenfield, 2015.

Opposite
Models pose in windows, wearing new Diane von Furstenberg relaunch designs, 1997.

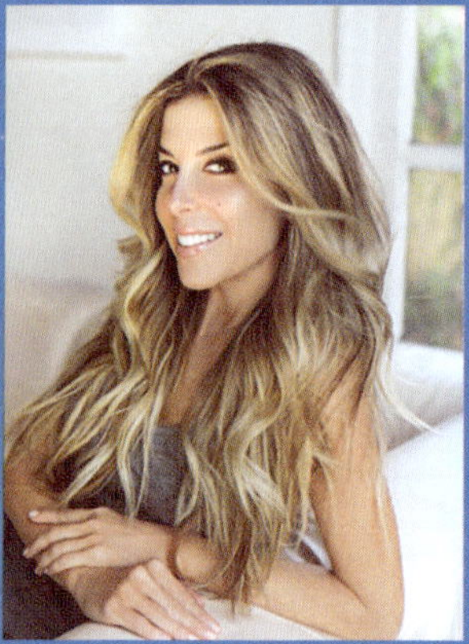

STEFANI GREENFIELD

Stefani Greenfield (b. 1967, United States) is a businesswoman and entrepreneur. After working for Donna Karan and Susie Tompkins at Esprit, she opened her store Scoop NYC in New York City in late 1996. Greenfield and Scoop played a major role in relaunching the wrap dress trend, giving a new understanding of Diane von Furstenberg's vision. Greenfield was regularly featured on the E! TV show, *House of DVF* from 2014 to 2015. She launched My Next Act, a brand-building agency, in 2013.

Can you explain the origins of your specialty retail store?

In October 1996, my partner and I opened Scoop NYC in Soho on lower Broadway. This area back then looked nothing like it does today. We wanted to launch something new: a retail store that had the look and feel of Soho's art galleries with a shopping platform that was all our own. Everything in retail at that time was very traditional. I was inspired by stores like Charivari and Barneys and the brilliant designers whom they discovered and cultivated, but I had a different vision for how I wanted to promote Scoop and the story we would tell to the customer. For my whole life, people have always said to me that they would love to shop in my closet. This was my launchpad for the entire Scoop concept and building the ultimate closet. I merchandised by color, classification, trend, and storytelling—not by designer name or brand logo.

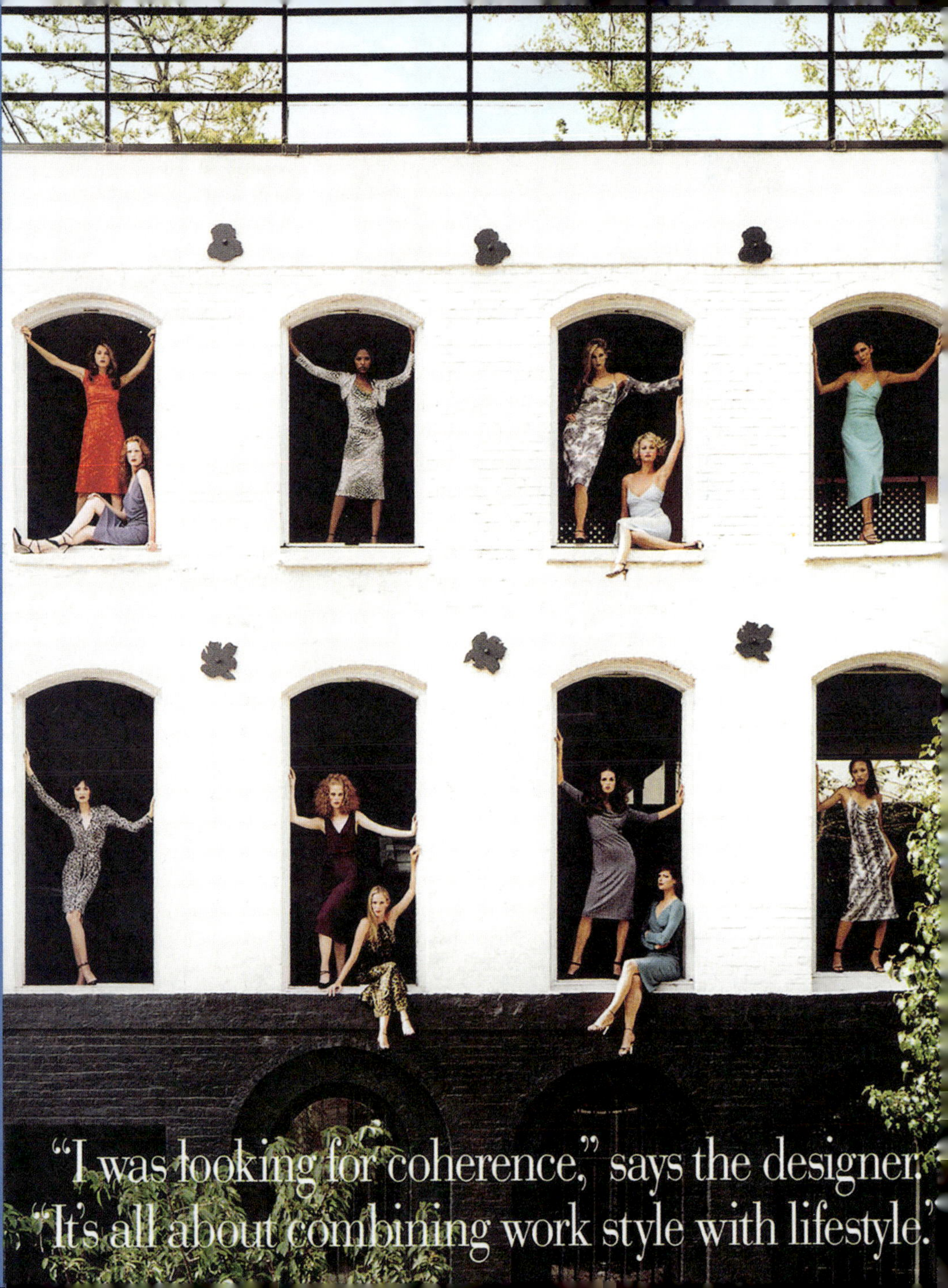

"I was looking for coherence," says the designer. "It's all about combining work style with lifestyle."

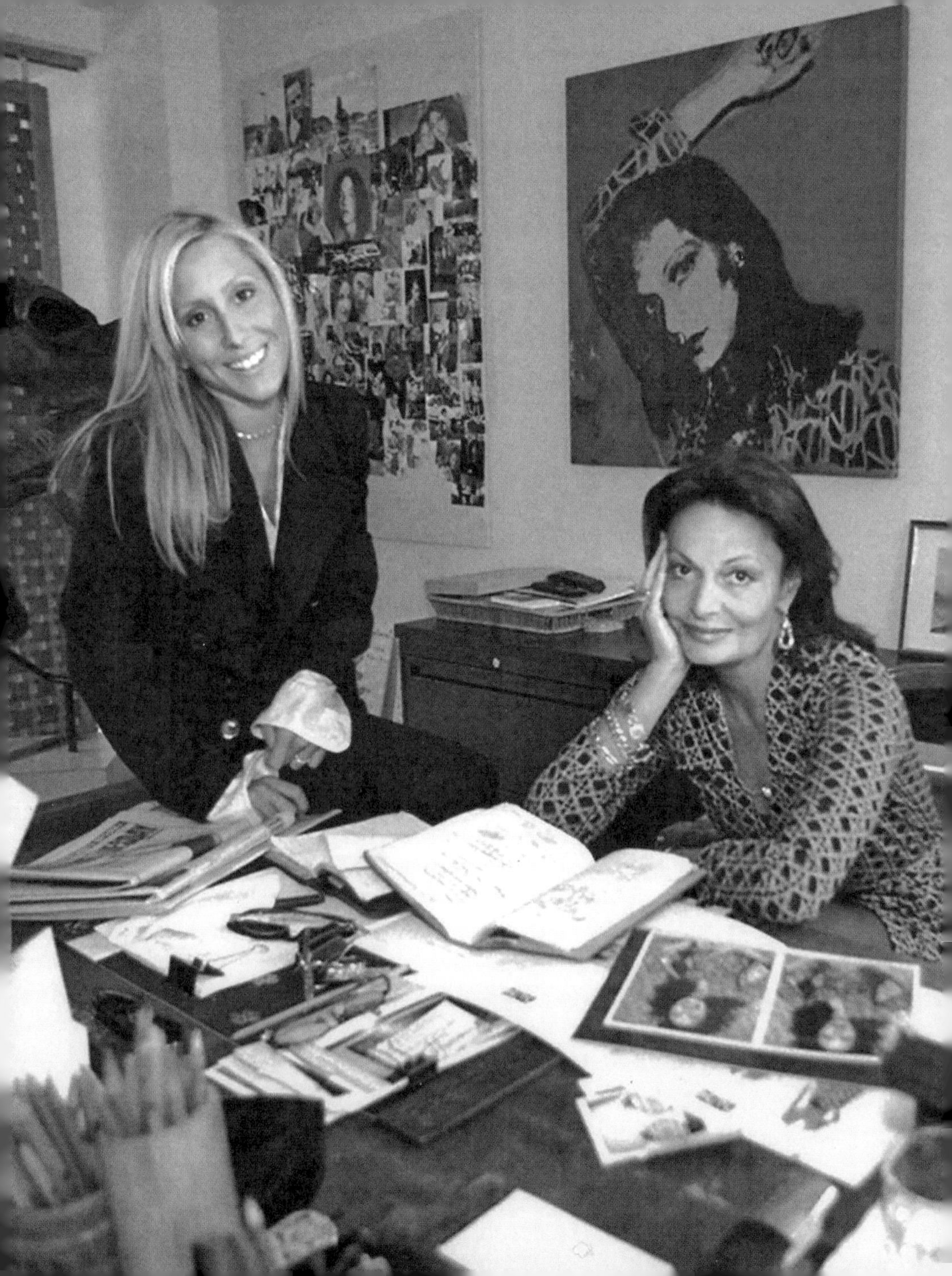

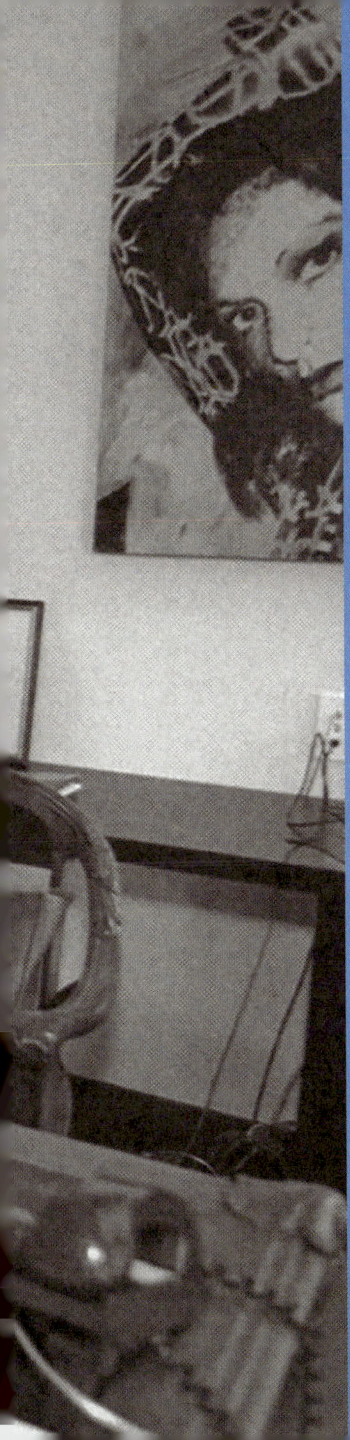

How and when did you start working with Diane von Furstenberg?

I was 27 years old in the spring of 1996, and a great customer and friend of mine was best friends with Alexandra von Furstenberg, Diane's daughter-in-law at the time. I heard they were relaunching the wrap dress, and I absolutely had to have them in my store. I asked my friend to introduce me to Diane and Alexandra. We met over lunch. They agreed to take a chance and work with us at Scoop. It was my dream come true! From the moment we unpacked the first box of DVF's wrap dresses and put them in the window, it became a phenomenon. No one could have predicted what was about to happen. Diane's dresses with vibrant colors and prints contrasted with everything in Scoop, which was an all-black, downtown NYC glamorous grunge aesthetic. Customers were lining up outside the windows to take pictures and at the registers to purchase Diane's dresses.

We could not keep the wrap dresses in stock to meet the crazy demand—even with weekly reorders on repeat! It got to a point where we had to remove the wrap dresses from the window because customers immediately demanded whatever we had available to sell.

Diane and Alexandra von Furstenberg at work in the DVF office, ca. 1998.

How was your business at Scoop selling Diane von Furstenberg?

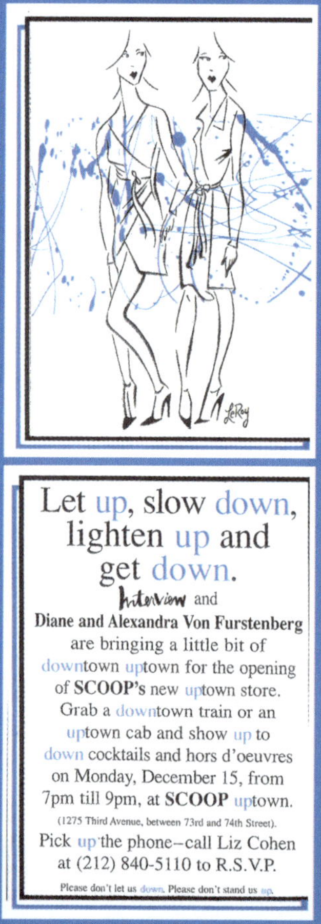

My team and I were curators. Our goal each season was to build the ultimate closet for women. The wrap dress was a business within a business at Scoop. We would take polaroids of our customers in their looks and tack them on a wall. Every dress and every woman told a story.

There was an art of wearing the wrap dress. I was taught by the master herself how to tie it. We trained our salespeople how to tie the wrap dress so they could assist the customers. It was the most versatile fit and democratic style we had in Scoop at the time. Our customers personalized their wrap dresses according to their own vibe: open, closed, layered, with belts, over jeans. They made it their own, customizing this major dress in a whole new way.

This new generation took the Diane von Furstenberg collection to the next level of work to street style, making it day-to-date, 24/7, timeless dressing. It was epic.

Scoop also collaborated on unique styles with Diane von Furstenberg in exclusive prints. Together, we designed collectible dresses that our customers would covet and that they could not find anywhere else.

Above
Scoop invitation, December 1997.

Opposite
Four Scoop advertisements, ca. 2001.

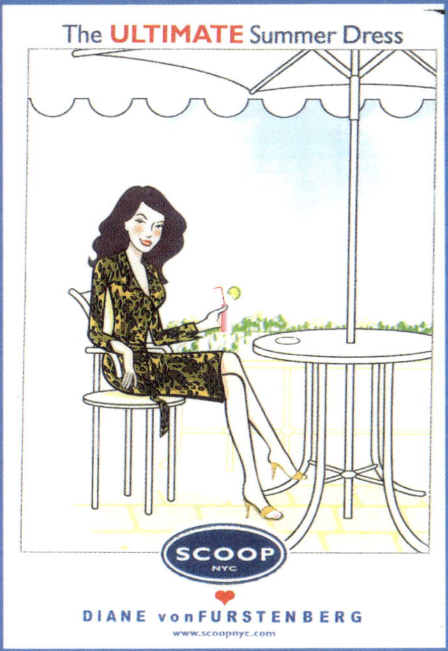
The ULTIMATE Summer Dress
SCOOP
NYC
DIANE vonFURSTENBERG
www.scoopnyc.com

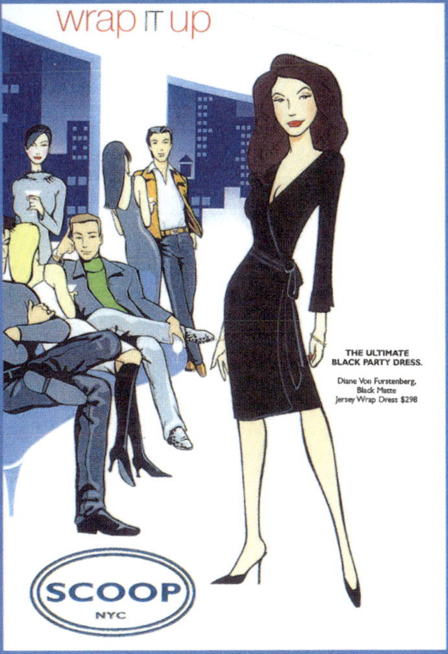
wrap IT up
THE ULTIMATE
BLACK PARTY DRESS.
Diane Von Furstenberg,
Black Matte
Jersey Wrap Dress $298
SCOOP
NYC

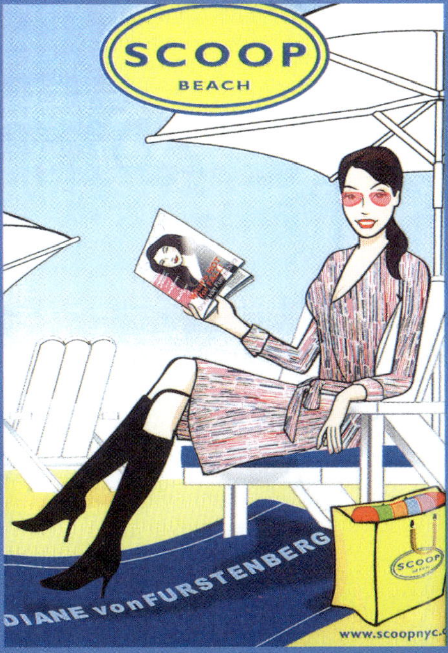
SCOOP
BEACH
DIANE vonFURSTENBERG
www.scoopnyc.c

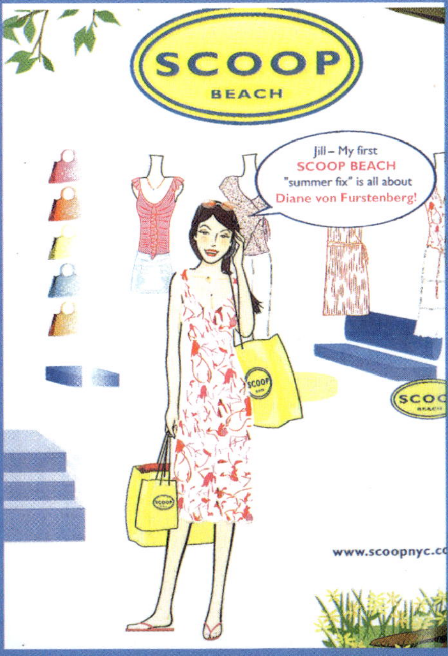
SCOOP
BEACH
Jill – My first
SCOOP BEACH
"summer fix" is all about
Diane von Furstenberg!
www.scoopnyc.c

How would you explain Diane von Furstenberg's great success?

Diane is a shrewd businesswoman. She is educated and immersed in all aspects of global culture. Diane has traveled, learned from, listened to, and been surrounded by people who have shaped our world. She is interested and interesting. She is a seeker, learner, teacher, and motivator. Diane is involved in every aspect of the business. She would set the design tone each season and drive the marketing vision and mission for the brand. DVF the woman is the brand. The brand represents all women.

Connecting to women from every corner of the world is what she loved. Diane's personal appearances and trunk shows in the stores are huge happenings and events. She listens to women, hears them, and understands them. Her true joy is the activation and empowerment of women. She says, "A successful brand is not delivered as a monologue." Diane remains in constant dialogue with the customer.

Opposite
Diane von Furstenberg in front of the Statue of Liberty in New York City, 2016.

Next page
Diane von Furstenberg superimposed on the Empire State Building, ca. 1980.

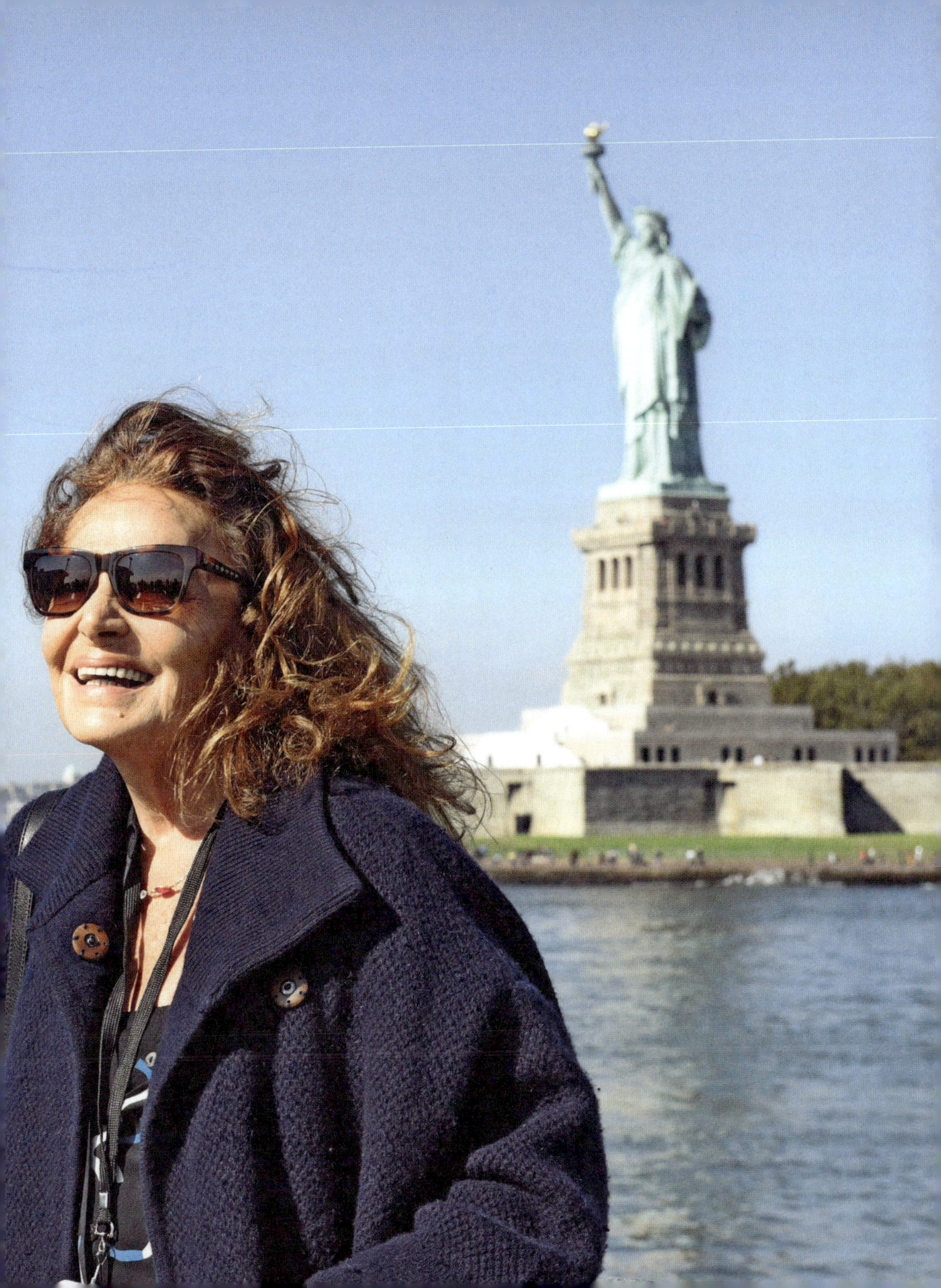

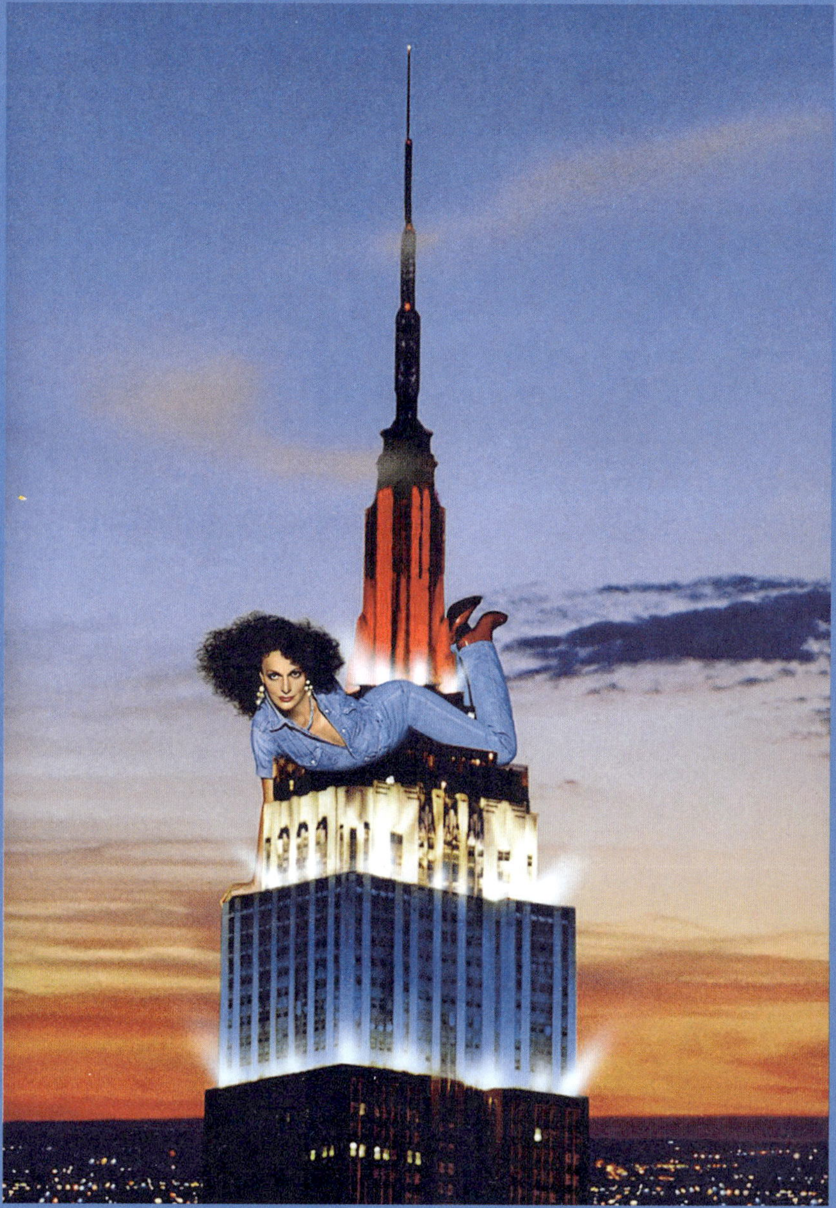

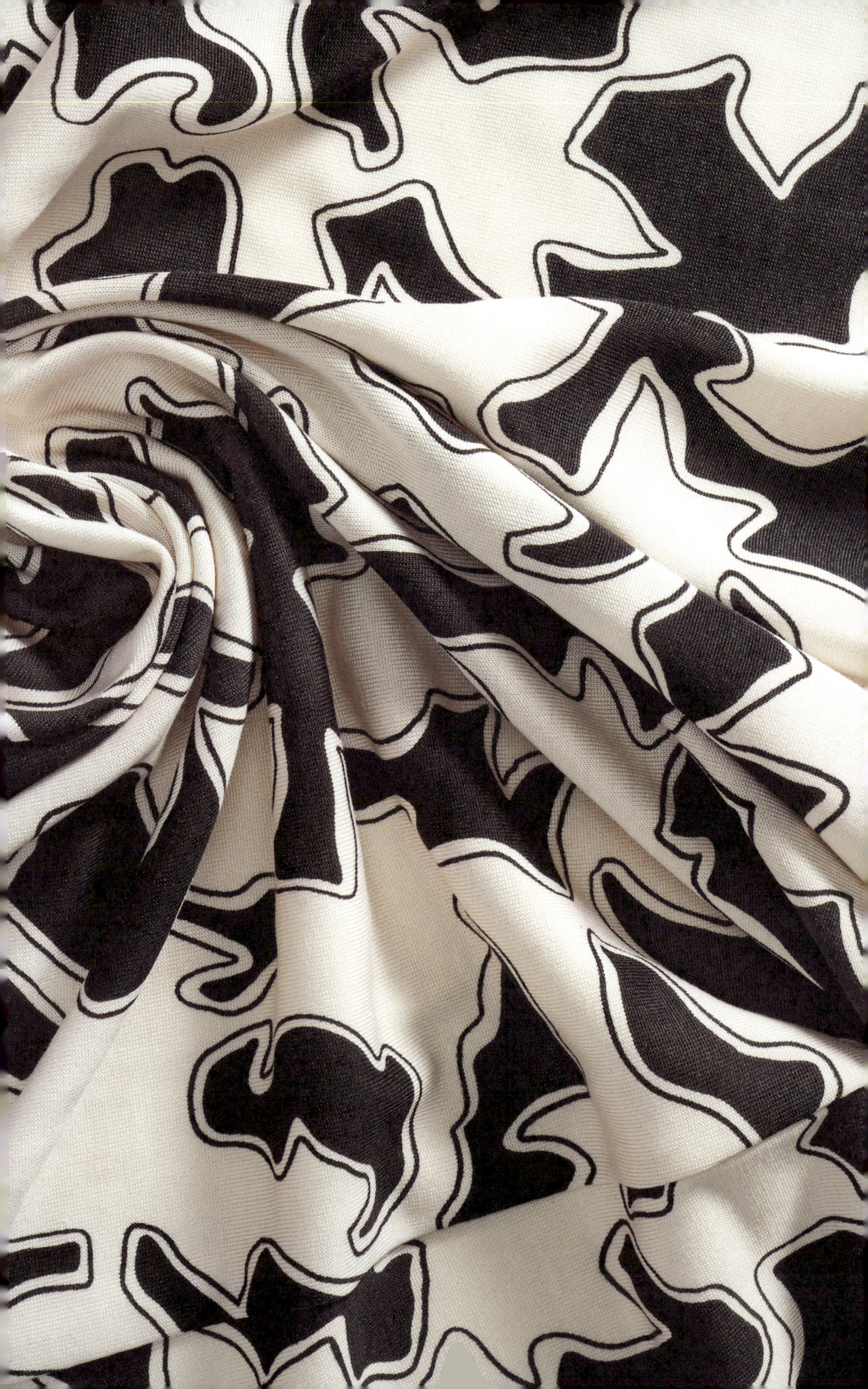

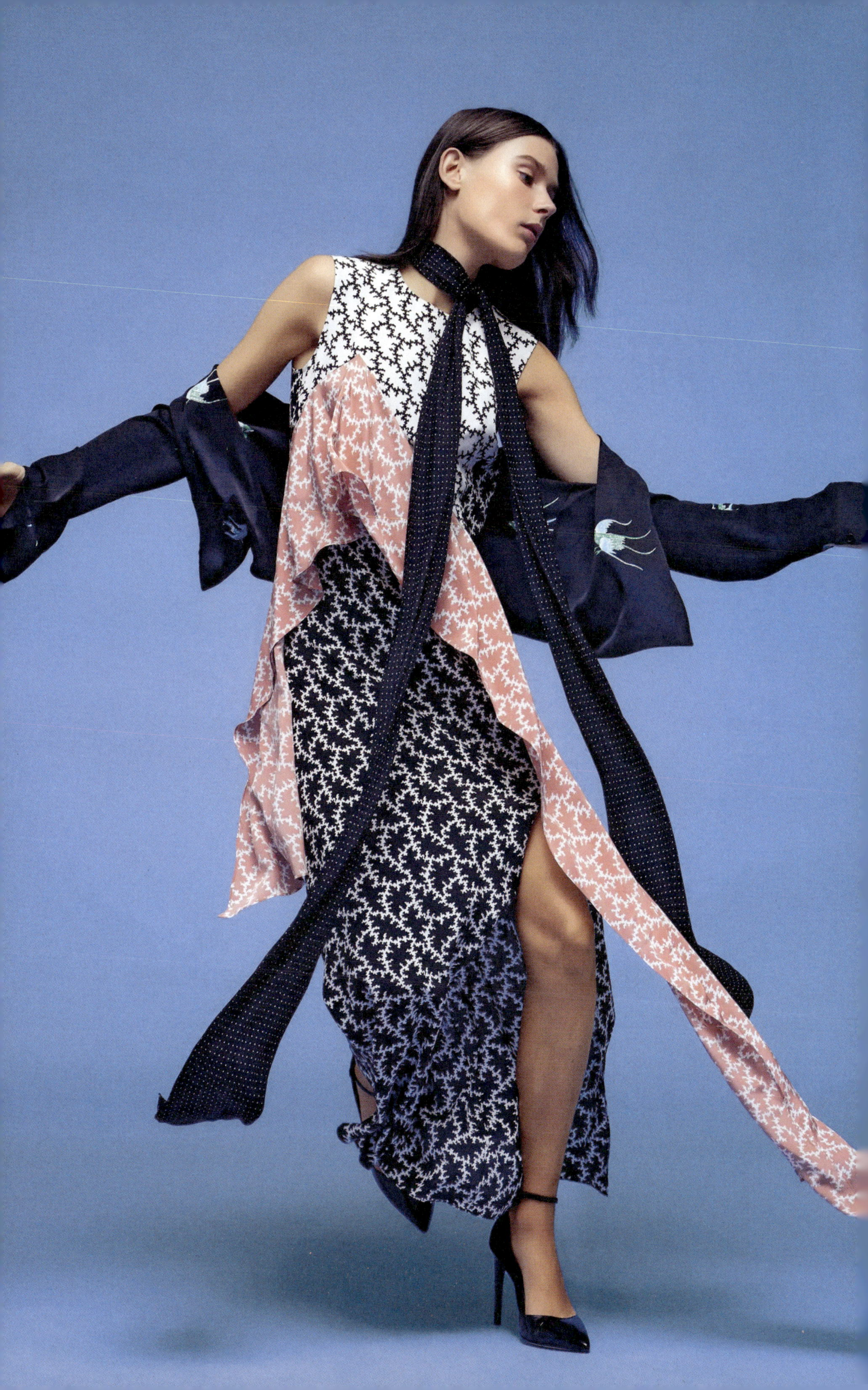

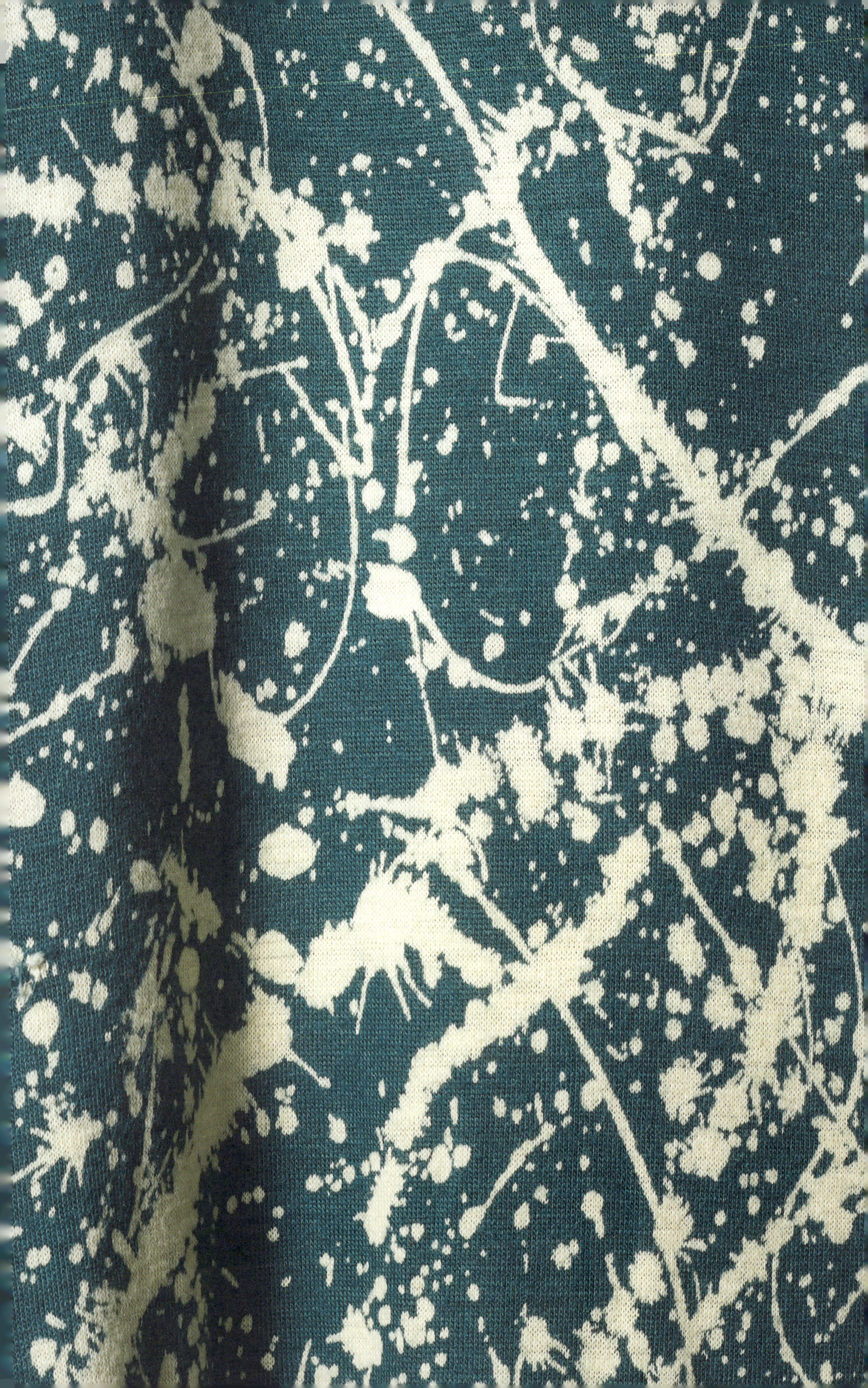

“

I came to America with a suitcase full of dresses and hope . . . thanks to the wrap dress I lived the **AMERICAN DREAM**.

”

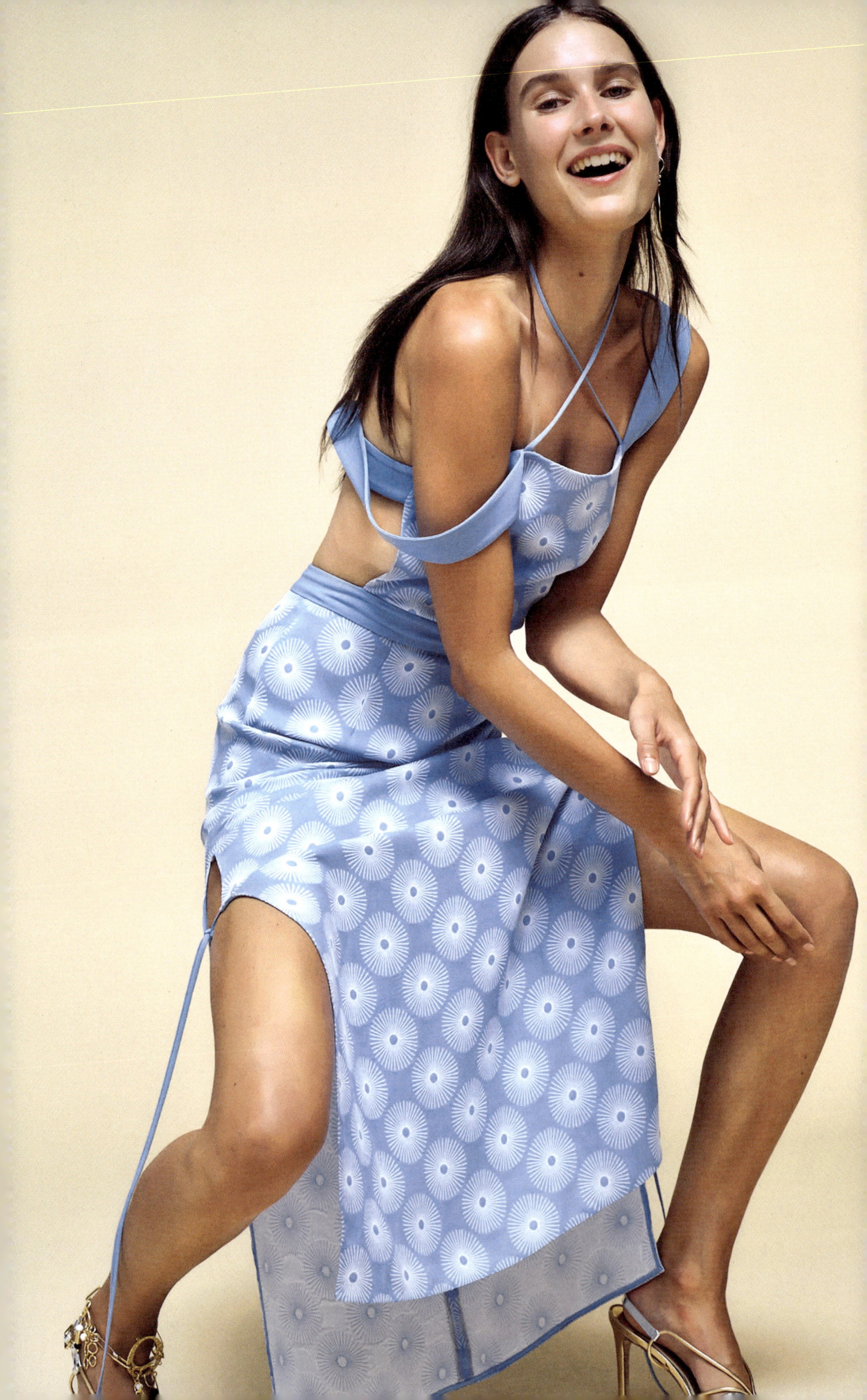

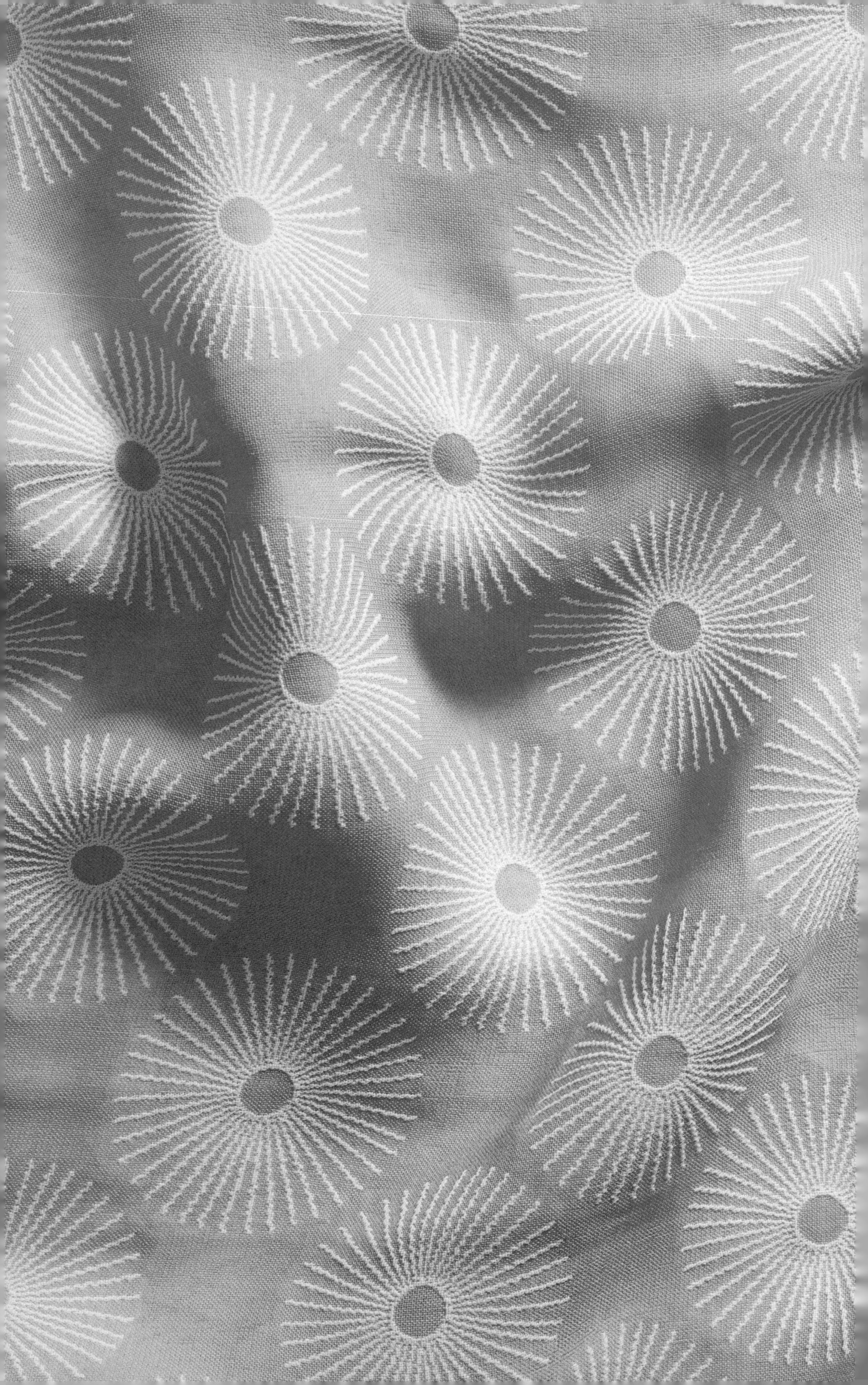

“*I was born in* **BELGIUM.**

Studied in **ENGLAND, SWITZERLAND,** *and* **SPAIN**

before I came to **AMERICA.**

I consider myself a citizen of the **WORLD.**”

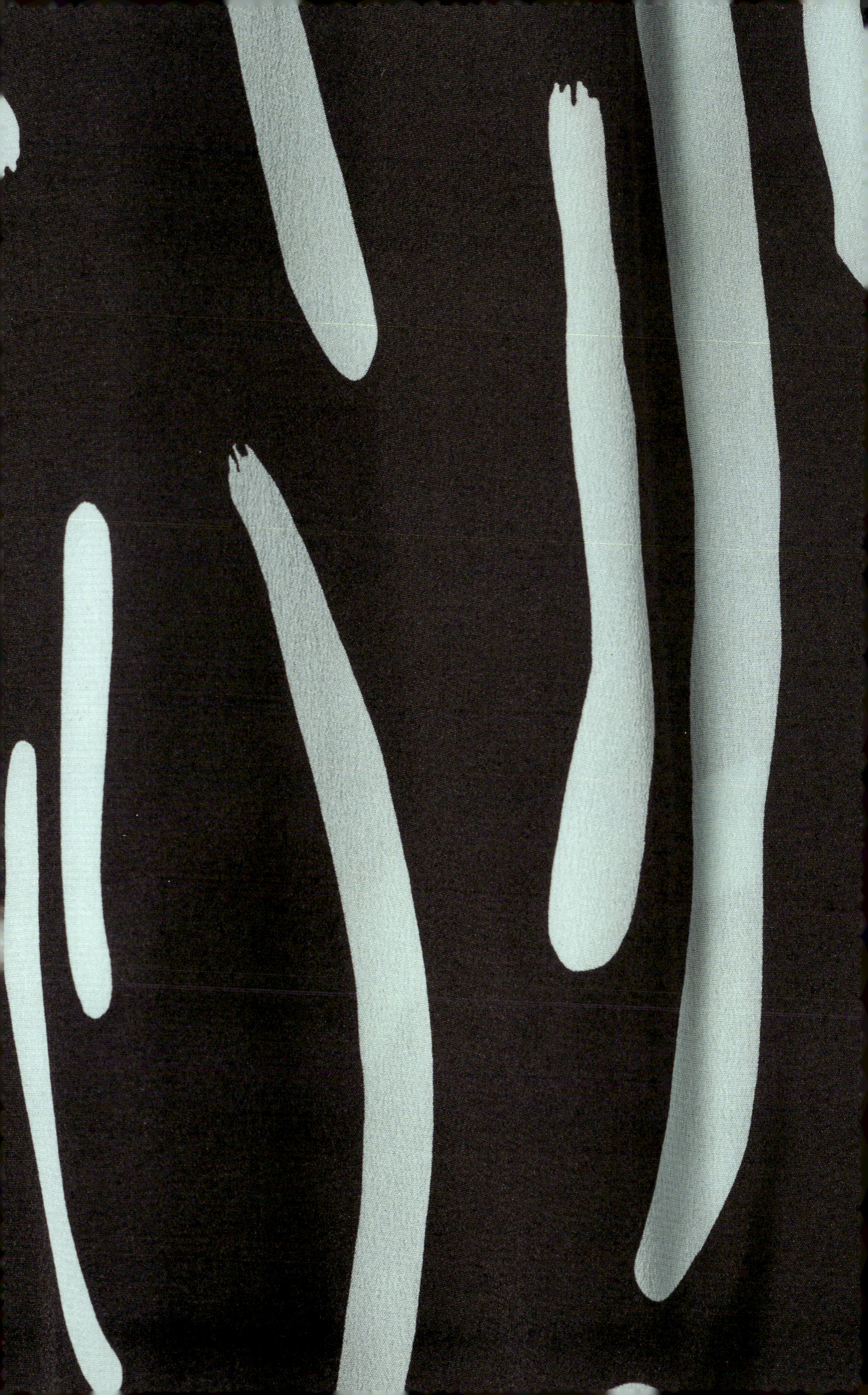

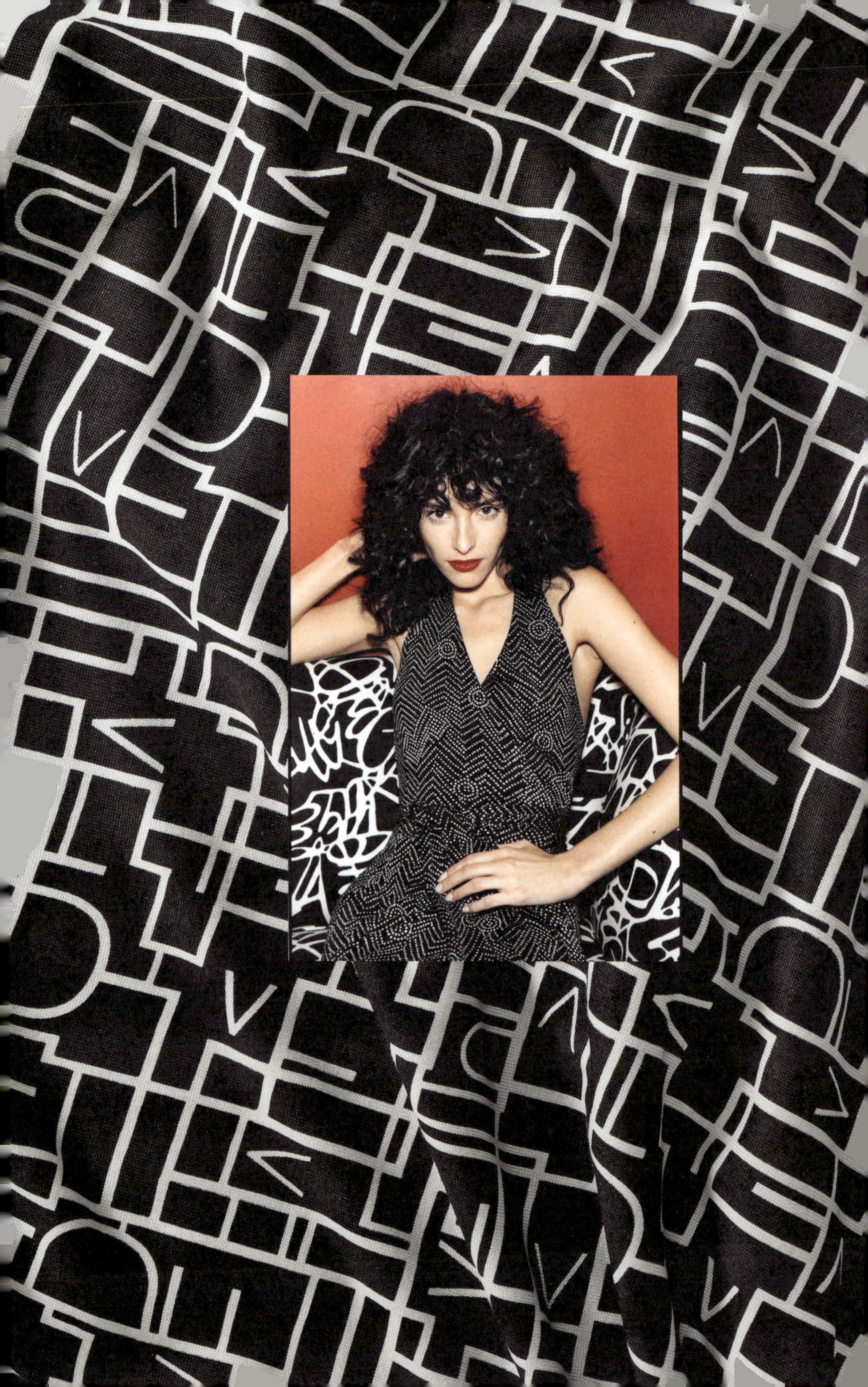

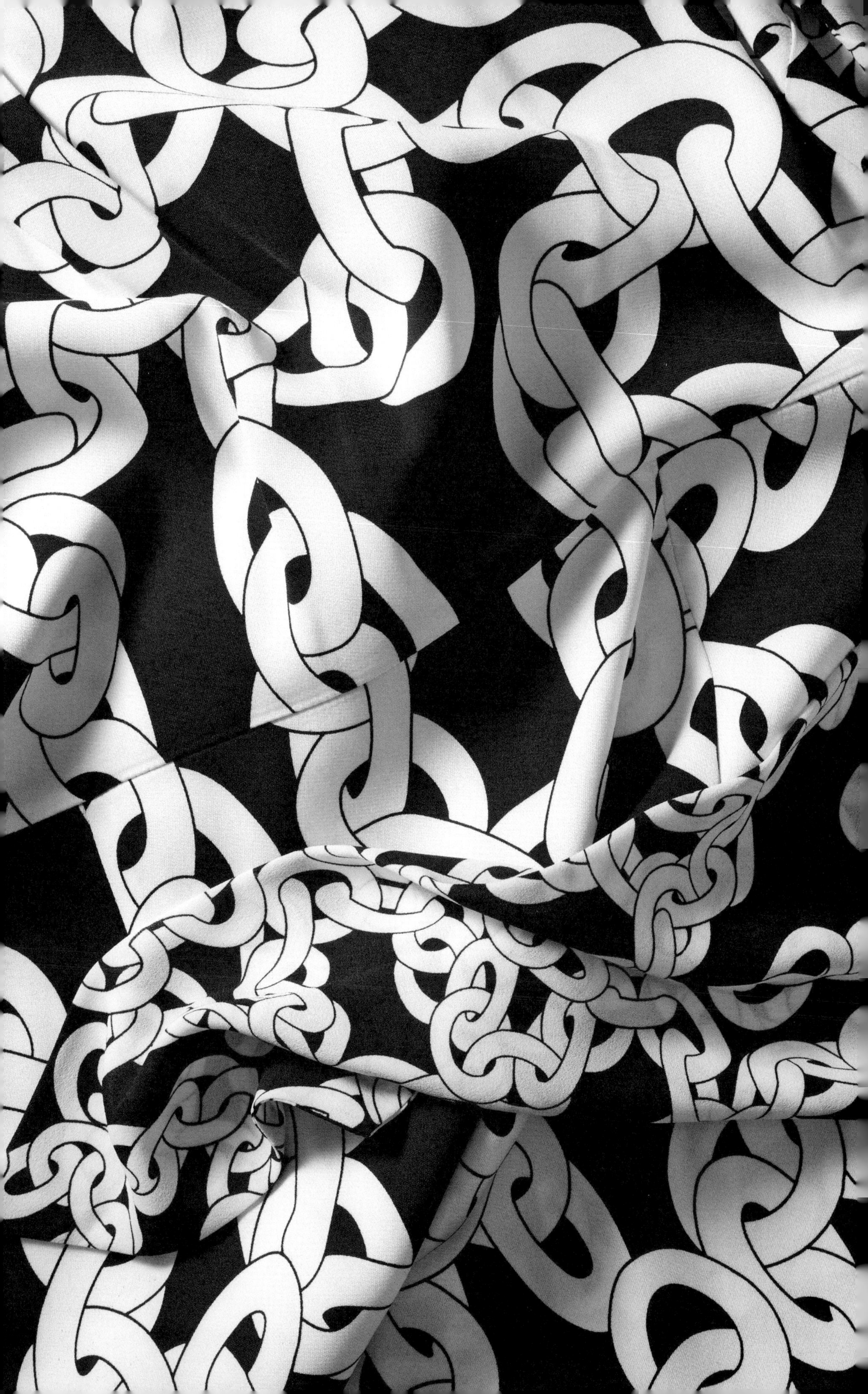

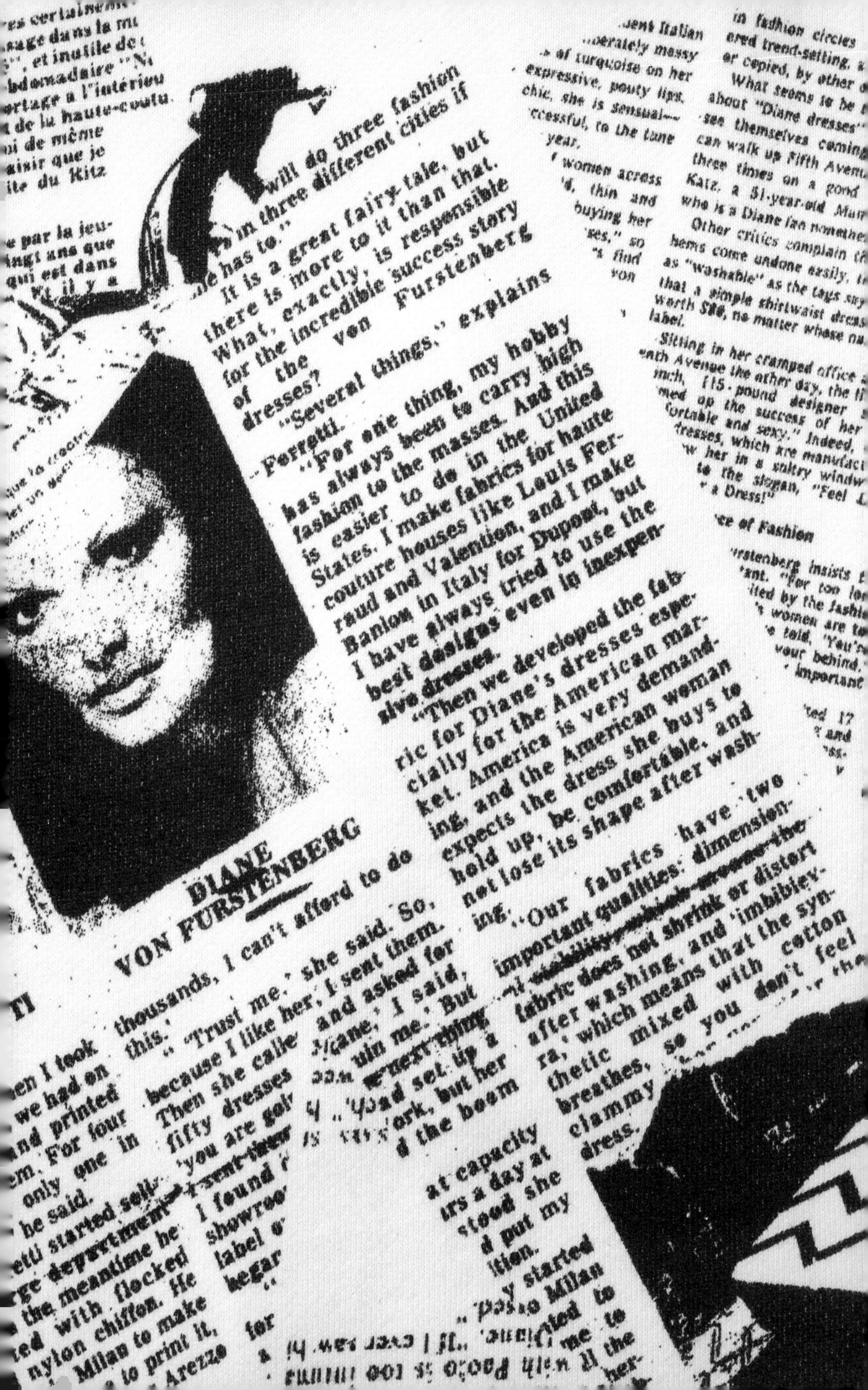

will do three fashion
in three different cities if
he has to."
It is a great fairy-tale, but
there is more to it than that.
What, exactly, is responsible
for the incredible success story
of the von Furstenberg
dresses?
"Several things," explains
Ferretti.
"For one thing, my hobby
has always been to carry high
fashion to the masses. And this
is easier to do in the United
States. I make fabrics for haute
couture houses like Louis Feraud and Valentino, and I make
Banlon in Italy for Dupont, but
I have always tried to use the
best designs even in inexpensive dresses.
"Then we developed the fabric for Diane's dresses especially for the American market. America is very demanding, and the American woman
expects the dress she buys to
hold up, be comfortable, and
not lose its shape after washing.
"Our fabrics have two
important qualities:
fabric does not shrink or distort
after washing, and
ra,' which means that the synthetic mixed with cotton
breathes, so you don't feel
clammy
dress.
DIANE
VON FURSTENBERG
thousands, I can't afford to do
this.'
"'Trust me,' she said. So,
because I like her, I sent them.
Then she called and asked for
fifty dresses

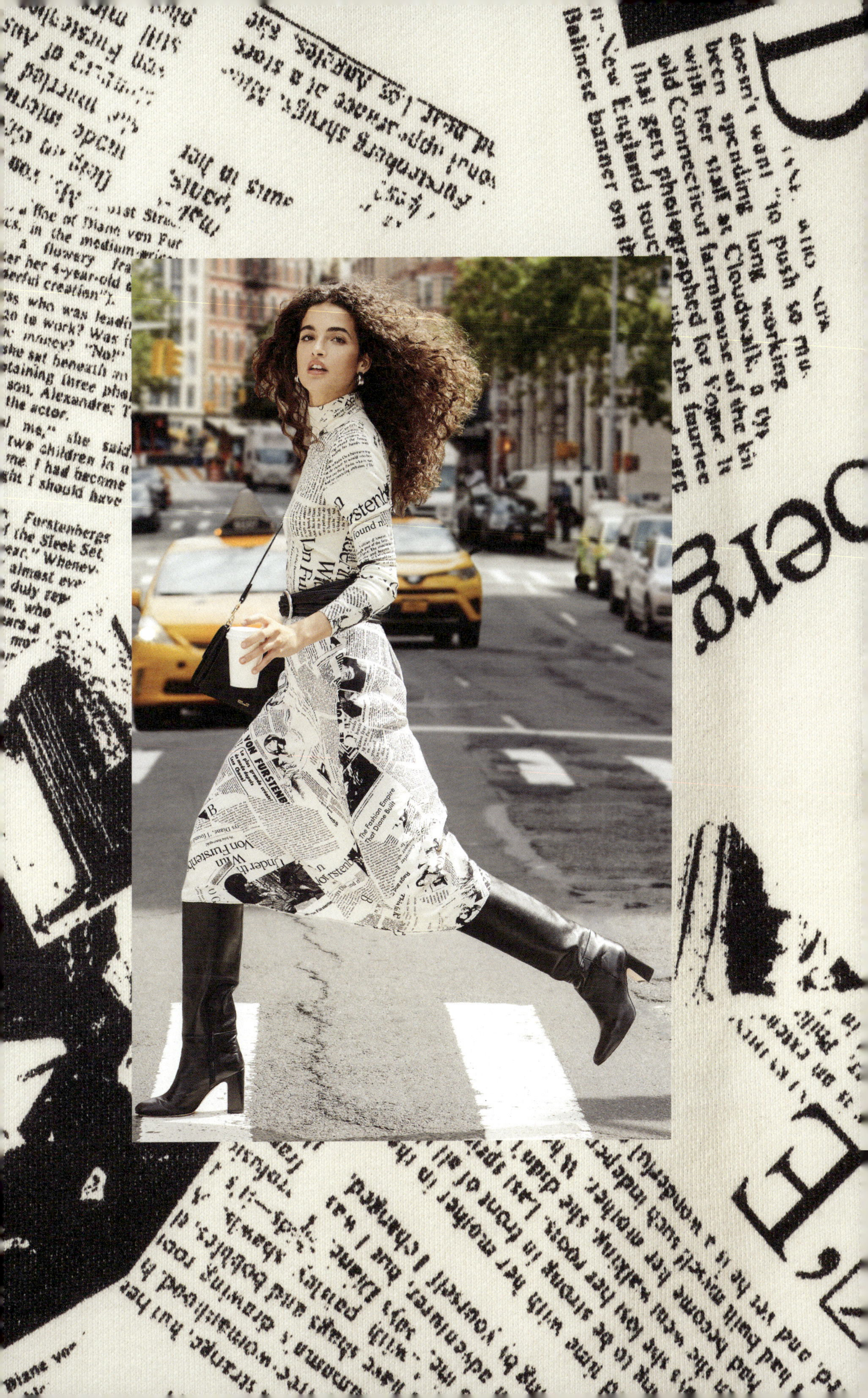

diane von furstenberg

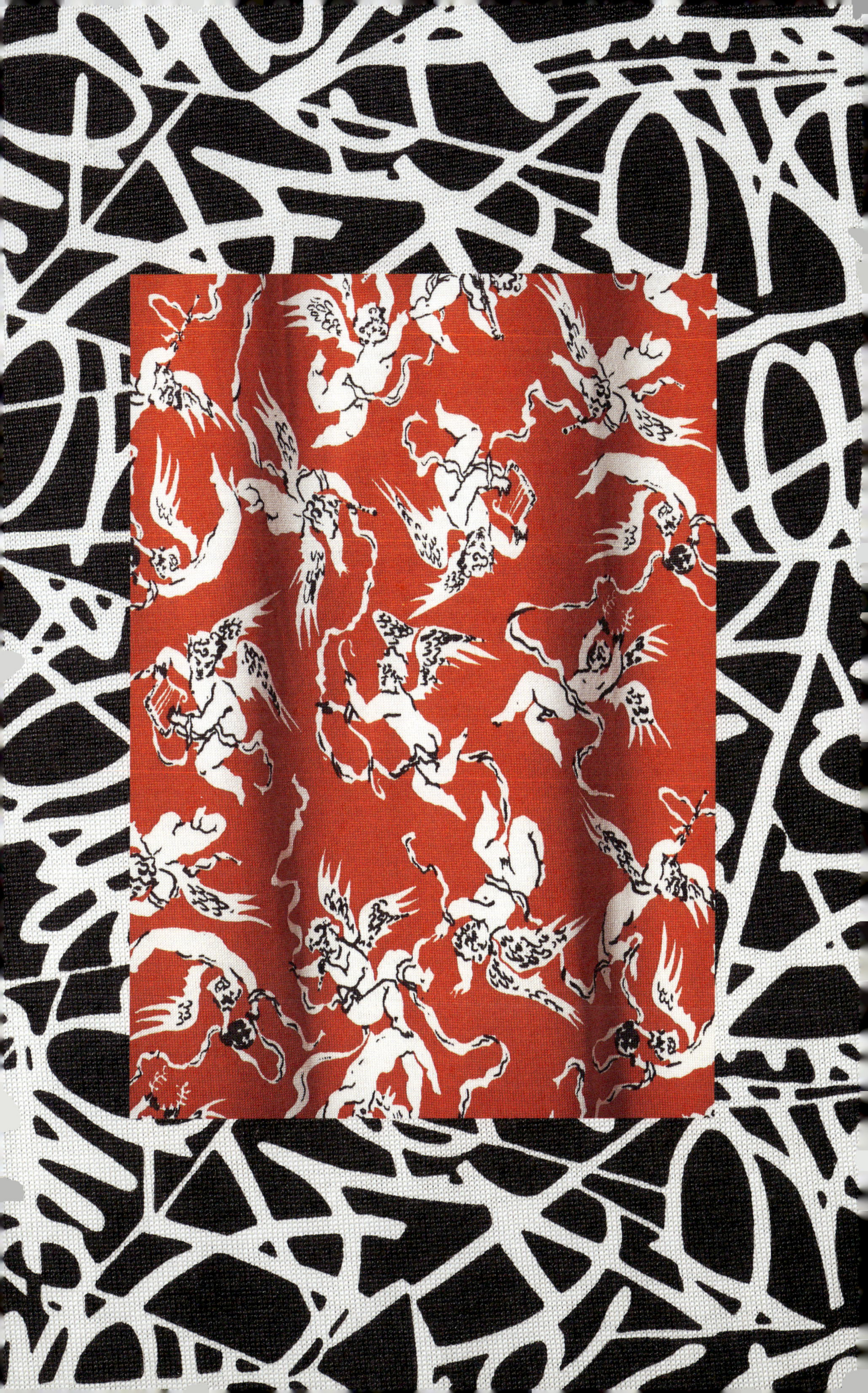

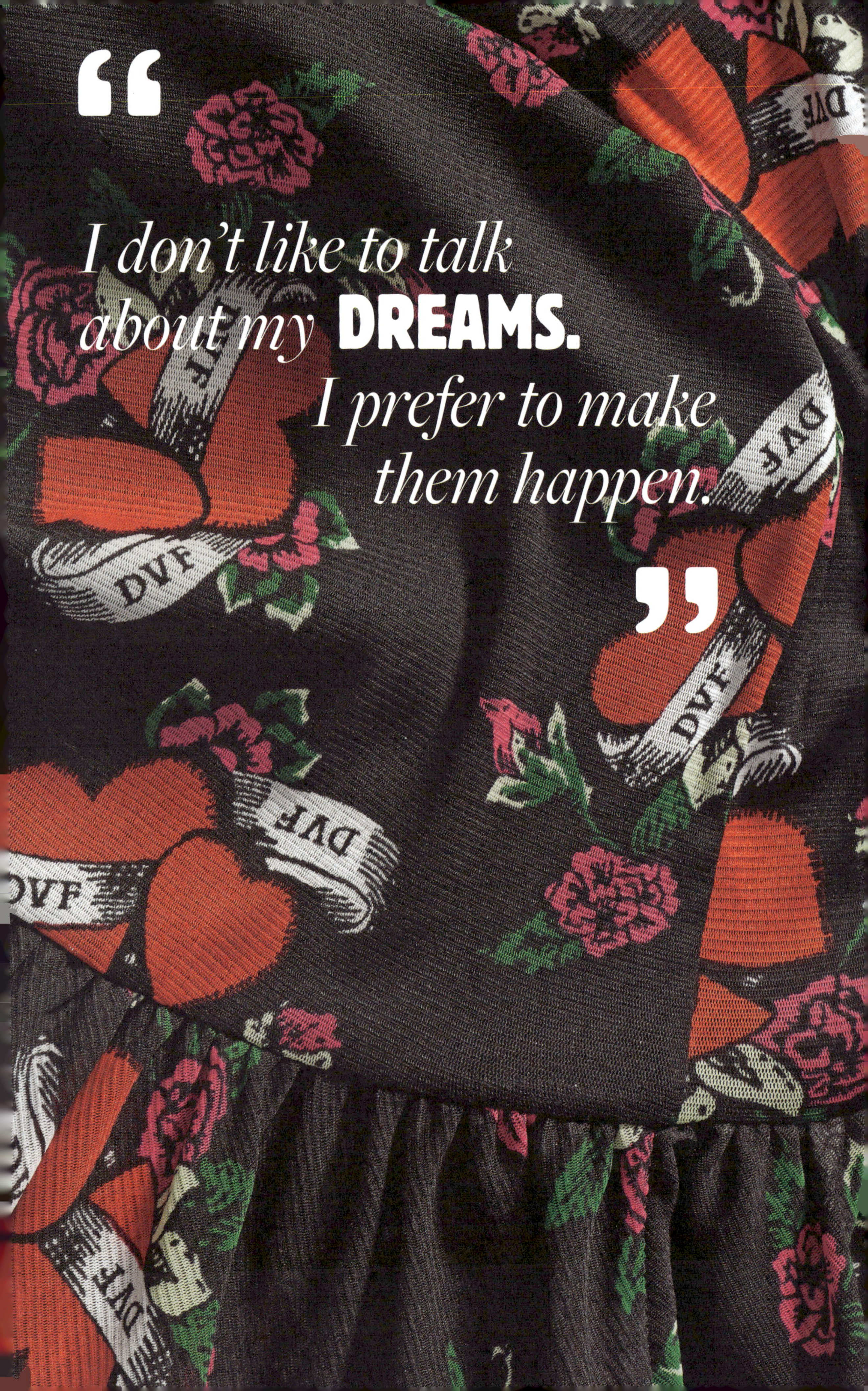

"I don't like to talk about my **DREAMS.** I prefer to make them happen."

03

WRITTEN BY
Alexis Romano

Designing the American Dream

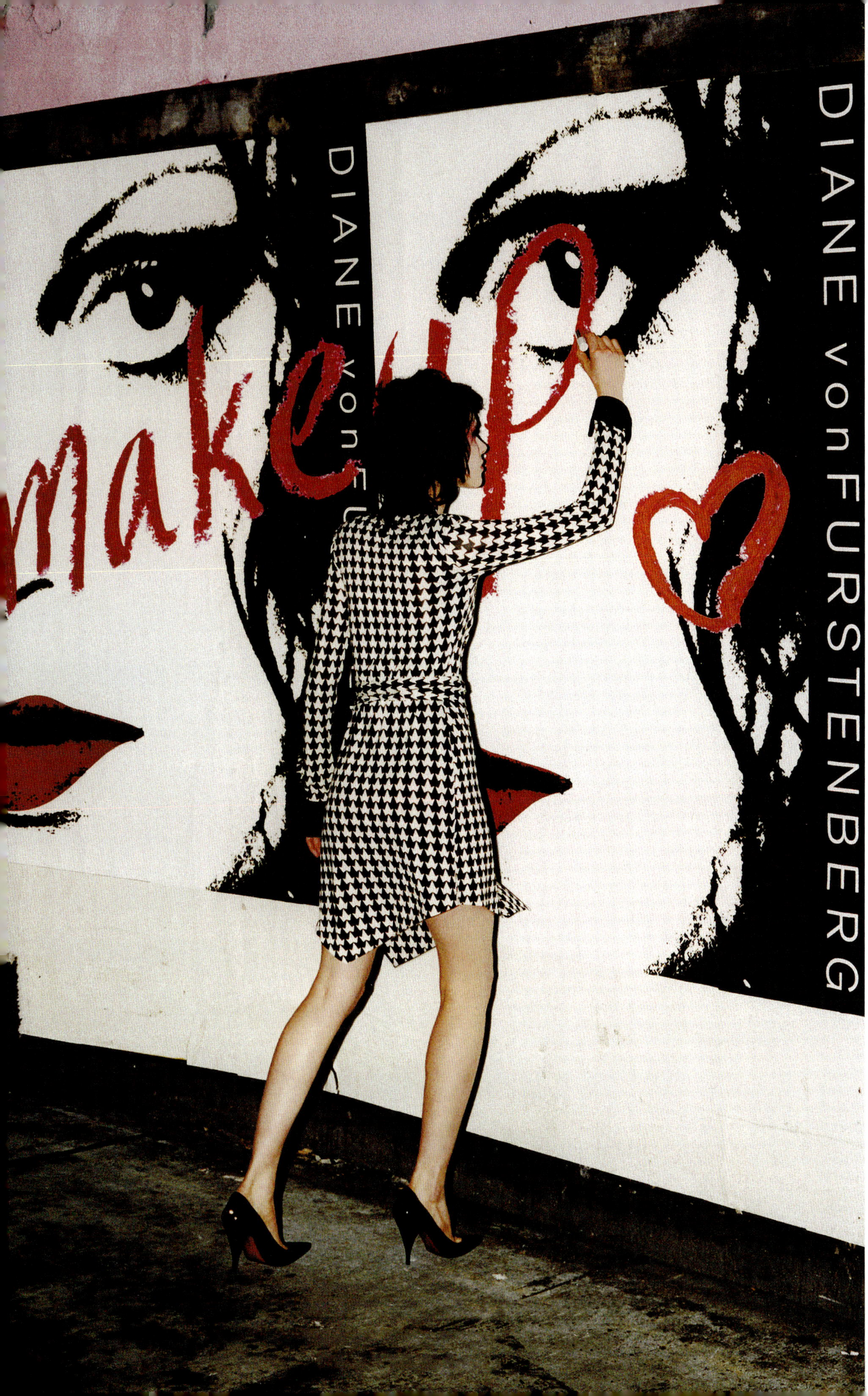

"When DVF arrived in America as a young Princess, she found a life of privilege. She became a world renown designer and used that privilege to lift up women all over the world."

EDWARD ENNINFUL

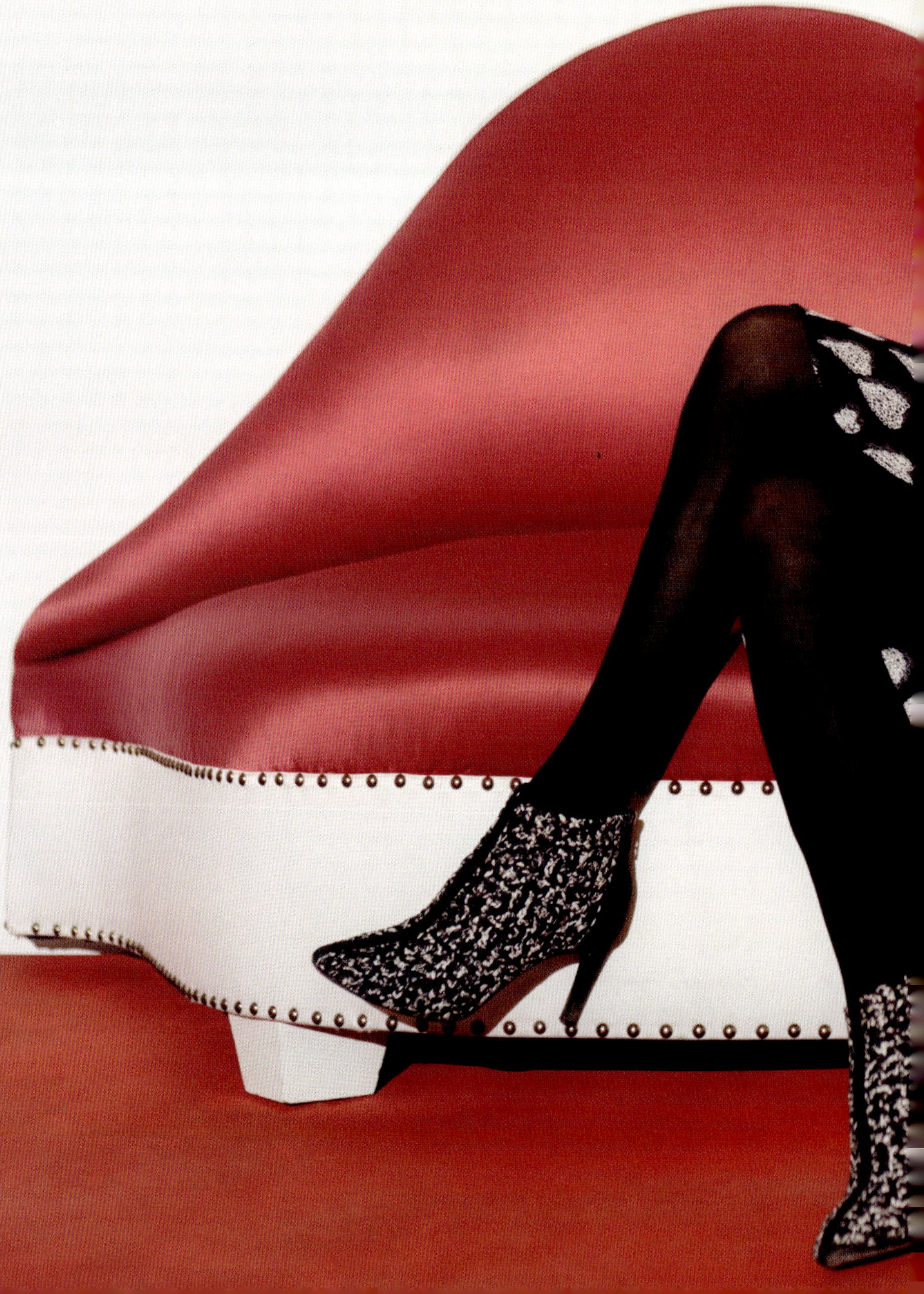

Previous page
Diane von Furstenberg 2003 advertisement campaign.

Diane von Furstenberg sitting on a Dali sofa, 2022.

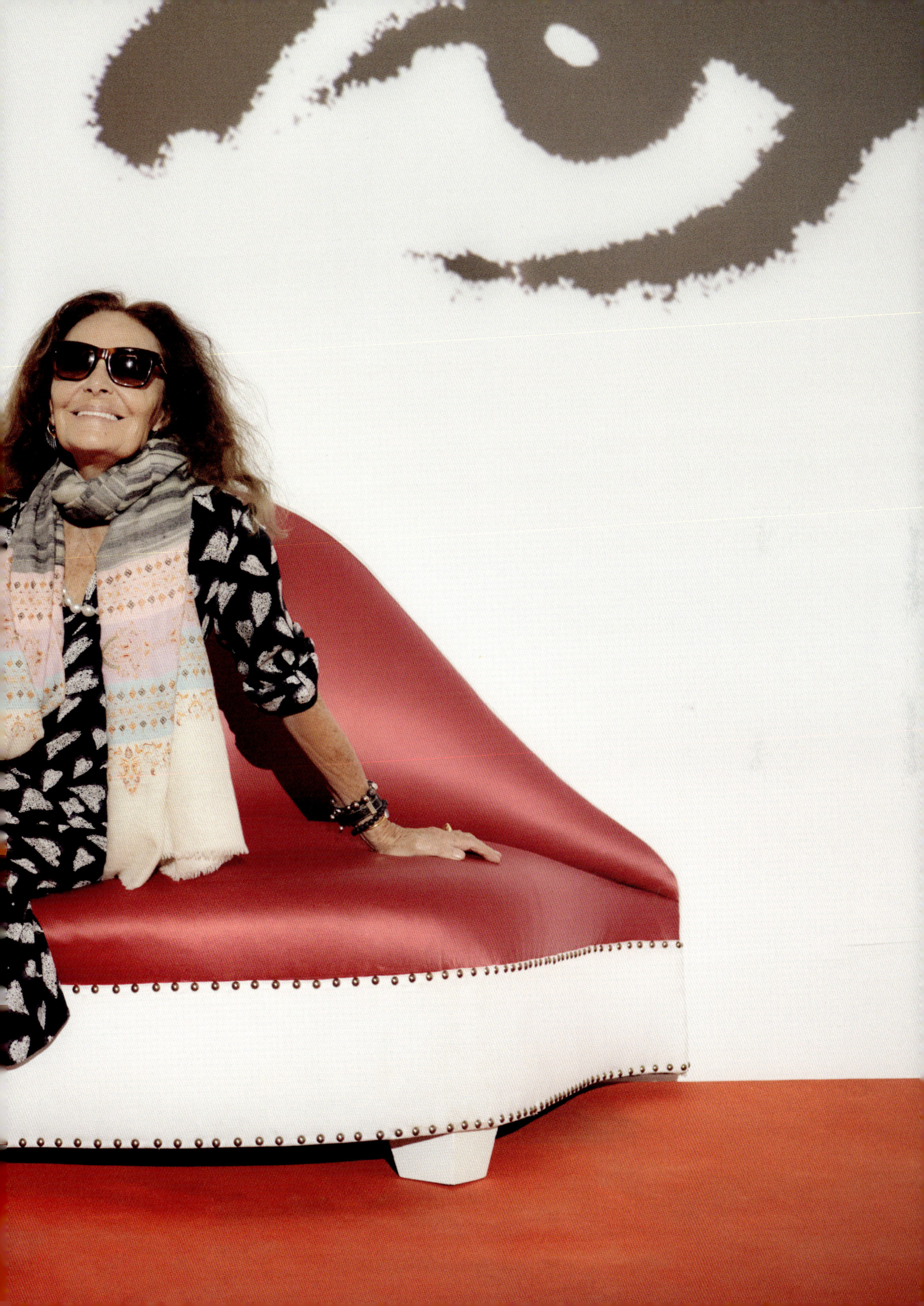

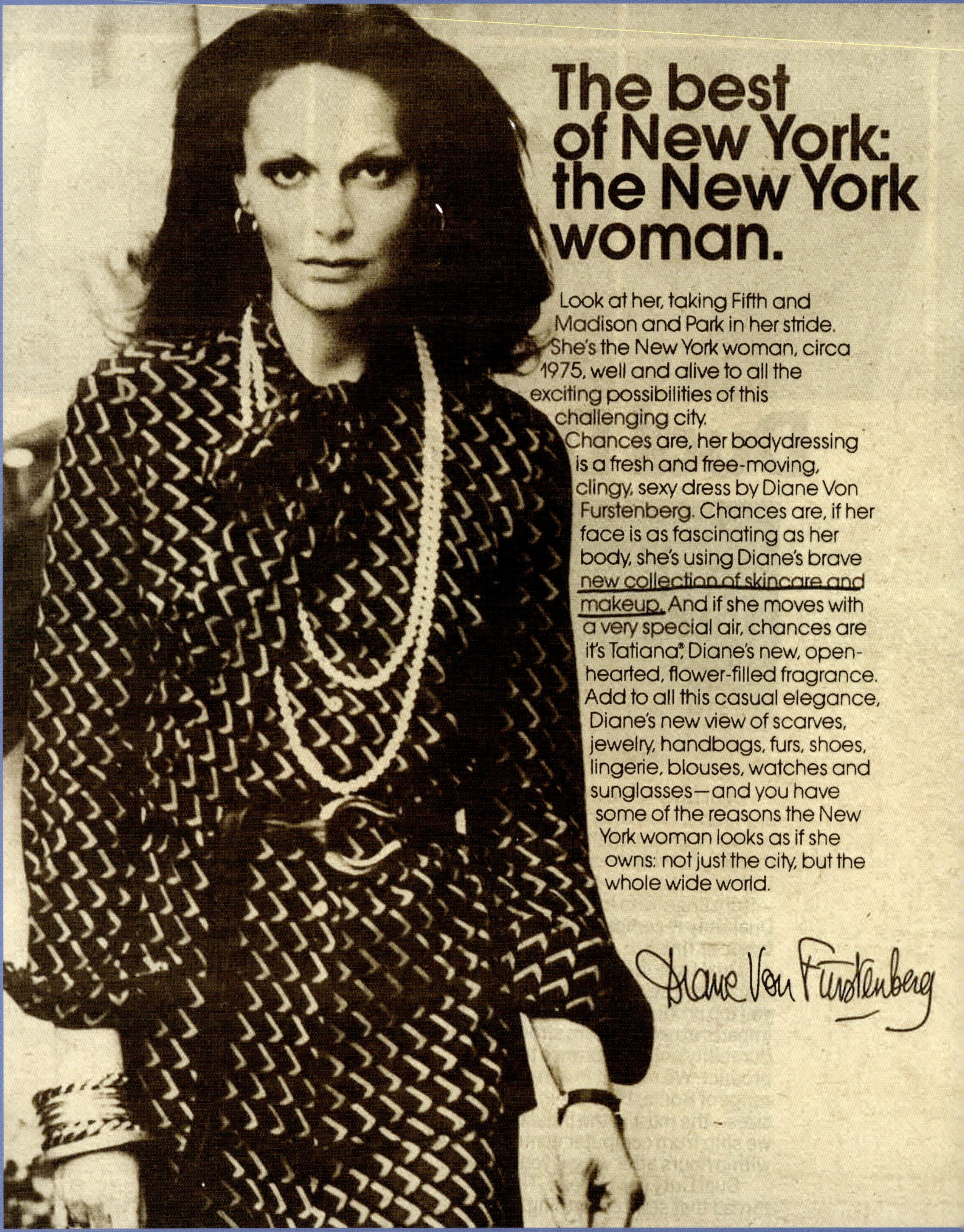
The best of New York: the New York woman.
Look at her, taking Fifth and Madison and Park in her stride. She's the New York woman, circa 1975, well and alive to all the exciting possibilities of this challenging city.
Chances are, her bodydressing is a fresh and free-moving, clingy, sexy dress by Diane Von Furstenberg. Chances are, if her face is as fascinating as her body, she's using Diane's brave new collection of skincare and makeup. And if she moves with a very special air, chances are it's Tatiana®, Diane's new, open-hearted, flower-filled fragrance. Add to all this casual elegance, Diane's new view of scarves, jewelry, handbags, furs, shoes, lingerie, blouses, watches and sunglasses—and you have some of the reasons the New York woman looks as if she owns: not just the city, but the whole wide world.
Diane Von Furstenberg

Designing the American Dream: Diane von Furstenberg's Career in 1970s New York

Opposite
"The Best of New York: The New York Woman" Diane von Furstenberg advertising campaign, 1975.

Next spread
Diane von Furstenberg poses with a Wonder Woman statuette, 2008.

"Look at her, taking Fifth and Madison and Park in her stride. She's the New York woman, circa 1975, well and alive to all the exciting possibilities of this challenging city. Chances are, her body dressing is a fresh and free-moving, clingy, sexy dress by Diane von Furstenberg."

The persona described in this 1975 advertisement was encapsulated by a model in a blouse-skirt ensemble—her professional polish achieved by the string of pearls and tied bow at her neck. Caught mid-step, she walks with purpose. As the text instructs readers to "look at her," she returns their gaze, staring dramatically into the camera lens. The reflective gaze conflates model and viewer, who also becomes the glamorous urbanite, taking possession of New York's streets, though the city was hardly visible in the image. Many viewers of this ad would have recognized the model, the designer Diane von Furstenberg herself, whose likeness was central to her brand. This made the above persona all the more real for clients to buy into. Laid bare before her public, the ad copy captures von Furstenberg's own New York success story and her identity as a fashionable, confident, and independent American woman. Movement was a key component of this experience—physical movement enabled through dress, which translated into a readiness to react to whatever was in store as she faced the unknown, inventing her path forward.

From a privileged European background, a young von Furstenberg came to New York City in 1969, determined to stay in the city that represented modernity and possibility for her. Prior to this, she worked for a Paris photography agency, where she was introduced to the workings and ambiance of the fashion industry and image-making. She later recounted, "It was a lot of fun, but my dream was to go to America. America was having its own problems in 1968, but to me, it seemed full of hope. Students were pressing for civil rights for minorities and women and protesting the Vietnam War. America was the new world where anything was possible."[1]

Seizing this spirit, von Furstenberg saw her entrance via the portal of fashion. In 1971, the US womenswear industry was valued at more than $13 billion wholesale.[2] However, von Furstenberg entered the industry during a precarious moment, with manufacturing and retail fluctuating alongside an inflation-laden economy. She learned to maneuver the tools of publicity and merchandising to stand out in a competitive arena of well-known designers and womenswear firms. Her major contribution—the wraparound dress—had staying power during the 1970s, a period of social and political tumult, and still signifies today. She described this period of her life as "The American Dream": the 1970s launch of her career, including her product development, marketing style, and wholesale approach. In these areas, she was a "conduit," conveying ideas to clients, largely based on her own story, through words, images, and fabric.[3]

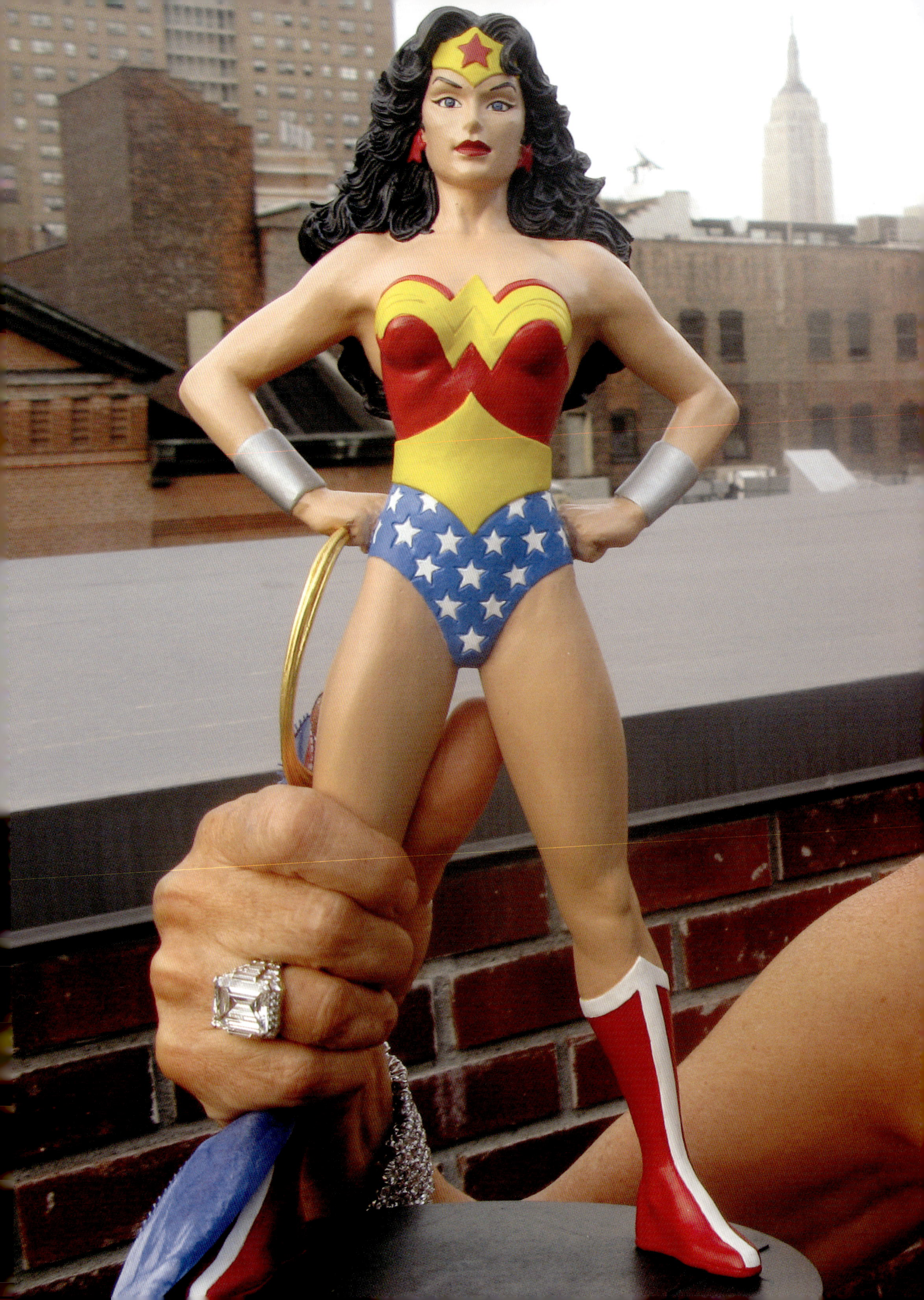

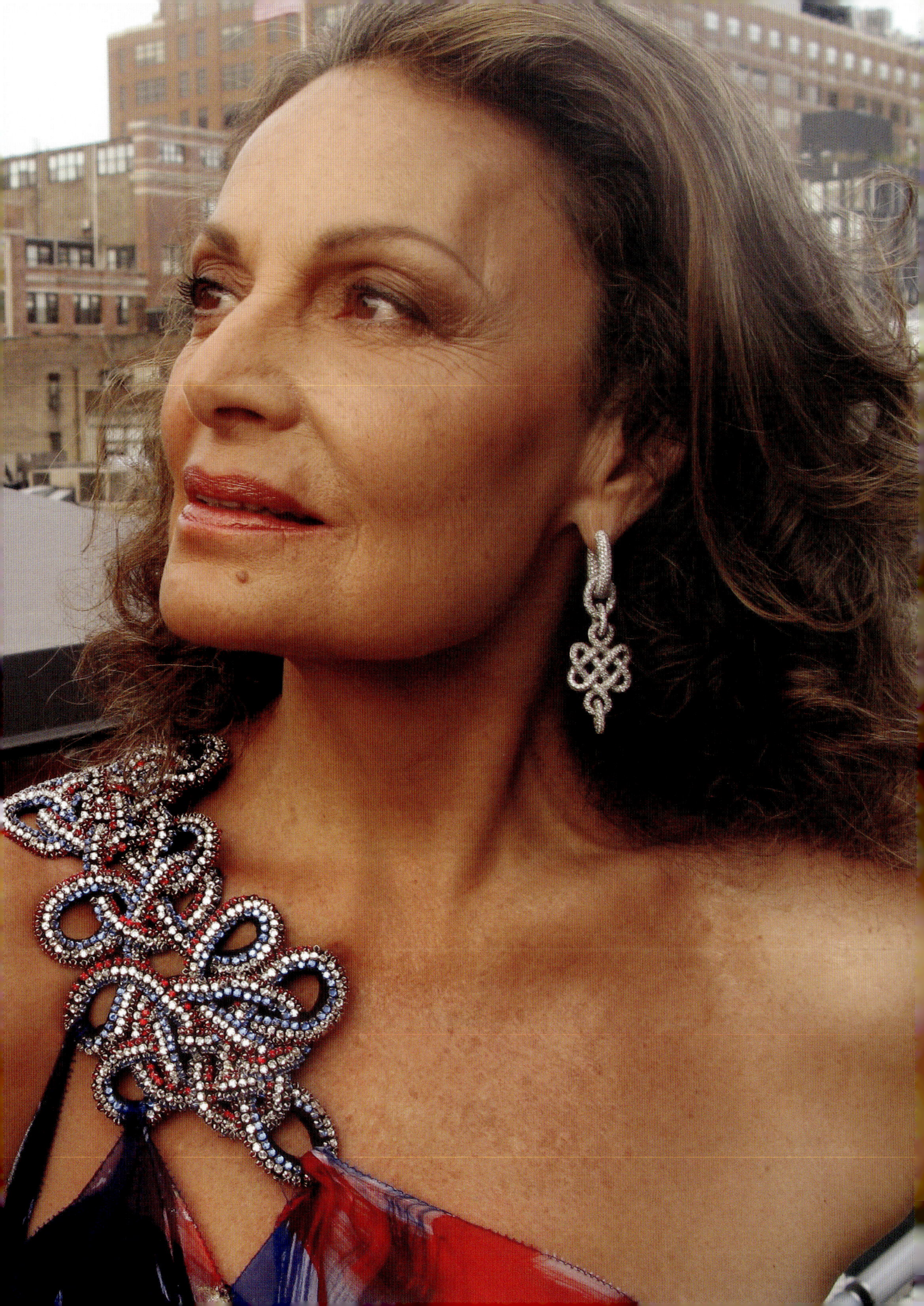

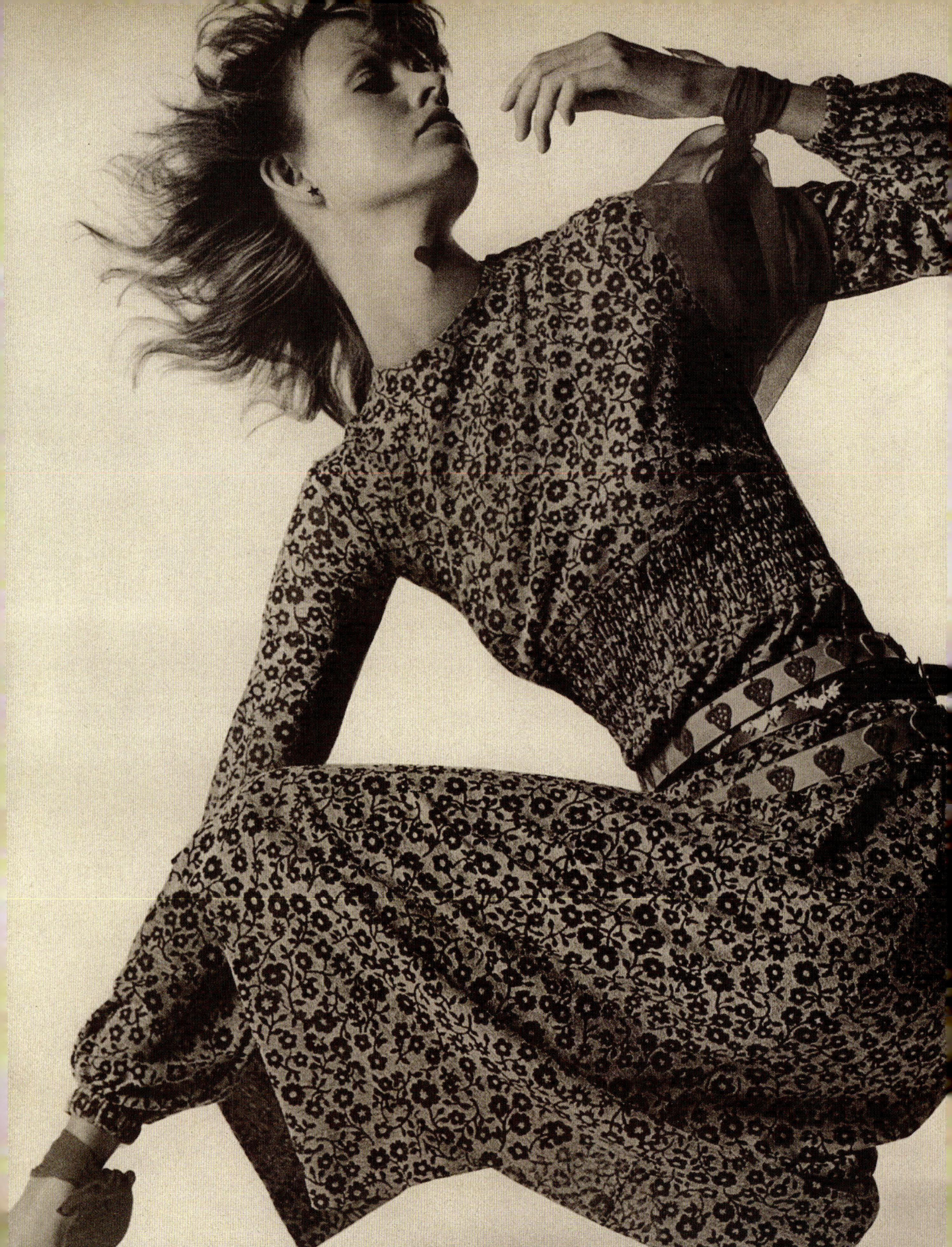

$100 and you're in violets, this page, acres and acres of them covering a pale-violet midi elasticized at the wide waistband and cuffs. With narrow strawberry and flower belts to hold it over matching pants. Turnout by Diane von Fürstenberg. Of cotton. At Bloom-

SEVENTH AVENUE IN THE 1970s: "HOW TO SUCCEED WITH A DRESS" [4]

When von Furstenberg came to the United States, the fashion industry was producing high volumes of products. "All the clothes we saw, however, were either hippie, designer, or drip-dry polyester," recalls von Furstenberg. "There was nothing in between, and I sensed an opportunity."[5] These ideas aligned with those of the Fashion Group, who described "The changing consumer" as a measured yet sophisticated woman in a 1971 *FGI Bulletin*: "Gidget is gone. The Youthquake girl of the 60s. Replaced by the woman of the 70s. A member of the fast-growing 20—34-year-old group. Married and a working woman who's already changing the composition of the American working force."[6]

Below
Models walk the Diane von Furstenberg Fall 1976 runway in leopard print dresses.

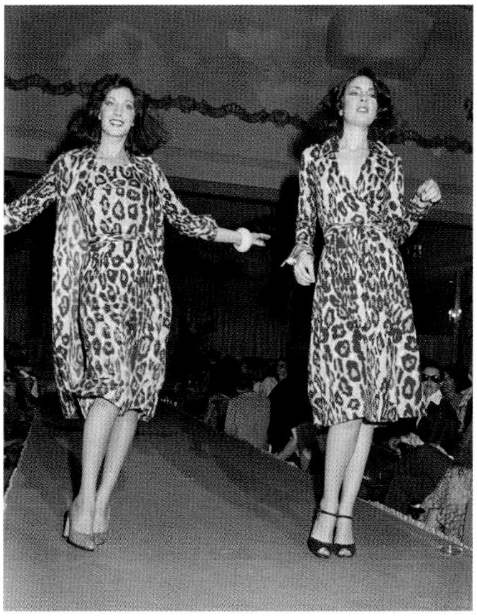

Informed by the jersey creations of American designers Stephen Burrows, Giorgio di Sant'Angelo, and Halston, along with the cotton T-shirts in vibrant prints and everyday dresses she had seen in Europe, von Furstenberg sought to negotiate the values of quality, price, and style, not to mention the various pulls of womanhood, which were not dissimilar to the Fashion Group's consumer forecast. Vital was the knowledge that she acquired about jersey, printing on knitwear, and designing with prints at Angelo Ferretti's factories outside of Como, Italy. She brought garments made from Ferretti's fabric back to New York: a T-shirt dress, a shirtdress, a long tented dress, and a tunic with pants—her vision for the 1970s American "professional" womenswear market.

After *Vogue* editor Diana Vreeland saw her garments, von Furstenberg made her debut in the magazine in 1970, offering visibility and authenticating her position as a designer. These examples illustrated the "language of color and print" that would be a mainstay in her work, including a tunic covered in a pattern of violets over matching pants, adorned with elasticized decoration and belts. That year, she made her first sales after a show at the Gotham Hotel in New York City, following advice to list her name in the Fashion Calendar, another vital gateway into the New York fashion industry.

Opposite
A model poses in a Diane von Furstenberg early design, 1970.

Still, combing through the many companies in New York's Garment District to be taken in as a division proved unsuccessful so she established her own business and Seventh Avenue showroom with entrepreneur Richard Conrad in 1972. A metaphor for the young and determined brand might be read in the expression of model Pat Cleveland, who also launched her career at that time, photographed by Irving Penn in 1972 for *Vogue*.

Clad in a shirtdress by von Furstenberg with an allover chain-link pattern, Cleveland was future facing: she looked outward in anticipation, as though to mimic von Furstenberg's own aspirations. She used the dress to access the American industry, where everything was unknown and necessitated invention.

Opposite
Model Pat Cleveland poses in a Diane von Furstenberg chainlink print dress, 1972.

That same year, von Furstenberg conceptualized the design that would propel her company to the forefront of the industry: the wraparound dress. The first came out in 1973 in a wood-grain print, an evolution of her wrap top and skirt ensemble developed with the patternmaker Bruna Sequalino and designer Susanna Feinberg at the Ferretti factory.

The garment's simple construction was ideal for "assembly line" production, with workers separately fabricating panels, sleeves, collars, and cuffs until the whole could be assembled. The first and most popular was the T/72, a fashion Model T. Fitted around the chest and arms, and tied to emphasize the waist and V-neck, the design featured a full skirt that allowed for easy movement. The variety of motifs available lent the design an infinite scope. It was a surface upon which von Furstenberg could test her "language" of color, print, fabric, and silhouette, through which she constructed sentences to tell a story.[7]

The effects of von Furstenberg's structuralist approach were borne out on the body and the wearer's psyche: prints inspired by the outside world only functioned in movement, on a body in motion; and the way the jersey draped over it and felt on, incited confidence in mind and body language. This was a modernist undertaking: simple, good design to fit a wide number of body types, budgets, and activities—whether professional or leisure, daytime or evening.

The garment's adaptability was widely propagated in the press, including a 1974 article that described the "simple jersey dresses being worn by all ages and figures," due to their style, motifs, and price, which between $70 and $90, was aspirational yet (relatively) accessible.[8] Journalist Pat Collins lent "real life" commentary, modeling the wrap in 1976 in *Harper's Bazaar*. "I wear lots of easy jersey dresses like this on my afternoon talk show," Collins explained to readers. "They hold up so well—won't wrinkle or be too hot under the TV lights. I'd probably wear this with a scarf for the show, then take off the scarf and change my jewelry and go out for the evening."[9]

As such, the wrap dress conformed to the long-standing ideology of twentieth-century American sportswear. Scholars such as Rebecca Arnold have connected sportswear's practical garments with innovative yet seemingly simple construction to the shaping of a modern, active femininity.[10] Indeed, wrapping was a part of an established design language, illustrated in the work of designers—notably, Claire McCardell—from the 1930s onward. von Furstenberg reinvigorated this style in a new historical context, remapping the arena of women designers. Publications such as *Women's Wear Daily* enable fashion's real and symbolic mapping, and a 1973 issue showed her wrap, illustrated by Stephen Cervantes, alongside one by the veteran sportswear designer Vera Maxwell, in the column "The Best of New York."

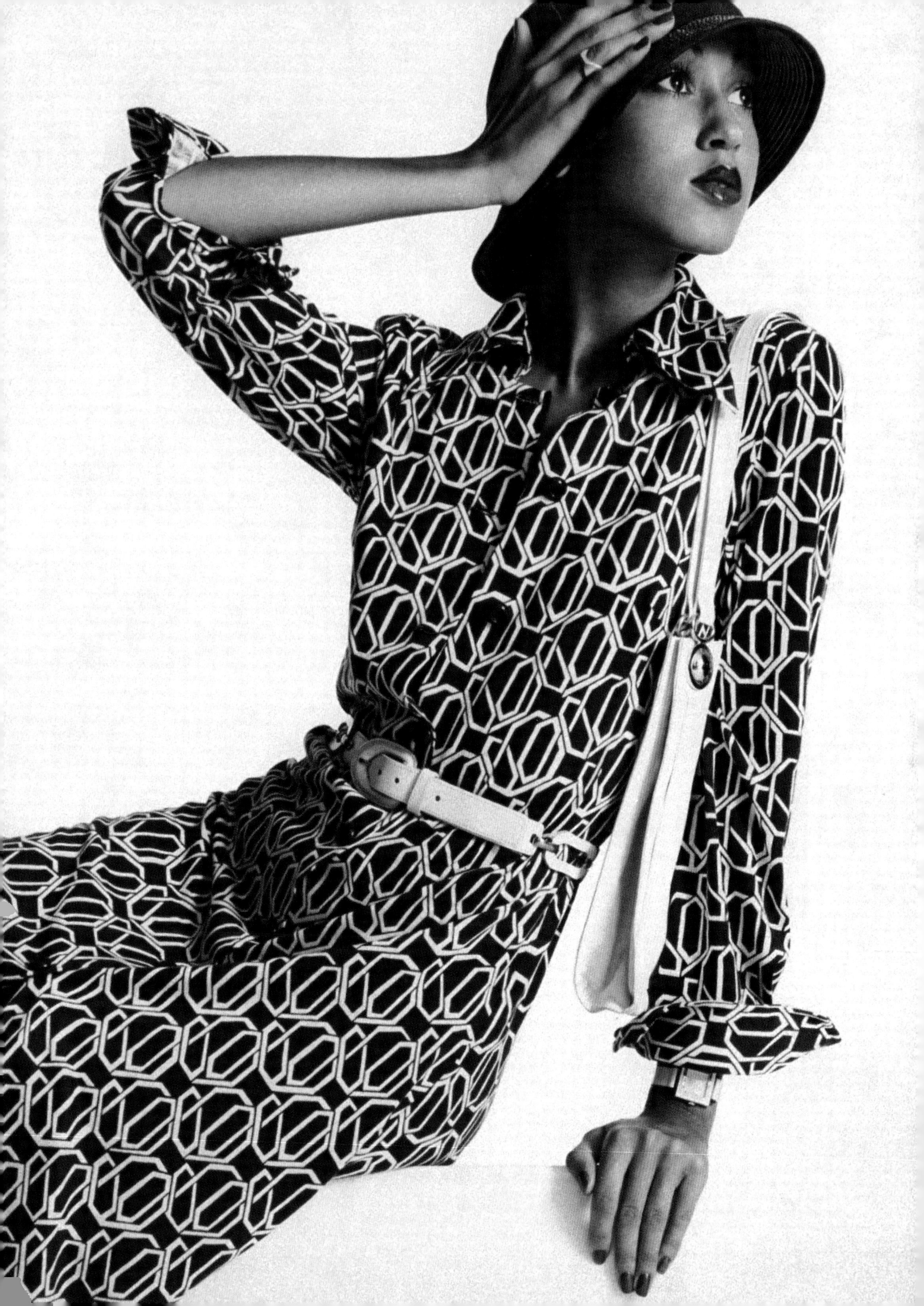

Opposite
Stills from Martin Scorsese's 1976 film *Taxi Driver*, starring Robert de Niro and Cybill Shepherd. Shepherd wears a Diane von Furstenberg wrap dress in several scenes in the film.

Next spread
(top left)
A 1977 Kreeger's New Orleans advertisement for Diane von Furstenberg lines and show.

(top right)
An advertisement for a Diane von Furstenberg eyewear line, ca. 1976.

(bottom)
Advertisement featuring a Diane von Furstenberg wrap dress design, 1973.

(opposite)
"Love the Mansion. But Do I Really Want to Be Mayor," Diane von Furstenberg advertisement, ca. 1988.

Against the throes of feminism's second wave, 1970s fashion was a core feature of debates on gender and identity. The wrap dress encapsulated von Furstenberg's wider messaging, promoting the traditional attributes of women within the framework of feminism. For her, it negotiated between body-conscious sexiness and the masculine authority lent by the collar and cuff. It was an alternative to the skirted suit and pants, which were increasingly pervasive amid transitioning gender roles and representations. According to one article, "Many women are still wary of returning to dresses, but many thousands across the country are happily wearing the dresses called 'Dianes.'"[11]

With its varying colorways and motifs, the wrap dress became an item to collect in multiples. Through this diversity, they acted as expressions of identity for the consumer who, according to the Fashion Group in 1971, "wants clothes that emphasize her personal identity in a world that often seems computerized, mechanized, dehumanized."[12] In parallel, they functioned as uniforms whose in-betweenness could cater to a range of consumer needs. At the end of 1972, Diane von Furstenberg, Inc. had reached wholesale revenues of $1.2 million and, after the introduction of the wrap, it grossed $10 million in 1974. By 1975, 300,000 dresses had been sold. It held a place in collective mentalities and visual culture by 1976, appearing on the covers of *Newsweek* and *New York Magazine*, and being worn by the beautiful, serious Betsy (played by Cybill Shepherd) in the Martin Scorsese film Taxi Driver. By 1977, von Furstenberg was already "long known for literally 'dressing' America."[13]

The dress became the unifier tying together, in the words of New Orleans shop Kreeger's "the world of Diane von Furstenberg,"[14] that, from 1975, grew to include cosmetics and the perfume Tatiana, which had its own Madison Avenue shop. von Furstenberg also embarked on a licensing program for other product lines, dispersing control of design and production to different companies for furs, jewelry, handbags, lingerie, raincoats, umbrellas, shirts, scarves, shoes, patterns, and fabrics. Some of these were illustrated in the 1977 Kreeger's advertisement alongside a wrap dress—clad model, described as a "female, un-fluttery way to go, borne of the von Furstenberg genius for well-wearing chic and parlayed into a look that reaches quite literally from head to toe."[15]

Thanks to aggressive sales and marketing schemes, consumers were familiar with the brand's visual and symbolic presence, which the addition of ancillary items reinforced. Optique du Monde, who held the license for glasses, conveyed how the Diane von Furstenberg label was a way of looking, and being perceived, through the transformative mechanism of clothing and accessories. One 1976 advertisement instructed viewers, "Change the way you see the world/Change the way the world sees you."

In 1976, *Women's Wear Daily* projected the licenses would gross $10 million that year.[16] The company growth needed to sustain this turnover ended in financial strain, furthered by the market saturation of the wrap. In 1977, von Furstenberg sold the dress license to Puritan Fashions Corporation, which held it until 1982, moving production from Italy to Hong Kong. In 1983, von Furstenberg licensed cosmetics, ending her control over the company, and added lines for children's clothing, sleepwear, hosiery, nurse uniforms, luggage, stationery, and furniture. With these, however, came a loss of design control, and a departure from the brand's original message of dressing American women.

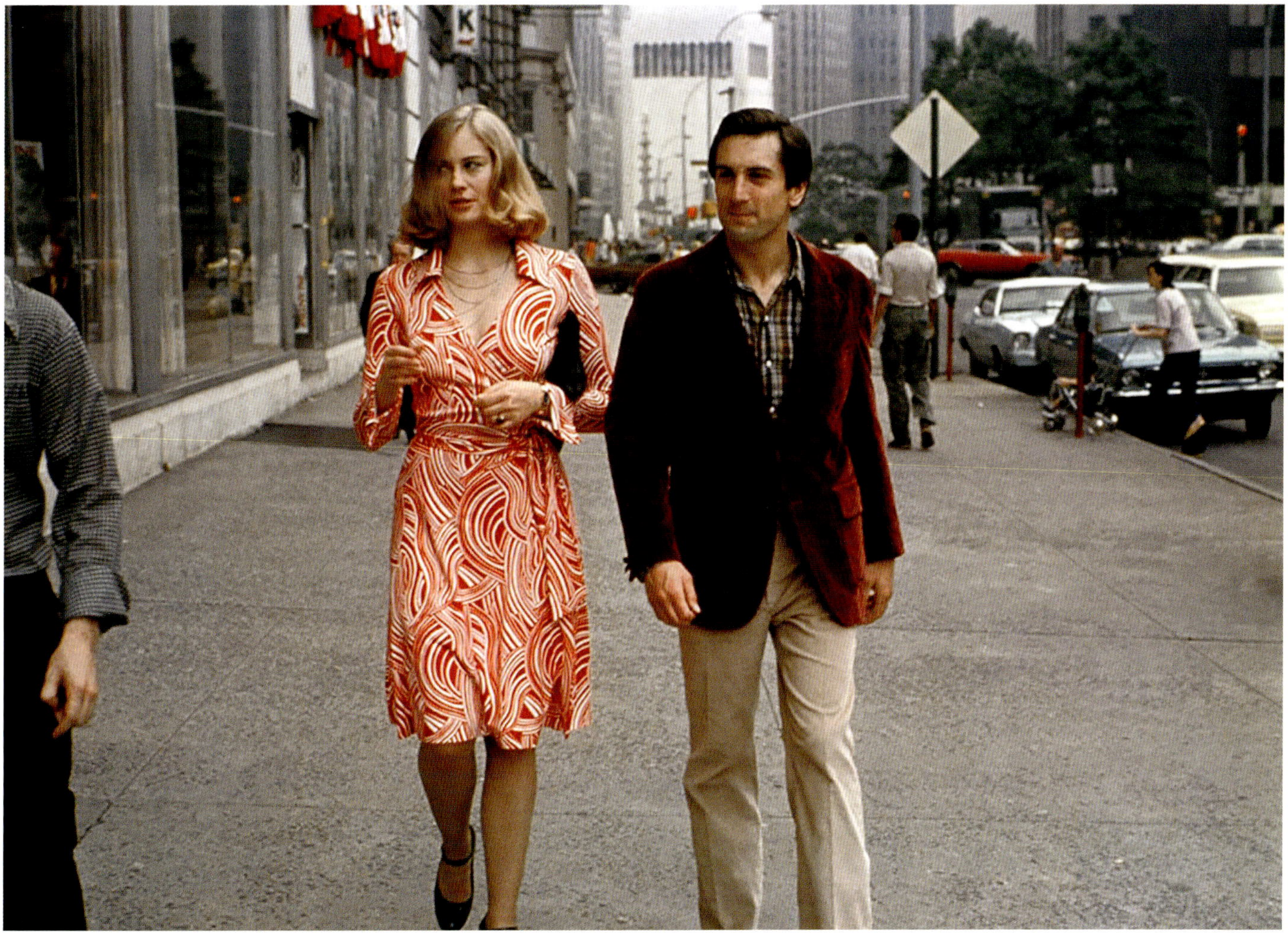

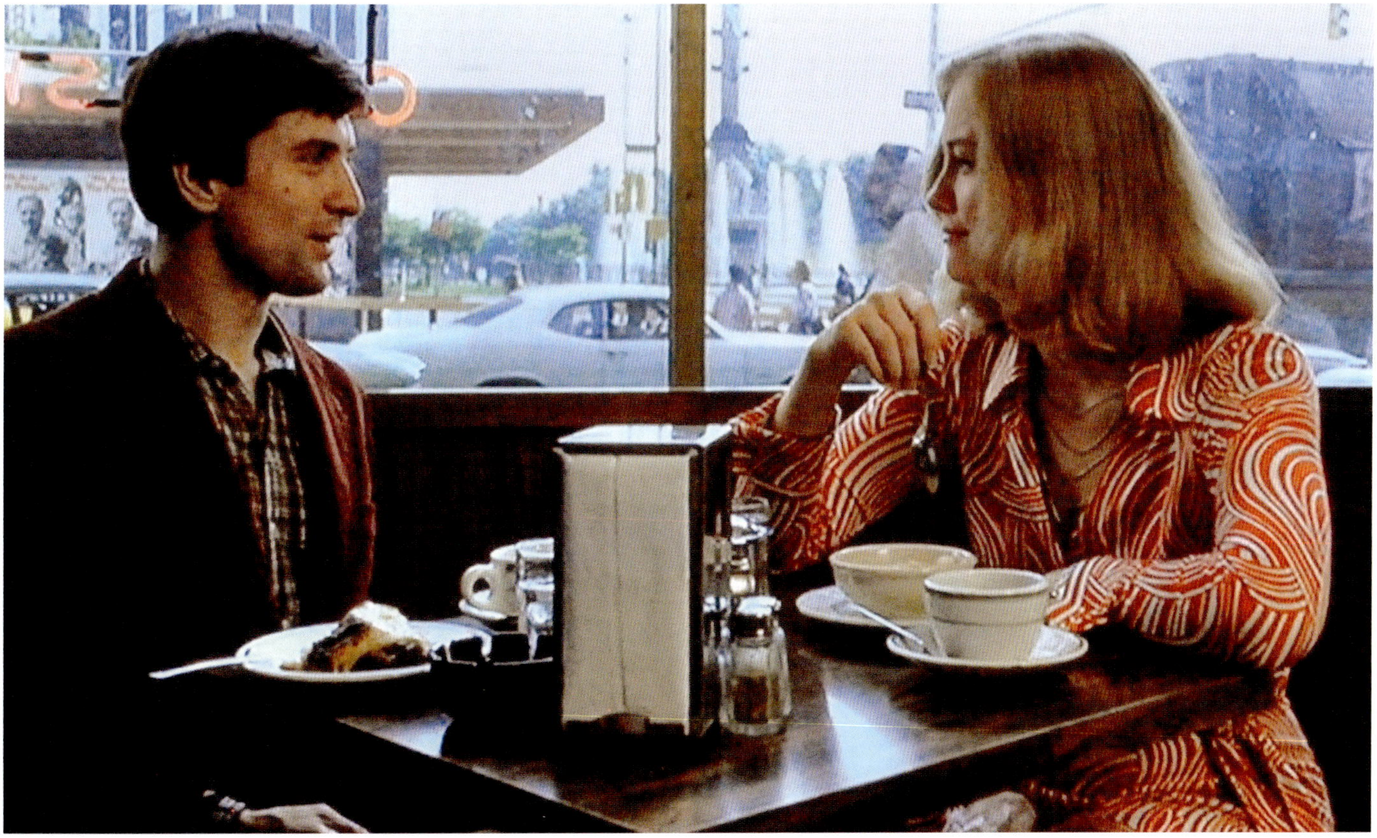

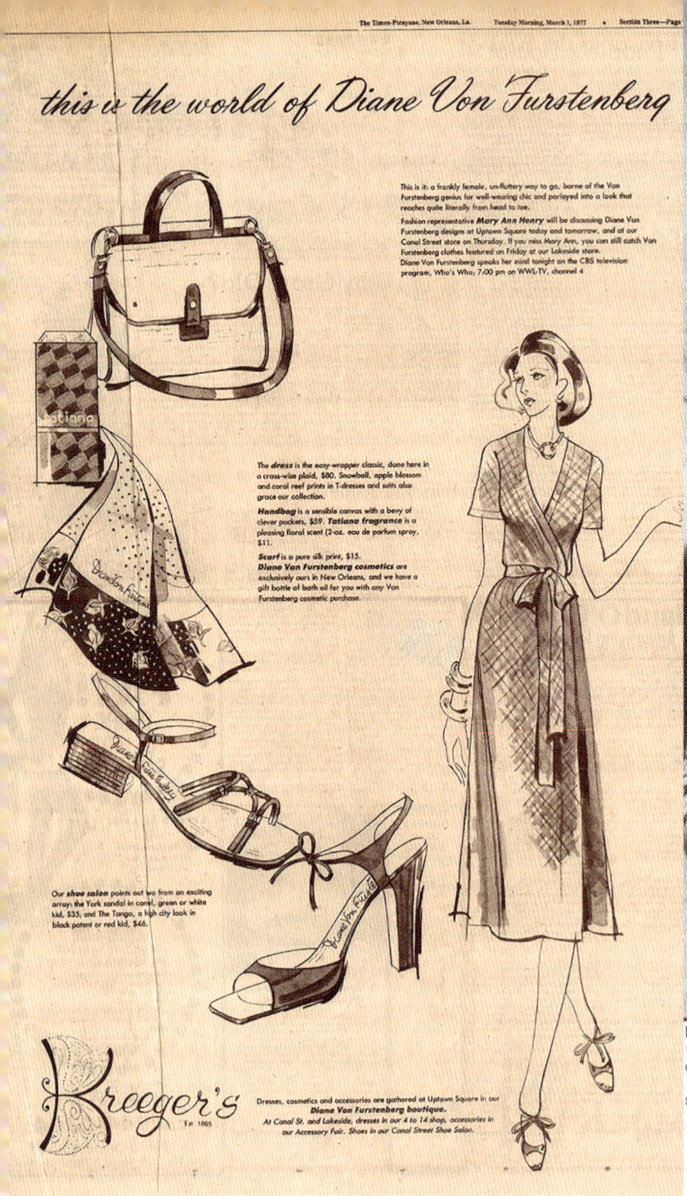
The Times-Picayune, New Orleans, La.   Tuesday Morning, March 1, 1977 • Section Three—Page
this is the world of Diane Von Furstenberg
This is it: a frankly female, un-fluttery way to go, borne of the Von Furstenberg genius for well-wearing chic and parlayed into a look that reaches quite literally from head to toe.
Fashion representative **Mary Ann Henry** will be discussing Diane Von Furstenberg designs at Uptown Square today and tomorrow, and at our Canal Street store on Thursday. If you miss Mary Ann, you can still catch Von Furstenberg clothes featured on Friday at our Lakeside store.
Diane Von Furstenberg speaks her mind tonight on the CBS television program, Who's Who; 7:00 pm on WWL-TV, channel 4
The **dress** is the easy-wrapper classic, done here in a cross-wise plaid, $80. Snowball, apple blossom and coral reef prints in T-dresses and suits also grace our collection.
Handbag is a sensible canvas with a bevy of clever pockets, $59. **Tatiana fragrance** is a pleasing floral scent (2-oz. eau de parfum spray, $11.
Scarf is a pure silk print, $15.
Diane Von Furstenberg cosmetics are exclusively ours in New Orleans, and we have a gift bottle of bath oil for you with any Von Furstenberg cosmetic purchase.
Our **shoe salon** points out two from an exciting array: the York sandal in camel, green or white kid, $35, and The Tango, a high city look in black patent or red kid, $46.
Kreeger's
Est 1865
Dresses, cosmetics and accessories are gathered at Uptown Square in our
Diane Von Furstenberg boutique.
At Canal St. and Lakeside, dresses in our 4 to 14 shop, accessories in our Accessory Fair. Shoes in our Canal Street Shoe Salon.

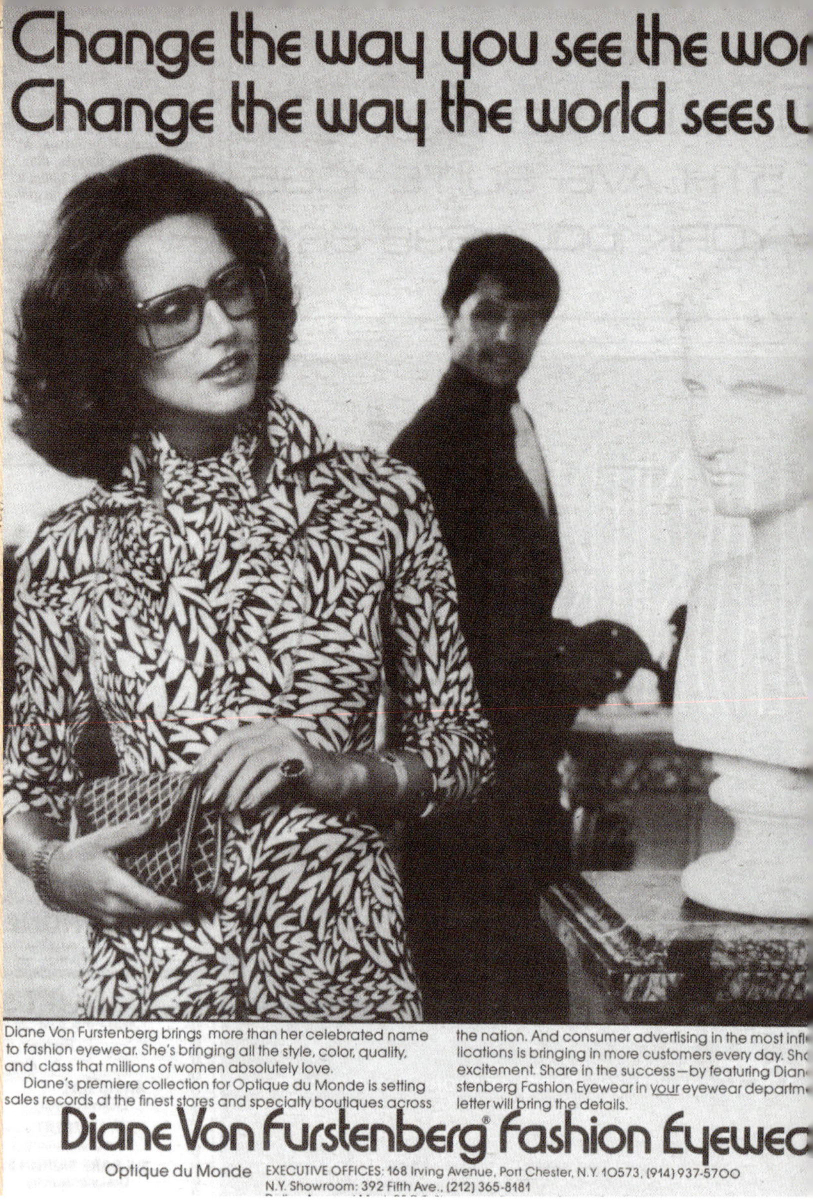
Change the way you see the wor
Change the way the world sees u
Diane Von Furstenberg brings more than her celebrated name to fashion eyewear. She's bringing all the style, color, quality, and class that millions of women absolutely love.
Diane's premiere collection for Optique du Monde is setting sales records at the finest stores and specialty boutiques across
the nation. And consumer advertising in the most infl
lications is bringing in more customers every day. Sh
excitement. Share in the success—by featuring Dian
stenberg Fashion Eyewear in your eyewear departm
letter will bring the details.
Diane Von Furstenberg® Fashion Eyewea
Optique du Monde
EXECUTIVE OFFICES: 168 Irving Avenue, Port Chester, N.Y. 10573, (914) 937-5700
N.Y. Showroom: 392 Fifth Ave., (212) 365-8181

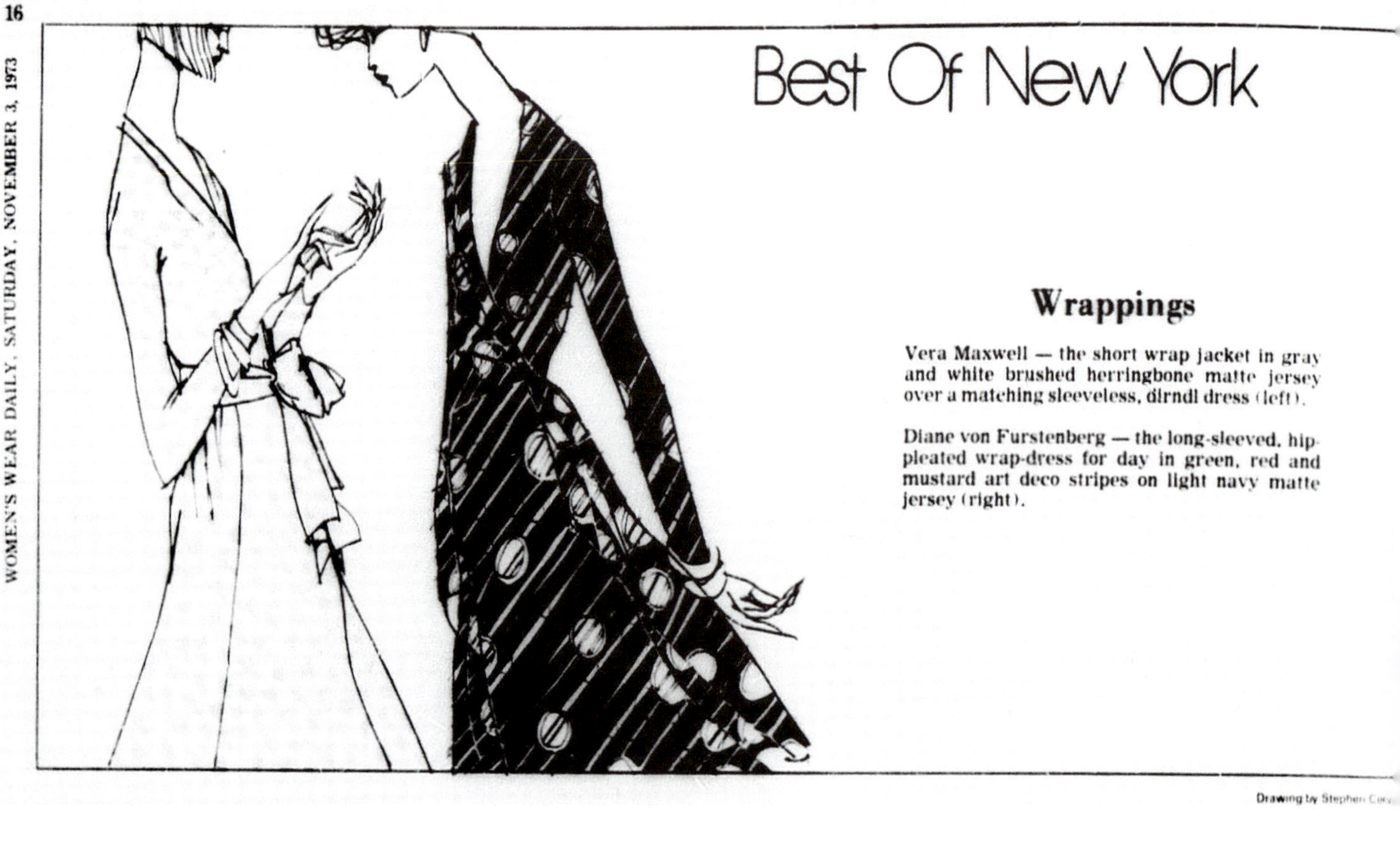
16
WOMEN'S WEAR DAILY, SATURDAY, NOVEMBER 3, 1973
Best Of New York
Wrappings
Vera Maxwell — the short wrap jacket in gray and white brushed herringbone matte jersey over a matching sleeveless, dirndl dress (left).
Diane von Furstenberg — the long-sleeved, hip-pleated wrap-dress for day in green, red and mustard art deco stripes on light navy matte jersey (right).
Drawing by Stephen Cer

LOVE THE MANSION.
UT DO I REALLY WANT TO BE MAYOR?

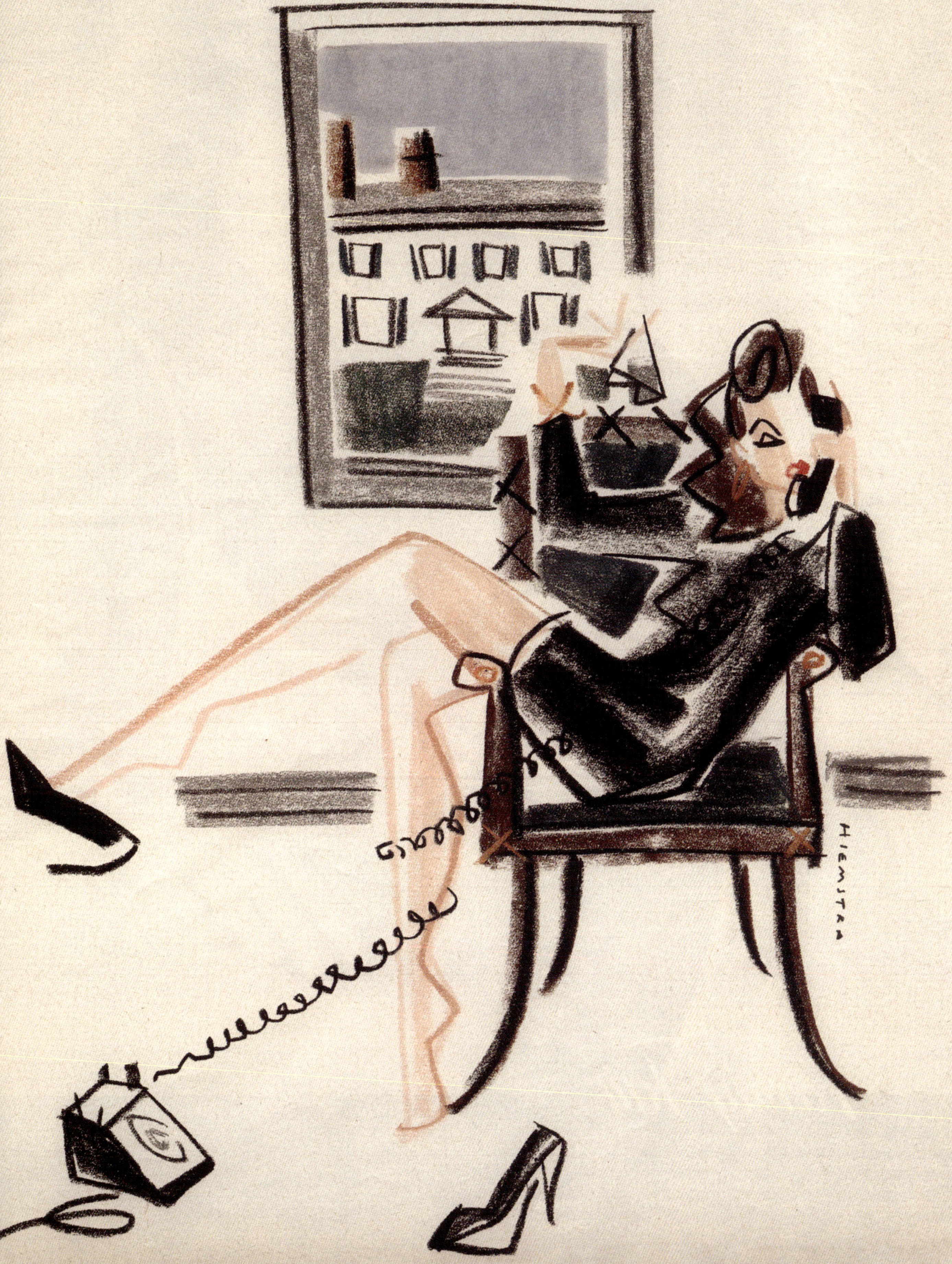

International
New York City

TIMES
NEW YORK, N. Y.
M-910,000
S-1,515,000

MAY-17-77

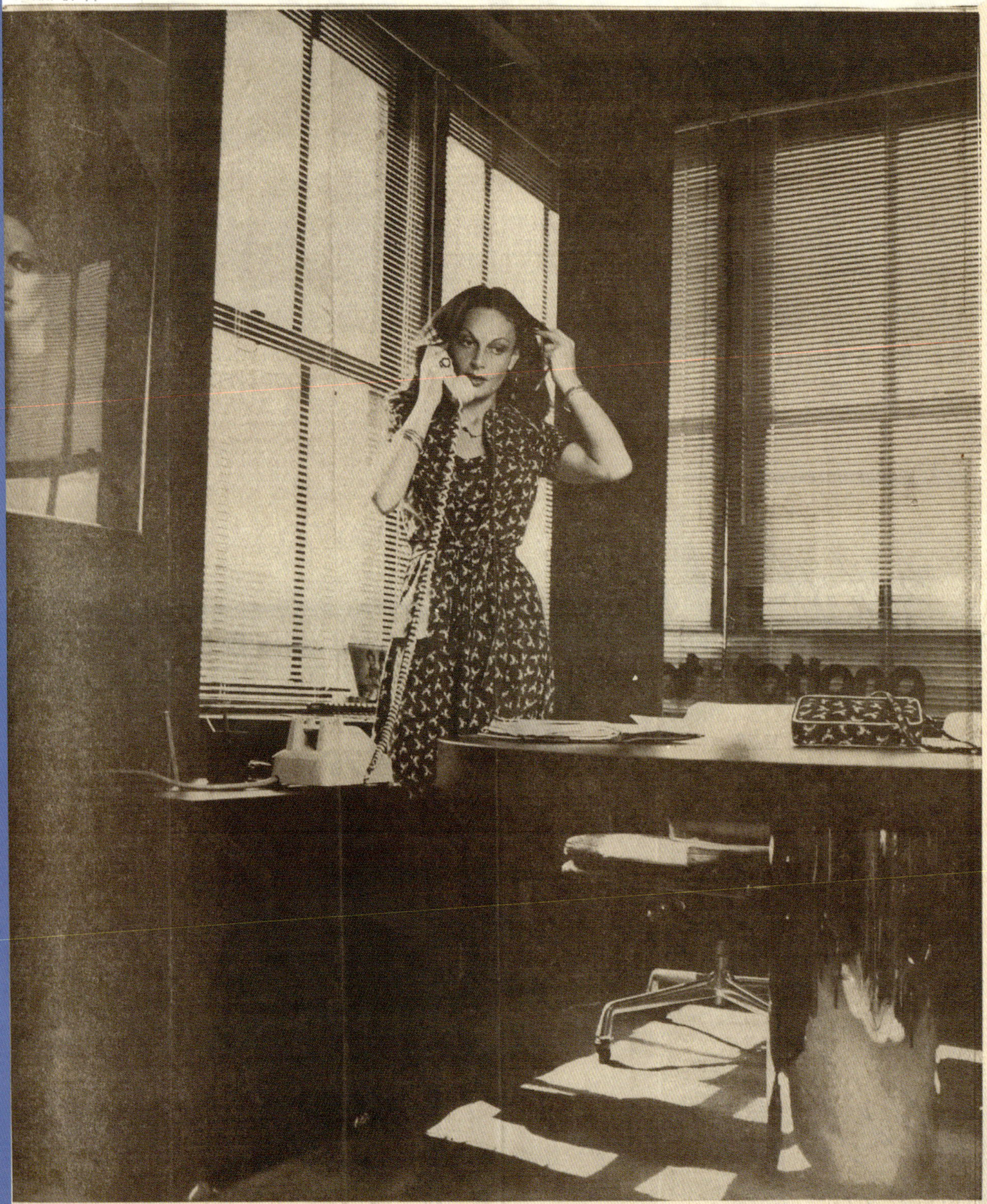

The ultimate Von Furstenberg print. Diane initialed it for us, with DVF's and SFA's. So we have the whole collection—and the only collection—in many styles and colors, in that soft imported cotton and rayon jersey—now more unmistakably hers (and ours) than ever. Here, Diane's wearing the brown sleeveless sundress with its matching short sleeve jacket, sizes 4 to 14, $118. On the desk, a small shoulder bag with detachable straps, covered in the same exclusive print, in red, black, brown or navy, $39.

Von Furstenberg Boutique, Third Floor.
Handbag Collections, Street Floor.

Saks Fifth Avenue

New York (212) PL3-4000 open Thursday until 8:30 p.m. • White Plains, Springfield and Garden City open Monday and Thursday until 9 p.m. • Bergen open Monday, Thursday and Friday until 9:30

SELLING AND MARKETING TO THE FEMALE CLIENT: "SHE'S IN STEP WITH TODAY'S WOMAN"[17]

In a 1977 photograph, von Furstenberg is pictured in her office, seemingly engrossed in a phone conversation as she runs a hand through her hair. The viewer entered into the private, professional space of the designer, which was disseminated into the public sphere in newspapers and magazines. Blurring the boundaries between a snapshot and a fashion photograph, this advertisement also illustrated the close relationship von Furstenberg held with her retailer partners—Saks Fifth Avenue, in particular. In it, she is modeling one of her dresses that is made from a fabric in collaboration with the department store—an allover pattern of their interlocked initials. A textile detail was also featured to reinforce the partnership to the reader, who need only head to the von Furstenberg boutique on the third floor to purchase her own.

During the 1970s, department stores discontinued some of their long-standing divisions, such as couture, millinery, and fabrics, in favor of cultivating designer culture. von Furstenberg excelled at the wholesale model and never opened her own womenswear shop during this time. She had a strong presence in New York, but also around the country in cities and thriving suburban shopping centers, where the wrap dress was a popular item for buyers of department and chain stores, and boutiques—from Gus Mayer in Birmingham to Loretta Blum in Dallas. In her concession spaces, garments were displayed alongside other brand products and images of herself, crystallizing the designer-fashion experience these shops increasingly offered.

Below (right)
Diane von Furstenberg window at Lord & Taylor in New York City, 1974.

Below (left)
Diane von Furstenberg's corner in a department store, 1977.

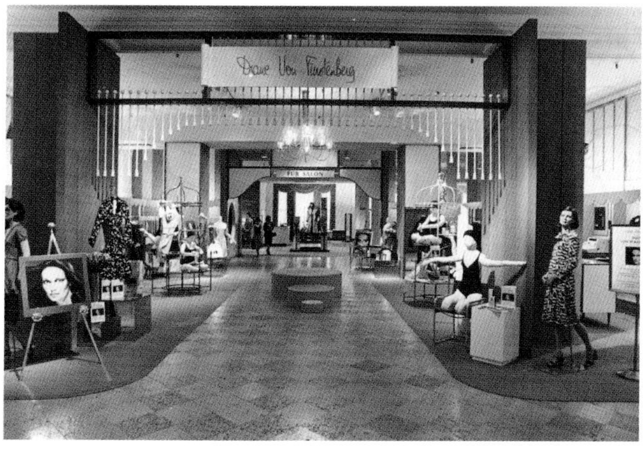

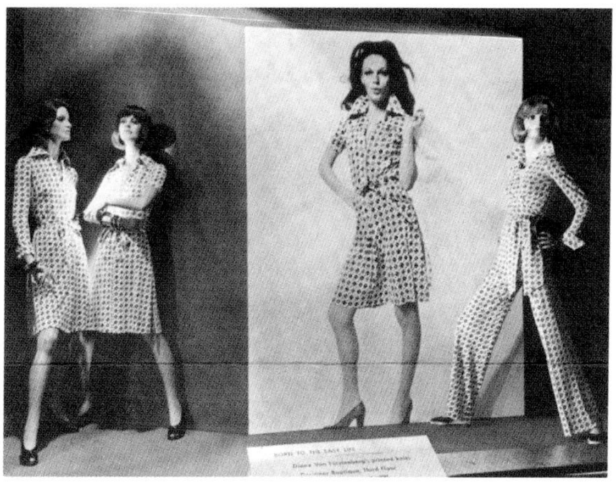

Opposite
Saks Fifth Avenue advertisement for Diane von Furstenberg new SFA and DVF print, 1977.

Von Furstenberg traveled extensively around the country to introduce her collections. These events were intimate encounters between designer and client, who discussed and tried on clothing together. Advertised widely in regional newspapers, they were framed as exclusive invitations to meet a princess. According to Bloomingdale's, "Chatting with this dynamic designer will add many new avenues to your fashion know-how."[18] Such wording suggested that personal interaction would enrich purchases, as *The Birmingham Patriot* reported on the crowds at Detroit's Bonwit Teller: "What brought them was a real-life princess who graciously shook a hand, arranged a sash, or sprayed cologne on a wrist. [...] Her customers, she knows, are buying, not just a product, but a piece of her image, her aura, her exciting life."[19]

Von Furstenberg's embodied approach to sales extended to marketing: the communication of her message persistently in advertorial imagery and copywriting that relied on the heavy use of her physical image, signature, and persona. She capitalized on a shared gender relationship to speak directly to her female client and communicate a message of empowerment and sex-positivity, as a 1976 ad illustrated: "For you, and Diane von Furstenberg, the most important job is being a woman. Diane is one woman you can really relate to. A lady. And a tiger. Yet always superbly, supremely feminine. And she creates clothes for women who want to feel the same way. Clothes that never forget the woman underneath."[20] According to the ads, her gender was a mark of assurance for clients, who could rely on her having tested the garments out, so that they "fit in so well with today's lifestyle."[21]

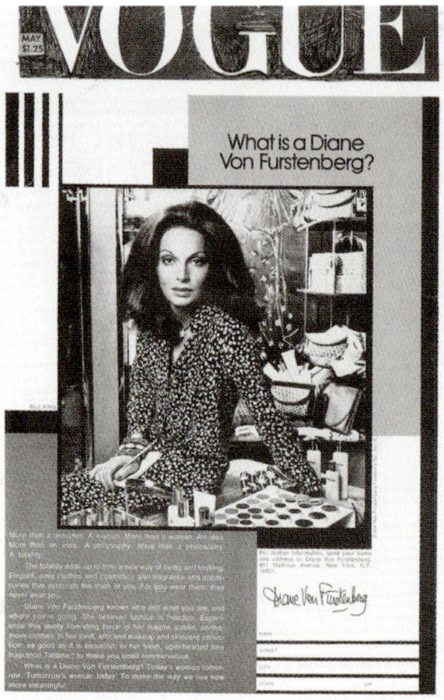

Above
"What Is a Diane von Furstenberg?" advertisement, 1975.

Some advertisements went further, characterizing the designer and brand as a concept and lifestyle. One posed the question, "What is a Diane von Furstenberg?" Alongside, the designer wore and was surrounded by her various product lines—an object scape charged with symbolisms. "More than a designer. A woman. More than a woman. An idea. More than an idea. A philosophy. More than a philosophy. A totality. [...] A new way of living and looking."[22] Such language echoed the psychology and self-help books on personal fulfillment and sexual awareness pervasive during what would become known as the "Me Decade." Even von Furstenberg added to this landscape with her *Book of Beauty* (Simon & Schuster, 1976). It contextualized advice on beauty and health against her life story. Like her personified ads, it imbued her consumer products with meaning and value. This was the first of several autobiographical texts authored by von Furstenberg, who recognized the power of language to communicate to the public. Throughout the 1970s, ads included a mail-in feature to amass a mailing list of loyal customers.

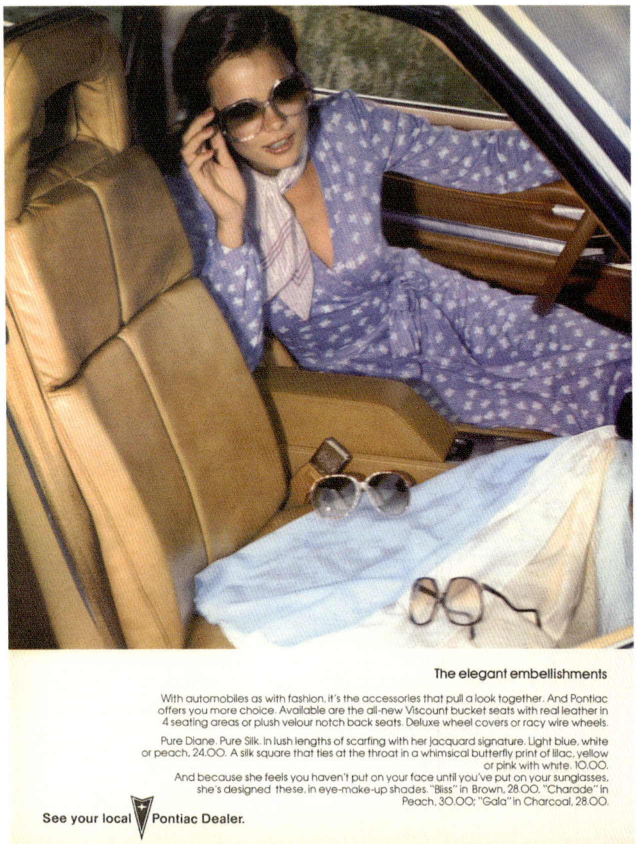

Left
A combined Diane von Furstenberg and Pontiac advertisement, 1977.

Opposite
Diane von Furstenberg "That Face" cosmetics and sunglasses advertisement, 1976.

Next spread
"Whatever Diane's got, I want" advertisement, 1979.

Cross-promotions were another means of powerful marketing, connecting clothing to other products to reinforce lifestyle narratives. In one 1977 example, von Furstenberg paired with Pontiac and Bloomingdale's in an eight-page spread featuring models against and inside car models. One image pictured a woman at the steering wheel in a lilac wrap dress, cushioned by plush tan leather car seats. Scarves and sunglasses were strewn about—a mix of textures and items to paint a complete picture of female empowerment and high-end living. As the "Me Decade" approached the wealth-obsessed 1980s, a new slogan combined aspirational marketing and designer embodiment: "Whatever Diane's got, I want."

That face.

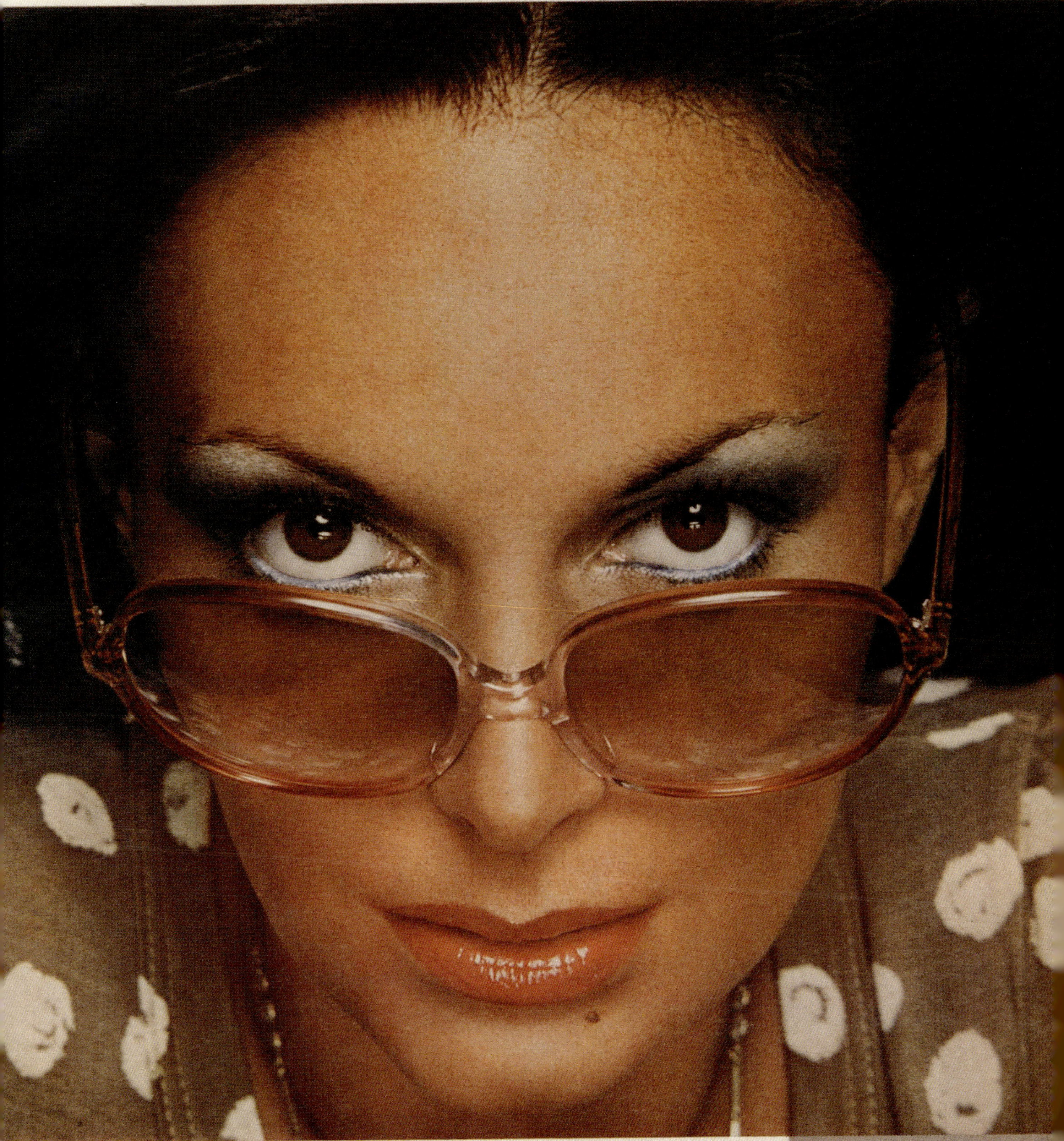

It's Diane Von Furstenberg, who believes "if your makeup and sunglasses don't complement one another, they don't compliment you."

Diane Von Furstenberg®
Cosmetics and Sunglasses
For women who want to be complimented

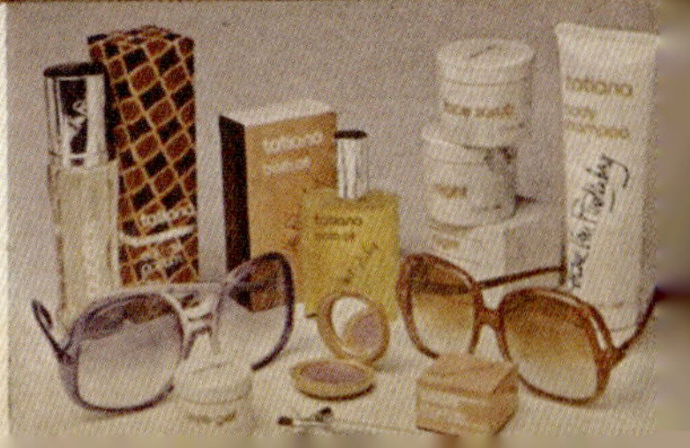

Available at all fine stores.

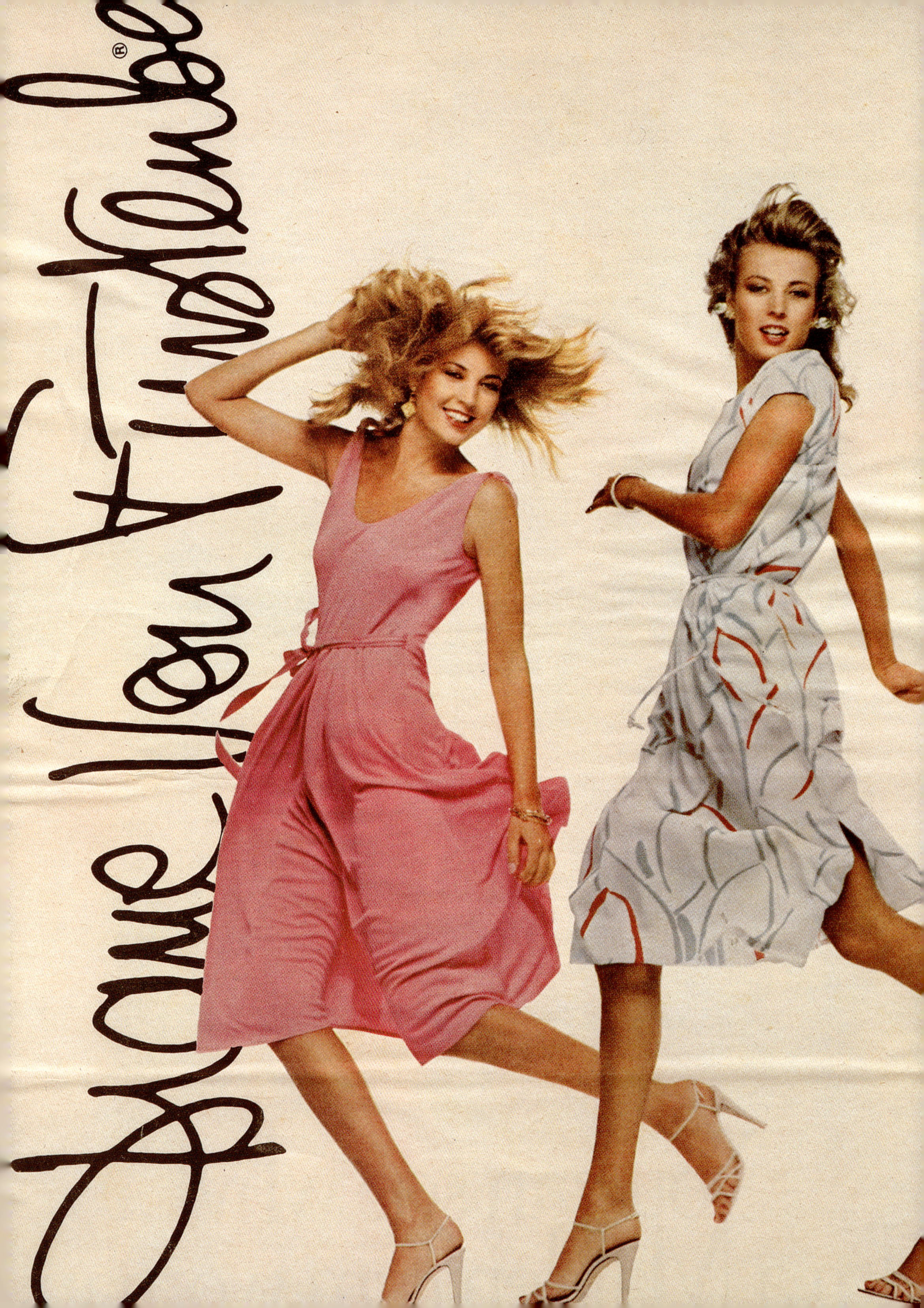
Diane Von Furstenberg®

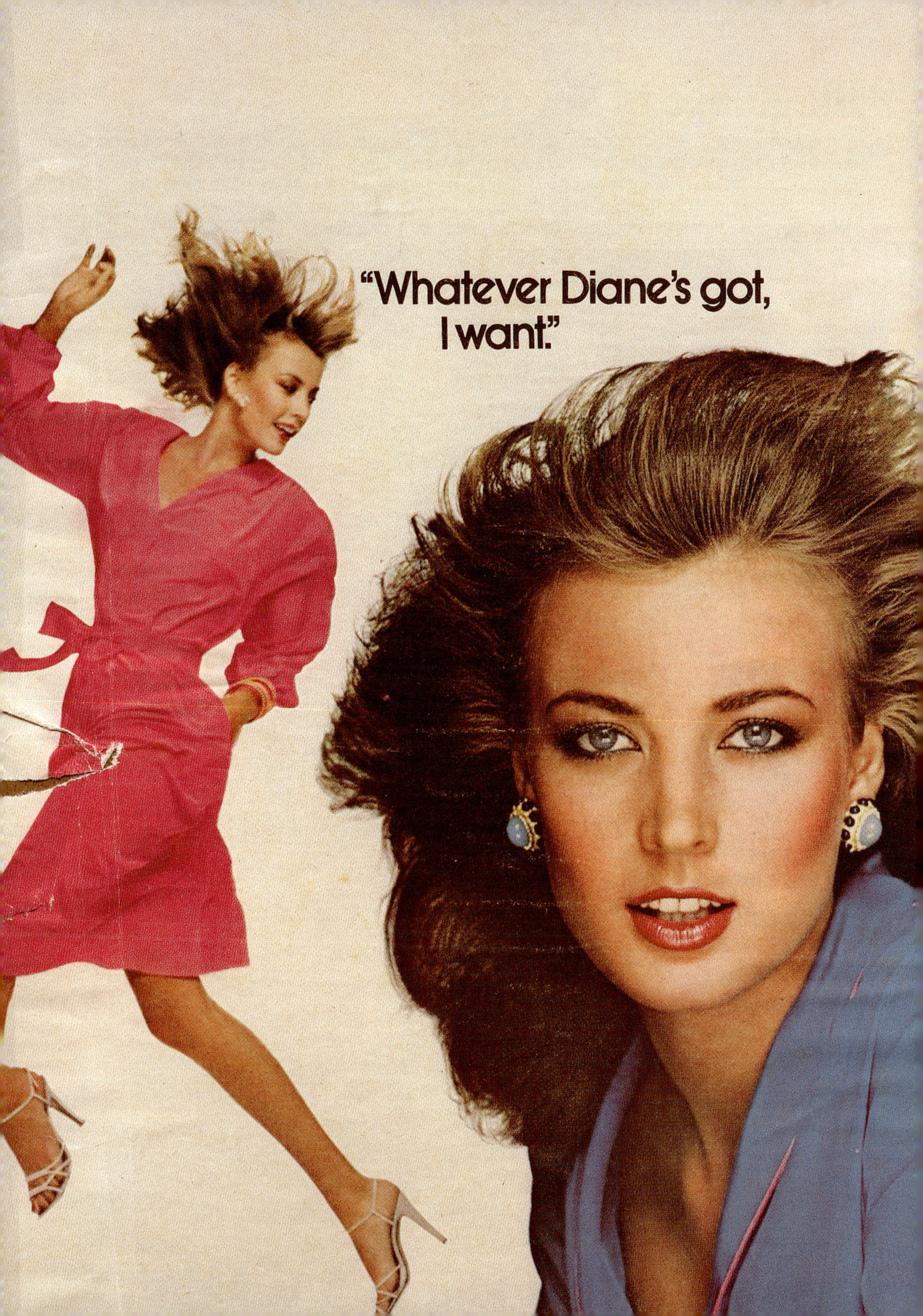
"Whatever Diane's got,
I want."

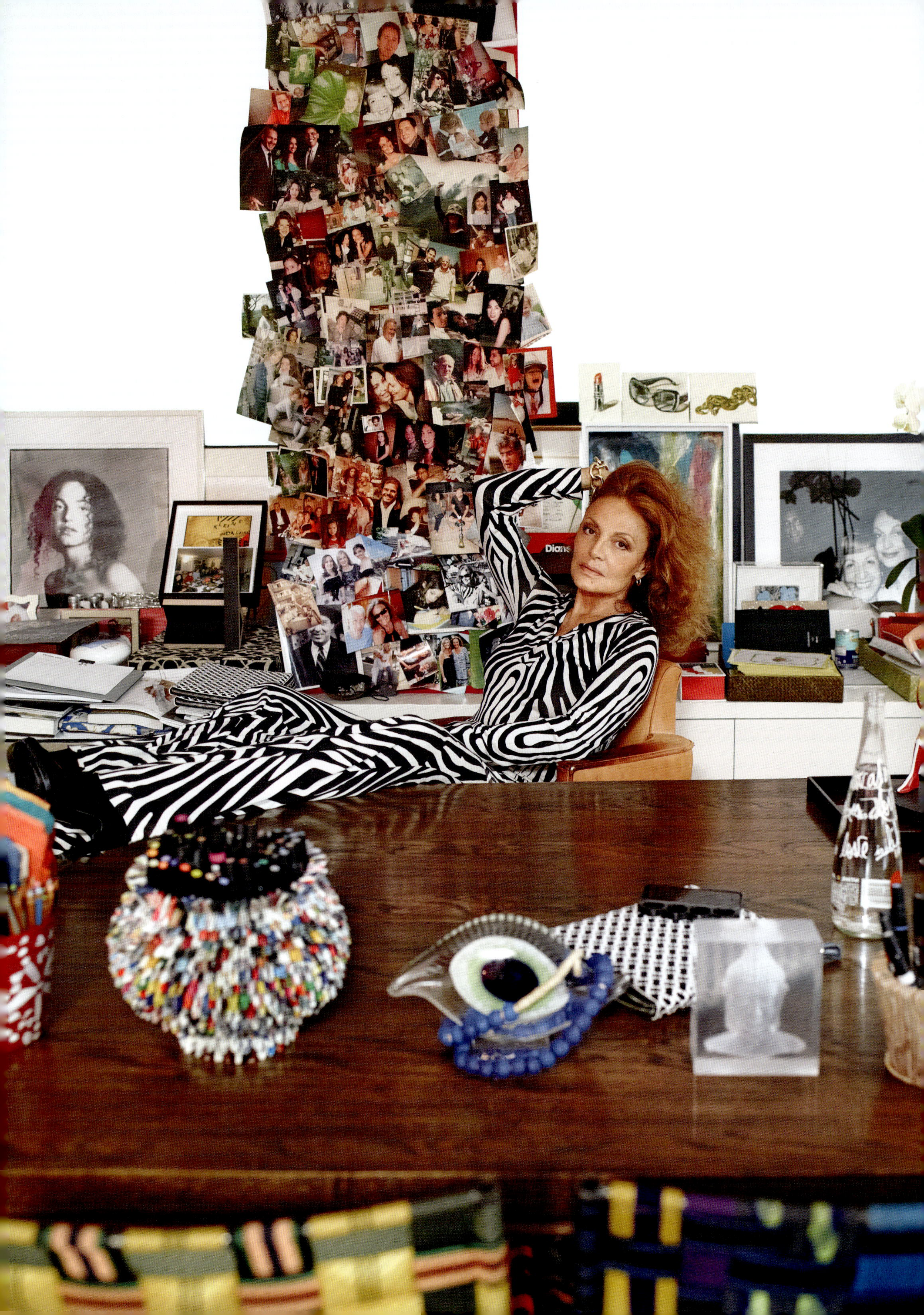

A SIGNATURE LIFE AND HERITAGE DESIGN IN THE 1990s AND 2000s

Opposite
Diane von Furstenberg in her office, 2014.

Below (left)
Advertisement for Diane von Furstenberg couture line: Diane Fifth Avenue, 1985.

Below (right)
An article about Diane von Furstenberg relaunching the wrap dress, titled "Talking Fashion," 1997.

Following her short-lived 1980s couture and 1990s home shopping collections, von Furstenberg revisited her roots and relaunched the wrap dress in 1997, which she reimagined slightly to align with changing styles.

This was fed by a culture captivated by retro style and vintage—the 1970s, in particular—as well as heritage branding and fashion archive-building.[23] von Furstenberg replicated this process in writing her memoir, *Diane: A Signature Life* (Simon & Schuster, 1998), which recounted her life and messaging to new audiences during the relaunch.

Some dresses were photographed in a 1997 feature for *Vogue*, which reported, "The Diane von Furstenberg wrap dress is back with a vengeance."[24] The company, whose leadership was then and now largely in the hands of women, moved to New York's edgy, bohemian Meatpacking District, where the flagship stands today.

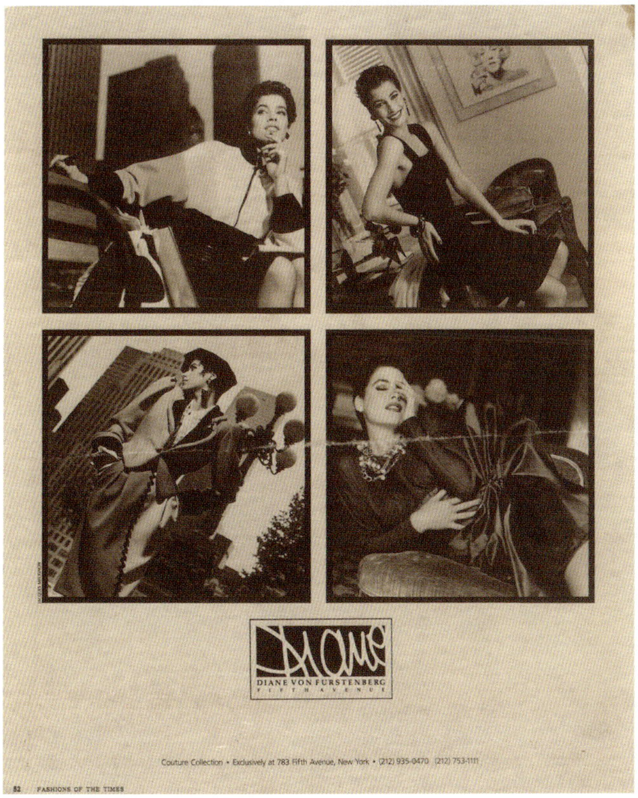

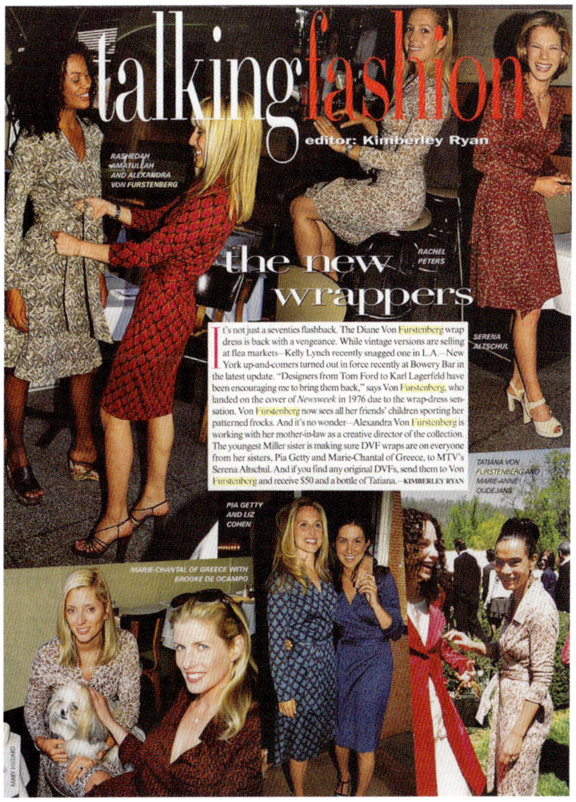
talking fashion
editor: Kimberley Ryan
RASHEDAH AMATULLAH AND ALEXANDRA VON FURSTENBERG
RACHEL PETERS
the new wrappers

It's not just a seventies flashback. The Diane Von Furstenberg wrap dress is back with a vengeance. While vintage versions are selling at flea markets—Kelly Lynch recently snagged one in L.A.—New York up-and-comers turned out in force recently at Bowery Bar in the latest update. "Designers from Tom Ford to Karl Lagerfeld have been encouraging me to bring them back," says Von Furstenberg, who landed on the cover of *Newsweek* in 1976 due to the wrap-dress sensation. Von Furstenberg now sees all her friends' children sporting her patterned frocks. And it's no wonder—Alexandra Von Furstenberg is working with her mother-in-law as a creative director of the collection. The youngest Miller sister is making sure DVF wraps are on everyone from her sisters, Pia Getty and Marie-Chantal of Greece, to MTV's Serena Altschul. And if you find any original DVFs, send them to Von Furstenberg and receive $50 and a bottle of Tatiana.—KIMBERLEY RYAN

SERENA ALTSCHUL
TATIANA VON FURSTENBERG AND MARIE-ANNE OUDEJANS
PIA GETTY AND LIZ COHEN
MARIE-CHANTAL OF GREECE WITH BROOKE DE OCAMPO

In 2005, von Furstenberg's contributions were acknowledged with a Lifetime Achievement Award from the Council of Fashion Designers of America (CFDA), for which she served as president from 2006 to 2019. During her term, she gave back to the industry and city where her American Dream was first staged including design copyright protection, improving Fashion Week, and mentoring designers. New York City features thematically in her work as a background in campaign imagery or seen, for example, in the 2019 Liberty Collection, an homage to the statue that symbolized the dream for so many immigrants.

Below
Diane von Furstenberg at the 2019 CFDAs.

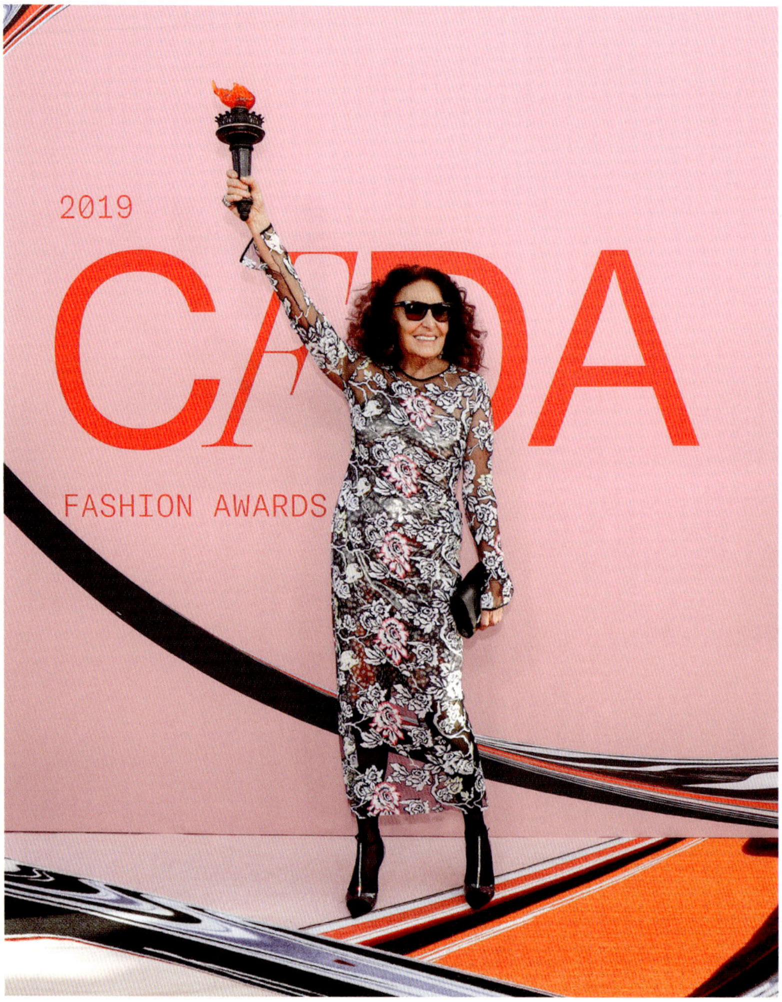

Such dreaming inspires future reflection. When von Furstenberg was imagining and fashioning what she would be, could she have foreseen her legacy in American history and its material culture? The wraparound dress is a remarkable garment in that it exists in most museum clothing collections throughout the country—a testament to her shop traveling days—regardless of collecting policy and mission statement. It also has a place in collective notions of the 1970s, used prevalently by film costume designers. Although capturing the early strengths of her career has posed challenges, as the global fashion industry undergoes vast changes, von Furstenberg's core messages promoting women's sense of self and empowerment, using herself as a conduit, are timely. In her latest book, *Own It: The Secret to Life* (Phaidon, 2021), she spreads these and other ideas in dictionary format—just as the modernist designer spoke through the semiotics of color, print, fabric, and silhouette. Her favorite word, "intention," connects directly to her American Dream and to that 1975 advertisement in which she walked forward with purpose.

Opposite
Three models in one-sleeve maxi Diane von Furstenberg wrap dresses in front of the Statue of Liberty, 2019.

Next page
Diane von Furstenberg lying inside a DVF logo sculpture, 2012.

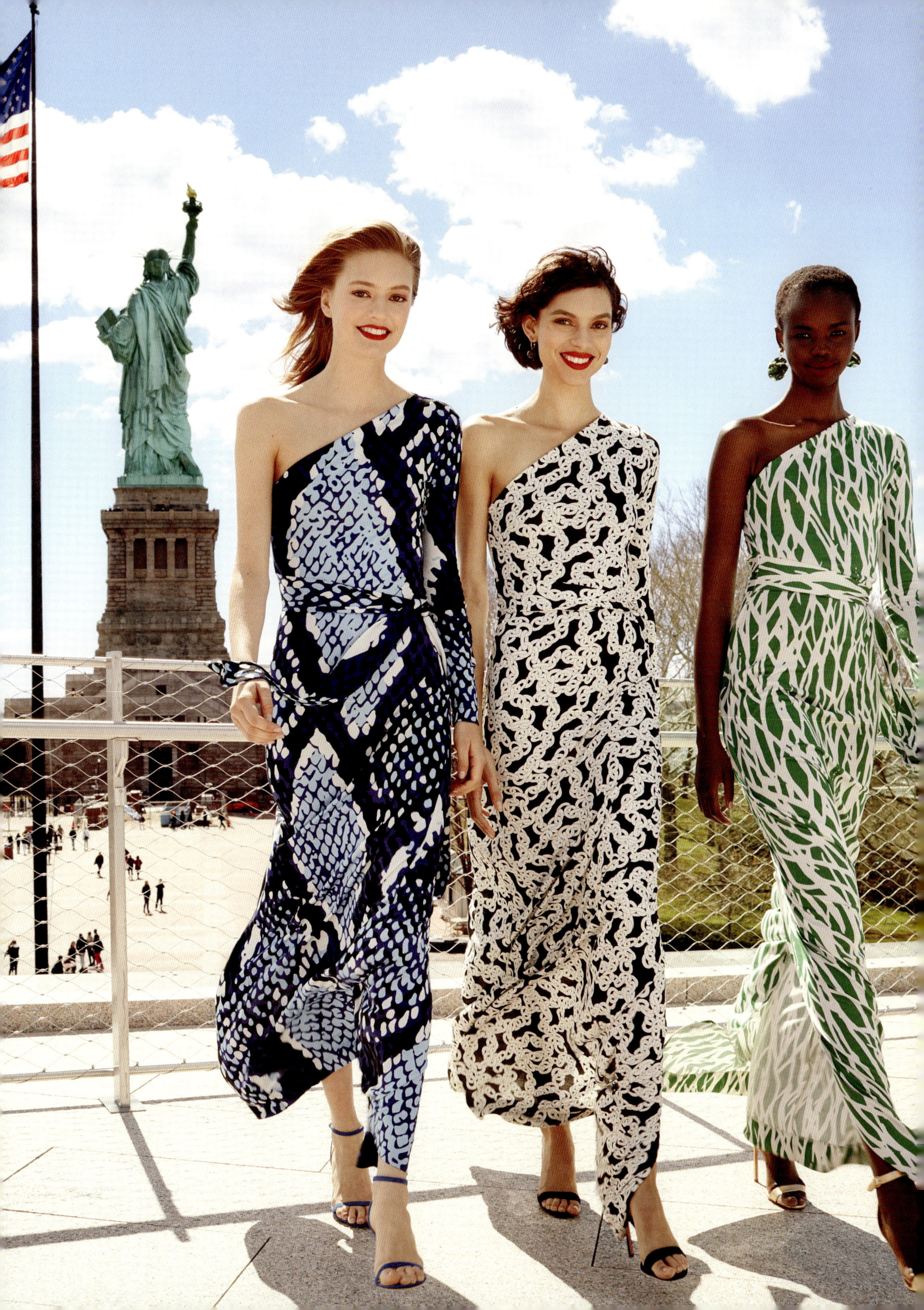

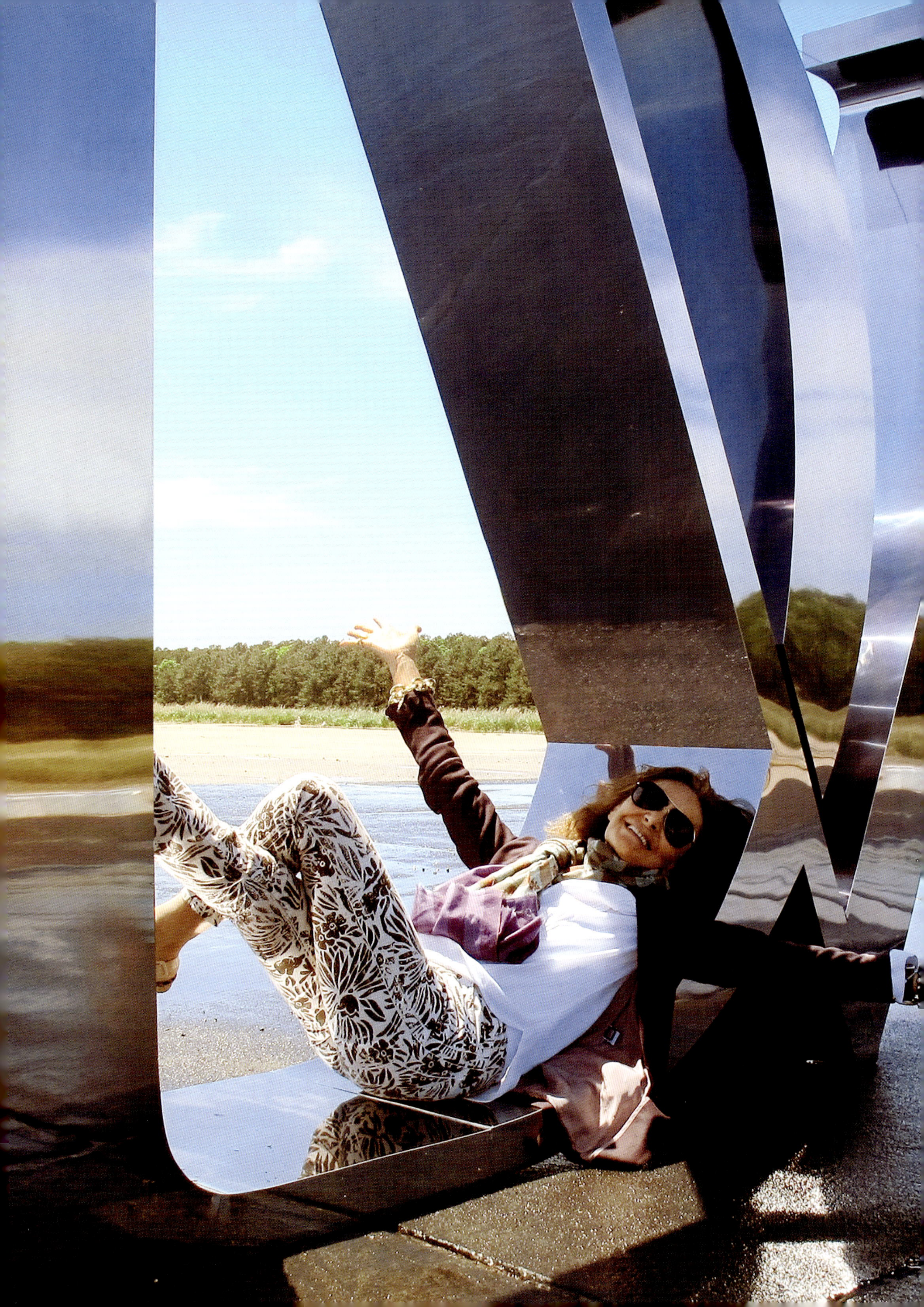

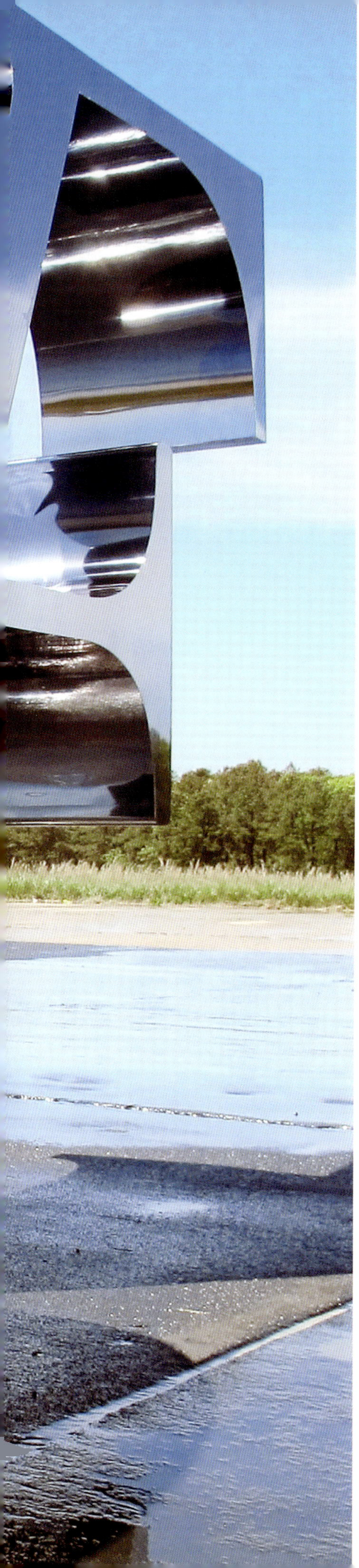

ACKNOWLEDGMENTS

Diane von Furstenberg: Woman Before Fashion is the result of hard work and dedication by many accomplished people. Producing the book has been an incredible journey of deep conversations, new discoveries, and encounters for me. I am so grateful to Diane von Furstenberg for supporting and trusting me to share her story in this book.

I would like to thank all of the DVF team for their unconditional support: Luisella Meloni, for sharing her knowledge and experiences at DVF; Costanza Reiser, for unveiling all the secrets from DVF Archives, which was begun by Franca V. Dantes; Laura Harvey, for her sharp, creative eye; and Morgan Hill.

Such a book could only have seen the light under the master orchestration of Rizzoli New York. I would like to thank Charles Miers, for his witty point of view and ideas, and Anthony Petrillose and Gisela Aguilar, for managing the editing and production.

This book is a beautiful visual object because of the creative vision of the design team. I wish to thank Diego Marini and his colleagues at YummyColours, especially Leo Cunningham and Anna Simonse, for the beautiful design.

The original content of this book came from great collaborations. I would like to thank writers Karen van Godtsenhoven, Lydia Kamitsis, and Alexis Romano for their research, which provided a comprehensive vision of Diane von Furstenberg's work and how it is connected to the history of fashion, feminism, sociology, and history of retail. For taking the time to share their personal, intimate stories and records in a unique way, I would like to express my gratitude to Naomi Campbell, Cindy Crawford, Stefani Greenfield, Mimmo Ferretti, Jerry Hall, Karlie Kloss, Elizabeth McKenzie, Bruna Sequalino, and Natalia Vodianova.

Last but not least, I would like to thank Veerle Windels and John Jay for their very instructive and inspiring thoughts, my colleagues from the Fashion & Lace Museum, and my loved ones for their daily support.

Nicolas Lor

NOTES

DRESS IS A DRESS IS A DRESS

[1] *Marie-Claire*, May 28, 1937, 46.

[2] Madeleine Vionnet.

[3] Linda Birde Franck and Diane von Furstenberg, *Diane: A Signature Life* (New York: Simon & Schuster, 1998), 86.

[4] Oscar Wilde, "The Philosophy of Dress," *The New-York Tribune*, 1885.

[5] Diane von Furstenberg, DVF: *Journey of a Dress* (New York: Rizzoli International Publications, 2014), 49.

[6] Dexter C.Bloomer, *The Life and Writings of Amelia Bloomer* (Boston: Arena Publishing Co., 1895), 72.

[7] Franck and von Furstenberg, *A Signature Life*, 74.

[8] Simone de Beauvoir, *The Second Sex* (Harmondsworth: Penguin, 1949).

[9] Franck and von Furstenberg, *A Signature Life*, 76.

THE DRESS MAKES THE WOMAN: DIANE VON FURSTENBERG'S FEMINISM, FASHION AND POLITICS

[1] A title coined by radical feminists Shulamith Firestone and Anne Koedt in 1970, for an essay by Carole Hanisch from 1969, which they published in *Notes from the Second Year*.

[2] Diane von Furstenberg in Diane von Furstenberg and Evelyn Portrait, *Diane von Furstenberg's Book of Beauty: How to Become a More Attractive, Confident and Sensual Woman* (New York: Simon & Schuster, 1977), 33.

[3] Bertrand Meyer-Stabley and Laurence Catinot-Crost, "Diane von Furstenberg, l'élégantissime," in *Créatrices de légende. De Jeanne Lanvin à Stella McCartney* (Paris: Editions Bartillat, 2019), 174.

[4] von Furstenberg and Portrait, *Book of Beauty*, 33.

[5] The author is aware of the problematics residing with the wave metaphor for intersectional and intergenerational feminist movements; however, because its name, motto, protagonists, and politics are so entangled with the era of von Furstenberg's youth, it is still deemed relevant in the context of this essay.

[6] Simone de Beauvoir, *The Second Sex* (Harmondsworth: Penguin, 1949).

[7] Gioia Diliberto, *Diane von Furstenberg: A Life Unwrapped* (New York: Dey Street Books, 2015), 129.

[8] Luce Irigaray, *Ce sexe qui n'en est pas un* (Paris: Editions de Minuit, 1977).

[9] Hélène Cixous, Keith Cohen, and Paula Cohen, "The Laugh of the Medusa" in *Signs* (Chicago: University of Chicago Press, 1976).

[10] Author's conversation with Diane von Furstenberg, 2022.

[11] Diliberto, *A Life Unwrapped*, 68.

[12] Diliberto, *A Life Unwrapped*, 78.

[13] Annemarie Strassel, *Redressing Women: Feminism in Fashion and the Creation of American Style, 1930–1960* (New Haven, CT: Yale University Press, 2008), 144.

[14] Originally coined by Michael Denning in *The Cultural Front: The Laboring of American Culture in the Twentieth Century* (London: Verso Books, 1997), 146.

[15] Linda Birde Franck and Diane von Furstenberg, *Diane: A Signature Life* (New York: Simon & Schuster, 1998), 80–81.

[16] Diliberto, *A Life Unwrapped*, 64.

[17] Franck and von Furstenberg, *A Signature Life*, 180.

[18] Judith Butler, *Gender Trouble, Feminism and the Subversion of Identity* (London: Routledge, 1990).

[19] Diane von Furstenberg in von Furstenberg and Portrait, *Book of Beauty*, 13.

[20] Diliberto, A Life Unwrapped, 146.

[21] Marji Kunz, "Diane: Princess, Mom, Dressmaker, Feminist," *Detroit Free Press*, May 19, 1976.

[22] Franck and von Furstenberg, *A Signature Life*, 195–196.

[23] Diane von Furstenberg, *The Woman I Wanted to Be* (New York: Simon and Schuster, 2014), 114.

[24] Franck and von Furstenberg, *A Signature Life*, 160.

[25] von Furstenberg and Portrait, *Book of Beauty*, 14.

[26] von Furstenberg and Portrait, *Book of Beauty*, 32.

[27] Diliberto, *A Life Unwrapped*, 108.

[28] Marc Karimzadeh, "Diane von Furstenberg Means Business in Soho," *Women's Wear Daily*, May 27, 2011.

[29] Franck and von Furstenberg, *A Signature Life*, 85–86.

[30] Carrie Donovan, "Feminism's Effect on Fashion," *The New York Times*, August 28, 1977.

[31] Franck and von Furstenberg, *A Signature Life*, 1974.

[32] Three Women, *Women's Wear Daily*.

[33] Franck and von Furstenberg, *A Signature Life*, 159.

[34] Franck and von Furstenberg, *A Signature Life*, 93.

[35] Diliberto, *A Life Unwrapped*, 122.

[36] *The San Francisco Examiner*, November 13, 1977.

[37] Franck and von Furstenberg, *A Signature Life*, 95.

[38] Franck and von Furstenberg, *A Signature Life*, 30.

[39] Franck and von Furstenberg, *A Signature Life*, 147.

[40] Diliberto, A Life Unwrapped, 242.

[41] Franck and von Furstenberg, *A Signature Life*, 82.

[42] Franck and von Furstenberg, *A Signature Life*, 95.

[43] Diliberto, *A Life Unwrapped*, 78.

[44] Franck and von Furstenberg, *A Signature Life*, 86.

[45] Franck and von Furstenberg, *A Signature Life*, 110–111.

[46] Franck and von Furstenberg, *A Signature Life*, 74.

[47] Elizabeth Hawes, *Why Women Cry*, or *Wenches with Wrenches* (New York: Reynal & Hitchcock, 1943).

[48] Diliberto, *A Life Unwrapped*, 3.

[49] Franck and von Furstenberg, *A Signature Life*, 86–87.

[50] Franck and von Furstenberg, *A Signature Life*, 86.

[51] https://joinincharge.com.

[52] Karimzadeh, "Furstenberg Means Business, 2011.

[53] "ABZUG, Bella Savitzky," US House of Representatives, Office of the Historian and the Clerk of the House's Office of Art and Archives. Retrieved February 12, 2019.

[54] Mellody Hobson, "Diane von Furstenberg Talks Bringing the New Statue of Liberty Museum to Life," *Harper's Bazaar*, May 13, 2019.

[55] Hobson, *"Bringing the New Statue of Liberty Museum to Life."*

[56] Hobson, *"Bringing the New Statue of Liberty Museum to Life."*

[57] von Furstenberg, *The Woman I Wanted to Be*, 56.

DESIGNING THE AMERICAN DREAM: DIANE VON FURSTENBERG'S CAREER IN 1970s NEW YORK

[1] Linda Birde Franck and Diane von Furstenberg, *Diane: A Signature Life* (New York: Simon & Schuster, 1998), 52.

[2] Jane Farrell-Beck and Jean Parsons, *20th-Century Dress in the United States* (New York: Fairchild, 2007), 193, 295.

[3] Author's conversation with Diane von Furstenberg, December 22, 2022.

[4] Title borrowed from an article on von Furstenberg that appeared in *Sunday* (Wappingers Falls, NY), December 22, 1974.

[5] Franck and von Furstenberg, *A Signature Life*, 55.

[6] "The Changing Consumer," *FGI Bulletin*, October 29, 1971.

[7] These ideas were gleaned from the author's conversation with Diane von Furstenberg, December 22, 2022.

[8] "How to Succeed with a Dress," *Sunday* (Wappingers Falls, NY), December 22, 1974.

[9] "How 8 Single Women Make Fashion Work for Them," Harper's Bazaar, March 1976, 70.

[10] Rebecca Arnold, The American Look: Fashion, Sportswear and the Image of Women in 1930s and 1940s New York (London and New York: I.B. Tauris, 2009).

[11] "How to Succeed with a Dress."

[12] "The Changing Consumer."

[13] Carrie Donovan, "The Success of the Dress," *The New York Times*, October 16, 1977, 118.

[14] Advertisement appeared in *The Times-Picayune*, March 1, 1977, 3.

[15] *The Times-Picayune* advertisement, 1977.

[16] Sandy Parker, "Furstenberg Licensing in Rapid Growth," *Women's Wear Daily*, September 22, 1976, 76.

[17] Advertisement appeared in *Women's Wear Daily*, May 8, 1976.

[18] Advertisement appeared in *The New York Times*, March 12, 1971.

[19] Sandy Tessler, "A Royal Show," *The Birmingham Patriot*, May 26, 1976, 15.

[20] Advertisement appeared in *Harper's Bazaar*, September 1976.

[21] *Women's Wear Daily*, May 8, 1976.

[22] *Vogue*, May 1975.

[23] See Anne D'Innocenzio, "Cashing in on the Seventies Retro Rage," *Women's Wear Daily*, November 20, 1997, 6.

[24] Kimberley Ryan, "Talking Fashion: The New Wrappers," *Vogue*, July 1, 1997.

CREDITS

© Michel Arnaud: page 6, 66-67

© François-Marie Banier: page 106, 107

© Chris Bartlett: (fabric swatches) page 33, 35, 36-37, 38, 40-41, 42, 44-45, 47, 48, 97, 100, 101, 102, 103, 104-105, 106, 107, 109, 110-111, 112, 161, 162, 164, 165, 167, 168-169, 170, 171, 174-175, 176

© David M. Benett/Getty Images: page 88 (bottom middle)

© Randy Brooke/WireImage/Getty Images: page 60

© Brianna Capozzi/REP: page 102

© Kenneth Cappello/Art Department: page 177

© Alex Phillipe Cohen: page 88 (bottom right)

© Terence Connors: page 135

© Ryan Dorsett: page 15, 16, 17, 46, 48, 76, 77, 80, 88 (bottom left), 96, 178-179, 208

© Matt Easton/August Images: page 140-141

© Todd Eberle: page 14, 153

© Elliott Erwitt/Magnum Photos: page 150

© Charles Eshelman/FilmMagic/Getty Images: page 89 (bottom left)

© Billy Farrell/BFA.com: page 89 (middle right)

© Murray Feierberg/WWD/Penske Media/Getty Images: page 11 (top)

Courtesy Chiara Ferragni: page 74

Courtesy of Mimmo Ferretti: page 26

Courtesy of Diane von Furstenberg Archive: page 9, 11 (bottom), 13, 18, 20, 23, 25, 27, 29, 30, 32, 34, 54, 58-59, 62-63, 65, 68, 70-71, 72, 79, 88 (top right), 89 (bottom middle), 114-115, 116, 118-119, 121, 122, 124, 126, 127, 130, 131 (left), 132, 134, 136-137, 138, 142 (bottom right), 143 (top left; bottom left; bottom right), 147, 148, 151, 159, 172-173, 180, 182-183, 190, 192, 193, 194, 195, 196-197, 199 (left), 202-203

© Tatiana von Furstenberg: page 64

© Ara Gallant: page 120, 160

© Burt Glinn/Magnum Photos: page 113, 128, 129, 131 (right)

Courtesy of Stefani Greenfield: pages 156, 157

© Laura Harvey: page 145

© Bob Hiemstra: page 69, 191

Mary Hilliard and Staff, Vogue © Condé Nast: page 199 (right)

©InDigital Images: page 93

© Mikael Jansson/Truck Archive: page 37

© Troy Jensen: page 152

© Dimitrios Kambouris/Getty Images: page 89 (bottom right)

© Jingyu Lin/Trunk Archive: page 88 (middle left)

© Kristin Loken: page 146

© AP Photo/ Dario Lopez-Mills: page 88 (top left)

© Alexi Lubomirski/August Images: page 201

© Christopher Macsurak: page 84

© Jacques Malignon: page 199 (left)

© Olivia Malone/Trunk Archive: page 39

© Wayne Maser/Trunk Archive: page 108

© Patrick McMullan: page 143 (top right)

© Ed Molinari/NY Daily News/Getty Images: page 123

© Chris Moore/Getty Images: page 61

© NikiForos: page 144

© John Nollet/Figarophoto/Getty Images: page 73

© Josh Olins/Trunk Archive: page 81

© OpticPhotos: page 88 (top middle)

© Tony Palmieri/WWD/Penske/Getty Images: page 185

© Oliver Hadlee Pearch/Art Partner: cover, 43, 98, 163, 166

Irving Penn, Vogue © Condé Nast: page 186-187

© Angelo Pennetta/Art Partner: page 90

© Matteo Prandoni/BFA.com: page 200

© Roger Prigent: page 49

© Marc Regas: page 75

© Coliena Rentmeester/Art Department: page 173

© Bettina Rheims/Trunk Archive: page 4-5, 170

© Norman Jean Roy/Trunk Archive: page 149

Francesco Scavullo/© 1976 IBT Media/PARS: page 12

© Pierre Schermann/WWD/Penske Media/Getty Images: page 10

© Joe Schildhorn/BFA.com: page 89 (top center)

© Tom Schirmacher/Trunk Archive: page 56

© David Seidner: page 2

© Bob Seligman: page 133

© Sonia Sieff/Figarophoto/Getty Images: page 52

Courtesy Aimee Song: page 89 (top left)

Bert Stern, Vogue © Condé Nast: page 184

© Kelly Taub: page 95

Taxi Driver courtesy Columbia Pictures/Sony Pictures Entertainment: page 189

© The Washington Post/Getty Images: page 50-51

© Mario Testino/Art Partner: page 86

© Steffen Thalemann: page 154

© Jennifer E. Trahan: page 88 (middle right)

© Stefano Trovati/SGP: page 85, 142 (top; bottom left)

© Asli Tunaman: page 55

© Yannis Vlamos/InDigitalImages: page 31

© Theo Wargo/Getty Images: page 89 (top right)

© Thomas Whiteside/Trunk Archive: page 88 (middle), 198

© Susan Wood/Getty Images: page 8

© WWD/Penske Media/Getty Images: page 82, 83

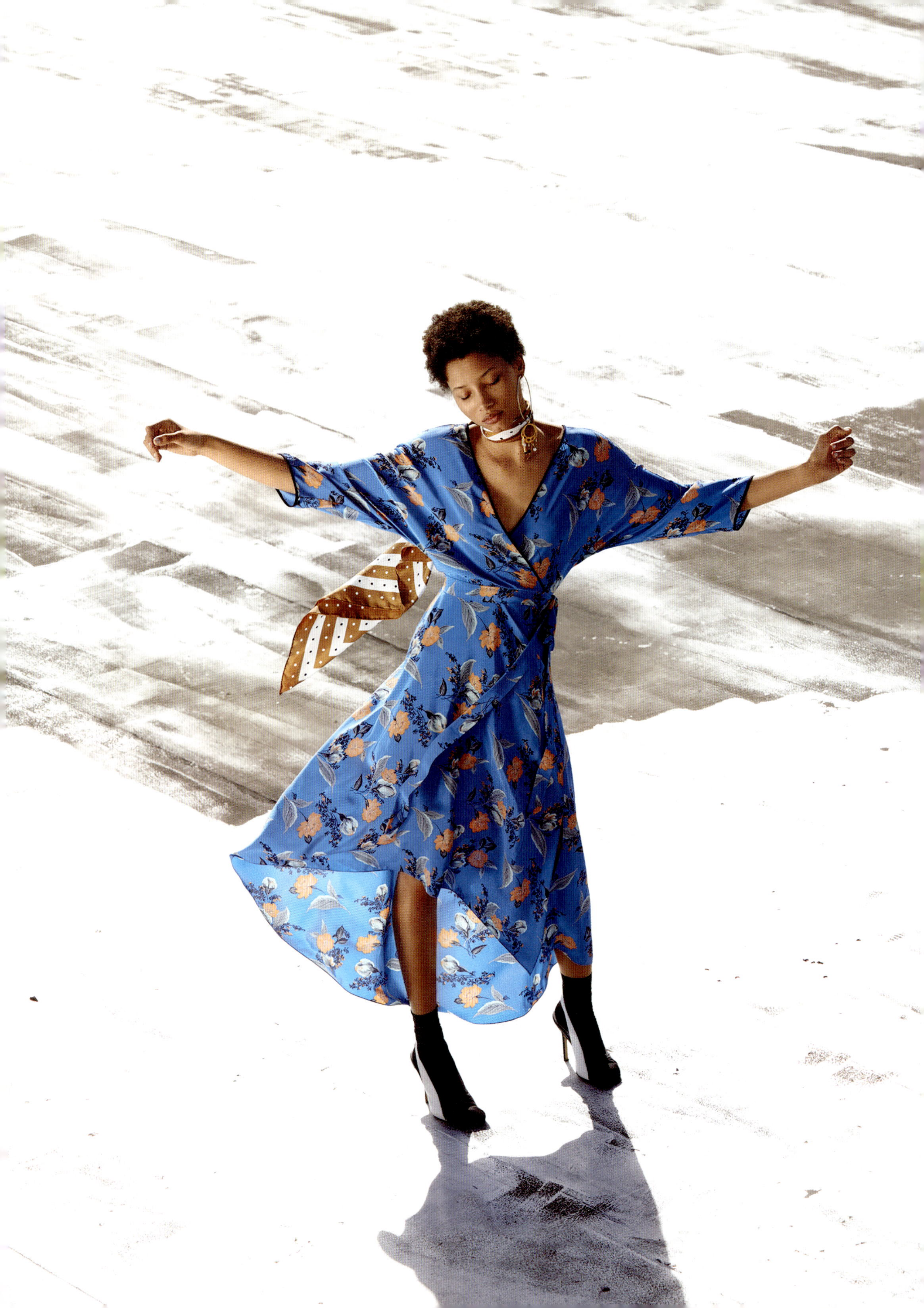

JOIN INCHARGE

To be InCharge is first a **COMMITMENT TO OURSELVES**. It is **OWNING WHO WE ARE.** It is respecting and trusting our character, knowing that it is forever the home and **THE CORE OF OUR STRENGTH.**

The practices that we commit ourselves to:

CONNECT: Make a habit of trying to make a miracle a day by connecting someone with a person they could not have met on their own.

EXPAND: Arrange a meeting or a call each week with someone that we don't know or would not typically engage with.

INSPIRE: Share our experience, vulnerability and strength through storytelling.

ADVOCATE: Take action on causes that matter to us, rally, speak up, organize and make an impact.

Diane

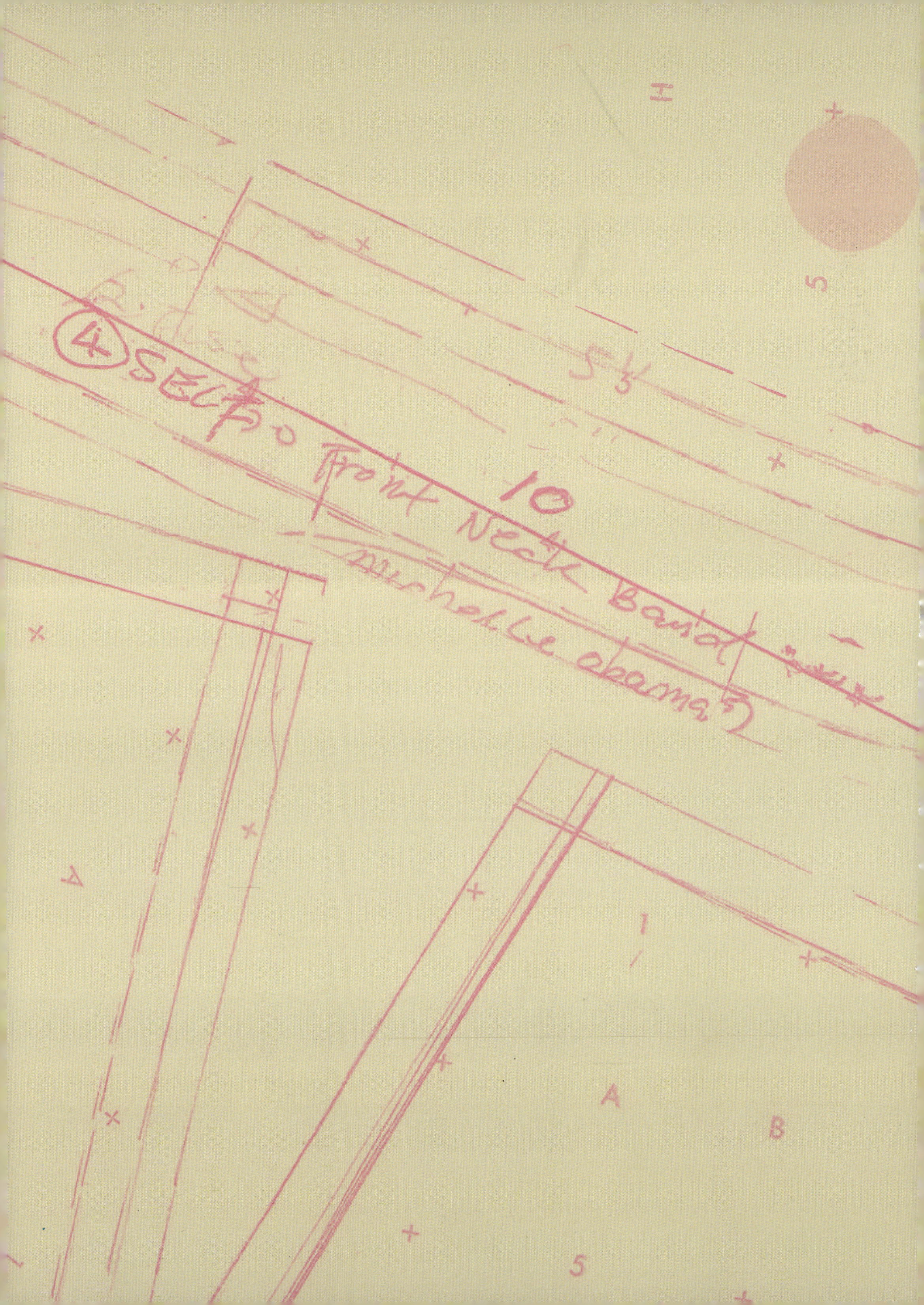
4 SELF
Front Neck Band
10
michelle obama?
A
B
1
5